JOURNAL FOR THE STUDY OF THE OLD TESTAMENT SUPPLEMENT SERIES
213

Sheffield Academic Press

A Blemished Perfection

The Book of Job in Context

Yair Hoffman

Journal for the Study of the Old Testament
Supplement Series 213

Copyright © 1996 Sheffield Academic Press

Published by Sheffield Academic Press Ltd
Mansion House
19 Kingfield Road
Sheffield S11 9AS
England

Printed on acid-free paper in Great Britain
by Bookcraft Ltd
Midsomer Norton, Bath

British Library Cataloguing in Publication Data

A catalogue record for this book is available
from the British Library

ISBN 1-85075-583-3

הרבה למדתי מרבותי,
ומחברי יותר מהם
ומתלמידי יותר מכולם
בבלי, מכות, י, א.

Much have I learnt from my teachers,
and more from my colleagues,
but most of all from my students
Babli, Makot 10.1

—to all of them this book is devoted.

CONTENTS

The present study is concerned with literary, theological, and linguistic aspects of the book of Job, and its place in biblical and ancient Near Eastern literature. It developed from my examination of the unique features of these aspects of the book of Job and the attempt to determine whether there is any interrelation among them and, if so, of what sort. I did not initially set out to prove any particular overall thesis. However, during the course of my study it became increasingly clear that the conclusions derived from the individual chapters combined into an overall picture, to which I gave expression through the title of the book. It was clear to me that this title needed to encompass two opposing concepts, for only thus could it reflect the central salient feature that I found in the book. Upon further consideration, it became clear to me that, in order to express properly the overall conclusions which I had reached, it was not enough merely to combine two opposites, and that only a truly paradoxical title would accurately reflect my intention. My conclusion was that the unique feature of the book of Job is its blemished perfection. While this formulation may sound absurd, in reality it is not so. Like any paradox, it seems vague and provocative. If 'blemished', then in what sense can it be 'perfect'? Yet such, to the best of my judgment, is the book of Job. My claim that its perfection is achieved, not in spite of its blemishes, but precisely because of them, relates both to the figure of Job as a believer and to the literary character of the book itself. Moreover, the phrase 'blemished perfection' also alludes to my contention that rigid, uncompromising attachment to a theory, to aesthetic rules whose theoretical force are universally recognized, may result in an inferior work of art, whereas lack of attention to these rules, whether deliberate or not, may actually yield a great work of art. This principled aesthetic may also be addressed, in a slightly different formulation, to the realm of religious faith, as it presents itself, in my view, in the book of Job. It is my contention, therefore, that the book of

Job is *prima facie* filled with faults in the literary, ideological, and linguistic realms—including those which originate in confusion in the transmission of the text. Nevertheless, all of these, through their combination into one unity—including the latter, which are a kind of peculiar response of the development of the book to its original nature—create the book's unique perfection.

This argument concerning blemished perfection is not explicitly articulated in all of the discussions in this study. This is so in order not to make the discussions dependent on the argument, and in order to facilitate the free flow of the discussion according to the particular requirements for the elucidation of each specific topic. By doing so, I may have diminished somewhat the impact of the claim. It is nevertheless sufficient that my position be understood, even if not everyone accepts it.

The study unites a variety of different aspects, which in many studies are generally separated and treated as distinct areas: theology, poetics, biblical literature, and literature of the Ancient Near East (Mesopotamia, Ugarit, Egypt). This approach also implies a certain methodological statement: even if there may be disciplinary justification for defining each of these areas as an independent realm, this diminishes our overall understanding of the book of Job. True, at times there may be no option but to separate the various subjects for didactic reasons, as I have also done, but this must be understood as a purely technical constraint.

I could have greatly extended the discussion by surveying the various studies, adding proofs, examples, arguments, and explanations to buttress my position. In refraining from doing so, I have adopted the conclusion suggested by Jerome about the book of Job: 'Ut si velis anguillam aut merenulam strictis tenere manibus, quanto fortius presseris, tanto citius elabitar'. That is, 'If you attempt to hold onto an eel by force—the harder you press, the more readily it will slip out of your hand'.

It is my pleasant duty to thank several of my colleagues at Tel-Aviv University who greatly assisted me: Dr Frank Pollak of the Bible Department, who spent many hours of his time helping me with the Mesopotamian texts; Dr Rafi Ventura of the Department of Archeology and Ancient Near Eastern Cultures, who made some important comments regarding 'The Protest of the Eloquent Peasant'; and Professor Abraham Tal of the Department of Hebrew Language, for his sound advice on several matters, including his comments on the sixth chapter concerning the difficult language of the book of Job; and last but not least to the translator of this book, Jonathan Chipman. It is superfluous to add that in the final analysis everything stated here reflects my own personal conclusions, and that I alone am responsible for any errors that may be found.

Yair Hoffman
Tel-Aviv, April 1995

ABBREVIATIONS

AB	Anchor Bible
AJSL	*American Journal of Semitic Languages and Literatures*
ALUOS	*Annual of Leeds University Oriental Society*
ANET	J.B. Pritchard (ed.), *Ancient Near Eastern Texts*
ATD	Das Alte Testament Deutsch
BKAT	Biblischer Kommentar: Altes Testament
BZAW	Beihefte zur *ZAW*
CBQ	*Catholic Biblical Quarterly*
EncBib	*Enzeqlopedyah Miqraʾit*
EncHeb	*ha-Enzeqlopedyah ha-ʿIvrit*
HAT	Handbuch zum Alten Testament
HKAT	Handkommentar zum Alten Testament
HTR	*Harvard Theological Review*
HUCA	*Hebrew Union College Annual*
ICC	International Critical Commentary
JBL	*Journal of Biblical Literature*
JHS	*Journal of Hellenic Studies*
JSOTSup	*Journal for the Study of the Old Testament*, Supplement Series
JSS	*Journal of Semitic Studies*
KAT	Kommentar zum Alten Testament
OTL	Old Testament Library
TOTC	Tyndale Old Testament Commentaries
TRev	*Theologische Revue*
UF	*Ugarit-Forschungen*
VT	*Vetus Testamentum*
VTSup	*Vetus Testamentum*, Supplements
ZAW	*Zeitschrift für die alttestamentliche Wissenschaft*

Chapter 1

THEORETICAL CONSIDERATIONS

1. *The Understanding and Interpretation of a Literary Work*

It is the goal of the present work to contribute to the understanding of the significance of the book of Job. In today's intellectual climate, anyone using the terms 'understanding' or 'significance' with regard to a literary work as if these referred to something understood in an unequivocal manner is likely to be considered naive and lacking in the basic knowledge required in order to engage in the interpretation of a text. This is so due to the various rival theoretical schools regarding, on the one hand, the nature of a literary text and, on the other, the nature of 'understanding' and the task of the exegete.

This problem is extensively discussed in works concerning the area of general poetics, as has been noted by Weiss in his study on the Bible. In the introduction to his book, Weiss raises the question, 'What is "correct" interpretation of a literary work?' (Weiss 1984: 12-17). Since then, the question has become even more complicated. The central issue around which this dispute revolves is that of the objectivity of the exegete. Weiss's approach leaves considerable room for the creative imagination of the reader, for his or her associative world and personal feelings towards the written text. At the same time, as Weiss has noted, his approach avoids 'the danger of arbitrariness, of excessive subjectivity, or of all kinds of anachronisms' (p. 18). That is, he understands absolute subjectivity on the part of the exegete to be a negative quality; hence, any literary approach likely to lead to it is seen by him as highly questionable, if not to be ruled out entirely. Yet in recent years there have been those who question this very principle: the deconstructionist theory of the school of Barthes, Derrida, and others praises subjectivism, going so far as to state categorically that the reader is the only authority regarding the text, that the reader must apply his or her own subjectivity, and that only thus may the work achieve realization and completion. Weiss

denied the superior authority of authors and their contemporaries
regarding the interpretation of the work, pleading on behalf of its right
to speak for itself beyond the limitations of the time and circumstances
in which it was composed, whereas deconstructionism went so far as to
deny the authority of the flow of the text to determine the correct
interpretation, leaving it entirely to the decision of the reader-exegete.[1]

To the 'objective' approach to a text, which sets out to interpret it in
terms of its anchoring in the particular circumstances in which it was
written, there has been added a theoretical dimension which attempts to
apply to literature, including biblical literature, the 'act-speech' theory of
language developed by Austin and Searle.[2] The main literary application
of this theory lies in the attempt to understand how it acted upon the
consciousness of the reader who was a contemporary of the author .

Thus, as a result of the profound theoretical debate concerning the
nature of the concepts 'understanding', 'correct interpretation', and the
like, anyone who sets out to write a work with the aim of contributing
to the understanding of any given work must first of all define the nature
of the understanding which is aimed for. Apparently, this would seem to
require an extensive theoretical discussion giving a well-reasoned formulation of the author's approach to the nature of literary understanding,

---

1.   See, for example, Derrida (1979: 84) who opposes the separation of text from
context, refusing to treat the text as if it were 'a finished corpus of writings, some
content enclosed in a book or its margins'. For him, the text 'overruns all the limits
assigned to it so far...everything that was to be set up in opposition to writing
(speech, life, the world, the real, the history and what not)'. A theoretical attempt to
navigate between the tendency towards 'objective' exegesis and the 'anarchistic'
approach to a text appears in Fish 1980. He defends the right of the reader to be freed
of the 'tyranny of the text' (p. 7), but argues that this does not threaten anarchy,
because the creative imagination of the reader-exegete is in any event limited by
'exegetical communities' composed of readers who follow the same exegetical
strategies. These strategies exist *a priori* to the act of reading and therefore determine
the manner of reading, rather than the opposite (p. 41). Because of the different
nuances among the various deconstructionist approaches, there are those who prefer
to categorize them all under the rubric of 'post-structuralism' or 'post-modernism'.
See *Semeia* 51 (1990), which is devoted to these approaches, under the heading
'Post-Structural Criticism and the Bible'. For more on the deconstructionist approach
to biblical research, see Greenstein 1989.

2.   See *Semeia* 41 (1988), which is devoted entirely to discussion of the theoretical and exegetical implications of this theory for biblical research. A polemic against
this, concluding with a long list of 'all the things it can't do', appears in Fish 1980:
197-245.

the purpose of interpretation, and the like, while rejecting other approaches. I shall not, however, attempt to do so: first, because I am not a literary theorist; and second, because I do not claim that the exegetical principles that I have used in this work are the only ones permitted in dealing with a literary text, and that all others are improper. Nevertheless, I cannot exempt myself completely from a brief explanation of the methodological principles upon which this study is based—and it is to this discussion that I have devoted the opening chapter.

At this preliminary stage it is worth noting one of the rules that I have established for myself: namely, that preference will be given to literal interpretation over homiletics, whether in the case of traditional exegesis that draws its power from axioms in the area of faith and belief, or that of modernistic exegesis, based upon various psychological, cognitive and philosophical theories, acknowledging the exclusive right of the reader to enjoy a free hand in the written word. It follows from this that, when I use such terms as 'understanding' and 'significance', I essentially refer to that realm within whose framework those readers who were contemporaries of the author were meant to interpret the work for themselves. This range may be quite broad. Did the author write only for contemporaries, or perhaps imagine a 'trans-temporal reader'? Or did the author perhaps not write 'for' at all, but 'because', without having any particular reader in mind? I do not intend to answer these questions here, as they are bound to entangle me in a theoretical discussion which I would rather avoid. I shall content myself instead with a general definition of my exegetical preferences in principle. During the course of this chapter these will be elaborated in greater detail, but without explicit connection to any specific school concerned with the theoretical understanding of literary documents. Those who find it important to classify exegetes within a theoretical framework may, during the course of their reading, judge whether my arguments are consistent with the positions of one or another school, or whether perhaps they do not fit into any strict classification of this type. In any event, it is sufficient for me that my work be found consistent and coherent.

One further point needs to be clarified: my intention to contribute to a better understanding of the book of Job does not touch upon one of its most important aspects—namely, the purely literal exegesis. There is no doubt that the understanding of this book would be advanced, more than anything else, by the solution of its lexicographical riddles. However, the contribution I wish to make is not in this field, even though where necessary I also discuss various matters pertaining directly to textual interpretation, and an entire chapter is devoted exclusively to the problem of the difficult language of the book. Nor do I follow another path which might contribute to the understanding of this book—namely, that of close reading—both because of my objections to the exegetical dynamic created by this method, and because I find it less interesting.[3]

2. *Circles of Cultural Exigency*

The present contribution to the understanding of the book of Job consists primarily of the attempt to take note of the various systems of constraint within which it was composed, and which affected its contents and literary fashioning. These constraints—whether known to the author or hidden from him—determined not only what he would write and how, but also what he would not write and how he was not to write. Hence, our understanding of the book will be facilitated by observation of their nature. I would suggest drawing a distinction among three such circles, which are predominant in any work of art; the more familiar we are with them, the better we are able to understand the work. The broadest circle, determining the limits of the possible in every human creation, whether artistic or technological, is that of the historical givens; the second circle is that of the art form within which the artist expresses himself; while the innermost circle is that of the specific genre.

The circle of historical data is concerned with the social, cultural, and technological background of the work. Without knowing the framework of limitations established by these factors, we cannot properly evaluate any human accomplishment. Why did the Assyrians bother to improve their chariots, adding horses and so forth, rather than making them move by means of mechanical engines? The answer to this innocent question is only self-evident if one is aware of the technological reality of the ninth century BCE. Anyone proposing an answer other than 'because motors had not yet been invented' (such as, 'because they were worried about air pollution', etc.) will be rightly accused of a total misunderstanding of the subject, evidently based upon ignorance of the circle of historical limitations. Anyone who, upon examining ancient drawings from Egypt, Assyria, or Greece, attempts to explain the absence of

---

3.   Examples of continuous close reading of a lengthy biblical text, which indeed drew its author into an excess of literary exegesis, may be found in Fokkelman 1975 and 1986.

perspective on religious, social, or similar grounds betrays a lack of awareness of the historical constraints within which artists of that period operated, the laws of perspective being first noted only in the fifteenth century by the Italian architect Filippo Brunelleschi. On the other hand, anyone who would explain the distorted perspective in the paintings of de Chirico, or the lack of perspective in many of the works of Picasso and Matisse, on the assumption that they did not yet know the laws of perspective not only reveals ignorance of the history of art, but will also entirely misconstrue the intention of these artists, for whom the foregoing of perspective represents a deliberate artistic statement. Similarly, anyone who seeks an internal literary answer to the question as to why Bialik, the greatest modern Hebrew poet, did not allude to the atrocities of the Nazis in his poem 'The City of Slaughter', ignoring the obvious fact that the poem was written before their occurrence, will end up with a significant misinterpretation of the poem. The same holds true for anyone who, while reading Eccl. 1.1-5, seeks a sophisticated (and *ab initio* incorrect) exegetical explanation for the question as to why these verses imply that the earth is stationary and the sun revolves around it, when it is known that the opposite is the case. Here too, the explanation must be sought in historical circumstances—in this case, the limitations of scientific knowledge during that period. Again, we find in the Bible a struggle against paganism, but no struggle against atheism. Anyone explaining this point outside of the historical and cultural circumstance of the time (namely, the lack of an atheistic world-view) will necessarily arrive at a distorted notion of the biblical world-view.

Moreover, knowledge of the circle of historical compulsions is also a necessary prerequisite for aesthetic evalation. Were one of Mozart's symphonies to be presented as a twentieth-century composition, it would not enjoy the same aesthetic valuation as it does when it is known that it was composed during the eighteenth century.[4] Hence, familiarity with the historical context also contributes to a better understanding of the work of art, because it is a precondition for clarifying connections among artists, which may at times be helpful in interpreting their works. Anyone who is unaware, listening to the opening of Mahler's Fifth Symphony, of the clear connection to the opening of the Fifth Symphony of Beethoven (albeit not necessarily as a result of knowledge or deliberate

---

4.   The example is taken from Zemach 1970: 38. A philosophical discussion of the relation between aesthetic evaluation and the date of the work appears there, pp. 7-41.

planning) understands the work of Mahler less well. But this knowledge becomes of exegetical importance primarily if we know that Beethoven preceded Mahler and not vice versa, as otherwise we are likely to err in our understanding of both works. In brief, historical and cultural circumstances are a constraining factor, knowledge of which is essential for the understanding of any work, including artistic works. Without this, it is difficult for us to understand the approaches expressed by artists in their work, and we are certainly unable to trace possible covert, indirect polemics with other views which were current in their time.

It follows from this position that, prior to any discussion of the book of Job, one must determine the period of its composition, and then take note of the cultural, social, and ideological characteristics of the period in which the book was written.[5]

5.   M. Weiss refers extensively to the exegetical importance of recognizing the historical background of an artistic work. In his introduction (1984: 13-18), he articulates a reserved, if not dismissive, stance towards the tendency to judge and to understand artistic works on the basis of their time of composition. This position is presented in the body of the book as well. Thus, for example, on pp. 50-73, he criticizes the prevalent view in biblical exegesis that 'by understanding the situation in which a psalm was created, we can understand the psalm' (p. 51), but his remarks do not refer exclusively to the psalm literature. His main polemic is directed against Gunkel and his approach, regarding both the uncovering of the historical and cultural background of the artistic work, and its classification by genre, a point to which we shall return later. The connection between the historical background of an artistic work and its understanding also relates to the question as to whether exegesis requires familiarity with the biography of the artist, or even whether it benefits from it. On this question, too, Weiss's view is negative: 'Hence also the objection to determining the intention of a literary work on the basis of the "sources" upon which the creator "drew". The details of the poet's life are irrelevant to an understanding of his poem, because that event in his life which moved him to create is not the source from which it is derived' (p. 24). Again (noting the opinion of Staiger, against that of Goethe): 'Biography is outside the scope of the literary critic...The poem cannot possibly be explained on the basis of biographical facts about the writer' (p. 50). On the other hand, one may present an opposite viewpoint, according to which the exposure of the author's biography is an important element in establishing the exegetical background for understanding the work. One finds the testimony of an involved party, namely, that of the poet, in Browning's study of Percy Shelley. He distinguishes between an objective artist, such as Shakespeare, knowledge of whose biography is a matter of mere curiosity because his work speaks for itself, and the exegetical need to know the biography of the subjective poet. In such a case, says Browning: 'in our approach to the poetry we necessarily approach the personality of the poet...both for love's and for understanding's sake we desire to know him, and as readers of his

At this point, I shall simply state that the book was written during the 'late biblical period'. Such is the view of the majority of scholars dealing with the book, who state that it was written between the sixth and fourth centuries BCE.[6] The question of date will not be discussed here *in extenso*, for several reasons. First, I have nothing new to add to what has already been written about the subject. Secondly, such a discussion will take us too far afield of the central theme of the present book. Thirdly, and most importantly, our knowledge of the biblical period does not allow for a precise chronological mapping of widely held viewpoints, nor of literary development, according to a clear chronological order. Hence, the present work would in any event not benefit from any more precise closure on the time of composition of the book, even were such a thing possible. For this reason, I find it preferable to forego any attempt at greater precision *ab initio*. It will become clear further on that even an extension of the chronological range of the composition of the book (such as, between the seventh and fourth centuries) will not influence my determination of the boundaries of the cultural background of its writing, which in this context is my main reason for interest in the circle of historical constraints. Hence, any comparisons to biblical and to ancient Near Eastern literature, as well as attempts to establish the literary influences which contributed to shaping the nature of the book of Job, will be based upon the above time framework, without its lack of precision affecting the arguments raised.

Before turning to the second circle of exigency, we need to reiterate that which does not belong to the realm of historical constraints: to wit, the sensitivity and intelligence of the artist. This comment relates to a feeling sometimes expressed by contemporary readers: namely, that 'it is

---

poetry must be readers of his biography also'. On this question, I tend to accept the opinion represented by Weiss, particularly as we do not have all the biographical data concerning the majority of the biblical authors, and certainly not the anonymous author of the book of Job.

6.   Thus, among others, Budde 1913: lv; Driver and Gray 1921: lxxx (5th century BCE); Eissfeldt 1964: 636 (4th century BCE); Weiser 1959: 292 (between the 5th and 3rd centuries BCE); Gordis 1965: 216 (500–300 BCE); Tur-Sinai, *EncBib*, I, pp. 247-48, 255 (composed in Aramaic in the Babylonian exile and translated into Hebrew no earlier than the 4th century BCE); and also Kleinert, Cheney, Dillman, Koenig, and Gunkel. On the other hand, there are those who set the date of the book in an earlier period. Thus Pfeiffer 1941: 675-78 (ca. 600 BCE); Kaufmann 1960: II, 623, who fixes its date in the First Temple period; Pope 1973: xl (7th century BCE). For further views, see Chapter 6, pp. 188-91.

not possible' that at such an early period the author could have 'such
subtle' psychological or aesthetic sensitivity; 'it is not possible' that the
author could have used such sharp and indirect irony, because this is, so
to speak, a sign of later times. On more than one occasion, this
unjustified feeling of superiority has been translated into a statement that
anyone who thinks that they have found these qualities in an early text is
guilty of anachronistic exegesis. To refute such arguments, it is enough
that one mention the delicate and multi-layered design of the narrative of
the Binding of Isaac; the psychological depth of the story of the Garden
of Eden or of the Joseph cycle; the irony of the words placed in Elijah's
mouth by the narrator when he tells the prophets of Baal, 'Cry aloud,
for he is a god; either he is musing, or he has gone aside, or he is on a
journey, or perhaps he is asleep and must be awakened' (1 Kgs 18.27);
as well as similar features in the works of Homer, Aeschylus, and others.
For this reason, it is important to distinguish between developments in
the technological areas or those of artistic, religious, and social conventions, and those qualities which pertain to the human spirit. Any attempt
to place the latter within a fixed developmental scheme is highly
questionable, if not disproven outright.

The second circle of exigency is that of the art form which the artist
chooses. The classification into music, verbal arts, and the plastic arts is
first and foremost a distinction among the various limitations (and
possibilities, which is the other side of the same coin) determining the
nature of the artistic medium.[7] One might argue, on the face of it, that
Beethoven's instrumental works do not express any particular world-
view because they do not contain any explicit statement, but merely an
orchestration of tones and rhythm. However, that would be to ignore
the restrictions which this art form imposes upon those working within
it. In Edvard Munch's painting, *The Scream*, one does not hear any
sound—not because there is any claim made that when one screams one
does not make any sound, or that a scream without sound is stronger
than a scream that is heard. Rather, what is expressed is the attempt to
explore the limits of painting as a silent art: How can one express
thereby the sound of a scream, despite its limitations? Recognition of the
substantive limitations imposed upon Munch by the medium of painting
will contribute to a better understanding of *The Scream*. One of the

7.   This is in practice the point of departure of Aristotle, who begins the *Poetics*
by drawing a distinction among the various arts on the basis of their means of
imitation (mimesis).

important characteristics of great works of art is the artist's struggle with the substantive limitations imposed by the chosen art form.[8] How can one convey an idea or story through instrumental music? How can one 'make a sound' in a painting? The attempt to express softness, round lines, and folds of clothing in a marble statue is a struggle with the limitations dictated by the hardness of stone. The attempt of the mime artist to 'say' things without words is a struggle with the substantive constraints imposed by the art of mime. Artur Rubinstein's piano-playing is not only the maximal exploitation of the possibilities offered by the instrument, but an attempt to overcome its technical limitations as a percussion instrument. In the same way, but in the opposite direction, one needs to judge the rendition of Bach by Glenn Gould, who attempts to overcome the softness of the piano, a softness which does not suit the sharp enunciation of the works of Bach (which were written before the development of the pianoforte). We may better understand a story by Faulkner if we are aware as he is of the substantive limitations of litera-ture in the description of simultaneous events or in the presentation of the same event from various points of view at one and the same time. This consciousness is certainly necessary for an intellectual and artistic evaluation of the work, which is in practice no more than an additional stage of its understanding.

It is therefore desirable that, in the course of our discussion of the book of Job, we take into account the fact that we are dealing with a work whose instruments are words: symbols bearing clearly defined meanings, as well as less clearly defined associations. This knowledge is of some importance when one attempts to understand various phenomena in the

---

8. A dogmatic presentation of the view regarding the substantive limitations unique to poetry and the plastic arts appears in the book by Lessing, *Laokoon* (1766), who is critical of those artists who attempt to break them, thereby denying their own art. This viewpoint is expressed in the sub-title of his book: *An Essay on the Limits of Painting and Poetry*. Other expressions of this dogmatic approach appear in a number of streams of contemporary art: to remove from the work whatever is not 'most essential' for its artistic value. It follows from this that painting must be with-out a 'story', music without 'contents', poetry without any defined subject, etc. The understanding of works of this type will also benefit from consciousness on the part of the art consumer of the limitations of the type of work in question, in order to better understand the 'essential' thing towards which the artist aims. Indeed, in this approach too one may uncover the artist's struggle with substantive limitations, that is, with the constraints of his or her art. Against the approach which sets boundaries and limitations upon the various different arts, see Croce 1965: 113-15, 436-58.

book—particularly, but not exclusively, in the realm of the use of language.

The third circle, that of genre, is subject to greater controversy among literary scholars. Since a number of subjects discussed in the present work pertain in one way or another to generic aspects of the book of Job, it is appropriate to dwell upon this problem at some length.

The long tradition of genre classification, beginning with Greek philosophy, particularly in the *Poetics* of Aristotle,[9] has been severely attacked by Croce.[10] However, his criticism thereof in principle did not cause literary scholars to renege entirely on the genre approach, although there were those who did so, of course.[11] Rather, it stimulated interest in philosophical and methodological aspects of the issue of genre

9.   Classification by type appeared in Plato's *Republic* (3.391-94, 396-97, 399-400). He classifies poetry according to subject, form, the viewpoint of the poet, etc. However, he does not undertake the same degree of detail and systematization as Aristotle, because his aim is different. Aristotle, who in the introduction to *Poetics* distinguishes the art of imitation in words and the art of imitation in colours, forms, or melody, thereafter classifies those arts which perform mimesis in words, setting aside a special place for tragedy as a genre in its own right. See chs. 4, 5, 6. For more on the classification and characterization of Aristotle, see below.

10.   Croce 1922: 111-52. A critical survey of the approaches toward classifying the arts appears on pp. 422-52. On pp. 436-37, he relates to Aristotle, and on pp. 439-40, 449-52 to Lessing. See also Croce 1965: 39-47. It nevertheless follows from several of his comments that his opposition to genre classification derives primarily from the tendency of theoreticians (such as Lessing, as mentioned above) to dictate obligatory rules, a kind of aesthetic law from which one is not allowed to depart: 'It is not scientifically incorrect to talk of tragedies, comedies, romances...if it only be with a view to be understood, and to draw attention to certain groups of works...To employ words and phrases is not to establish rules and definitions' (p. 38). His opposition is therefore not to genre classification as a didactic method; he objects to those 'who seek out the aesthetic laws which must in their belief control literary and artistic kinds'.

11.   See, for example, Blanchot (1959: 293) who states that the only important thing is the book itself, as it is, beyond genre and without classification into prose, poetry, novel, etc. The isolated story is literature itself. In this case too one may cite Weiss (1984) as the explicit spokesman of this approach to Bible studies in Israel. He exemplifies this both in his actual method of treatment of the biblical text, and in those notes and appendixes which bear a programmatic and methodological character. Weiss is critical primarily of Gunkel's method of study of literary types in the Bible, against which he poses the method of total interpretation (1967: 136-40, 245-49). It follows from his remarks that the 'New Criticism' refers to the school of Croce, while the genre approach is *passé*. As will be explained below, this description does not reflect contemporary literary research.

classification. Such involvement is one of the distinguishing signs of a number of scholars and schools within contemporary literary study,[12] who see genre classification as a necessary step accompanying any aesthetic study of literature.[13] The lack of agreement among scholars regarding the identification of principal genres[14] is not in principle a valid argument against genre classification *per se*. It only indicates the need to refrain from excessive dogmatism, to recognize the flexible nature of the generic entities,[15] and thus to refrain from giving unequivocal validity and force to these divisions, but to be content with descriptive, explanatory and interpretive uses.[16]

12. Such as the structuralist approach. See, for example, Todorov (1976: 151-70), who states that there was never literature without genre, and there was never a 'pre-genre' state—and thus also others. See also the collection of papers edited by Strelka (1978). For a recent principled discussion justifying genre classification, see Rosmarin 1985. An interesting theoretical discussion is given by Hirsch (1967: 68-126). Among other points, he explains the exegetical advantage to be gained from awareness of the genre of the work to be interpreted; see on this esp. pp. 89-102.

13. See, for example, the remarks by Bonnet (1978: 3) that without drawing distinctions among basic genres there would be total confusion in the aesthetic realm. Nevertheless, one need not accept his definitive approach concerning the dichotomy between poetry and prose: 'Art is dual because we are dual' (p. 12); 'The distinction between fiction and pure poetry... will be perpetuated until the end of the world' (p. 15).

14. See Bonnet 1978. Another dichotomistic distinction—between didactic genre and mimetic genre—is proposed by Carin and Olson (cited in Reichert 1978: 61). Sacks (1964: 46) suggests a different division: that prose be classified into three principal genres: satire, apologia, and representative activities, the boundaries between which are extremely sharp. According to him, the definitions of the different genre categories naturally exclude one another, making it impossible to place a work of the type of 'representative activity', for example, under the rubric of 'satire', just as it is impossible in English to write an active sentence which is also passive.

15. As noted by Marino (1978: 54), literary genre definitions, like literary approaches, are historical, and hence subject to change. They are conventional, and therefore not exact; they are relative, and hence do not fit completely. See also the remarks by Hirsch: 'and thus the terms tragedy, comedy, etc., are valid, even if they are not precisely defined' (1967: 109).

16. To 'dictate' in the sense that these are the rules of the genre and it is forbidden to deviate from them. An example of a dictating approach is to be found, for example, in Horace (*Ars Poetica*, pp. 189-92): 'Let no play be either shorter or longer than five acts...nor let a fourth actor essay to speak'. On the role of Horace in the shaping of Western poetics, see Boyd (1968: 35-49). I have already mentioned the dogmatism of Lessing, but this relates to distinctions between different areas of art, and not to intra-literary genres.

Genre distinction is an important element in the aesthetic evaluation of the work, in addition to recognition of the characteristics and limitations of the art forms, and for the very same reason: genre likewise creates a framework of dialectical constraints through which the artist attempts to express himself, on the one hand; and from which he wishes to be freed, on the other hand. This struggle is at the very heart of art; thus, anyone who ignores the perception of genre as a constraining, limiting, directing element is unable to describe the realm of the artist's most important struggle, which determines to a not inconsiderable degree the nature of the completed work.[17] A poet writing a classical sonnet consciously accepts a set of strict generic constraints relating to the structure and length of the poem; readers who are unaware of these limitations will not appreciate the sonnet to the same extent as those who are aware of them. Their understanding will be particularly lacking if the artist breaks out of the strict boundaries of the genre (for example, if he adds a line, omits a line, or deviates from the conventions of metre). Without knowing the 'laws' of the sonnet, the reader will be unable to interpret the use of these very strong means of expression. The breaking of artistic conventions as an expressive tool is only possible when the consumer of art recognizes their limiting, constraining nature. Hence, the genre forces upon the artist a system of artistic conventions (which, it is true, is at times flexible), and at the same time creates in the reader a model of expectations, which is in itself an important factor for the understanding of the work.[18]

17. See on this Hoffman 1986. This does not contradict, but even explains the statement by Kant (*Critique of Judgment*, sects. 46-47, 58) that the artistic genius is not subject to aesthetic laws, but creates a new aesthetic law. Similarly, Gombrich (1960: 52) claims that, 'Variants can be controlled and checked only against a set of invariants'. It is interesting to note the following quotation, cited by Croce (1922: 443), from a letter of Giambattista Marino from 1627: 'I am convinced that I have more profound knowledge of the rules of literature than all the meticulous ones in the world. But the only correct rule is to know how to break the rules in the right place and in the appropriate time.'

18. See the remarks by Todorov cited above, n. 12, as well as: 'It is because genres exist as an institution that they function as 'horizons of expectations' for readers and as models of writing for authors' (1976: 163). The exegetical value of genre examination in the realm of the Bible has been noted by Gerhart, who states among other things that 'readers have perceived that different kinds of texts give rise to different kinds of expectations...Generic analysis would seem to be important, than, for opening up alternative versions and visions of the text for the penultimate purpose of understanding it better' (1988: 31, 41).

It is not my intention to argue here that, for example, a reader needs to establish a book's genre classification before reading it. Precisely because the conventions of genre are not an artificial demand of the theoretician, it is possible during the course of reading to formulate a system of comparative judgment, and from this, a correct system of expectations, which will assist in the understanding of the work by its proper location within a scheme of genre coordinates. Anyone who begins to read a detective novel without knowing at the outset what kind of book it is can nevertheless guide her or himself during the course of reading to the correct questions (such as: Who is the murderer? Under what circumstances will he be discovered? What mistakes did he make in the committing of the crime?), and will realize that one ought not to expect here a tragic love story or profound philosophical reflections. In this respect, readers who know of the existence of a genre called 'detective stories' enjoy an advantage, because they will arrive at a correct set of expectations more quickly than will readers who do not know of the existence of such a genre. At first glance, this latter assumption seems to contradict our claim regarding the exegetical importance of recognizing the genre of the work. Theoretically, when speaking of the 'ideal' reader, who directs her or himself to the correct genre like a radio which automatically tunes itself to a particular station, there is no need for advance classification or consciousness of the genre. However, this characteristic of the 'ideal reader' is primarily an acquired one; only someone who has read a great deal and has acquired familiarity with a variety of genres will arrive at a system of proper sensitivities and become an 'ideal reader'. That is, the fact that the reader did not initially know to which genre the work belongs is for her or him a purely technical fact. Moreover, there are few 'ideal' readers; hence, genre classification serves us as an important tool. Moreover, any person who is unwilling to forego the intellectual experience of reading and understanding a work, that is, its aesthetic judgment, will inevitably seek the answer to such questions as: Why did I enjoy (or not enjoy) this work? Do I 'believe' the work? What created the aesthetic experience for me? In other words: what was it that caused the work to be as it is? The answers to these questions are to be sought, among other things, in the manner in which the artist used the particular genre. Was it adhered to strictly? Where was there deviation from the expectations of the genre? To what extent was the expressive power of the work enhanced by strictness or flexibility in the use of genre?

One should not conclude from what I have said thus far that every literary work necessarily belongs to a defined genre. On the contrary: one of the arguments of the present work is that the book of Job does not belong to any genre, but is a unique work,[19] the fruit of the feeling (not necessarily knowledge) of its author, who would have been unable to attain his goal by means of the traditional genre tools that were available to him. But even this statement requires a certain classification of the book of Job: it does not belong to any genre, not only because nobody wrote in a similar manner prior to its writer, but because there were no other works written according to its exact model thereafter. Thus, its non-belonging to any genre is to a certain extent a purely 'statistical' statement, not a phenomenological one. In any event, the understanding and aesthetic evaluation of the book require elucidation of the genre possibilities available to the author, which he confronted and in the final analysis rejected (in my opinion, not consciously) because they did not satisfy him as an artist.

3. *The Work, the Artist, and the Exegete*

In the course of outlining the basic framework of my study, I feel the need to add several remarks concerning the question to which I have already addressed myself, and whose elucidation is important: namely, to what extent must the exegete who sets out to interpret a given work take into consideration the author's own intentions? What exegetical authority ought to be given to the author? Plato was evidently the first one to deny the artist, in a caustic way, any exegetical authority regarding his work.[20] The modern version of this argument, while not requiring

19. The argument concerning the 'uniqueness' of every great artistic creation (see on this matter Haezrachi 1954: 105-106) is of course correct, but does not contradict the possibility that it may belong to a clear and well-defined genre. *Hamlet* is a 'unique' drama (genre), just like *Macbeth*. Their classification within the same genre does not refute their uniqueness, but establishes a proper point of view from which to observe the nature of this quality.

20. Plato, *Apologia*, 22: 'After the politicians I went to the poets: tragic, dithyrambic, and all sorts…Accordingly, I took them some of the most elaborate passages in their own writings, and asked what was the meaning of them…I am almost ashamed to confess the truth, but I must say that there is hardly a person present who would not have talked better about their poetry than they did themselves. Then I knew that not by wisdom do poets write poetry, but by a sort of genius and inspiration; they are like diviners or soothsayers, who also say many fine things, but do not understand the meaning of them. The poets appeared to me in much the same case…'

contempt for the creative artist, consists in the empirical-pychological assumption that, while artists can indeed know what they wish to write, they have no control over those things which will in the final analysis emerge from their work. Such critics speak in theoretical terms of the autonomy of the artistic work: after it has been written it is an entity unto itself—it has left the control of the author, it speaks for itself, and the author's intention is no longer relevant to its interpretation.[21] This approach must be viewed with great circumspection. I do not think that the autonomy of the work can justify an anachronistic interpretation (e.g., 'Amos was a socialist'), nor do I see any justification for ignoring in principle that which the author may have intended to express in his or her work. Concerning this matter, I accept Hirsch's distinction between 'meaning' and 'significance'.[22] Nevertheless, in attempting to understand the meaning of a work one cannot ignore the difficulty in determining exactly 'what the author intended'. Therefore, as an auxiliary exegetical tool, one must content oneself with understanding the author's intention in a negative way, as a limiting factor. That is, rather than asking, What

21. See Weiss (1984: 15-17): 'Whoever undertakes to interpret a literary creation should not ask: "What were the intentions of the author in his work?" nor "How did his contemporaries understood it?" but rather: "What is written in the text?"' (compare also p. 192 n. 24). Cf. Beardsley (1958: 17-28, 456-69), who deals with the issue of the intention of the artist in the various arts from the point of view of the exegete and the performer. His position is similar to that of Weiss: one ought not to ask, 'What is this supposed to be? But, What have we got here?' (p. 29). Nevertheless, he does not reject such formulae as 'the author attempted, but did not succeed, in forming images...' because such an impression may be derived from the work itself (p. 28).

22. See Hirsch 1967: 8. Under the heading, 'In Defense of the Author', he writes the following: 'Meaning is that which is represented by a text; it is what the author meant by his use of a particular sign sequence'. As against that, 'significance' is concerned with the relationship between meaning and the reader, which may also include errors in understanding. Such an explicit stance is likewise taken by Fox (1981). In his later work, Hirsch altered several of his earlier positions. Thus, for example, he states that at times there is a gap between that which is represented by the text and the intention of the author ('Jack can mean "Datsun" when he says "Toyota"'). See on this Hirsch 1986: 628, as a reaction to the papers of Battersby-Phelan and Leddy. On the semiotic stance, according to which there is no room at all to speak of a text as 'having meaning', see Patte 1990: 35. Without accepting his approach in its entirety, I do accept his conclusion that it is indeed permitted to read a text in various ways, but one may nevertheless rule out certain readings entirely and see them as illegitimate (p. 32).

did the artist mean? one must ask, What could the artist definitely not have intended? Or, How would the work definitely not have been understood by the writer's contemporaries? Thus, if due to historical exigencies the author of Job could not possibly have intended to express a stance concerning the suffering of Jesus, then anyone who attempts to interpret the book along such lines, invoking the autonomy of the work, presents thereby a distorted interpretation. This position is likewise true with regard to literary and aesthetic criteria. Of course, there is also a danger of injudicious use of this assumption, as in those cases where the exegete posits on inadequate grounds that which the author could not have wished to express (such as a deviant religious viewpoint, or a literary technique which is seemingly only contemporary). However, the possibility of such injudicious use of a tool does not invalidate the tool itself, but only gives notice of the need for cautious use thereof. It is clear from this why, at the beginning of my remarks, I rejected the deconstructionist approach which allows the reader to interpret the text, not only contrary to the intention of the author, but also against the given structure of the text.

At this point, I would like to make a comment concerning the gap between exegetical theory and practice. Among all the various theoretical works which have attempted to justify one or another approach towards textual exegesis, I have not found even one which succeeded in providing adequate answers to all of the counter arguments in such a way as to make the approach entirely coherent from a logical viewpoint. On more than one occasion, one finds outstanding literary analyses, with which the reader can agree completely, in a book whose theoretical framework is not necessarily acceptable. On more than one occasion, by the critic's own declaration, an illuminating analysis of a literary text stands in blatant contradiction to the theory upon which it is meant to be based. This would seem to be a characteristic of any philosophical teaching: there will always be someone who will uncover its weak points, attempt to improve it or to present another one in its place—but again, without absolute success. But whereas in philosophy the theoretical discussion is the very essence and goal, in literary exegesis it is no more than a framework for the main thing.[23]

---

23. On the opposition between literary theory and involvement in creativity itself, see Rosmarin 1985: 3-6. In the light of this, some have concluded that one ought to abandon the theory of literature completely. See, for example, Knapp and Michael (1982: 723), who propose an end to involvement in literary theories. De Man reaches

The principles which have been outlined here in brief are intended to assist in understanding the arguments to be presented below, even if one finds there certain points which have not been fully developed, and even if they reflect a certain tendency to 'compromise' which refuses to draw the 'ultimate' logical conclusions as required of a philosophical theory. I have already noted that it is not my aim here to engage in theoretical discussions, but merely to provide the theoretical framework for my own work. This framework does not stand on its own, and I trust it will be supported in the discussions which follow. In any event, the reader must not confuse essential and tangential issues. Thus, even someone who does not agree with the theoretical framework which is implied in the principles I have presented may examine my arguments on their own merit, and decide his or her stance regarding them in light of an exegetical theory which he or she accepts. Such an approach may perhaps provide an answer to one or another claim, as well as to the general approach which underlies my research. That should be determined on the basis of an awareness of the central problem which underlies the work, which is the key to the understanding of any artistic work: namely, what is the aesthetic problem which the artist wished to solve? In this formulation of the problem, the search for whose answers constitutes the central theme of my study, I follow the approach of Haezrachi:

> The 'artist' problem is to express in his own medium, whatever it may be, something suggested to him by his own spirit, or by the order of a customer. He solves this problem by following the rules of his art, the rules of harmony and counterpoint, of prosody and brush work, such as he has learnt them from his masters or as he has invented them himself to suit his own needs. The solution is an artifact, a construction. What the artist has constructed will be a work of art, will possess aesthetic merit, if the problem set by the medium, ideas, technique has been successfully solved. Or rather, elegantly solved. That is, solved with a brilliance, an economy, and a seeming ease which belie the difficulty of the problem, and make this solution and no other seem the right, inevitable, perfect one.
>
> The aesthetic quality of a work of art, the beauty of a work of art, can be defined as elegance of solution. And since no two artists have the same problem, no two solutions are alike, and therefore the beauty of a work of art will always be unique…The creative genius, formulating his own problems, cannot follow any rules in their solution. He establishes the rule

another conclusion (1982: 770). In his opinion, the conflict between exegetical theory and practice is 'inherent in language, in the necessity which is also an impossibility to connect the subject with its predicates or the sign with its symbolic manifestation'.

by which he is afterward judged himself, and by which his imitators may
be measured. He creates and establishes his own kind of perfection…
        In order to evaluate a work of art the critic first notes that it represents
the solution offered by a given artist, at a given point in history to a given
problem. He then tries to gauge the qualities of this solution: is it appropriate to its problem? (Haezrachi 1954: 81-84)

What aesthetic problem did the book of Job set out to resolve? This
question is the leitmotif connecting all the chapters of this work, and is
the key to its coherent understanding.

Such a formulation may mislead the reader into thinking that I am only
concerned here with the aesthetic realm rather than with the contents of
the book, its religious outlook or its place in biblical thought. This is not
the case! In any literary work, the aesthetic problem is related to the
contents, and may be defined as follows: what is the best way to express
the content within the constraints accepted by the author? The aesthetic
problem confronting a modern-day author who would wish to express
contents similar to those of the book of Job would be entirely different
from those that confronted the author of the book of Job; the aesthetic
problem confronting the author of Job would likewise have been different had he wished to express other contents in his book. Therefore, in
focusing upon the central problem which I wish to confront in the
aesthetic area, I am not ignoring other aspects of the book of Job. On
the contrary: without examining the realm of beliefs and principles, it is
impossible to represent properly the aesthetic problems, and certainly
not to identify the solutions given in the book of Job.

Chapter 2

GENRE DISTINCTIONS

1. *Genre and Aesthetic Judgment*

In this chapter, I shall begin to discuss the genre classification of the book of Job *per se*. In the previous chapter, I elaborated an approach which in principle recognizes the importance of genre limitations for the formation of a poetic stance suitable to the aesthetic evaluation of a work. However, with regard to the book of Job, the examination of genre is of secondary importance, for reasons that go beyond pure aesthetics. One of the issues which has troubled students and exegetes of the book over recent generations has been the extent to which the extant text is 'original' and not the result of corruptions and additions during the course of its transmission.[1] This problem is of course not unique to the book of Job, but it acquires therein a unique form: it pertains not only to individual words or verses, but to the composition of the book as a whole. Doubts regarding its authenticity have been raised primarily regarding the prose chapters, the third cycle of exchanges with the friends, the speech by Elihu, and God's answer out of the whirl-

---

1.   I have placed the word 'original' within quotation marks in order to bypass the question of the number of stages in which the book was shaped by its author— that is, whether a number of different editions were 'published' prior to it. Thus, for example, Snaith (1968: 69-71, 92-99) and others have stated that the author himself 'published' three different editions, of which only the last survived. I believe that we are incapable of drawing such distinctions, for which reason I shall from here on utilize the term 'original' without quotation marks to refer to everything circulated to the public. This position is based upon the methodological assumption that it is more reasonable that deviations, structural imperfections, etc., originated at the hands of a person whose sensitivity to the work was less than that of the author himself. On the other hand, editing, changes and additions performed by the author himself were presumably incorporated in the book so smoothly that it is impossible to distinguish them at all.

wind.[2] And indeed, anyone who does not accept as axiomatic—whether religiously or methodologically—that exegetes must relate only to what they see, and that they need not even consider the possibility that what they see is a corruption,[3] must deal with the question of the present text of the book of Job. Examination of this issue will require us to determine as clearly as possible both the genre of the book and the constraints which determined its image.

The following are two examples of elucidations of this question.

1. Knowledge of the fact that the book of Psalms is an anthology confutes outright any claim that the present order of its hymns is 'corrupt' (for example, that in the original text Psalms 1, 15, and 23 were adjacent to one another, as all three deal with the righteous), as there is no strict thematic relation between one psalm and the next. On the other hand, in another genre (such as biblical narrative) a lack of thematic connection might serve as definite proof of corruption of the original sequence of the composition.

2. The method of reconstruction of biblical texts in the school of Albright, Cross and Freedman is based upon the attempt to identify models which might serve as criteria for purposes of reconstruction (Goodwin 1969: 9). These models constitute the literary and linguistic norms through which one may see the exigencies pertinent to the period and genre of the work in question. In the wake of studies of earlier literature which has come down to us in fragmented form, knowledge of genre conventions has become one of the most important tools for reconstructing damaged texts. The following passage from the Ugaritic myth of Baal and Anath, for example, is based upon the reconstruction of Cassuto:

> [I beseech you! Call to the bullock, to his father]
> [El the King shall establish him]
> [and call to Asherah and her sons]
> [To Aleh and the community of her offspring]
> [For now Baal has not a house like the gods]

2.   A systematic discussion of these elements appears below, Chapter 8.
3.   I reject this 'fatalistic' approach. I do not see any methodological justification (as opposed to a religious dogmatic one) for imposing an explanation upon a text whose corrupted nature is beyond doubt. This being so, and since it is clear that there are more than a few corrupt texts in the Bible, their correction and the interpretation of the corrected text represent an important goal. Thus, in principle. To what extent it is possible to realize this goal and to achieve adequate results is of course a separate question. See on this Tov 1990: 1-13, 215-80.

[nor a courtyard] like the sons of [Asherah.]
[The seat of El is a bower] for his son;
And the se[at of the mistress, Asherah-of-the-Sea.]
A seat for the mule[s of the daughter of Ar]
[A bower] for Tali daughter of the gre[at one]
[A dwelling place for my land] the daughter shall serve;
[A dwelling] for the correct [brides].
Then answered [the virgin Anath]
Return me a bullock to [my father...] (Cassuto 1971: 70, ll. 9-14)

In the introduction to his translation and reconstruction of this passage, Cassuto writes: 'Several lines are lacking, but it is possible to reconstruct them on the basis of parallels' (1971: 69). Such reconstruction was only possible because the redactor noticed one of the important genre characteristics of Ugaritic epic literature—namely, the use of repetitions (the phenomenon is described in his book on p. 34). He completes the lacunae based on the knowledge that this epic repeats what has been said in the identical words. Other Ugaritic scholars follow the same principle.[4]

Through analysis of this example, we reach the following conclusions. (a) The Ugaritic work in question has undisputably come down to us in fragmentary and corrupted form. Hence, (b) the missing elements need to be reconstructed in order for one to understand it. (c) Reconstruction is only made possible through the redactor's knowledge of the genre conventions of Ugaritic epics. For this reason, for example, he does not use prose in restoring the missing lacunae, as there are no mixed poetic and prose works in the genre of the Ugaritic epic. (d) The reconstructions are also based upon the recognition of the aesthetic norms of the particular work, with the awareness that they do not deviate from the 'expectations' for works written within the same circle of historical and cultural exigencies. (e) Any scholar in the field will see such a reconstruction as purely conjectural; that is, they will be perceived as of lesser worth than the extant original text.

The analogy to the book of Job is not complete, the situation there being far more complicated. First of all, the most basic facts are not the same for the two texts, as we do not know with any certainty that the extant text of Job is in fact corrupt; and even if it were so, unlike the Ugaritic text there is no agreement regarding the location of these corruptions. Hence, if both the very existence of corruptions and devia-

4.   See, for example, the reconstructions of Driver (1956: 34) to the Epic of Aqhath, and many others there.

tions from the text as well as their location is a matter for speculation, how much more so the suggested emendations. Hence, point (c) is particularly important, and we may now reformulate it in broader theoretical terms. In order properly to criticize a work of art that seems corrupt, one needs thorough knowledge of the system of constraints and conventions which determined its original character. But in this respect as well there are at least two decisive differences between the book of Job and the Ugaritic epic. First, the book of Job was not written with the same schematic strictness as the Ugaritic epic poem, so that the critical statements regarding it cannot have the same force as the proposed reconstructions concerning the epic. Secondly, once the epic of Baal was inscribed on tablets during the fourteenth century BCE, it was frozen and no changes whatsoever were introduced into it (with the exception of those physical changes caused by the ravages of time). Hence, the distinction between the original and proper text and the corrupted text is sharper (albeit there is no absolute certainty that the copy from the fourteenth century was free of errors). On the other hand, the book of Job was copied numerous times before its text was canonized and fixed, so that deliberate changes may have been made during the course of copying. Such changes are not as striking as random corruptions, making their identification more difficult, and their very existence more questionable. Moreover, since genre conventions are dynamic, and sensitivities regarding matters of faith and religion change from generation to generation, the book may have been reshaped during the course of its transmission in accordance with changing approaches and views. That which seemed 'impossible' (in terms of structure, theological position, etc.) to the original author may have appeared correct and proper to one of the later copiers (redactors?) of the book. The above analysis, intended to note the seriousness of the methodological problems involved in a critical approach to the book of Job, is also intended to answer the argument in principle raised by those scholars who are opposed to all change. They ask did not the redactor who allegedly added passages—beautiful as they may be in themselves—feel that he was thereby damaging its ideational coherence? In their opinion, the necessary conclusion to be drawn is that whatever a later redactor or copyist allowed himself, so to speak, to introduce into the book could have been done by the author himself. It follows from this that we can never know for certain which were the secondary additions. Such an argument is refuted, as I said, by the above analysis.

Hence, examination of the genre of the book of Job touches upon both its aesthetic evaluation and its critical examination, which are two sides of the same coin. Anyone who argues that the present composition of the book is not original must do so on the basis of aesthetic judgment: he or she initially states that there are faults in the present text, and in the wake of this assumes that these stem from unreliable transmission of the original text. For this reason, he or she proposes restoring the original text, clean of faults. Hence, whenever I speak here of 'examination' or 'judgment' of the book of Job, I refer both to aesthetic evaluation of the book as well as to the critical conclusions which scholars are liable to derive therefrom.

2. *Suggested Genre Classifications of the Book of Job*

A considerable number of scholars have addressed their attention to the question of the genre classification of the book of Job, whether as a whole or with regard to specific sections. These studies expose the essential problematics involved in any genre classification: the blurring of the boundaries between genre and sub-genre; the overlapping of the various sub-genres; the attempt to impose a specific cultural anchor (*Sitz im Leben*) upon a literary genre; and more. Nevertheless, these studies have contributed substantially to our understanding of the artistic nature of the book. I will content myself here with a brief survey of the various opinions regarding the subject, as background to the following stance (which will be fully presented further on). Even though the book eludes any attempt at strict genre classification, the very attempt to determine its genre contributes to our understanding thereof and helps to establish criteria for clarifying questions connected with its composition, its structure, and the theological positions represented thereby.

Any classification is based upon comparison. Hence, the most accepted means of genre classification of the book of Job is to contrast it with other works whose literary type is more clearly defined and accepted by the majority of scholars. Through such comparisons, there emerged the accepted view within Bible scholarship that the book of Job belongs to biblical Wisdom literature.[5] Even though it is doubtful whether this

5.   Thus, for example, Driver and Gray 1921: xxi-xxii; Kaufmann 1960: II, 606; Tur-Sinai, *EncBib*, III, p. 132. Gordis (1965: 41-45) distinguishes between high, speculative wisdom, and simple, practical wisdom, attributing the book of Job to the former type. Thus also von Rad (1972: 206-209) albeit he also notes elements of the psalm of lament.

constitutes a precise classification, it certainly represents a definite genre association. Volz (1911: 22-26, 61-76) emphasizes the relation of the book of Job to lament psalms, as does Westermann (1956: 22-25, 72-75)—this alongside other psalmic sub-genres, such as hymn, supplication, confession, etc. In the opinion of Westermann, only ch. 28 belongs to Wisdom literature.[6] Weimer (1974), following him, emphasized the relation of the book of Job to the genre of lament, even devoting a monograph to this topic.[7] He nevertheless notes as well the dramatic character of the book, in the wake of Bentzen (1959: 182), who saw it as a cultic drama, similar to the Babylonian work, 'I Will Praise the Lord of Wisdom'.[8] Other scholars note that the book is composed of several genres, and that it is in this that its uniqueness lies. Thus Fohrer (1963: 50), who stated that the speeches were composed according to the principle of 'mixing of types' (*Gattungsmischung*). In fact, several recently published studies concentrate on the genre classification of specific sections of the book. Thus, Von Rad (1960: 293-301) observed the relation of ch. 38 to the catalogue genre, even though his final conclusion is that this chapter, like the book as a whole, belongs to the Wisdom literature.[9] Dick (1983), in examining chs. 29–31, stated that even though they appear to be homogenous, they are in fact a combination of several genres—judgment speeches, laments, and wisdom, and that ch. 31 is wisdom in its essence. From here it is not a great step to cast doubt as to the very possibility of a genre classification for the book. Pope stated that from a literary viewpoint the book of Job is composed of fragments, and even wondered whether there is any justification for attempting to ascertain the genre of a book whose literary unity is in doubt—that is, *sui generis*—and which is lacking in terminology to define it. While there is justification for the statement regarding the generic uniqueness of the book of Job, there is some doubt as to whether this may be

6.   Westermann rejects the opinion of Baumgartel (see below, Chapter 8), who sees the laments as constituting an alien and secondary element in the book. For more on the issue of the relation of Job to the hymnal literature, see below, Chapter 5.

7.   He uses the term 'complaint'. On pp. 7-18 he briefly surveys the research on this subject. Further on, he offers a discussion of the genre of laments and its biblical contexts (pp. 55-67) and that of ancient Near Eastern literature (pp. 67-83).

8.   In his opinion, 'The dialogue is a 'dramatization' of the psalm of lamentation, more accurately of the prayer of the accused placed in the frame of the narrative'.

9.   He found a resemblance between ch. 38 and Papyrus Anastasi I, and thought that the 'school for training sages' was its *Sitz im Leben*. The fifth chapter of the present work is devoted to the relation between the book of Job and the catalogue genre.

attributed to the corruptions and changes which the work underwent over the course of generations, as Pope thinks—a point to which I shall return further on. In his commentary, Dhorm quotes Renen, who observed the literary norm of genre confusion in Israelite literature (which he saw as a somewhat 'primitive' characteristic). In noting the lack of generic uniformity, Renen stresses that it would be a serious error to describe the author as working according to a strict programme; we are not dealing here, he says, with a Platonic dialogue or an oration by Cicero, nor should one expect to find here Western laws of logic. Dhorm therefore stresses that one cannot expect the book of Job to follow strict poetic laws; rather, it is a literary type which allows for extremely free and variant movement, following the dictates of the artist's poetic imagination. Muller suggested several genre classifications for the cycles of debates (wisdom, hymnal, judgment), and attempted to arrive at a synthesis among the various approaches.[10]

In attempting to describe the literary nature of the book, there are those who forego genre classification, limiting themselves to comparison to extra-biblical ancient Near Eastern literature, primarily Mesopotamian. Thus Snaith states that the author of the first edition of the book derived his inspiration from the Babylonian 'I Will Praise the Lord of Wisdom'.[11] Gray (1970: 251-69) likewise emphasized the close connection between the book of Job and Mesopotamian literature. Unlike Snaith, Crenshaw (1970: 388) noted that it is precisely the connection of the book of Job to Mesopotamian literature that provides it a clear genre anchoring, and it is therefore doubtful whether it ought to be called a distinct *gattung*.

In the light of the multiplicity of nuances regarding the issue of genre identification of the book, it is doubtful whether the book of Job may be classified generically on the basis of comparison to other works, especially as the literary type of the latter is not itself always clear. In any event, it is impossible to determine how the book needs to 'behave', what

10. H.P. Muller 1978: 73-100. On pp. 23-72, he surveys studies concerning the genre relation of the book of Job to ancient Near Eastern literature, a subject which I will elucidate below.

11. Snaith 1968: 26ff. He notes that the genre classification of a Mesopotamian work such as 'I Will Praise the Lord of Wisdom' and 'The Babylonian Theodicy' is also subject to controversy among Assyriologists. See pp. 60-61 for the opinions of Gese, von Soden, and others. On the relationship of Job to 'I Will Praise', see Weimer 1974: 11-14, 76-78. Discussion of these texts and their relation to the book of Job appears below, in Chapters 4 and 5. For a comparison of the concepts of recompense presented therein and in the book of Job, see Chapter 7.

anticipations the reader ought to develop in relation to it, and what
phenomena may be defined as those for which there is no place in the
book from the genre viewpoint, and therefore as requiring exegetical
treatment of one sort or another. Under these circumstances, it is clearly
impossible to determine anything regarding the relation between the
extant text and the 'original' version of the book.

3. *The Book of Job and Aristotle's Poetics*

Another possible option for classifying and evaluating a literary work is
to examine it on the basis of the theoretical criteria which were established for a related genre. This method may only be implemented in the
case of those works within whose cultural milieu theoretical works pertinent to them or to similar works were also written. But what theoretical
work exists upon whose basis one may examine the book of Job and its
genre status? Clearly, no such works on literature were composed in
ancient Israel.

In the light of these considerations, I shall utilize for this purpose the
Poetics of Aristotle.[12] The most important consideration in making this
choice is didactic: comparison to Aristotle's work will illuminate certain
literary characteristics of the book of Job, a result which will not follow
from its comparison to other basic works in the realm of aesthetics. The
other reasons are theoretical, and may well explain the didactic advantage to be gained specifically from this comparison. (a) Due to the lasting
admiration enjoyed by Aristotle's *Poetics*, it is fitting that ancient and
modern works be judged according to it (I do not refer here to judgment in the value sense). The degree of authority enjoyed by the *Poetics*
is suitable to a confrontation with a book such as Job, whose literary
value is likewise beyond doubt. (b) While there is a great geographic and
cultural distance between classical Greece and biblical Israel, the chronological distance is not at all great. One may reasonably assume that the
Poetics was written around 330 BCE, a date that lies within the range of
the late biblical period, the period during which the book of Job was
composed (see above). (c) As I shall clarify below, there are cogent
methodological reasons for examining the book of Job on the basis of
criteria set forward by an aesthetician who did not know the book, and

---

12. An examination of the qualities of the book of Job in relation to the *Poetics* of
Aristotle was performed in the eighteenth century by R. Lowth (1787: 389-92) under
the interesting heading, 'The Poem of Job not a Perfect Drama'.

was not known to its author. (d) Aristotle's *Poetics* is devoted primarily to tragedy; there is likewise no dispute regarding the generally tragic character of the book of Job. Moreover, we have already seen that a number of Bible scholars see it as a drama. Even those who are reluctant to define the book in such terms are forced to admit that the essential element of drama is a central feature of the book of Job: everything which occurs or is stated therein is articulated by the figures in the work, and is advanced by them; the author himself is not involved at all. In this respect, the book of Job is unique within the biblical context, a point to which I shall return below. (e) Critical biblical research is a strictly Western-cultural product. As such, it is both directly and indirectly influenced by the literary norms established within Greek culture, and developed in the classical culture that flourished in its wake. From this vantage point, there can be no doubt that Aristotle's *Poetics* greatly influenced the formation of the literary criteria used by biblical scholars, and to large measure determined the stance of research towards the book of Job, even if in indirect and in many cases largely invisible ways. An examination of the book in the light of Aristotle's *Poetics* is therefore likely to uncover some of the hidden factors influencing the study of the book of Job.

Indeed, quite a number of non-biblical scholars have argued that Job was generically a Greek drama in the full sense of the word,[13] and there were even those who attempted to alter the book on the basis of this assumption.[14] While these approaches are exaggerated, they do contain a

---

13. According to Pope (1973: xxix), this claim was first made by Theodotius of Mopsuestia (350-428 CE), one of the Church fathers who dealt with Bible interpretation in a rationalistic way, while polemicizing with the allegorical approach, and thereafter by Theodor Bazet (1519-1605), a friend and disciple of Calvin.

14. For example, Kallen. The declared purpose of his work is 'to reconstruct the biblical Book of Job to what was in my opinion its original form—a Greek tragedy in the manner of Euripides' (1918: vii). In his opinion, the original drama was adjusted to the literary norms of the Bible by later redactors. He likewise states (in his introduction to the 1959 edition) that 'I have not yet found any sufficient reason for altering my statement…that we have here a Hebrew poet who knew the tragic form of Euripides'. In the reconstruction itself, Kallen brings a Greek chorus of priests; Elihu is the conductor and choir leader, who sings, among other things (sic!) 'Shema Yisrael' (p. 912). Kallen was a philosopher and aesthetician rather than a Bible scholar, but even a serious Bible scholar such as G.F. Moore suggests, in the introduction to Kallen's book (p. xxvi) that one should relate to his words as a serious conjecture in the realm of Bible studies.

certain element of truth in terms of the nature of the book of Job. There
were also those who saw it as an epic.[15] This too derives from its
'objective' character (that is, the demonstrative non-involvement of the
author in the course of the work) which is among the essential elements
of both drama and epic.

Hence, the point of departure suggested here is the following: What is
the picture to be derived from comparison of the norms articulated in a
sublime and influential theoretical work such as Aristotle's *Poetics* with
a work such as the book of Job, which has been seen by readers and
aestheticians of all generations as a classic work of genius? In other
words we shall attempt as a didactic exercise to evaluate the book and
ponder its generic characteristics on the basis of the criteria which
Aristotle established for tragedy.

a. *Aristotelian Principles Fulfilled by the Book of Job*
Aristotle imposed the following requirements upon tragedy, all of which
are well fulfilled in the book of Job.

1. Aristotle states that tragedy should deal only with elevated themes—
suffering, struggle between humans and the gods, or between conflicting
truths of high, great, moral power: 'The structure of the artistically finest
tragedy should not be single but complex...it should be an imitation of
fearful and pitiable happenings (for that is the special trait of this variety
of imitation)...' (ch. 13, 1452b31-34); 'Tragedy, then, is an imitation of
an action which is serious' (ch. 6, 1449b24-25).[16] See further the
examples cited by Aristotle in Chapter 14, referring to the confrontation
between conflicting values as subjects suitable to tragedy, as in Antigones
and Medea.

There is no doubt that the book of Job fulfils this requirement, as its
very essence is the struggle between suffering man and his god. Job, the
friends, God in his response—all represent truths of great power, whether
it be ethical power (Job), or power based upon intellectual dogmas that
have acquired the status of social norms (the friends).

2. The language of tragedy must be 'attractive...[with] speech that has
rhythm and melody [and song]'[17] (ch. 6, 1449b29-30). That is to say,

15. Thus the poet Milton (according to Pope 1973: xxix).
16. All of the quotes from the *Poetics* are based upon the translation of G.F. Else
(1957), except where otherwise noted. The matter mentioned above is discussed at
greater length by Halperin (1978: 36-39).
17. *Melos*, and see Halperin (1978: 74) for the translator's note regarding the

even though Aristotle includes tragedy among the genres which create mimesis 'using only prose or verses unaccompanied' (ch. 1, 1447a27-b8), it must forego imitation of the style of everyday speech, using elevated, 'artificial' language. The book of Job clearly fulfils this requirement.

3. Aristotle demands 'unity of plot': 'Hence, just as in the other mimetic arts a single (unified) imitation is of a single object, so also the plot, since it is an imitation of an action, should be an imitation of an action that is unified, and a whole as well...' (ch. 8, 1451a30-33).[18] This requirement too is met by the book of Job.

4. Aristotle stresses, 'But in the use of tragedy they cling to the historically given names. The reason is that what is possible is plausible' (ch. 9, 1451b15-16). Job, too, was chosen as the protagonist in this work because he was a 'known', 'historical' figure, as may be seen from Ezekiel (14.14, 20).[19] The names of the friends as well, taken from the Edomite *onomasticon* (Gen. 36), serve the same purpose: to relate the book to a known tradition and to lend it credibility by basing it upon 'historical' figures.

5. 'Thus the artistically shaped plot must necessarily be single, rather than double, as some maintain, and the shift must not be from bad fortune to good but the other way round, from good fortune to bad, and not caused by villainy, but by a big mistake' (ch. 13, 1453a12-16). It is clear that the book of Job is based upon a transition from good fortune to bad; Job becomes more and more entangled in misfortune, until he loses his property, his family, his health, and finally also his friends. (On the epilogue, which involves his return from ill fortune to good, see

question as to whether harmony and melody are equivalent concepts for Aristotle in this context.

18. A more extensive discussion appears in Halperin 1978: 62-65. Regarding the unity of time, Aristotle presents this as a characteristic of the tragedy (as opposed to the epic), but does not formulate it as an obligatory rule (ch. 5, 1449b12-15). Cooper concluded from this that this is not at all an aesthetic requirement of Aristotle, but only a description of the situation. Only the poetic theorists of sixteenth-century Italy, and thereafter Corneille and Racine in seventeenth-century France, saw this as an aesthetic rule. See Cooper 1962: 15-16. However, it seems to me that we should not be misled by the descriptive formula given by Aristotle. He in fact intended to establish the unity of time as a 'natural' rule, which exists in practice in every tragedy, making it superfluous to formulate it as an imperative. See on this Halperin 1978: 65-67. Regarding the unity of place, Cooper is correct in noting that this is not mentioned at all by Aristotle, but is a requirement of the later classicists.

19. See on this below, Chapter 8.

below.) Job's disaster did not come about because of his wickedness but, on the contrary, because of his outstanding righteousness, without which he would not have become a subject for discussion between God and Satan.

6. Aristotle states that the appropriate element of pathos is lacking in a tragedy if the disasters are caused by enemies or by people who are indifferent to one another. 'But when the painful deed is done in the context of close family relationships, for example, a brother kills or intends to kill a brother, or a son a father, or a mother a son, or a son a mother, or does something else of that kind—these are the acts one should look for' (ch. 14, 1453b19-22). This happened in the case of Job: God, who loved him, brought upon him disaster; his faith in God is at the same time the source of Job's emotional distress. See Job 29.1ff.; 30.1; 20–21; etc. The same is true of the feeling that his friends have betrayed him: 6.21-30; 19.1-2; 21.1-2; etc.

7. Aristotle formulates his demands of the heroes of tragedy in four rules: (a) that they be good; (b) the appropriateness of the image, that is, that it not be artificial or forced (such as, that an ignorant or simple man not declaim philosophical thoughts); (c) 'naturalness (likeness) of the individual'—that the figure be unique and archetypal; (d) consistency— 'In the character also, in exactly the same way as in the structure of the incident, one must seek constantly either for the necessary or the probable, so that it will be either necessary or probable that the kind of person say or do a certain kind of thing, and either necessary or probable that this incident follow that one' (ch. 15, 1454a33-36).

The thinness of the plot of Job (on which see below) does not allow for real character development. However, the very fact of the reader's empathetic identification with Job and rejection of the character of the friends teaches us that, at least with regard to Job (and possibly also with regard to Eliphaz),[20] the author succeeds in creating a consistent figure with individual characteristics beyond stereotypes, despite Job's being an archetype of the righteous man. Job is a judge, a respected figure, for which reason his character is suitable to elevated language and profound theological thoughts. This is evidently also the assumption with regard to his friends.

8. As for the structure, Aristotle mentions the 'prologue', which is 'a whole part of tragedy which comes before the entrance (*parodus*) of the chorus' (ch. 12, 1452b19-20) This refers to a kind of exposition similar

---

20. On the fashioning of the images of the friends, see below, Chapter 5.

to the prologue in the book of Job. As for the number of speakers in each scene, it is worth noting that the book of Job fits the period before Sophocles, as described by Aristotle, when only two speakers participated in the exchange of words. However, despite the praise that Aristotle gives Sophocles for introducing a third speaker, he does not demand this of every tragedy (ch. 4, 1449a15-21), nor does he limit the number of actors to three, unlike Horace.

The similarity between Aristotle's poetic rules and the book of Job bears testimony to the literary intuition of the author of the book of Job and to the analytic ability of Aristotle, who knew how to direct his remarks to substantive rather than to chance aspects. This resemblance justifies the comparison between them.

b. *Aristotelian Principles not Followed in the Book of Job*
There are several of Aristotle's principles that are not fulfilled in the book of Job.

1. Aristotle sets forward six rules for tragedy, which he ranks in order of importance as follows: plot, character, thought, use of speech, adornment of physical appearance, song–composition (ch. 6, 1450a29-30). The last two principles do not apply at all to the book of Job, and I shall ignore them. I would rank the other four elements by their order of importance in the book of Job as follows: thought, use of language, characterization, plot—a ranking that is almost the exact opposite of that required by Aristotle.

2. Examination of each of these four elements also indicates the great distance between the book of Job and Aristotle's demand of tragedy. (a) Plot: the definition of tragedy is opened by Aristotle in the following words: 'An imitation of an action which is serious, complete, and has bulk...and since it is the plot which is the imitation of the action (for by 'plot' I mean here the arrangement of the events)...But the most important of these is the structure of the events. For tragedy is an imitation not of men as such but of an action, a career, a man's happiness...' (ch. 6, 1449b25, 1450a4-5, 15-17). That is to say, what is important are the activities which take place, the scope of the plot. Therefore, Aristotle asks that the plot have some length (so long as it is still clear as a whole), and that it be developed and have some complication (ch. 7, 1450b31). All this is absent, of course, in the book of Job, whose plot may be summarized (apart from what appears in the frame-story) in one sentence. This being the case, there is also no complication, and hence no resolution

of the complication in the plot. If, however, we define the ideological complication in the book of Job as a kind of substitute for the complication in the plot (which is not really accurate), then the solution, too, the unravelling of the complication, is distinctly anti-Aristotelian: namely, the appearance of God out of the whirlwind. Not only is this solution not unequivocal,[21] but it belongs to that type of solution which Aristotle explicitly rejects. This is referred to by him as a *deus ex machina*—the appearance of God from the machine, brought about in an artificial way so as to resolve the complication.[22] (b) The images, that is the objects of imitation in tragedy, says Aristotle, are the acts of man, by means of which we must know his character: 'Hence they are not acting in order to represent their characters; they include their characters (along with the actions) for the sake of the actions. Thus the course of events, the plot, is the goal of tragedy, and the goal is the most important thing of all' (ch. 6, 1450a21-23). In the book of Job there is no activity on the part of the characters, except for talking. Hence, this condition is not fulfilled at all. Still another requirement of Aristotle regarding the characters is that the transition of the protagonist from success to failure be caused by a serious error he committed. This condition is not fulfilled in the book of Job.

c. *Conclusion*

It follows from this brief examination that the book of Job may be judged on the basis of the criteria established by Aristotle for tragedy, as we have found many common elements. But if we do so, we will also need to state that as a tragedy it is marred by numerous flaws, that it is a poor work of art. Yet the literary intuition of numerous generations completely rejects such a conclusion as based upon the attempt to examine the book of Job according to inappropriate criteria, notwithstanding its relationship to the ideal tragic model described by Aristotle. In the same way, any sonnet will be found inferior if examined according

---

21. Lowth (1787: 393, 395) compares the book of Job to the complex and convoluted plot of Sophocles' *Oedipus Rex*, showing that there is no resemblance between Aristotle's expectations in this area and the book of Job. His conclusion is that the book of Job does not contain any plot or action, not even of the simplest type. In practice, says Lowth, the very subject of the book eliminates any possibility of dramatic development.

22. Albeit the appearance of God does not constitute interference on the part of a factor taken from outside the plot, because throughout the length of his speech Job calls upon God to appear.

to the criteria for ballads, and vice versa.[23] This being so, by what aesthetic criteria ought one to examine the book of Job, if not by those of tragedy? As there is no other genre closer to the book of Job—that is, one by which, were one to judge the book of Job by its 'rules', it would be evaluated more properly—our judgment must be based upon those rules that the book sets for itself.[24] This known aesthetic rule[25] requires us to examine the aesthetic norms presented by the book of Job itself, according to which it ought to be judged. 'To be judged' in both senses: both aesthetic judgment (which is essentially a particular level in the understanding of the work),[26] and critical judgment, regarding the relation of the present version to the original version. Proposals for correction of the text are certainly not meant to be based upon alien criteria, for then one arrives at absurd conclusions, such as those arrived at by Kallen, as shown above.

23. In the formulation of Lowth (1787: 403): 'Criticising it according to foreign and improper rules would make this composition appear lame and imperfect'.

24. Lowth concludes that the book is a poem (1787: 405). But even here he applies alien criteria, and it follows *ipso facto* that the praises he gives to it are reserved and relative, based upon an indulgent attitude in the light of the antiquity of the book. Greece, says Lowth, did not succeed in reaching such a level of art prior to the days of Aeschylus, but thereafter, 'whatever rank may be assigned to Job, in a comparison with the poets of Greece, to whom we must allow at least the merit of art and method; amongst the Hebrews, it must certainly be allowed, in this respect to be unrivalled' (p. 404).

25. See the remarks of Haezrachi, cited above, pp. 29-30.

26. On the relation between exegesis and poetics, see Berlin 1983: 15-20.

Chapter 3

POETIC CONVENTIONS:
THE BOOK OF JOB, THE BIBLE, AND THE ANCIENT NEAR EAST

To what extent may the poetic criteria inherent in the book of Job itself be utilized for its aesthetic evaluation? A precondition for answering this question is the identification of its outstanding artistic characteristics, in which one may see norms immanent to the work. These means will enable us to assign it a suitable exegetical context, be it for critical purposes—the suggestion of changes and emendations—or for harmonistic treatment of its difficulties.

At this stage, I would like to note two salient characteristics of the extant version of the book of Job, whose striking nature makes it probable that they also characterized the original text, even if it did differ to a greater or lesser degree from the extant text. These are (a) a strong emphasis upon schematism and symmetry as structural elements, and (b) unusually difficult language. There is also a third characteristic, less striking at first glance, which I shall not consider at this stage of the discussion. I would argue that these characteristics should be seen as immanent poetic norms which may be utilized for a better understanding of the book, or even to establish a position regarding controversial questions concerning possible differences between the extant version and the original version.

The present chapter deals with questions relating to the first of these characteristics—the structure of the book. For a discussion of its linguistic characteristics, see Chapter 6.

1. Structural Elements in the Book of Job

The tendency towards schematism assumes several different forms in the book of Job, a multi-faceted quality strengthening the assumption that this is indeed a substantive aesthetic norm for the entire work.

Many observers have noted the schematic elements in the frame-story, chs. 1–2 and 42.7-17 (see Weiss 1959: 9, 22-29, 56):

i. The prologue is composed of several scenes of similar length, whose venues—heaven and earth—alternate with one another: Earth: 1.1-5; Heaven: 1.6-12; Earth: 1.13-22; Heaven: 2.1-6; Earth: 2.7-13.[1] To a certain extent, this schematic quality is also continued in the epilogue: God's words to the friends (42.7-8) are uttered from heaven, while vv. 9-17 close a circle, in that they parallel the description of the situation on earth in the opening scene of the prologue.

ii. There are several examples of the use of the typological numbers three, five, seven, and ten: (a) In the description of Job's wealth and happiness: 7 daughters + 3 sons = 10; 7,000 sheep + 3,000 camels = 10,000; 500 cattle + 500 she-asses = 1,000. (b) The verb ברך, which serves as a leitmotif or key word in the story, is repeated seven times, being alternately used in the opposite meanings of blessing and of curse (1.5, 10, 11, 21; 2.5, 9; 42.12).[2] (c) The description of the restoration of Job's fortune stresses the exact doubling of his property (42.12), while regarding his sons and daughters the typology is preserved by means of the numbers seven and three (v. 13). (d) The years Job lived after his restoration, one hundred and forty (42.16), are a multiple of the number 70, which is archetypical of the normal human life-span, as in Psalms: 'the years of our life are threescore and ten...' (90.10). (e) The number seven is repeated in the story seven times: 1.2, 3; 2.13 (twice); 42.8 (twice), 13.[3]

iii. There is repetition of the same linguistic formulae: 1.6-8 is repeated

---

1. See Weiss's note (1959: 71-72) concerning the exceptional manner of changing scenes in 2.7.

2. The seventh time the meaning is ambiguous: either curse God and bring an immediate end to your sufferings; or, with bitter sarcasm, continue to praise God until you die. This ambiguity is a means of focusing the dramatic problem of the prologue, which will accompany us throughout this work: does Job continue to bless God, or does he perhaps in the wake of his suffering dare to 'curse Him to his face', as Satan expected. By this, we are given a hint of the proximity that may exist between these two contradictory responses.

3. Weiss similarly noted the seven trials undergone by Job, but in this he also included the turning away of his friends, which I find somewhat forced. One who is not apprehensive of exaggerations of this type may also examine the repetitions of the number three; the repetition of the word 'land'; and other details which in a sophisticated (and to my mind homiletical) manner may be incorporated in the series of use of typological numbers.

verbatim in 2.1-3. The formula, 'a blameless and upright man, who fears
God and turns away from evil', which appears in these verses, also
appears at the beginning of the book (1.1). The phrase, 'but put forth
thy hand now, and touch' (1.1; 2.5); the idiom, 'Now there was a day'
(1.6, 12; 2.1); the sentence, 'and I alone have escaped to tell you' (1.16,
17, 19); and 'while he was yet speaking there came another' (1.16, 17,
18) are all repeated twice or more.

The literary norm of schematism and of clearly drawn structural
features also dominates the other chapters of the book, albeit in a different form, in which it has a strictly symmetrical direction. (a) The underlying structure of the book is symmetrical: that is, prose narrative–
poetical speeches–prose narrative. (b) The basic structure of the cycles of
arguments is strictly schematic, and repeats itself three times (chs. 3–11;
12–20; 21–37): Job–Friend A–Job–Friend B–Job–Friend C / D. (c) The
identical sentence is repeated in the opening of each of the twenty-five
speeches: 'Then X answered'.[4]

All these data seem to me to justify the statement that schematism and
accentuation of the structural framework are a striking and authentic
aesthetic characteristic of the book.

To what extent may this conclusion be used in the exegesis of the
book? This question arises because in a number of cases one finds
striking exceptions to this literary feature. In order to concretize this
matter, I shall describe the structure of the book in such a way as to
emphasize the exceptions to this schematism.

i. In the third cycle of debates, the speech of Zophar is missing,
thereby disrupting the model found in the two first cycles.

> 1st Cycle: Job–Eliphaz–Job–Bildad–Job–Zophar.
> 2nd Cycle: Job–Eliphaz–Job–Bildad–Job–Zophar.
> 3rd Cycle: Job–Eliphaz–Job–Bildad–Job–

ii. Seven of the eight speeches of the three friends are at least twenty
verses long, while Bildad's speech in the third cycle (ch. 25) is only six
verses long. Below are the number of verses in the speeches of each of
the friends:

	1st Cycle	2nd Cycle	3rd Cycle
Eliphaz	48	35	30
Bildad	22	21	6
Zophar	20	29	0

---

4.   In 27.1, 29.1, and 36.1, a different formula appears: 'And X again took up his
discourse, and said'. See on this Chapter 8.

iii. There is no symmetrical parallel in the opening of the cycles of debates to the speech of the Lord. Thus: Prose [Prologue]–[   ]– Speeches of the friends–the Lord's Speech–Prose [Epilogue]

iv. Chapters 32–37 introduce the speech of a figure not previously mentioned, thereby breaking the schematic structure of the cycles of debates:

1st Cycle:	Eliphaz–Bildad–Zophar
2nd Cycle:	Eliphaz–Bildad–Zophar
3rd Cycle:	Eliphaz–Bildad–Elihu

v. The longest of Job's first eight speeches is 75 verses long (chs. 12–14), while his final speech (chs. 26–31) deviates completely from the usual length, occupying 161 verses.

vi. Of the speeches of the three friends, the longest is 48 verses (Eliphaz, chs. 4–5), while the speech of the fourth friend, Elihu, is three times as long—159 verses (chs. 32–37).

Does the totality of all these facts require exegetical treatment? That is, must one ask the question as to why, in a book characterized by a literary norm of structural rigidity, there are exceptions from this norm, and whether each 'exception' demands explanation? In order to clarify the problematics underlying these questions, I shall compare it to an even stricter literary model, that of the acrostic.

Together with full, strict acrostics,[5] we find in the Bible a number of acrostics bearing exceptions to what one would expect on the basis of

---

5.   Such as Ps. 119; Prov. 31.10-31; Lam. 1; 2; 3; 4. In these poems the acrostic is complete without fault (albeit in Lam. 2 and 3 there is a change in the order of letters; the ‏פ‎ precedes the ‏ע‎, and it may be that there was once such a system of arranging the alphabet). An attempt to describe the metric characteristics of acrostics appears in Freedman 1972. I do not share his position that one may speak of 'non-alphabetical acrostics'—i.e., works (such as Pss. 33 and 94) which have certain metric characteristics in common with true acrostic works, but which lack the most important characteristic of the acrostic—alphabetical order (and see Freedman 1987). Deissler (1955) devoted a comprehensive study to Psalm 119 and its acrostic nature. In his wake see also the article of Mays concerning the Torah psalms (1987). Hurvitz has recently observed the wisdom nature of Psalm 119, as well as the relation of the acrostic model to Wisdom literature (1991: 131-34). For a comparative study of acrostics in the Bible and in Mesopotamian literature, and for additional bibliography, see Soll 1989: 315-18. He discusses 'The Aesthetics of Acrostic Poetry'. I do not agree with his conclusion that 'The name/sentence acrostic has the advantage of having its structure individually tailored to the *contents* [my emphasis] of the poem.' The acrostic in 'The Babylonian Theodicy' has nothing to do with its contents.

this model. Thus, for example, in Psalm 25 the hymn is basically acrostic, but its arrangement is less strict, containing several exceptions: the letters ר, ב and ק are missing; the letter ר is repeated twice (vv. 18-19); and following the letter ת there is another verse beginning with the letter פ. Psalm 34 is likewise acrostic, but with two exceptions: the letter ו is missing (albeit there are those who find it in the word ופניהם in the second half of v. 6, which opens with the letter ה, rather than at the beginning of a separate, independent verse), while following the verse opening with the letter ת there appears, as in Psalm 25, a verse beginning with the letter פ. There are those who see the final verses (beginning with the letter פ) of those two psalms as a late liturgical addition; it is interesting that in both cases the opening word is taken from the root פדה, followed by the name of God.

The careful reader would expect to find explanations for striking exceptions of this type, while ignoring them is tantamount to poor reading. One possible explanation is that, by unanticipated skipping of a letter, the author wished to draw the reader's attention to an important and central element in the poem as a whole. But in order for this explanation to be convincing, one not only needs to prove that there is a complete overlap between the place of the missing letter and the unusual importance of the idea conveyed by this omission; one also needs to demonstrate that such an artistic means is not entirely alien to the literary tactics of the period. If such an explanation cannot be found when one is speaking of an ancient poem whose text was circulated in numerous copies, one may be justified in offering a second, critical type of explanation: namely, that a line was omitted here due to an error in copying.

Theoretically, there is also a third possible approach: that the author did not pay sufficient attention to the demands of the model which he chose, and therefore did not bother to bring a verse beginning with the appropriate 'missing' letter. However, it seems to me that such an explanation must be rejected out of hand, as the very choice of such a stringent model as the acrostic indicates that the author deliberately undertook to open every verse with the letter that was required by the model.

Returning now to the subject of our comparison, the book of Job: here the third approach cannot be unequivocally rejected. While there can be no doubt regarding the strict conventions upon which the acrostic model is based, no such certainty exists regarding the book of

Job. Unlike the acrostic, we are unable to cite any clear model for comparison which would indicate the stringency of the conventions within which the author of the book of Job may have been working. Thus, in order to arrive at a position regarding the essential question—namely, whether 'lack of order' in the book of Job demands exegetical involvement, or whether the very fact of such involvement constitutes an excessive degree of interference—we require greater familiarity with the literary conventions upon which the book was shaped. But as the present text may be corrupt, it is impossible on its basis to provide a definitive answer to the question of the literary conventions of the original book, apart from the general characteristics cited above. In other words: is one to relate to the book of Job as one would to an acrostic, in which every exception to the strict scheme must be seen as a difficulty requiring exegesis, or may one assume that, notwithstanding its tendency toward schematism and symmetry, the basic norm of the book is one of non-insistence upon structural rigidity, making any exegetical involvement with these phenomena superfluous? This question becomes even more serious because a theoretical answer is insufficient. The decision as to when one needs to engage in exegesis, and when the very wish to 'interpret' is excessive and unnecessary, is itself not an unequivocal one, but a matter of judgment. The determining factors are the power of the exception, and the degree to which it is unequivocal—that is, something which might indeed be considered an 'exception' demanding exegetical involvement (whether critical or harmonistic). In principle, the answer is quite clear: any phenomenon which readers feel to be contrary to their anticipations, based upon the norms clearly set out in the work, requires exegetical intervention. However, in practice these anticipations differ from one reader to another, particularly because not everyone distinguishes between subjective anticipations and those which follow objectively from the work and its literary conventions.

A clear example of that approach which sees the original version of the book of Job as being based upon strict and rigid structural norms, any departure from which requires explanation, may be inferred from the various suggestions proposed by exegetes for reconstructing the original structure of the book. I shall exemplify this approach on the basis of one of the recent papers published on this subject, which attempts to set up objective criteria for a system of expectations to be applied by the would-be exegete when he or she sets out to reconstruct the original version of the book. The author of this article, M.P. Reddy, sets forth as

axiomatic the following criteria, upon which any reconstruction is to be
based (1978: 60-61):[6]

> i. Because of the very nature of Hebrew poetry, verses may be expected to
> occur in groups (strophes) connected by thought content, rather than
> singly.
>
> ii. In any speech the thought is expected to be continuous and the strophes
> ought to follow one another in the natural sequence of thought.
>
> iii. The chapters are expected to follow one another in a harmonious
> sequence of thoughts.
>
> iv. The chapters range in length from twenty to forty verses, with an aver-
> age length of twenty-six. If a chapter contains much less than twenty
> verses this is a fair sign of mutilation of text.
>
> v. Within each cycle of the Dialogue of the Book the discourses occur
> according to a pattern demonstrably the same, so that an approximately
> cyclic development of the argument can be seen, which will be found to be
> of great value in placing some of the disordered chapters.
>
> vi. There are numerous themes developed in the poem, some of which
> occur several times over with interesting variation. A pattern can be traced
> in the recurrence of the themes. From the content of a theme it is often
> possible to identify the speaker.

Examination of these principles reveals that, notwithstanding that they
appear to be excessively strict and rigid, they are not fundamentally
untenable, and some of them are evidently derived from norms inherent
in the work itself: for example, that the text of the book of Job is in fact
not composed of verses devoid of context, such as are found in several
of the collections in the book of Proverbs. Hence, one may reasonably
expect a certain logical continuity of subject between one verse and
another (i), between strophes (ii), and between one speech and another
(iii). The schematism that we have found in the book of Job seems to
confirm (iv) and (v), and even (vi) seems based upon this poetic norm.
However, despite the fact that these methodological assumptions seem
to make sense, when they are used in practice by Reddy to reconstruct
the 'original' edition of the book of Job, results are obtained which it is
difficult to accept.

The following, for example, are the conclusions regarding the original

6.   For additional proposals for reconstruction see, among others Tur-Sinai 1941.
In the second edition (1972), he is more cautious about making statements concerning
the 'correct' structure of the book. See also his remarks in *EncBib*, I: pp. 248-50.

constitution of the first cycle of debates which he reaches on the basis of these principles (Reddy 1978: 67):

> Job: ch. 3
> Eliphaz: 4.1-21; 5.1-7, 17-27.
> Job: 9.1-4; 5.8-10; 9.5-24, 32-35, 25-26; 10.1-13; 9.27-31; 10.14-22.
> Bildad: ch. 8.
> Job: 6.10; 7.9-12, 17-18, 1-4, 13-15, 5-6, 16, 19, 7, 20-21, 8; 6.2-30.
> Zophar: 11.1-12; 5.12-15, 11, 16; 11.13-20.
> Job: 12.1, 11-12, 2-10, 13-25; 13.1-24, 26-27; 14.16-17, 13, 14b, 15.

I would argue—and I shall attempt to substantiate this claim below—that this proposal is absolutely arbitrary. Notwithstanding the fact that it is based upon reasonable aesthetic-theoretic principles, one should completely refrain from presenting it as a 'reconstruction' of the original book. How does it come about that reasonable principles lead to unreasonable conclusions? The answer is, first and foremost, that they have been established in isolation from the literary-generic milieu of the book, rendering their application deficient. The main confusion derives from incorrect (and inconsistent—but this fault is irrelevant to the theoretical issue with which we are concerned here) judgment of the phenomena which ought to be defined as 'deviations' from the expected aesthetic norms. In other words, incorrect judgment regarding the definition of what should be considered an authentic deviation requiring exegetical intervention.

Is it indeed legitimate to assume that the book of Job was written with such great strictness as to justify rearrangement of the speeches simply to make them almost equal in length?[7] My own intuitive answer to this question is negative, but is there any ground for this intuition? One may indeed argue that such a claim is the result of being trapped in the logical circle to which we have already pointed: if we assume that the book was corrupted during the course of its transmission, it is difficult to infer clear-cut aesthetic intuitions and guidelines from the present version

---

7. According to Reddy's claim, the editors deleted certain verses in order to soften the criticism in the speeches, which is likewise the reason for the confusion introduced *ab initio* into the original version of the book. In the conclusion of his article, he even states the number of verses missing in the second and third cycles, since the average number of verses in each chapter is lower than the average of the chapters of the first cycle (1978: 86): in the first cycle, the average number of verses is 28 per chapter; in the second cycle, 25.9; in the third, 26.5. It seems strange that Reddy relates to the chapters rather than to the speeches, as if the division into chapters originated with the author.

regarding its structure and order prior to having become corrupted: that is to what extent was it rigid, dogmatic, and lacking in 'exceptions'? It follows from this that one may only break out of this logical circle by turning to the framework of historical and generic exigencies within which the book was created, in order to arrive at the literary norms which influenced its shaping. (Thus, for example, one may reject out of hand the seemingly plausible interpretation that the book is an absurd play in the style of Beckett or Ionesco, and therefore is 'confused' and 'incomprehensible', because such an explanation ignores the historical, cultural and generic framework of the book.)

An examination of the literary norms within whose framework the book of Job was created indicates that there is no justification for assuming that it originally had such a strict and schematic structure as assumed by Reddy. On the other hand, one cannot simply ignore the tendency of the book to emphasize systematic structural lines; hence, one needs to take a stance regarding the striking deviations from the anticipated structure which we mentioned above. The exegetes have dealt extensively with these exceptions, suggesting various solutions— whether by means of harmonistic exegesis or in a critical manner. I will not discuss here in detail the various proposals which have been raised, but will simply exemplify the directions of the solutions. A complementary and more detailed discussion, as well as my own conclusions regarding the relation between the extant version of the book and the original text, appears below in Chapter 8.

The following are a number of scholarly positions regarding the structural deviations which we have noted.

The absence of the speech by Zophar and the extremely short speech of Bildad, which are answered by an extremely long speech by Job, are seen from the harmonistic perspective as the author's allusion to the fact that the arguments of the friends have been played out. Eliphaz's speech in the third cycle is also shorter than his previous speeches; Bildad mumbles a few words containing nothing new; and Zophar is completely silent (see, for example, Segal 1942). In support of this interpretation, one may say that the literary character of the work, in which everything is conveyed by direct speech of the principals, prevented the author from intervening and stating the reason for the brevity of the words of Bildad or the absence of the words of Zophar, allowing the reader to reach this conclusion by her or himself. The unusual length of Job's final speech in the third cycle may also be explained in principle in the same manner: it is a kind of grand finale of his arguments, and hence a fitting end to the entire series of speeches as a whole. What is common to these interpretations is their use of the aesthetic principle that deviation from the expected is a known means of artistic expression, and that one ought not to be surprised at the author for using it.

Against this approach, one may pose a number of arguments. This is an excessively sophisticated approach, unsuitable to the cultural milieu within which the book of Job was written; it is an 'aesthetic anachronism'. One may strengthen this argument through the fact that the author is nevertheless heard here and there, not only in the fixed formulae, 'And...answered', but also in explicit statements, such as, 'So these three men ceased to answer Job, because he was righteous in his own eyes' (32.1), in which there is no hint that the friends gradually ran out of answers. For this reason, most critical exegetes think that the division of speeches in the third cycle is a clear result of corruptions: the overall size of this cycle is similar to that of the two previous cycles;[8] thus, we simply need to divide it differently, and to assume that part of that which is erroneously ascribed to Job was recited in the original version by Bildad and Zophar. The simplicity of the solution in this case is a virtue not to be ignored.[9]

I do not wish at present to decide among these different options, but merely to illustrate the existence of a genuine problem which the reader needs to consider. What is in fact the correct approach to the solution of the problem? Such a question cannot be decided, as I mentioned, on the basis of the book of Job alone, but only through consideration of the artistic conventions within whose framework the author worked.

The speeches of Elihu likewise break the schematic structure of the book in a striking way, making it necessary to examine them from an exegetical viewpoint (even without taking into account another difficulty: namely, that Elihu is mentioned neither in the prologue to the book, chs. 1–2, nor in the epilogue, specifically in 42.7, 9). Here too, there are those who suggest a harmonistic explanation: Elihu's speeches 'are a natural transition from the end of Job's accusations to the appearance of God...he is evidently the poet himself', says Kaufmann. According to Snaith, these speeches are an expression of the author's good dramatic sense. Similarly, Segal argues that Elihu's speeches, in delaying the antici-

8. First cycle—224 verses; second cycle—226 verses; third cycle—273 verses.
9. It is clear that one still needs to examine whether the contents are suitable to this solution, a matter that will be judged further along.

pated reply by God, are another trial which afflicted Job, perhaps more difficult than the previous ones, and an inseparable part of the book.[10]

The critical exegetes find these solutions to be forced, and hence reject them. They argue that the speeches of Elihu are in fact a later addition by an author who wished to leave his impression upon the book, so much so that he overcame his reluctance to create an aesthetic-structural fault, or was too blind to see the fault.[11]

In this matter as well, familiarity with the literary-generic conventions in which the book of Job was composed may be helpful in deciding between these two approaches.

The speech of the Lord likewise breaks the symmetrical structure of the book. However, even someone who states that this speech is a late addition[12] must base this perception primarily upon reasons of content, rather than upon its deviation from an anticipated schematic structure. And indeed, we have here a clear example of a structural exception which, because it seems self-evident, is not to be seen as a difficulty requiring exegetical intervention. God's appearance, which has been awaited by Job throughout the length of the book, must by its very nature be presented as an exception to the routine model found throughout the book. Despite his marked tendency towards schematism, one cannot expect the author to preface Job's lamentation in ch. 3 by words of God merely in order to create a symmetry with God's speech at the end. The breaking of the schematic framework is almost necessitated by the uniqueness of the speaker—God—and is so natural that the reader does not at all feel that this is a problematic exception. In other words, it is not the breaking of the anticipated structural framework that emphasizes the speech of God, nor do we learn of its exceptional

10. Y. Kaufmann 1960: II, 609; Snaith 1968: 75; Segal 1942: 89. Fisch (1990: 33-34) argues the authenticity of Elihu's speech, based upon the assumption (which is to my mind incorrect) that one may understand the book of Job as a kind of cultured dialogue with the Greek tragedy: 'It seems sometimes, as though, in this, the Hebrew poet was trying to outgreek the Greeks' (p. 29). On the other hand, he argues that the function of Elihu is parallel to that of Hermes, who criticizes Prometheus before the appearance of Zeus, in Aeschylus's work *Prometheus Bound*.

11. Many follow this general direction. See, for example, the interpretations of Driver and Gray 1921: xl-xlviii; Kahana 1924: 14; Dhorm 1926: ci-cv. See also Kraeling (1938), and others.

12. On all the questions connected with the reconstruction of the third cycle and the speech of God, see Chapter 8, where additional bibliographical references are also given.

character from it; rather, this exceptional character exists in and of itself. Hence, unlike the two previous examples, any proposal to eliminate this speech (or to add a parallel speech at the beginning of the dialogues) merely in order to create symmetry must be rejected out of hand.

The distinction between the two previous exceptions and God's speech is clear: the third cycle of debates and the speech of Elihu depart from the dominant model in a manner arousing surpise, creating an authentic need for exegetical involvement, whether it be harmonistic or critical. This is not so in the case of God's speech.

Much as I have attempted to formulate a rule which would present in a theoretical manner the principle upon which my present argument is based, I have not been successful. Such a formula would have needed to include such parameters as the power of the exception (that is, its explicitness); the importance of the message which it emphasizes; the nature and degree of stubbornness of the genre; the literary conventions which guided the author; the simplicity or complexity of the critical solution. But it is impossible to weight properly all of these data in such a way as to create a real equation. In the final analysis, what will decide among the different exegetical proposals—those to be rejected out of hand because they create an imaginary difficulty, and those which are deserving of consideration and from among which one must select the appropriate solution—are the common sense and feeling of proportion of each reader. However, one must nevertheless strive for the maximal possible limitation of the subjective elements in this imaginary equation, something made possible through familiarity with the literary conventions within whose framework the work was written.

Our discussion in this chapter has thus far focused upon structural questions, while ignoring considerations related to the content of that which is written. However, it is clear that any proposal to retain or to alter the present version, as well as the question as to how to alter it, cannot be decided on the basis of structural considerations alone. One needs to ask whether the words attributed to Job in the third cycle are appropriate to him in terms of content. It is not sufficient for those who would suggest alterations in the cycle of debates merely to arrive at a structural balance; they must demonstrate that those things which they propose transferring from one speaker to another are suitable in the mouth of the latter. In the case of Elihu, one also needs to take into account extra-structural considerations, such as the fact of his not being mentioned in the prose prologue, the extent to which his style is unusual, whether the ideas and motifs in his speech are consistent with the book as a whole, and so on. These considerations have not been mentioned here, in order to isolate the structural issue and to present the methodological problems involved therein, as well as the theoretical conclusions to be derived therefrom. The application of these conclusions, as well as of other conclusions to be reached in the course of our examination, will be presented in Chapter 8, after discussing various other aspects of the book and offering a fuller picture of its character. In any event, it is appropriate to note here that, due to the difficult language, there are many passages which may be interpreted in a manner suitable to nearly every one of the speakers, thereby reinforcing the structural considerations.

To summarize: our comparison with Aristotle has confirmed the known aesthetic principle, according to which one ought not to examine the book of Job except on the basis of its own immanent aesthetic-literary norms. However, it became evident, through our examination of the structural questions, that any examination based upon these norms requires a better acquaintance with the broad literary circle within which the book of Job was created, namely, that of biblical and ancient Near Eastern literature. Only thus may the exegete properly evaluate the data in the book itself and determine the aesthetic norms which obtained before it became corrupted, if such indeed happened. There is a clear difference between taking our criteria for the examination of the book of Job from Aristotle, and deriving them from the Bible and from ancient Near Eastern literature. In the former case (unlike the latter), we are bringing the book of Job into an entirely foreign realm, outside of the 'circle of exigencies' within which it was created. It follows from this that we need to examine several of the circles of exigencies, whose recognition may assist us in shaping a balanced exegetical position with regard to fundamental problems in the structure of the book. In the light of this discussion, at the end of the chapter I shall draw certain conclusions in principle, examining their implications for the book of Job.

2. The Dialogues

Let us now examine several of the literary conventions within whose framework the book of Job was created, so as to establish an appropriate system of poetic expectations which will enable us to judge the book within its correct cultural context. The discussion will first concern itself with the dialogues and dialogic literature in the Bible and the ancient Near East, and thereafter I shall clarify questions of structure.

Nevertheless, due to the close relation between these two aspects, I shall not draw a sharp and unequivocal line between them in the course of the discussion.

The framework of the book of Job is essentially dialogic, consisting of exchanges between Job and his friends, and his God. The complete lack of plot elements between one speech and the next, with the exception of brief connective sentences, need not obscure the relationship between this framework and the genre of biblical narrative, which is also based upon dialogic scenes bridged by connective words of the author, whether these are long or short.[13] It is therefore also worthwhile to examine the book of Job according to the criteria and literary conventions of this genre. Such an examination will relate to two central matters in the shaping of the biblical short story: the continuity of the dialogues and the nature of the speech within them.

One of the central exegetical questions concerning the book of Job concerns the nature of the dialogue therein, and whether or not the present order of Job's speeches is corrupted. As I have already indicated, this question is generally analysed by scholars on the basis of the reasonable assumption that there ought to be clear connections and a firm relationship between one speech and the next, such as may be reasonably expected in any dialogic literature. In the absence of these, there are two kinds of solutions that may be proposed: the critical solution is to see this as evidence of corruption during the course of transmission of the text, in which case there is room for a reconstruction which will tighten the connection between the dialogues. The harmonistic solution, by contrast, is based upon the quest for literary explanations for the lack of a clear connection between speeches which are adjacent to one another. This may be seen as a mimetic tactic on the part of the author—that is, a means of indicating the difficult psychological state of Job, who is unable to respond in an orderly and systematic way to each argument; or as a mimesis of the process of debate. The more heated the debate becomes, the less its participants react to the words of their fellows, focusing only upon what seems important to them or that which particularly impressed them. Nevertheless, at one stage or another, they do return to deal with points which had already been mentioned in the earlier stages.[14] Thus, for example, the words of Job, 'Truly I know that

13. Licht (1978: 24-50) took note of this. And see Bar-Efrat 1979: 62, 159, 167.

14. On mimesis, which I see as an explicit feature of the book, in addition to the two features mentioned above (emphasis upon structural lines and

it is so: But how can a man be just before God' (9.2) may be seen as a direct reaction to the words of Eliphaz, 'Can mortal man be righteous before God? Can a man be pure before his Maker?' (4.17), albeit the speech of Bildad interrupts between these two speeches. Does this indicate a confusion in the transmission of the text (Reddy 1978: 66), or ought one to apply here the following mimetic principle: this is the author's means of conveying Job's psychological state; following the first speech of Eliphaz, being too agitated to respond to the arguments in a proper manner, Job only recovers after the words of Bildad and returns to deal with Eliphaz's doctrine of recompense (thus Dhorm 1926: xxxii)?

These two opposing approaches share the assumption that the book, as written by the author, required an inner logic and a suitable order of arguments and responses. Therefore, we need to reconstruct the source in such a way as to present a logical order, or else find a hidden logic, literary or psychological, for the present order.[15] Indeed, may we really interpret or reconstruct the book on the basis of a system of expectations that assumes a thematic and developmental connection between each speech, and between each of the details of the speeches? This question is deserving of examination through analysis of the structure of the cycle of debates in the book against the background of the generic conventions of the dialogic literature within whose framework it was written.

The structure of the cycles of debates presented the author with possibilities for several different kinds of connections among the speeches, from which there followed extremely strict compositional demands. The reader may anticipate the following connections:

a.   A dialogic connection between the speeches of each of the friends and the speeches of Job, and between the speeches of Job and those of each one of the friends.

b.   An internal development within each of the speeches of Job and the speeches of the friends, in those parts of the speeches which are not a clear response to that which preceded them.

---

schematism; difficult language), see below, esp. Chapter 5.

15. Such logic cannot be found in those cases in which an answer is given (according to the exegete) to a statement which has not yet been made. See, for example, the words of Tur-Sinai (1972: 113): 'The words of Eliphaz in ch. 4 are in effect a response to the claims made by Job in ch. 9; and it follows from this, evidently, that one ought to see these words of Job, like those in ch. 7, whose connection to chs. 9–10 are extremely striking, as part of a comprehensive speech of Job which preceded the replies of the friends…'

c.   Development from the words of one friend to the next—so
       that they do not all repeat the same thing.
d.   Development from one cycle of debates to the next.

Presented schematically, the picture will look as follows (the arrows
indicate anticipated influences):

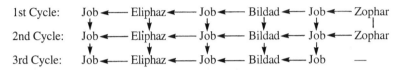

The system of possibilities represented by this model is not fully
exploited. I do not know of even one commentator, whether critical or
harmonistic, who argues that in its original version (whether that extant
here or not) the book realized all of these possibilities. Thus, the question
is why should one suppose that the author actualized one rather than
another system of interrelationships, if in any event he did not exploit all
of the possibilities inherent in the above structure? Perhaps he needed to
compromise and to relate to only some of them, because he was unable
to relate to them in full—and for this reason not every lack of connection
between one speech and the next requires 'interpretation' or correction?

Here, too, an examination of the dialogical literature within whose
framework the book of Job was written may assist us to create a more
reasonable system of expectations of the book, and thereby help to limit
the degree of arbitrariness involved in the exegetical decisions.

The biblical short story is filled with exchanges which do not involve
the structural complications of a multi-sided conversation. These
exchanges are generally speaking simple, brief and written in prosaic
language.

Simplicity is expressed in the fact that only two speakers participate in
the conversation, which was the accepted norm in Greece prior to the
period of Sophocles (according to the testimony of Aristotle, *Poetics*,
ch. 4). This is the case in the conversations between God and Cain (Gen.
4.6-16); between God and Abraham (Gen. 15; 18.20-33); between Jacob
and Esau (Gen. 33); between Moses and God (Exod. 3; 4.1-17); between
Moses and Jethro (Exod. 18.6-23); between Rahab and the spies (Josh.
3);[16] between Samson and Delilah (Judg. 16.4-17); and elsewhere.[17]

16. It is striking here that preserving the simplicity of the dialogue—no more than
two speakers—causes the author to forego mimesis in conveying the words of the
spies: they speak together, as a chorus to whom the text is dictated (vv. 14, 17-20, 24).

Even when the occasion demanded the presence of more than two speakers,[18] the conversation was usually constructed in such a manner that in any given scene one of the speakers filled the role of intermediary, who guides the dialogues. An example of this may be found in the story in Genesis 24: in the second scene, the servant of Abraham fulfils the role of 'intermediary', while in the third scene Laban and Milkah fulfil this role. Thus:

> (A–Abraham; B–the servant; C–Rebecca; D–Laban; E–Bethuel; F–Milkah).
> First Scene: A (24.2-4)–B (5)–A (6-8).
> Second Scene: B (17)–C (18-19)–B (23)–C (24-25)–B (33a)–D (33b)–B (34-49
>   [37-41: internal dialogue between A–B; 45-47: internal dialogue
>   between B–C])—D + E (50-51).
> Third Scene: D + F (55)–B (56)–D + F (58a)–C (58b)–D + F (60).

This brief survey, intended to clarify the meaning of the term 'simple dialogues', illustrates that, even though the biblical narrative is not excessively strict on this point, and certainly does not consciously conform to any aesthetic 'law', the accepted literary tradition preserved a simple structure for dialogic exchanges.

The dialogues are, generally speaking, brief. Sometimes, indeed, one of the participants speaks at some length, but then the reply of the second speaker is usually brief, pertaining to only one aspect of what has been said. Thus, Moses responds in brief to the relatively lengthy words of God (Exod. 3.5-10, answered in v. 11; vv. 14-22 answered in 4.1); the Edomites respond with great brevity to the detailed speech of Moses (Num. 20.14-17, answered in v. 18b); similarly, the spies' response to the words of Rahab (Josh. 2.9-13 answered in v. 14; vv. 17-20 answered

A similar phenomenon is found in other dialogues, such as that between Jephthah and the elders of Gilead (Judg. 11.4-11); between Rehoboam and the representatives of the people (1 Kgs 12.1-14); between Jonah and the sailors (Jonah 1; but compare v. 7, which is a mimetic attempt to convey the situation of verbal exchange; as likewise in Gen. 42.21); Baruch to the princes and the king to the princes (Jer. 36); and the like.

17. See Bar-Efrat (1979: 115-21), who notes 2 Sam. 19.19-24 as an exceptional multi-sided conversation, in which there participate three speakers—David, Shimei son of Gera, and Abishai son of Zeruiah.

18. It would seem that this literary practice even influenced the formation of stories and images *ab initio*. It thus seems to me that the story of the revelation of the angel to the parents of Samson (Judg. 13) is divided in two in order to 'allow' both Manoah and his wife to speak with the angel. For a detailed analysis of this chapter, see Zakovitch 1982: 19-84.

in v. 21); David's brief response to the Tekoite woman (2 Sam. 14.5-7, answered in v. 8; vv. 11-17 answered in v. 18a); Ruth's brief response to the words of Naomi (Ruth 3.1-4, answered by v. 5); and the like.

iii. Unlike the case in Ugaritic and Mesopotamian epics, the dialogues are characteristic of biblical prose and are not commonly found in poetry. In the prophetic literature, which is primarily poetic (apart from the non-prophetic genres found in the prophetic books, such as the biographical stratum in the book of Jeremiah), dialogues are only found in the reports of visions, mainly call visions.[19] And, in fact, in these visions the responses of the prophets, which create the dialogue, are also in prose, unlike the generally poetic framework of the prophecies (see Isa. 6.5, 8b, 11a; Jer. 1.6, 11b, 13b; Amos 7.2b; 8.2; Zech. 1.9-17; 2.1-4, 5-9; 3; 4; 5; 6). In the poetry found in the Wisdom literature and in the Psalms there are also no dialogues.[20]

We may therefore state that dialogues are a technique characteristic of biblical prose, rather than of biblical poetry. Perhaps this is because dialogue is fundamentally understood as a mimetic means unsuitable to the elevated language of poetry, which by its very nature is not the language of speech.[21]

Nevertheless, biblical poetry does contain an alternative technique to dialogue: the debate. In this technique, the author creates a dramatic monologue, placing words in the mouth of one side alone.[22] The substantive difference between such a monologue and a true debate is that

19. I have found an exception to this only in Amos 7.12-17—the words of both Amos and of Amaziah contain poetic parallelisms.

20. Alter (1985) notes Proverbs 7 as an exceptional example of a kind of story written in poetic parallel. But here too there is no dialogue, only the quotation of the words of the seductress. On quotation as a substitute for dialogue, see below.

21. Rendsburg (1982) attempted to prove that a dialect of spoken language existed in Israel alongside the biblical language, which was a separate literary dialect. This is not the place to examine his conjectures, which seem to me incorrect. In any event, even if one accepts his view, within the framework of the limits of use of a literary dialect alone, it is clear that prose is more appropriate than poetry for the imitation of everyday speech.

22. Such as Isa. 28.14ff.; 40.27; 44.16-17; 45.10, and *passim*; Jer. 2.23, 27; 11.14-15; 12.9, 26-28 (and perhaps these are not poetic fragments?); Hos. 2.7, 14; 14.8; Amos 6.13; Mal. 1.1-2, 12-13; etc. Crenshaw even defined the genre of the book of Job as dialogue-debate (*streitgesprach*), which is in his opinion a wisdom genre that assumed new dimensions in prophetic literature, especially in Second Isaiah.

this technique makes no pretence to objectivity: the author formulates the response as he or she wishes. At times he deliberately formulates them in an absurd or sarcastic manner,[23] while at other times he uses a sophisticated technique of 'negative quotation'—citing what the other side should have said but did not say, such as 'They did not say, "Where is the Lord who brought us up from the land of Egypt..." ' (Jer. 2.6; see also v. 8, etc.).

It would appear that, apart from the book of Job, one may note only one outstanding exception to the biblical rule of resorting to dialogue within the prose framework alone—the Song of Songs. Even though here too there are no dialogues creating a consecutive plot, the frame structure of the book is dialogic, a fact which may be connected with its late date of composition, which was certainly several generations after the book of Job.[24]

With regard to the dialogues, like several other areas of literature (see Hoffman 1979a: 96-99), the Bible seems closer to Egyptian literature than it does to north-eastern Semitic literature (that is, Mesopotamian and Ugaritic). In Egyptian literature, the dialogues are primarily a technique of prose narratives,[25] whereas in Mesopotamia and Ugarit they are more widely used in the poetic realm. One may therefore describe them as a technique of epic literature, whether in poetry (Mesopotamia; Ugarit) or in prose (the Bible; Egyptian literature).

The biblical dialogues are also closer to those of Egyptian literature in terms of their nature: they are brief, mimetic-dramatic. Such dialogues appear both in the autobiographical genre that was common in Egypt[26]

---

23. Such as Isa. 28.15b. An exceptional case, on the boundary between dialogue and quotation, is found in Judg. 5.28-30, where there appears a fictitious dialogue between the mother of Sisera and her wise ladies, whose polemic-ironic (that is: one-sided) intention is very clear.

24. For further discussion of the Song of Songs and its structure, as well as its compositional relation to the book of Job, see below, pp. 97-98, 388. The literary nature of this book has recently been discussed at length by Fox 1985: 186-90. Even though he notes the striking genre connections between it and Egyptian love poetry of the second millennium BCE, he shares the general opinion which pushes the date of composition of the Song of Songs forward to the Second Temple period.

25. Within the Egyptian stories, there are incorporated at times poetic sections. These do not advance the plot, but praise the king of Egypt. See *ANET*, p. 19, lines 45-74. Nevertheless, they are not alien bodies that were incorporated within the work at a later date.

26. See the report of Wen-Amun, in *ANET*, pp. 25-31; Sinhath, *ANET*, pp. 19, 21.

and in stories of other types. We thus find dialogues in the story 'The Tale of the Shipwrecked Sailor' (Lichtheim 1973: I, 211-15), and in various miracle tales (for example, 'The Magician Djedi' [Lichtheim 1973: I, 217-20]). In the story 'The Two Brothers', the dialogues between the seductress (the wife of Anpu) and the younger brother, Bata, fulfil an important role in the course of the plot, as do the dialogues between the two brothers (Lichtheim 1973: I, 203-11). In all these, as in the Bible, the exchanges are only two-sided, even though here and there one finds that one of the sides in the dialogue is a group rather than an individual, such as the youths in 'The Doomed Prince' (Lichtheim 1973: I, 200-203) or the princes in the story of Si-nuhe (Lichtheim 1973: I, 222-33).[27]

In north-eastern Semitic literature matters seem different. The Mesopotamian epic poem is constructed of numerous dialogues, differing both in length and in their mimetic nature from those found in biblical and Egyptian prose. They are long and very convoluted. The main complication is created by the repeated inclusion of quotations and secondary quotations, so much so that at times it is difficult to understand who is speaking, what he is quoting, what comes earlier and what comes later.[28] One sees here the authors' struggle with the details of the plot, resulting in an extremely complicated story. These qualities are also characteristic of the Ugaritic epic poem.[29] In it, as in Mesopotamian literature, the exchanges are only between two sides; unlike the biblical narrative, one does not find there more complexly structured chains of dialogues, such as A-B-A-C-A-D.

A striking exception to these characteristics of dialogues in Mesopotamian literature is found in the prose of the proverbs. Here one finds dialogues of a very complex structure, reminiscent both of that found in the biblical narrative and of the structure of the dialogues and the

---

27. An interesting exception is the myth of the 'Contest of Horus and Seth', in which numerous participants take part in the exchanges alongside the group of 'nine' (the group of primary gods) which speaks as one group. See *ANET*, pp. 14-17.

28. See, for example, the words of Anshar to Gaga in Annuma-Elish III, 3-66; the conversation between Gaga and his parents Lahmu and Lahamu, 71-124; between Marduk and the great gods, the Igigi, VI. 21-29. See II.10-48—the long speech of Ea to Anshar and, following intermediary comments of the narrator—Anshar's answer, 35b (the tablet is broken). All references are according to *ANET*, pp. 60-72.

29. See Cassuto 1971: 66, 67-68, 69. The complication of the plot, and not only the state of preservation of the tablets, also makes it difficult to understand the course of the plot in these epics. See, for example, the discussions concerning this matter in a new study of the epic of Aqhat in Margalit 1989: 3-92.

general situation in the book of Job: thus, for example, in the story, 'The Fox and the Animals', whose background is a trial. The animals appeal to the gods Shamash and Enlil to judge among them, speaking to one another while the god-judges hover in the background. Thus, there is created a kind of multi-sided conversation in which one of the partici- pants, the fox, plays a more prominent role, functioning as an interme- diary guiding the exchanges. Nevertheless, the structure is not entirely orderly.[30] While the primary participants are the fox, the dog, and the wolf, there is also a lion, whose function is unclear. According to the reconstruction and translation of Lambert, the structure is as follows:

> A brief prologue, presenting the appeal of the fox to the gods Enlil and Shamash.
> Exchanges: Fox–Lion–Fox–Dog–Wolf–Fox–Dog–Wolf–Dog–Wolf– Fox–?–Dog–Wolf–Fox–Lion–Fox–?–Fox–Dog–Wolf–Fox–Dog–Wolf– Fox.
> A brief epilogue, in which Enlil is again mentioned.

Another Mesopotamian work, consisting entirely of dialogues, is known by the name, 'The Babylonian Theodicy'. At its centre is a man who bemoans his suffering to his friend, who attempts to comfort him. The poem consists of 27 stanzas, of 11 lines each. It is built on the model of an acrostic: the opening syllables of each of the stanzas of the poem are identical, and when combined together one arrives at the sentence *anaku saggilki [namu]bbib masmasu karibu sa ili u sarri* ('I Saggilkinamubib, the incantation priest, an adorant of the god and the king'). The meaning of the personal name, according to Romer and von Soden (1990: 143) is 'Sangil, the pure and faithful one'.

According to Lambert (1960: 63), the work was written around 1000 BCE; according to Romer and von Soden (1990: 142), its date is ca. 800- 750 BCE. The earliest extant copy is from the eighth century BCE, while there are also later copies beginning from the period of Assurbanipal, in the seventh century BCE, on to the Seleucid period (300-300 BCE), or even the Parthian period (100 CE). It follows from this that it was known and attracted great interest during the period of composition of the book of Job.

30. The exact structure is difficult to reconstruct because of the state of preserva- tion of the tablets. The date of the work is also subject to controversy: 1200-1500 BCE? 1700 BCE? The tablet preserved is from the seventh century, meaning that, despite the antiquity of the work, it was known and accepted even later. See Lambert 1960: 186-209.

Romer and von Soden emphasized that 'Dem Buch Hiob steht kiene babylonische so nah wie diese' (1990: 146). Yet, as our concern in this section of the work is with structural issues, I will not discuss here other connections between 'The Babylonian Theodicy' and the book of Job. The most important characteristics of this work which, as we shall see below, may contribute to our understanding of the structure of the book of Job are the following:

i.   The work has a very rigid structure, both in terms of the length of the stanzas and in terms of its being an acrostic.
ii.   The dialogic structure is extremely simple and clear, as only two speakers participate in the conversation alternately.
iii. Even though we have here a dialogic model, there is an extremely weak connection between the words of the friend and those of the sufferer.
iv.   There is no development of any kind in the work, such as exacerbation of the argument, complication of the problems, or an approach to a solution.
v.   It follows from the latter two features that one could change the order of the stanzas without harming or altering the contents.
vi.   The connective function of the acrostic, which alone requires the specific present order of stanzas, follows from this.
vii. Deviation from the schematic structure is never used as a means of expression or emphasis. A striking example is found in lines 83 and 87. Instead of *ki*, which is the regular opening sign in the eighth stanza, a *qi* is used, but this deviation from the required acrostic model seems minor and insignificant, and is certainly not meant as a means of emphasis.
viii. The work does not have any distinctive sections (prologue; epilogue) which would create a narrative framework. Nevertheless, it is possible to extract various statements of an autobiographical nature from the words of the sufferer: that he is the youngest son, that he was dependent upon the kindnesses of the first-born, who rejected him, and his difficult material situation, despite his honourable origin.
ix.   Apart from the equal length of the stanzas, the highly schematic nature is not expressed in symmetry.

Another Mesopotamian work deserving of mention here due to its structural relation to the book of Job is the dialogue between a master and his servant known as 'The Dialogue of the Pessimist' or 'A Pessimistic Dialogue between a Master and his Servant'.[31] This work consists of a series of dialogues in which the master turns to his servant with various requests, to which the latter responds, hastening to agree with everything his master says—while the former always says a thing and its opposite . Thus, for example, the first stanza:

1 ['Slave, listen to me'.] 'Here I am, sir, here [I am]'.
2 ['Quickly, fetch me the] chariot and hitch it up so that I can drive to the palace'.
3 ['Drive, sir, drive...]...will be for you.
4 [...] will pardon you.
5 ['No, slave, I] will by no means drive to the palace'.
6 ['Do not drive,] sir, do not drive'.
7 [...] will send you [...]
8 And will make you take a [route] that you do not know .
9 He will make you suffer agony [day and] night.

And so on. Subsequent stanzas refer to the caprices of the master in various other areas, such as eating, hunting, the appropriate reaction to a rival, etc. In the final stanza, the master asks a general question—What is good? To which the servant replies—death.

This is not the appropriate framework within which to elaborate upon the various problems involved in this work, which do not pertain directly to the book of Job. I shall only note here several structural characteristics:

i.   Schematic nature. Each stanza opens with the same words: *arad mitanguranni annu beli annu* ('"Slave, listen to me". "Here I am, sir, here [I am]"'). In each stanza, the master asks the servant to do something and its opposite, while the servant expresses agreement to both proposals.

ii.   While there are repetitive elements which contribute to its schematic nature, these do not appear in all the stanzas, and their appearance is inconsistent: the command, *sisirma dikannima* ('quickly bring me...') is repeated in stanzas 1, 2, 3. In stanza 7 the same phrase appears with slight change: *sisir dikannima*. In the other stanzas there is no indication of this combination.

iii.   The length of the stanzas is uneven, varying between 6 and 12 lines.

31. See Lambert 1960: 139-43 (Introduction), 144-49 (translation and transcription). Pfeiffer's translation appears in *ANET*, pp. 437-38.

iv.   Unlike the 'Theodicy', the dialogues here are very short, each
        stanza focusing upon only one thing: the bringing of a sacrifice;
        the raising of a family; eating; travel in a chariot; etc.
v.   As with the 'Theodicy', there is no inherent significance to one
        or another order of the stanzas; apart from the final stanza,
        which constitutes an ironic climax, the order can be changed
        without the content of the work thereby being harmed or
        falsified.
vi.   There are no clear lines of symmetry.

3. *The Cyclical Model*

The dialogues, which constitute the basic framework of the book of Job,
are arranged in cycles, so that one may state that the basic structure of
the book is cyclical: the debates repeat themselves three times in a fixed
order, with the exception of the absence of Zophar's third speech. I
have already mentioned the other difficulties found in this cycle, which
in several other respects deviates from the anticipated model. Since
cyclical structure is alien neither to biblical literature nor to its readers, it
is worthwhile noting the pertinent literary conventions which were
among the exigencies of the book, and which created the system of
anticipations among its readers.

It is a known characteristic of biblical narrative that it repeats similar
situations or similar formulae a number of times: the story of Samson
and Delilah (Judg. 16.4-20), the story of the divine call to Samuel
(1 Sam. 3.4-10), and the story of Balaam and his ass (Num. 22.21-34)
are but a few of many examples of this literary method (see Licht 1978:
51-95). One may distinguish between two basic models of situational
repetitions: the gradual developmental model, and the model of 'three
and four'.

In the first model, each repetition entails a certain novelty in comparison to that which preceded it; there are new data or new emphases,
creating a feeling of development towards a certain climax. An example
of such a model is found in the story of Joseph and his dreams (Gen.
37): the second dream adds to the first the bowing down of the parents,
serving to deepen our recognition of Joseph's hidden wishes and making
us better understand his brother's hatred towards him. Another example
appears in Genesis 24: the fourfold repetition of the business of the oath
and the servant's encounter with Rebecca (vv. 13-14, 17-22, 42-44, 45-

47)—in each case the exact formulation of the words being changed somewhat according to circumstances—creates a dynamic of anticipation of what will be said and done in the course of the plot.

The second model, 'three and four', creates the impression that the most important cycle of events is the last one—the third or fourth, those which precede it serving the nature of an introduction. This is the basis for the formula 'for three...and for four', intended to emphasize that which is stated in the last line.[32] An example of narrative use of this model appears in the account of the divine call to Samuel (Zakovitch 1979: 93-100), in the story of Samson (Zakovitch 1982: 171 and n. 15), in the brief episode of God's revelation to Elijah (1 Kgs 19.11-12), in the story of Elijah and the captain of the fifty men (2 Kgs 1.9-14), and elsewhere. The story of Balaam is an example of a sophisticated combination of both models: the story of Balaam's refusal to go and curse follows the first model: when God eventually 'gives in' to Balaam and allows him to go, while stipulating to him the condition, 'but only what I bid you, that shall you do' (Num. 22.20), a certain tension is created leading towards the decisive stage—will he curse, or not? By contrast, the story of the ass in ch. 22 is based upon the model of the three and the four: v. 25 does not add anything essential to the situation depicted in v. 23 (the phrase, 'so he struck her again', merely emphasizes the repetition of the identical situation), while only in the third cycle (vv. 26-30) does the important development emerge.[33]

Other data which may be helpful as background for understanding questions of structure in the book of Job may be derived from examination of the story of the plagues of Egypt (Exod. 7.15–12.36). Both earlier commentators and contemporary scholars have noted that the first nine plagues are clearly divided into three groups of three.[34] This being so, the account of the tenth plague, which is the longest and most complicated in terms of its motifs, represents the fourth and final stage

32. E.g., in Amos 1–2; Prov. 30.15-33; etc. On the various varieties of the model and the broad literary use made thereof in the Bible, see Zakovitch 1982.

33. See the analysis of the Balaam narrative in Zakovitch 1979: 123-24; Licht 1978: 69-74. Licht proposes a somewhat different division, according to which the decisive stage in this episode is the fourth and not the third.

34. See the respective commentaries of R. Samuel b. Meir (Rashba'm) and Abravanel to Exod. 7.26. Of the contemporary exegetes, see Cassuto 1959: 60-62; Loewenstamm 1965: 35; Greenberg 1981: 65-75; Bar-Efrat 1979: 123-25; Licht 1978: 64-69.

in the model of the three and four, and as such is both part of the structure as a whole, and a striking (and significant) deviation from it.[35]

The following is the basic model for the three triplets in the account of the first nine plagues (*a* indicates the motif of going to Pharaoh and giving warning prior to the plague, while *d* indicates the motif of the hardening of Pharoah's heart).

	First Three	Second Three	Third Three
First Plague:	*ad*	*ad*	*ad*
Second Plague:	*ad*	*ad*	*ad*
Third Plague:	*d*	*d*	*d*

However, this model only presents the most frequent and orderly motifs in the chapter, ignoring the less orderly repetition of other motifs. A fuller presentation of the model[36] will be of interest to our discussion of the structure of the book of Job. I will present this here using the following key, as well as *a* and *d* mentioned above:

b	command concerning the execution of the plague by stretching forth the hand (or staff) of Aaron (*b*), or of Moses (*b'*).
c	motif of the attempts of the magicians to imitate the miracles of Moses and Aaron (*c'* indicates lack of success).
e	motif of Pharaoh's attempt at appeasement—his agreement to free the people—and regret.

The distribution of the motifs in the chapter of the plagues of Egypt is as follows:

I. 7.15-25	IV. 8.16-28	VII. 9.13-35
a	*a*	*a*
b	-	*b'*
c	-	-
d	*e*	*e*
-	*d*	*d*

---

35. In this I disagree with Licht, who stated that the account of the plague of the first-born does not belong from a structural viewpoint to the narrative pattern of the nine plagues that preceded it.

36. It is not my intention here to elaborate upon all the details of this model (such as the use of the word נבא in the first plague of each group of three, or of השׁכים in the second plague of each group). I will likewise not take note of everything that might be considered a deviation from the expected pattern; the large number of details does not further my methodological aim.

II. 7.26–8.11	V. 9.1-7	VIII. 10.1-20
a	*a*	*a*
b	-	*e*
c	-	*b'*
e	*d*	-
d	-	*e*
	-	*d*

III. 8.12-15	VI. 9.8-12	IX. 10.21-29
-	-	-
b	-	*b'*
c	*c'*	-
d	*d*	*e*
-	-	*d*

Thus, the account of the plagues contains other repeated motifs besides *a* and *d*. Motif *c* appears in different variations in four plagues; after reading the account of the first three plagues, it would seem that it is about to create a fixed model, as with motifs *a* and *d*, but this is not the case. Its variant appearance in the third and sixth plagues does not create a model, nor an exception containing a hidden content message. The same holds true with regard to motif *e*: on the face of it, we would anticipate that in such a story, one of whose striking characteristics is its schematic structure, this motif would appear in some sort of orderly manner (for example, only in the first three plagues), but in fact this is not so. One may go on to note other variants stressing the non-orderly elements in the model, but this seems to me to be superfluous.

How may one explain the creation of a schematic story such as this with so many non-schematic 'exceptions'? Based upon all existing methods of biblical research, it seems that this may be attributed to the literary conventions through which the story took shape. Those who accept the simple principle of a single author, as do the harmonistic exegetes, are certainly required to say that this author chose thus to shape the story. By contrast, those who accept the approach of classical source criticism or one of its later variants will ascribe the task of final redaction to a later editor, but even there it is clear that this redactor must have had an explicit literary reason for shaping the section according to a sophisticated model. If so, then this feeling must also have guided him with regard to exceptions to this model. This, without denying the necessary assumption of this approach, according to which the initial data for the final redaction were also dictated by the exigencies of the written sources. One of the outstanding proponents of a third approach is Loewenstamm. In his discussion of the composition of the narrative of the plagues, he resolved some of the disorders in the motifs in accordance with his general approach: namely, through the assumption that during the process of oral transmission of the different traditions of the story the motifs became confused, several of them being deliberately rejected from the Torah; even though a very strict literary model was thereby created, the different nuances of the original traditions were not completely abolished (Loewenstamm 1965: 25-79). His assumption is that in each one of the pre-Pentateuchal traditions of the story of the plagues there was greater unity in the primary narrative motifs (such as Pharaoh's reaction, the function of the staff, the division of tasks between Moses and Aaron), but he does not argue that every such tradition was organized in a schematic and rigid manner, especially as in his opinion the number of plagues differed from tradition to tradition.

Hence, according to all approaches, the one who left his final mark upon the structure of the account of the plagues was responsible for creating the basic model (*ad*), as well as for the partial arrangement of several of the motifs. Why then did he not fashion the chapter according to stricter and more tightly organized structural principles? This question may only be answered in one of the following two ways: (a) that the author (or redactor) did not intend to present a narrative based upon strictly schematic principles, either because he did not see this as an artistic value worth achieving,[37] or because he did not take account of the possibilities inherent in the tight and strict ordering of the totality of motifs; (b) that the author (redactor) attempted to create meticulous regularity, but due to the confusion inherent in the chapter and the absence of a narrative tradition exploiting a schematic structure with all its subtleties and possibilities, he did not succeed in utilizing all the niceties allowed him by the story.

In presenting these two alternative explanations, I have rejected a third theoretical possibility: namely, that the author made sophisticated use of exceptions from the anticipated order, making it incumbent upon us, the readers, to attempt to understand him fully by finding an explanation for each exception. Such a possibility is to be rejected for two reasons: first,

---

37. Thus Licht 1978: 66. He states that the narrator was aware of the artistic damage caused by excessive schematism, and therefore took care to disperse the various motifs with a certain freedom.

I have not found plausible explanations for any such 'exception'; second, the 'exceptions' are so numerous that they are not explicitly identifiable as such. Hence, the reader cannot be aware of the hidden messages which are supposed to emerge with their help. Yet, one should note that the basic model itself utilizes the artistic tactic of deviation from the anticipated model, as the division into triplets is created by eliminating element *a* in the third plague of each group. We therefore find that in the basic model, in those motifs which are extremely explicit, the narrator makes use of a tactic of exceptions, but he abandons this tactic as a general and sophisticated method with regard to the distribution of the totality of motifs in the narrative.

In the discussion of the structure of the book of Job, in which I attempted to describe various aspects of the generic-historical circle within whose framework the book was written, it is also worth mentioning the Egyptian story, 'The Protest of the Eloquent Peasant'. This story is concerned with a peasant who was attacked and robbed by a cruel, high-ranking official, and who complains of this to the ruler.[38]

The story occurs during the reign of Neb-kau-Re Khety III, who ruled in Herculopolis (the biblical Hanes; today, Itnasyah al-Medina), and was one of the claimants to the throne of Egypt during the twenty-first century BCE. The work sheds light upon an important period (the middle first kingdom), during which significant social and political changes took place. The king referred to was the ruler of Egypt only in theory. In truth, he only ruled over a few districts of middle Egypt. Political struggles and even fraternal warfare between the districts were rife. The extant manuscripts are from the twentieth to eighteenth centuries BCE.

The following literary characteristics of this work have bearing upon questions of the structure of the book of Job:

i.   A narrative framework whose style is one of simple praise, interspersed with speeches (concerning the obligation of the ruler to preserve righteousness and justice). According to Ventura, 'one is speaking of a difficult literary work. The story is merely a framework for the nine speeches, which are the true goal of the author. The difference between the story and the speeches is very strongly felt, because the language of the speeches is

38. See Lichtheim 1973: I, 169-70 (introduction and bibliography), 170-84 (translation and notes). For Wilson's translation of selected passages from this story, see *ANET*, pp. 407-10.

rhetorical, filled with images, and formulated in a complex style...Lichtheim is correct in saying that the addresses are written in poetic metre and rhyme'.[39]

ii. The speeches are not organized in any necessary developmental order; one may switch the order of appeals without harming its logical continuity or altering the contents.

iii. The abundance of words and of metaphors; the repetition of metaphors and ideas which were already said.

iv. The division into nine appeals is not necessary except for purely structural reasons, and to the same extent the things could have been concentrated in five, six or ten appeals.

v. There is no emphasis on symmetrical elements, such as an emphasis upon the fifth, central appeal, or the creation of a relationship between the first and last appeal.

vi. The appeals are of unequal length. There are those which are longer (second, third) and those which are shorter (fifth, ninth), without any particular order in this matter.

vii. One can see a clear tendency towards accumulation of parables and wisdom sayings which do not directly pertain to the peasant's complaint. According to Ventura, the entire story was written in order to serve as a framework for the appeals, which are the essence of the work and its purpose.

4. *Summary*

In this chapter we have discussed various questions associated with the structure of the book of Job. As a result, the discussion has *ipso facto* been concerned with the nature of the dialogues, which constitute the framework that carries the work as a whole. Our methodological point of departure has been that, in order to uncover the inner poetics of the book, one needs to recognize the literary field within whose boundaries it was created—that is, the literary conventions which consciously, and especially unconsciously, defined the author's means of expression; this, based upon the assumption that these fields were biblical literature and certain realms of ancient Near Eastern literature generally.

Our assumption is based upon the presumption that the author of the

---

39. This quotation is from a letter by my colleague, the Egyptologist Dr Rafi Ventura. I thank him for his assistance.

book of Job was an Israelite,[40] making it likely that he knew the biblical literature that preceded him. We likewise rely upon the view that the above-mentioned Egyptian and Mesopotamian works also belonged to the cultural milieu within whose frame the book of Job was written. To what extent is this assumption correct? Did the Israelite author know the Egyptian story of 'The Eloquent Peasant'? 'The Babylonian Theodicy'? 'The Fox and the Animals'? Or 'A Pessimistic Dialogue between a Master and his Servant'?

It is not impossible that the author of the book of Job was indeed acquainted with these works. These works stood the test of time over the course of centuries: they were evidently copied repeatedly, beginning from the time of their composition until the time of composition of the book of Job, and even thereafter. There is no evidence that they were translated into Hebrew, although it is possible, just as it is possible that the author of the book of Job was able to read at least some of them in their original language. Further on we shall find that there is great similarity—both in content and in the lexicon of metaphors and ideas—between the book of Job and another Babylonian work, 'I Will Praise the Lord of Wisdom'. Our author's particular interest in questions of divine justice, a subject to which the entire book is devoted, encourages the speculation that he was well acquainted with non-Israelite literature dealing with this question, including the above-mentioned works. If this conjecture is correct—and it is doubtful whether it will ever be possible to remove it from the realm of speculation—then the direct influence of these works upon the author of the book of Job certainly determined the manner of fashioning of his work to a considerable extent.

However, the claim that works of non-Israelite literature influenced the author of the book of Job need not imply that he knew them in an unmediated way. Biblical literature as a whole is part of the body of ancient Near Eastern literature. As is well known, several of its major characteristics give clear expression to this: the poetic parallelism; the repetitions in the narrative; shared idioms; similar narrative and mytho-logical motifs; identical wisdom proverbs; etc. Even when biblical litera-ture created more sophisticated techiques than those known in non-Israelite ancient Near Eastern literature, one can clearly see that these as the result of an encounter—at times even a struggle—with the widespread literary conventions of the region. The influence of these literatures

---

40. As against those who think that the book was not originally Israelite. A discussion of this matter appears below in Chapter 6.

upon the book of Job is thus only one of many expressions of this cultural reality. For our purposes, it is worthwhile mentioning especially one example—the relation of the Song of Songs to Egyptian literature, on the one hand, and to Sumerian literature, on the other. M.V. Fox has recently discussed this problem at length. From his study, it clearly follows that this literature, which preceded the Song of Songs by nearly a millennium, influenced it beyond any doubt, despite the distance in time. Fox is correct in noting that the influence flowed in different channels, and that over the course of generations numerous possible points of contact were created between Israelite and Egyptian literature. The fact that these are not clearly documented in biblical literature from the period of time between the composition of the Egyptian love songs and that of Song of Songs does not refute the claim of direct or indirect influence (Fox 1985: 181-93). The same holds true for Sumerian love poetry: despite its antiquity, it is difficult to ignore the relation of motifs, metaphors, and literary forms between it and the Song of Songs, even though we are of course unable to prove that the author of Song of Songs knew these works in an unmediated way (Fox-Klein 1987: 16-18, 34, 35, 39). Another example of the explicit relationship between a late biblical work and an extremely ancient Near Eastern work (even though it is difficult to trace the exact manner of its relation) is the resemblance between the description of old age in Ecclesiastes 12 and the opening of the collection of Egyptian parables of Petah-Hotef.[41] And of course, one should also mention the relation of Ugaritic literature to that of the Bible. All these confirm our basic methodological claim: even if it is impossible to prove that the author of the book of Job knew the above-mentioned Egyptian and Mesopotamian works, we may see them as part of the circle of literary factors influencing the poetics of the book in one way or another.

The following are the main conclusions pertaining to the structure of the book of Job which follow from our examination of the above-mentioned biblical and extra-biblical works.

The overall model of the book of Job is determined by the norms of biblical prose and poetry. In shaping the structure of the framework, the author followed the path of biblical prose: the omniscient narrator leads the plot from dialogue to dialogue. As against this, the lion's share of the book—the dialogues—is in the style of biblical poetry.

41. See *ANET*, p. 412. For more on the relation of Egyptian parable literature to the wisdom literature of Israel, see McKane 1986: 150-51.

The combination of narrative prose (chs. 1–2; 42.7-17) and poetic dialogues is an innovation of biblical literature, but it is not an unanticipated one, and certainly not an indication of a later stage of editing. The stories of 'The Eloquent Peasant' and 'The Fox and the Animals' indicate the use of a similar technique in ancient Near Eastern literature. The first conclusion cited also indicates that there is no objection to seeing the combination of poetry and prose as an element that was present in the book from the beginning.[42] This is so, notwithstanding the clear gap between the difficult poetic language of the speeches and the flowing prose of the frame story .

The very use of poetic dialogues is an innovation within biblical literature, albeit one accepted in Mesopotamian literature. However, since the basic framework of the book consists of debates, one may define the author's method as an expansion of the traditional technique of debate in biblical poetry. In any event, those who come to judge the dialogues, and who propose to correct them because they do not meet their aesthetic expectations, must take into account that the author was not trained in a biblical tradition of poetic dialogues.

The literary tradition of the Bible, as mentioned, is one of brief prose dialogues. The author of the book of Job created a new technique of lengthy dialogues, each one of which contains several motifs. But in so doing he did not create something out of nothing, as such dialogues appear in the Mesopotamian literature mentioned. However, this very innovation is a kind of 'burden' upon the author. One may not therefore assume that the dialogues will meet aesthetic expectations based upon recognition of a later dialogic tradition, which is far more developed and complex.

In examining the Mesopotamian dialogues, one finds that a close connection is preserved among them when they are brief, which is weakened as they become longer. Thus, for example in 'The Babylonian Theodicy', the connection between the words of the sufferer and those of his neighbour is tighter in the general subject than it is in his reactions to specific claims. Hence, change in the order of the dialogues is possible in terms of the contents, while only the formal framework of the acrostic creates an obligatory order of the speeches. The analogy to Job is clear:

---

42. Considerations of an entirely different nature brought me to the same conclusion concerning the close primary relationship between the prologue and the cycles of debate. See Hoffman 1981, and below, Chapter 8.

one should not anticipate a close and complete relation between one speech and the next, nor a systematic reaction to each and every detail. Here too there is a very strict formal framework—the model of Job–friend–Job–friend, etc.—which creates a feeling of continuity even when some of the things said have no direct bearing upon the previous speech.

In the absence of strong connections between the words of the participants, one certainly may not anticipate any development; such is the situation in the story of 'The Eloquent Peasant', in 'The Babylonian Theodicy' and in the 'Pessimistic Dialogue'. We may infer from this that this was an accepted literary norm. I do not claim that the author of the book of Job adopted this norm for himself. Having been acquainted with the ways of the biblical narrative, he certainly set out to create a gradual development among the speeches. However, in the light of the lack of such a literary tradition in the genre of long dialogues, one should not be surprised at the absence of an explicit development of this type throughout the course of the book.[43]

Simple structural elements are strictly observed in the above works: orderly exchanges of the two speakers in 'The Babylonian Theodicy' and the 'Pessimistic Dialogue'; repetitions of a fixed formula between one speech and another in 'The Eloquent Peasant'; the three-fold structure of the narrative of the first nine plagues in the narrative of the plagues of Egypt. However, with respect to those details which do not pertain to the basic framework there is no such strictness. Such is the case in the narrative of the Egyptian plagues, regarding the differences among the length of the speeches in 'The Eloquent Peasant' and the 'Pessimistic Dialogue', and regarding the repeated formulae in 'Pessimistic Dialogue'. As against this, when the structural framework itself is more complicated, as in 'The Fox and the Animals', there are times when even the basic structure does not preserve a fixed model.

There is no insistence on an even length of 'stanzas' unless the model itself requires it, as in a regular, double, eight-fold, or eleven-fold acrostic. Thus, we find that in the narrative of the plagues of Egypt there are very long and very short 'stanzas'. The same holds true for the story of 'The Eloquent Peasant': from the point of view of content, there was no difficulty in creating pleas of an equal or similar length, yet the author did not trouble to do so.

This point may be connected with another characteristic which follows from these works: despite their adherence to schematic elements, they

---

43. A discussion of these questions will appear in the next two chapters.

do not insist overly much upon structural symmetry, nor is symmetry used as an indirect means of expression.

From examination of biblical and Mesopotamian acrostic poetry, as well as of the narrative of the plagues of Egypt, the story of 'The Eloquent Peasant', and other works in which formal structure plays an important role, we find that there is an inverted relation between adherence to a strict structure and artistic mimesis. The more strictly a work adheres to a formal structure, the weaker becomes the mimetic, 'logical', 'expected' connection among its elements. This is not only because of the substantive contradiction between structural rigidity and the mimetic description of systems of relations, emotional development, and so on, but also because of the equivalent function played by structure and mimesis within the framework of the work: to tighten the connection among its various units. Therefore, if this function is fulfilled in one way, one may forego its realization in another way. This rule concerning the unavoidable tension between structure and mimesis is one of the keys to understanding many phenomena in the book of Job (see on this below, primarily in Chapter 8).

In none of the above examples have we found any sophisticated use of exceptions to the anticipated structure as an extra-linguistic means of expression. The exceptions—and they are numerous—flow from a free approach to the small details of the model.

This last conclusion touches upon the connection between structure and language, which I mentioned previously as being among the poetic characteristics of the book of Job. It would seem that adherence to strict structural models harms, not only the ongoing inner development of the work, but also the verbal economy of its expression. The generic constraint undertaken by the author of the 'Theodicy', namely, to write 27 stanzas of 11 lines each, leads to repetition of ideas, metaphors and linguistic forms. This is a characteristic feature in Psalm 119 as well and, in a not insignificant way, in the acrostic of the book of Lamentations. This issue and its methodological influences upon the study of the book of Job will be described below, in the chapter on the difficult language of the book. And indeed, there is some doubt as to whether one ought to attribute the verbosity of the book to structural exigencies alone. We have seen that this phenomenon also characterizes the story of 'The Eloquent Peasant', where it is not required by the structure, as the author could have reduced the number of appeals had he wished. Likewise the Mesopotamian work, 'I Will Praise the Lord of Wisdom' (discussed in the next chapter), is characterized by verbal excesses even without exigencies of structure. It would therefore seem that this feature is a characteristic of ancient Near Eastern literature dealing with the suffering of humanity. More on this below, in Chapter 6.

It seems appropriate that these conclusions should define our path as we set out to understand the structure of the book of Job and to uncover the literary conventions which characterized the book in its original form.

The most important statement following from an analysis of the above data is that the book represents a new innovation within the context of biblical literature in terms of composition, even though it is not at all isolated from the literary conventions of its cultural milieu. The striking-ness of this innovation lies in the fact that the book was a path-finder in a number of parallel realms: in that of the structure of the framework—excessive complications creating numerous literary possibilities (and *ipso facto* exaggerated expectations on the part of the contemporary reader); in that of dialogue—great length and poetic language; in that of narrative—in the creation of a kind of story from theoretical materials which are not characteristic of the biblical narrative, or of any ancient Near Eastern prose.

In the light of these data, there is a basis for assuming that the author adhered to a strict basic model so that the book would not 'fall apart'. The creation of this model—three cycles of debates, with a fixed sequence of alternation among the speakers in each cycle—was in itself a literary innovation, whose roots may be traced. Therefore, one should not expect the author to make sophisticated use of a technique of deliberate departure from the basic structure as a means of expression. A technique of deviation is only effective when there is a clear awareness of the convention from which the author is deviating; otherwise the deviation is not felt, making it impossible to express a non-verbal message thereby. Hence, there is no justification for interpreting the truncated structure of the third cycle as a structural means of expression. Such a conclusion is strengthened by the absence of such means of expression in the background literature to the book of Job. I must emphasize that I am not hereby claiming that, because this specific means of expression does not appear in the background literature, it is also impossible in the book of Job. Rather, through an examination of the book against its literary background, it is unreasonable to assume that such a tactic was used as an artistic innovation of the author.

These conclusions have bearing upon the question of the relationship between the extant version of the book of Job and the original version. The assumption that the prose chapters of the book of Job were a separate work from the poetic ones is not supported by claims related to structure (other considerations concerning this issue will be brought in Chapter 8, where my overall position on this question will be defended).

The assumption that there was a close connection in content between one speech and another in the original version is not supported by structural considerations; certainly, these do not confirm that there were full developmental connections, such as is made possible by the model (see above, p. 61). Therefore, one must reject out of hand any suggested reconstruction based upon a structural-content claim of lack of firm connection between one speech and another.

Similarly, various proposals to move passages from one speech to another in order to arrive at uniformity of the length of the speeches cannot be grounded in structural considerations. The basic model of the book is not an acrostic one, and therefore does not require full equality in the length of the literary units. However, this conclusion does not apply to the speech of Bildad in the third cycle (ch. 25). One needs to draw a distinction between the other speeches, in which precise comparison of their length is artificial, and this speech of Bildad, whose extreme brevity is inconsistent with the tendency of the book to schematicism and to strict structure. For this reason, one may reasonably describe this brief speech of Bildad as the outstanding exception to the basic structure of the book. The same holds true for Job's final speech in the last cycle: its extraordinary length compared with that of the other speeches is a striking exception to the structural model of the book. Thus, exegetical intervention—whether harmonistic or critical—is justified in both these cases. The full gamut of considerations and a final conclusion on this matter will be offered in Chapter 8. At this stage, I will limit myself to the following statement based upon structural considerations: one may not assume that the author utilized structural deviations as a tactic of expression; it is therefore reasonable to assume that these speeches, in the form in which they appear in the present version of the book, do not reflect the author's intention in the original book.

For a similar reason, one may state that the absence of the third speech of Zophar also evidently does not fit the taste of the author. The same holds true regarding the speech of Elihu. Examined in terms of structural considerations, it is difficult to find any basis for it in the compositional norms of the book. This is not true regarding the speech of God. I noted above that the absence of a symmetrical parallel to this speech is extremely natural. It is therefore doubtful whether there is any reason to see the speech as a structural element that breaks the anticipated symmetry. Examination of the various works has taught us that symmetry is not an absolute characteristic, and we have not found that tactical use is made thereof. This datum confirms the conclusion, that one ought not see in the speech of God a structural element alien to the book.

It must once again be stressed that these are purely provisional conclusions. First of all, because they are based exclusively upon considerations of structure, which are by themselves insufficient, as one needs also to examine considerations of content, ideas, and language. Secondly, I have not discussed the question as to whether or not one may reconstruct the original text, and how this ought to be done. A decision regarding this matter requires us to examine additional aspects of the work, to which the following chapters shall be devoted. In these chapters, I will attempt to illuminate the book from other perspectives, in the hope that expansion of our acquaintance with its characteristics will constitute an additional layer in its understanding. This will be yet another step towards fashioning our final conclusions on the question of the relation between the original book and the present version.

Chapter 4

JOB AND CATALOGUE LITERATURE

Several scholars have raised the issue of the relation of several chapters in the book of Job to catalogue literature. I believe that the first to draw attention to this question was Von Rad who, in his discussion of the literary character of ch. 38, noted its relation to Egyptian onomastic lists and to the papyrus of Anastasi I, both of which utilize the catalogue model. Following him, Gray also observed that several passages from God's speech are an expansion of these catalogues,[1] reflecting crypto-scientific activity in Egyptian wisdom circles. Against them, Fox argued that there is no justification for associating the Egyptian (or Mesopotamian) catalogues with any kind of 'scientific' activity. To the same extent, the reference to various natural phenomena in the speech of God (chs. 38–39) are not to be taken as indicative of parallel intellectual-'scientific' activity in Israel. Hence, he calls for greater caution in drawing conclusions regarding the direct influence of extra-biblical literature upon the Bible on the grounds of a purely superficial similarity or on the basis of a questionable identification of a similar *Sitz im Leben*.[2]

In this chapter, we shall observe the generic relation of the book of Job as a whole, and not only of one or another section, to catalogue literature in general. I will not discuss here all of the types of ancient catalogues, nor will I attempt to determine the origins of this model or its development in the ancient Near East. Such a discussion would take us too far afield from the focus of our concern, and is deserving of a

---

1. See von Rad 1960; Gray 1970: 251-52. On p. 295 von Rad gives a comparative list of catalogue entries in Job 38, in the Onomasticon of Amenophe (see below), in Ben Sira 43, in Psalms 148, and in 'The Prayer of Azariah and the Three Youths' (from the additions of the LXX to the book of Daniel).

2. Fox 1986. It is nevertheless worth mentioning that Fox himself devoted a comprehensive study to the influence of Egyptian love literature upon the Song of Songs (Fox 1985).

separate literary and historical study. I will hence limit myself to a brief survey of catalogues in ancient Near Eastern literature and in the Bible, as background to our discussion of the use of this model in the book of Job.

1. *The Catalogue Model in Ancient Near Eastern Literature*

The catalogue is among the oldest literary genres known to us from the recorded literature of the ancient Near East. One may define it quite simply as a list of terms, activities, names, etc., having a definite common denominator, usually noted in its introduction. I will refer here only to well-defined catalogues, the common denominator of whose components is substantive (names of mountains, kinds of animals, etc.)—that is, those which exist outside of the context of the list itself, so that anyone reading the list might easily distinguish its common denominator, even if it is not designated at its beginning.[3]

One of the characteristics of the catalogue is that the order of its items is inconsequential, the important thing being the fact of their being gathered and cited together in one context. However, as the catalogue was never an isolated genre but was influenced by other genres, there were also those catalogues created in which the order of items was important, such as lists of kings, which were arranged chronologically. Hence, the boundary between the catalogue and other types of lists is not always clear. For example, it would be incorrect to include genealogies within this genre, because in genealogies the chronological-developmental sequence, that is, the obligatory order of its items, is no less important than the overall common denominator—that is, their being members of one family.

The special advantage of the catalogue lies in its great economy—that

---

3.   Theoretically, any list of nouns, adjectives, verbs and the like may be considered a catalogue if they follow an introductory sentence, such as: 'These are the words which I remembered during my trip to Jerusalem'. Any combination of sentences may be considered a catalogue if one prefaces it by a phrase such as 'these are the sentences which…', or if it is given any other sort of general name. According to Hornby (1965: 106), the definition of a catalogue is as follows: 'A term to describe lists of persons, places, things, or ideas which have a common denominator such as heroism, beauty, death, etc.' On the theoretical aspects of the definition of a catalogue, see the first chapter in Arpali 1977. The basic model of the catalogue may be described schematically by the formula: x (a; b; c…n), where x designates the common denominator of the elements within the parentheses.

it conveys a large amount of information with great brevity. For this reason, and because of one of its most widespread uses, it is often thought of specifically within the realm of administration, and is assumed to have originated in those cultures which began to develop orderly administrative systems. And indeed, there are not a few ancient administrative catalogues.[4] However, alongside these there is early evidence for a good number of catalogues which are not essentially administrative. Lichtheim states that Egyptian literature generally began with catalogues of graves—lists of offerings, clothes, jewellery, biographical details of the deceased and of his family—without any relation to the realm of public administration. These in turn developed into independent literary types, such as prayers and autobiographies (Lichtheim 1973: I, 15-17). One of the most explicit examples of an ancient, non-administrative catalogue is the Egyptian list known as the Onomasticon of Amenope, from the twelfth century BCE (Gardiner 1947: 2ff.). This list is quoted here (in part) because of the interest it aroused in biblical studies, and because it will be mentioned again below in connection with our discussion of the book of Job.

The catalogue begins as follows:

> Beginning of the teaching for clearing the mind, for instruction for the ignorant and for learning all things that exist: what Ptah created, what Thoth copied down, heaven with its affairs, earth and what is in it, what the mountains belch forth, what is watered by the flood, all things upon which Re has shone, all that is grown on the back of the earth, excogitated by the scribe of the sacred books in the house of life, Amenope, son of Amenope.

According to Gardiner, the original version included some 2,000 items; even though not all of them were preserved in the manuscripts, one can clearly discern the nature of the work. The items are arranged into

---

4.   See, for example, the catalogue of Egyptian servants from the eighteenth century BCE, *ANET*, pp. 553-54; lists of food-stuffs and material in the Temples, *ANET*, pp. 261-62; etc. However, the boundaries between an administrative catalogue and other types of catalogues are not always clear. Thus, for example, the list of those paying tax to a victorious king (as in *ANET*, pp. 283a-291bc): is its main purpose administrative or political—that is, the exaltation of the king's name and memorializing his greatness? Similarly, the editing of lists of conquered cities, in the wake of Thut-mose III, was customary among the kings of Egypt (see *ANET*, pp. 242-43). Chadwick (1960: I, 276) enumerates the early catalogues under the general heading of 'study literature', whose purpose is not to entertain or to give pleasure. This classification is extremely broad, including under its rubric administrative, wisdom, political and other catalogues.

various sections: sky, water, earth; persons, court, offices, occupations; classes, tribes and types of human being; the towns of Egypt; buildings, their parts, and types of land; agricultural land, cereals and their products; beverages; parts of an ox and kinds of meat. The following are examples from three clauses (I have here and there skipped items which are unclear):

> *Section 2*: Sky, Water, Earth. Sky, sun, moon, Orion, the Great Bear [?], Cynocephalus Ape [a constellation], the Strong One [a constellation], Sow [a constellation], a storm loud, tempest, dawn, darkness, sun [light], shade, sunlight, rays of the sun, storm-cloud, dew, snow, rainstorm, primaeval waters [the Nile], flood, river [Nile], sea, wave, swampy lake, pond, well, basin [?], waters, pool, frontier...
>
> *Section 3*: Persons, Court, Offices, Occupations. God, goddess, [male] spirit, female spirit, king, queen, king's wife, king's mother, king's child, crown prince, vizier, sole friend, eldest king's son, dispatch-writer of Horus, mighty Bull, chief of department of the Good God, first king's herald of His Majesty, fan-bearer on the right of the king...
>
> *Section 4*: Classes, Tribes and Types of Human Being. Men, mankind, Phlebeians, sun-folk, commanders of troops, infantry, chariotry, Jjemah-people, Jjehnu-people, Meshwesh, Libyan, the Kehek, Keshkesh, Dene (Danuna), Khatti...

It would seem that this material was primarily intended for study and reflection, and may also have served scribes for exercise and practice in the art of writing. It is obvious that this was not an administrative catalogue. On the basis of the statement that appears at the beginning, there is a certain tendency to classify and to sort out things, but in practice the classification is superficial and at times confused, including repetitions.[5] Also notable by its absence is any hierarchical structure or inner logic— there is no order based upon importance, size, or the like, and the sequence seems to a great extent to be associative. Another literary characteristic of the Onomasticon of Amenope—which is a striking generic sign of the catalogue, even though it is not a necessary datum by its very definition—is the equal syntactic nature of its items, and the tendency insofar as possible towards brief items. This type of catalogue exploits the characteristic economy of this model, which allows for the recording of a great deal of data with the maximum brevity. However,

---

5.   There follows from this the suggestion of M.V. Fox (1986: 303) not to relate with excessive seriousness to the declaration of intentions at the beginning, but to see the catalogue primarily as material for exercise in writing rather than as the result of intellectual-scientific activity.

the use of a catalogue is not always based upon functional-pragmatic reasons, and not a few catalogues create the impression that the model is utilized specifically for an emotional reason. It seems that a flow of words, all of which have the same syntactical structure and a certain common denominator, serves to create a quasi-magical feeling, and has a cumulative power far beyond the information conveyed in the adding of parts to one another. This is particularly true with regard to lists in the realm of religion, such as those of deities, which form an important component in a number of types of ancient works—particularly treaty literature, in which lists of gods form an integral part.[6]

The extensive use of catalogues led to the creation of variations on the basic model.[7] This variety is expressed in three main forms: (1) the expansion of the individual items of the list through the addition of information pertinent to each element ('expanded model'); (2) the combination of two different catalogues, such as those of merchandise and prices ('combined model'); (3) the breakdown of the catalogue into its component units, creating an 'open model' which nullifies the advantage of the catalogue as the most economic genre.[8] An example of the 'expanded model' appears in the admonitions of the Egyptian sage Ipu-Wer: a catalogue of harms and disasters, each of whose elements is expanded beyond the simple listing of the harm.[9] The list of the prices of animals in the Hittite Law (sections 178-180)[10] and the list therein of

6.   See, for example, the list of gods at the end of the treaty between Mursilis the Hittite and Duppi Tessub of Amurru (*ANET*, p. 203); the treaty between Suppiluliumas the Hittite and Mattiwaza (p. 205); the treaty between Ashurnirari V of Assyria and Matiilu of Arpad (p. 533); and the introduction to the treaty between Esarhaddon and Ramataya (pp. 534-35). See also the lists of gods in ritual texts (pp. 331-35, 342, etc).

7.   Basic and not first. The terminology used here is not diachronic—i.e., development of the model—but phenomenological. Just as one cannot know in what connection the catalogue was originally created—cultic, administrative, etc.—so is it impossible to ascertain the earliest model of the catalogue.

8.   Corresponding to the formula of the basic model, the formulae of the other models will appear as follows: expanded model: x([a + expansion], [b + expansion],... [n + expansion]); combined model: xy (a, b, c,...n); open model: xa, xb, xc,...xn.

9.   Such as: 'Why really the Nile is in flood, but no one ploughs for himself... Why really women are dried up and none can conceive. Khun cannot fashion (mortals) because of the state of the land. Why really poor men have become the possessors of treasures...' etc. (translation by Wilson, *ANET*, pp. 441-42).

10.   Sect. 178: 'The price of a plough-ox is 12 shekels of silver. The price of a bull is 10 shekels of silver. The price of a full-grown cow is 7 shekels of silver. The

prices of clothing[11] are examples of the 'expanded model'. Examples of the 'open model' are the catalogue of praises of Bel recited on the New Year festival in Babylonia, each one of whose lines (about 11) opens with the words 'My Lord', which is thereafter repeated;[12] the table of sacrifices in the Marseilles Tariff;[13] and the list of kings of Assyria and the years of their reign.[14] There are also mixed models, in which the generic nature of the catalogue is somewhat obscured. An example of this is the list of the kings of Sumeria, which mixes the 'combined model' and the 'expanded model'.[15]

It was only natural that the dominance of catalogues and their use in a variety of areas of life should also have led to their use in artistic literature: there are numerous examples of the incorporation of catalogues in such works. Thus, the Sumerian myth of Anki and Ninurta concludes with a list of the gods;[16] towards the end of the epic of the

price of a one-year-old plough or cow is 5 shekels of silver. The price of a weaned calf is 4 shekels of silver' (*ANET*, p. 195).

11. Sect. 182: 'The price of a *happushanza* garment is 12 shekels of silver. The price of a fine garment is 30 shekels of silver. The price of a blue woollen garment is 20 shekels of silver. The price of an adulpi garment is 10 shekels of silver...'

12. See *ANET*, p. 332, in the translation of Sachs:

> My Lord... My Lord, king of the countries,
> My Lord... My Lord...
> My Lord... My Lord who gives, My Lord...
> My Lord who dwells in the chapel.
> My Lord... My Lord, he is my lord...

Further on, this model appears in the course of a catalogue of stars. See also the open catalogue of gods who are meant to bless the worshipper; *ANET*, p. 342, etc.

13. *ANET*, pp. 656-57.

14. *ANET*, pp. 564-66.

15. For example, in the introduction: 'When the kingship was lowered from heaven, the kingship was in Eridu. In Eridu A-lulim became king and reigned 28,800 years. Alalgar reigned 36,000 years. Two kings reigned its 64,800 years. I drop [the topic] Erido; its kingship was carried to Bad-tibira. In Bad-tibira En-men-lu-Anna reigned 43,200 years; En-men-gal-anna reigned 28,800 years; divine Dumuzi, a shepherd, reigned 36,600 years: three kings reigned its 108,000 years. I drop [the topic] Bad-tibira. Its kingship was carried to Larak...' Further on, there are other narrative expansions, such as (ll. 39-41): 'The flood swept thereover. After the Flood was lowered from heaven, the kingship was in Kish...', etc. (according to Jacobsen 1939: 71-127). Other examples may be found in the catalogue of gods and of curses in the vassal treaties of Assarhadon, *ANET*, p. 538; in the epilogue to the laws of Hammurabi, *ANET*, pp. 179-80, etc.

16. *ANET*, p. 41.

death of Gilgamesh[17] we find a catalogue incorporating a list of about twenty gods, some of which are presented according to the basic model, and others according to the 'expanded model'. In the epic of the descent of Innana to our world, there is a list of seven cities and seven temples of Innana formulated in the 'mixed model',[18] as there is in Mesopotamian literature. The phenomenon is known in ancient Greek literature as well. The catalogues in the second chapter of the *Iliad*—both Hellenic and Trojan—which enumerate the names of dozens of nations and tribes which came to war together with their ships, are a well-known example.

In these and similar cases, one is confronted with the question as to whether these represent the inclusion within the work of authentic independent catalogues, the artistic reworking of existing catalogues, or whether perhaps the author may have created his own catalogue—that is to say, he made use of the literary genre, but not of an existing catalogue. Of course, the preservation of lists of gods, cities, lands, or peoples is not in itself an indication that every catalogue in a given literary text is authentic or reworked, and that only its inclusion is new. Kramer observes[19] that the above-mentioned catalogue of cities and temples of Innana appears in a different order in the various copies of the work, but that the names of the places themselves do not change. It is difficult to know what conclusion one ought to draw from this. In his study of the Hellenic catalogue in the *Iliad*, Allen states that use was made there of an authentic document from the early pre-Doric period, which Homer reworked somewhat in order to include it in his work. The Homeric school continued to do this thereafter, but the authentic basis was still dominant.[20]

17. *ANET*, p. 51.

18. 'In Arakh she abandoned Annana and descended to the lower world. In Bad Tabira she abandoned Umushkalma and descended to the lower world. In Zeblam she abandoned Giguna', etc. (*ANET*, p. 53).

19. *ANET*, p. 53, n. 10.

20. Allen (1910: 70) notes that the catalogue appears there in a unit separate from the context as a whole, prefaced by the author's invocation of the muses. 'Tell me now, Muses, dwelling on Olympus, as you are heavenly, and are everywhere, and everything is known to you—while we can only hear the tales and never know—who were the Danaan lords and officers?' (*Iliad* II.455-459; R. Fitzgerald, trans.). See on this matter Simpson and Lazenby (1970), who attempt to clarify the precise early historical background of the original catalogue, which is in their opinion the vast bulk of the catalogue extant in the *Iliad*. See also Bowra (1930: 71), who likewise believes that the catalogue in the *Iliad* preserves extremely ancient material: it essentially dis-

As an example of the use of catalogues in a large artistic work, it is worth noting the Mesopotamian poem which I have mentioned previously—'I Will Praise the Lord of Wisdom' (*ludlul bel nemeqi*). Due to the numerous points of contact of this work with the book of Job, I shall compare the manner in which it incorporates catalogues with that found in the book of Job (in Chapter 7, I shall discuss other connections between this work and the book of Job).

The poem is a long one, written on four tablets, each one of which contains 120 lines. For details concerning the preservation of the poem, the tablets, early interpretations ('commentaries'), and the relation of the fourth tablet to the work as a whole see Lambert (1960: 21-27) and Romer and von Soden (1990: 110-14). The speaker in the poem is a person called *Shubshi meshre shakkan*, who is mentioned in Tablet III.43. According to the poem, he occupied a high office (I.60, 61, 103, 104), had slaves and fields (I.89, 101), a family (I.99), and spoke of the city as if it was subject to his rule (I.102). Nevertheless, he himself was subject to the king and saw in this, alongside his fear of the gods, a clear expression of his righteousness.

According to Lambert (1960: 15), the work dates from the Cushite period (1500–1200 BCE), while Romer and von Soden (1990: 112) date it from the twelfth century BCE.

In this poem, one may distinguish the following catalogues:

i.   A catalogue of human types (in the opening of the poem): a deaf person, master, servant, neighbour, magician, dream interpreter, necromancer, magician.

ii.   A catalogue of sins (also in the opening): failure to offer libation, failure to pray before eating, lack of decorum, failure to recite prayer, carelessness and contempt towards idols, failure to teach the people fear of God, forgetting God at the time of eating, abandoning the sacred terebinth, failure to offer the grain-offering, pride, taking the name of God in an oath light-heartedly. Further on in this catalogue (ll. 23-32), we find its opposite—those positive acts which were performed by the lamenter (compare to the catalogues in Job 29–31).

turbs the structure of the work; it includes names which are not at all mentioned further on in the work; and its incorporation involves a certain concession by Homer to the tradition of ancient poetry, so as to satisfy expectations of his listeners external to the work. On the artistic problem aroused by the use of the catalogue, see below.

iii.   Catalogue of organs of the body (or of pathological symptoms):
         head, gullet, face, eyes, muscles, throat, neck, forehead, bosom,
         flesh, diaphragm, kidneys, innards, lungs, ribs, fat, torso, eyes,
         ears, hands, knees, feet, mouth, lips, throat, ribs, sinews, arms,
         back (II.41-105). This catalogue is repeated towards the end of
         the work (Tablet III), in the list of pathological symptoms which
         have passed.
iv.   Catalogue of the gates of Babylon: IV.49-60.
v.   At the beginning and end, hymnic catalogues are brought listing
         elements of the cosmos, thereby establishing a framework for
         the work. At the end: earth, heavens, sun, fire, water, wind,
         human beings. At the beginning: night, day, stormy wind, a
         light wind, heaven, human beings.

'The Babylonian Theodicy', mentioned above, also contains several
catalogues, involving at least two subjects. The first is a catalogue of
human types: old man, wise man, scholar, counsellor, child, young man,
father, mother, friend, stupid person, poor man, first-born, wealthy man,
philanthropist (at the opening, strophes 1-2). A second catalogue of
human types appears in strophes 13-23: robber, beggar, friend, daughter,
mother, hunter, son and daughter, modest man, prince, unfortunate man,
naked, guardian of the malt, nobleman, son of the wealthy, honourable
man, owner [wearer?] of headdress [turban? mitre?], builder, learned
man, righteous man, son of evil-doers, cheat, property owner, scoundrel,
boat-man, first-born, donkey driver, heir, hoodlum, indigent person,
youngest son. And in strophe 25: strong, weak, evil, straightforward,
beggar, ruler, poor, nouveau-riche. The second is a catalogue of animals:
onager, wild ass, savage lion, the gorer who trampled down the fields,
lion, cattle.

I shall compare below the manner in which catalogues are incorporated in these works and the approach of the book of Job to these
matters.

2. The Catalogue Model in Biblical Literature

In the context of the distribution and variety of catalogues in ancient
literature, it is worthwhile examining the role played by this model in the
Bible as well. Here too, there are a variety of types of catalogues, so that
the question of their basic relationship to the texts in which they were
incorporated arises repeatedly. Did the catalogue of nations in Genesis

10 exist independently before its incorporation in the book of Genesis (or, according to many scholars, in the Priestly Source), or was it initially written as a part of the narrative of the history of the human race in the Torah (or in the Priestly Source)? Was the catalogue of the children of Esau and its chiefs and kings (Gen. 36.11-43) once an entirely independent document, and if so, when and for what purpose was it written? Such questions may be raised regarding many other biblical catalogues, such as the list of heads of families (Num. 1.5-16); the censuses in the desert (Num. 1.20-47; 26); the itinerary on the way from Egypt to the land of Canaan (Num. 33); the kings of the land who were smitten by Joshua (Josh. 12.9-24); the boundaries, cities of refuge, and levitical cities in the book of Joshua (chs. 15–21); and many other lists, from Genesis to Chronicles, which is particularly rich in lists. Several of the catalogues are well integrated within the fabric of the book as a whole, and in some cases even constitute an essential part of it; others seem out of place from a literary viewpoint, and it is difficult to know exactly what led the author (or redactor) to include them within the text. But these catalogues and the problem of their relationship to their present literary context are not our interest at the moment.

I shall discuss below those catalogue elements which are incorporated in the Bible as an inseparable part of their context, in such a manner that the model—and perhaps even the catalogue itself, which had previously enjoyed an independent existence—is completely subjugated to the artistic purpose of the biblical work. To this end, I shall coin here a new term—concealed catalogue. This term refers to a catalogue which underlies a literary work in such a manner that it is not immediately discernible as a catalogue. In such a case, the author may have consciously obscured the use made of the catalogue model, or it may be deliberately designed so as to show us that, while there is indeed a catalogue here, it is edited in such an artful manner that the substantive drawbacks of the catalogue model—its monotony and superficiality—are negated. In other cases, the concealed catalogue may be the result of an unconscious struggle of the artist with the routine model: that is, the confrontation with certain limitations and the liberation from them by means of the creative artistic imagination. It is superfluous to add that, in most of those cases in which a work contains a concealed catalogue, there is no sure way of determining whether the artist was indeed aware of it or not. It is moreover doubtful whether such a statement would be of much exegetical importance, even were it possible to substantiate it.

From the artistic standpoint, the use of a concealed catalogue is more sophisticated than that of an explicit catalogue. Nevertheless, in certain cases it is precisely the knowledge of the possibility of concealing catalogues that gives added weight to the use of an overt, basic catalogue. An example is the use made by the book of Joshua of the above-mentioned catalogues. Their citation in a straightforward manner, without any attempt at concealment, well serves the purpose of the book—namely, to create a feeling of trust in the historical data that is offered, as if to say we are not dealing here with 'literature', but with dry facts. The degree of sophistication in this 'simplicity' will be appreciated primarily by those who think that the data in this book are not in fact taken from authentic catalogues from the period of settlement. In any event, I will not discuss here the explicit catalogues in the Bible, but only those which are concealed, as this type alone appears in the book of Job.

A classic example of a concealed catalogue appears in the words of Ezekiel concerning Tyre (Ezek. 27). The framework of this prophecy is an allegory: Tyre is compared to a well-constructed ship which set out to sea loaded with much merchandise, and sank when it went out on the high seas (v. 26). However, the framework of the prophecy completely obscures the underlying catalogue framework. The latter is no more than a pastiche of several different catalogues, in a combined model: a catalogue of peoples and lands (Senir, Lebanon, Bashan, Cyprus, Egypt, the islands of Elisha, Sidon, Arvad, Gebal, Persia, Lud, Put, Tarshish, Javan, Tubal, Meshech, Beth-togarmah, Dedan [Rhodes], Aram [or Edom], Judah, the land of Israel, Damascus, Arabia, Kedar, Sheba, Raamah, Haran, Canneh, Eden, Asshur, Chilmad); a catalogue of professions (builders, rowers, skilled men, caulkers, mariners, men of war, tradesmen); a catalogue of merchandise (fir trees, cedars, oaks, pines, ivory, fine embroidered linen, blue and purple, silver, iron, tin, lead, vessels of bronze, horses, war horses, mules, ivory tusks, ebony, emeralds, purple, embroidered work, fine linen, coral, agate, wheat, olives, early figs, honey, oil, balm, wine of Helbon, white wool, wine of Uzal, wrought iron, cassia, calamus, saddlecloths, lambs, rams, goats, all kinds of spices, precious stones, gold). There are those who claim that this prophecy is based upon an authentic list of merchandise (Hoffman 1977: 141, n. 30); in any event, it is clear that the prophet reworked it with a free hand for the purposes of the prophecy, like an artist who takes stones from an old, broken mosaic and recomposes them according to the model which he has designed.

Less sophisticated use is made of the catalogue model—and perhaps of a ready-made catalogue—in the prophecy in Jeremiah 25.15-31. This consists of a list of nations—Egypt, Uz, Philistines (Ashkelon, Gaza, Ekron, Ashdod), Edom, Moab, Ammon, Tyre, Sidon, the kings of the coastline across the sea, Dedan, Tema, Buz, all who cut the corners of their hair, Zimri, Elam, Media, Sheshach (this evidently refers to Babylonia)—which some think may have once been a clearly defined catalogue, which served as a kind of table of contents of Jeremiah's collection of prophecies concerning the nations (Hoffman 1977: 108-10). Another prophecy with a catalogue framework is that addressed to Moab in Isaiah 15–16, and the parallel prophecy in Jeremiah 48, listing a series of Moabite cities (17 in Isaiah; 24 in Jeremiah). It is impossible to discern any geographical or other principle in the order of enumeration of the cities (Hoffman 1977: 204-208), a feature that is generally characteristic of the catalogue model. One may also clearly distinguish catalogic elements in many other prophecies, such as Ezekiel 16 (jewellery and beautiful clothing); 18 (sins); 30.13-18 (cities of Egypt); in Mic. 1.9-16 (cities); etc. In these prophecies, unlike the previous examples, the catalogue genre is distorted by the expansion of its elements ('expanded model'), thereby losing its identity through its incorporation within a non-catalogue genre.

Particularly variegated use of the catalogue model appears in the Psalms, in the Wisdom literature, and in the Song of Songs—collections whose universal character stands out in comparison to the Torah and prophetic literature. As in the above-mentioned catalogues, here too one can see that the author often attempts to convey a new character to the known catalogue model, suitable to his own unique creation. These cases provide an explicit model of the struggle between the literary conventions that were deeply rooted in the culture, and the artistic need to innovate, to pave a path beyond the usually accepted. The following are several examples.

From a generic viewpoint, Psalm 136 is a catalogue of God's mercies. However, the author utilizes the 'open model', thereby bringing out the tendency to praise God at length, and to repeat his praises over and over again. In other words, the structural advantage of the catalogue model—its economy of language—is here turned upside down, the catalogue being transformed into a model containing an abundance of information, for the sake of the sheer power of the experience. The author reworks the catalogue in Psalm 104 in a different manner: the 'expanded model' is here camouflaged by the use of a large number of explanatory sentences or phrases and the presentation of the catalogue items, not in a strict subject order (heavenly bodies, animals, etc.), nor in their order of creation according to the accepted tradition, but rather through the practical relation among the various items—that is, how one serves the other—a relation explained by means of the sentences elaborating upon the items of the catalogue, rather than by the catalogue itself. The following are the items contained in the catalogue: light, heavens, waters, clouds, wind, fire, flame, earth, the deep, mountains, thunder, valleys, springs, beasts of the field, wild asses, birds of the air, grass, cattle, plants, food, wine, oil, trees, cedars, birds, stork, fir trees, wild goats, rocks, badgers, moon, sun, darkness, night, beasts of the forest, young lions, man. The psalm reaches its climax in v. 24, which is essentially the 'title' of the catalogue, the common denominator of all of its elements: 'O Lord, how manifold are thy works! In wisdom hast thou made them all; the earth is full of thy creatures.' As a result of the attempt made to overcome the generic characteristic of a nondescript order of elements, or conversely an arrangement in groups which could be anticipated in advance, an inner tension is created, presenting the reader with the need to guess the principle of its arrangement from the reading of the cata-logue, a riddle that is only resolved in v. 24. This verse is more than a self-evident title for the catalogue, as the verse does not merely say, 'this is a list of items from the cosmos', but rather elaborates: these are the works of God, adding an allusion to the principle by which the catalogue is arranged: 'In wisdom hast thou made them all'. Moreover, all this is presented, not in a dry informative manner, but in a cry of amazement combining experience with the facts.[21]

Another psalm making sophisticated use of the catalogue model is Psalm 150. The phrase 'praise him' (הללו) repeated thirteen times with slight variations, creates a model similar to the 'open catalogue'. On the basis of the first two appearances of this word, one is led to believe that we have here a catalogue of those places in which one is to praise God ('in his sanctuary', 'in his mighty firmament'); but thereafter the psalm goes on to note the reasons for which one is to praise God ('his mighty deeds', 'his exceeding greatness', etc.),[22] and the heading of the catalogue

---

21. On this, and on the relation to the hymn of Ahanaton to Shamash, which is also based upon a catalogue, see Hoffman 1992. On the catalogic nature of Psalm 148, see von Rad 1960: 295-97.

22. In v. 3 the letter כ appears for the only time in this hymn, in place of ב—i.e

seems to change. However, a true catalogue only appears in vv. 4-6, which is a list of musical instruments—trumpet sound, lute and harp, timbrel and dance,[23] strings and pipe, sounding cymbals, loud clashing cymbals. We thus find that the structure of the psalm is primarily a catalogue of musical instruments, combined with a kind of catalogue whose concern is how and why one is to praise the Lord.

Explicit catalogue elements are also to be found in the dirges in the book of Lamentations. These contain a catalogue of parts of the body (3.1-48): flesh, skin, bones, heart, kidneys, teeth, soul, blood (נצח; usually 'eternity', but compare Isa. 63.3, 6), heart, mouth, cheek, foot, hands, nose, eye (I have skipped those organs mentioned more than once). Chapter 5 gives a catalogue of types of people: strangers, aliens, orphans, mothers, widows, fathers, slaves, women, virgins, princes, elders, young men, boys.

Catalogue elements appear in several different chapters of the Song of Songs. In Song 2.1, 5, 11-17 one finds a catalogue of plants (rose, lily, brambles, apple tree, flowers, fig tree, vines, lilies), combined with a catalogue of animals (gazelles, hinds, young stag, songbird, turtle dove, dove, foxes—vv. 7-17). There are five separate small catalogues in ch. 4: animals (doves, goats, ewes, fawns, lions, leopards); parts of the body (eyes, braid, hair, teeth, lips, temple, neck, breasts, heart, lips, tongue); items from the vegetable kingdom (pomegranate, lilies, garden, orchard, pomegranates, choicest fruits); mountains (Gilead, mountain of myrrh, hill of frankincense [גבעת הלבונה] Lebanon, Amana, Senir, Hermon, mountains of leopards); and various luxuries (scarlet thread, necklace, nectar, honey, milk, nard, saffron, calamus, cinnamon, frankincense, myrrh, aloes, chief spices). In ch. 5 there again appears a catalogue of parts of the body (heart, head, locks, feet, hand, innards, fingers, palms, soul, head, locks, eyes, cheeks, lips, arms, body, legs, mouth); while the first part of the chapter (vv. 1-6) speaks of the body of the female

כרב גדלו. I wonder if one ought not to prefer the formula ברב גדלו, which appears in the Peshitta and in several traditional manuscripts. In LXX there is a change in the preposition preceding גבורותיו (*epi*) and preceding רב גדלו (*kata*) while in other cases the preposition returns as *en*.

23. Mandelkern, in his concordance, interprets מחול as a musical instrument, similar to a pipe or flute. In Pss. 53, 88, we find the heading למנצח על מחלת ('To the Choirmaster: according to Mahalath...'), which is translated by Aquilas, Theodotion and Symmachus as if from the word *coros* like the LXX in our chapter. This word means either a particular dance or a chorus; hence, it is difficult to know how LXX understood it in our chapter.

beloved, the second half (vv. 11-16) refers to the body of the male lover. Chapter 7 also conceals a catalogue of the parts of the body (feet, thighs, navel, belly, breasts, neck, eyes, nose, head, locks, lips, teeth) and of plants and their parts (wheat, lilies, palm tree, clusters, branches, clusters of the vine, apples, vines, pomegranates, mandrakes). It seems that the catalogue framework of many of the chapters of the Song of Songs helps to explain the technique of the author: when he or she wishes to deal with erotic subjects which should only be spoken of indirectly, he or she softens the impact by using known catalogues from completely different areas. There is even something of a challenge—adding a dimension of riddle and of wisdom—in the assembling of numerous catalogue items and their incorporation within new contexts. At times, it even seems that the author's tendency to be swept up by bizarre images may be explained on the basis of his or her tendency to make use of a large number of catalogue elements—and this too may be seen as a kind of literary embellishment.

The catalogue model occupies an extremely important place in Wisdom literature. If we expand the definition of the term, as we shall see below, one might even say that biblical Wisdom literature is primarily catalogic.

The following are several catalogues incorporated in the book of Proverbs. In Prov. 8.22-32, there is a catalogue of elements of the earth: depths, springs, mountains, hills, earth, fields, dust, heaven, skies, fountains of the deep, sea, waters, foundations of the earth, inhabited world. In Proverbs 10 there is a catalogue of different human types: son, father, foolish son, mother, righteous, wicked, diligent, wise of heart, fool, he who has understanding, him who lacks sense, rich man, poor, sluggard, him whose way is upright. Chapter 15 contains a catalogue of parts of the body (15.1-7): nose, tongue, mouth, eyes, tongue, lips, heart; and again at the end of the chapter—mind, mouth, eyes, bones, ear. In Prov. 26.1-18 there is a list of animals: sparrow, swallow, horse, ass, dog, young lion, lion. In ch. 29 there is found a list of human types: he who is often reproved, righteous, wicked, he who loves wisdom, one who keeps company with harlots, king, one who exacts gifts, man, neighbour, poor, scoffers, wise men, fool, bloodthirsty men, one who is blameless, upright, fool, ruler, officials, poor man, oppressor, child, mother, son, servant, man of wrath, man given to anger, lowly in spirit, thief, ruler, unjust man, he whose way is straight. The structure of 30.11-14 is that of an 'expanded catalogue', following the model of an 'open catalogue'—a list of kinds of generations (or, if you prefer: characteristics of different

societies). The lists of 'three and four' (vv. 15-33) are essentially catalogues of extended elements. Similarly, the song of the woman of valour
(31.10-31) is basically a catalogue—a point to which I shall return further
on.

Ecclesiastes 2 is based upon a catalogue framework of various kinds
of property: houses, vineyards, gardens and parks, pools, forest of
growing trees, male and female slaves, slaves born in the house, herds,
flocks, silver and gold, treasures of kings and provinces, singers, both
men and women, concubines. The list of times in ch. 3 is an 'open catalogue' of activities and human reactions. As is the way of catalogues, it
is difficult to find a logical order here, but the principle of contrasting
pairs is clearly applied.

But beyond all the specific examples given, the relationship of wisdom
literature to the catalogue mode may be seen in the very act of assembling sayings and proverbs—that is, by its very anthological nature—a
point which I shall elaborate below.

3. *Catalogues in the Book of Job*

It is within this general context that we must examine the relation of the
book of Job to catalogue literature. The following are those passages from
the book which, according to our definition, are concealed catalogues:

i. Meteorological and astronomic phenomena: ch. 3.1-9: day and night,
darkness, light, gloom, clouds, blackness of the day, thick darkness,
months, stars, dawn, 'eyelids of the morning'; ch. 24.7-14: night, dark,
twilight, deep darkness; ch. 37: heaven, lightning, corners of the earth,
thunder, snow, shower, rain, whirlwind, cold, scattering winds, ice, broad
waters frozen fast, thick cloud, clouds, balancings of the clouds, south
wind. To this group one should also add ch. 38, which is a catalogue of
natural phenomena from the realms of meteorology, astronomy, and of
those things found upon the surface of the earth: whirlwind, foundation
of the earth, morning stars, sea, clouds, thick darkness, morning, dawn,
skirts of the earth, light, springs of the sea, recesses of the deep, gates of
death, expanse of the earth, dwelling of the light, place of darkness,
storehouses of snow, hail, east wind, torrents of rain, thunderbolt, desert,
waste and desolate land, grass, rain, dew, ice, hoarfrost, heaven, waters,
face of the deep, Pleiades, Orion, Mazzaroth, Bear, ordinances of the
heaven, clouds, flood of waters, lightnings, clouds, mists, waterskins of
the heavens, dust, clods.

ii. Human types: ch. 3: those who curse the day, kings, counsellors of the earth, builders, princes, an untimely birth, infants, wicked, weary, prisoners, taskmaster, small and great, slave, master, him that is in misery, bitter in soul, man; ch. 12: people, friends, just, blameless man, laughing stock, one who is at ease, those whose feet slip, robbers, those who provoke God, aged, length of days, deceived, deceiver, counsellors, judges, kings, priests, mighty, those who are trusted, elders, princes, strong, nations, chiefs of the people of the earth, drunken man; ch. 19.13-21: brethren, acquaintances, kinsfolk, close friends, guests in my house, maid-servants, stranger, alien, servant, wife, sons of my own mother, young children, intimate friends, those whom I have loved, friends; ch. 29.1–30.12: young men, aged, princes, nobles, poor, fatherless, him who was about to perish, widow, blind, lame, poor, him whom I did not know, unrighteous, men, chief, king, mourners, men who are younger, fathers, thief, disreputable brood, rabble.

iii. Organs of the body: ch. 3.9-12: eyelids, womb, eyes, belly, knees, breasts; ch. 10.3-19: hands, eyes, flesh, man, hand, skin, flesh, bones, sinews, spirit, heart, head, womb, belly; ch. 16: soul, head, mouth, lips, face, nose (אף: metaphorically, wrath), teeth, eyes, cheek, hands, neck, kidneys, gall, skin, eyelids, hands, blood, man, human being; ch. 20.9-16: eye, hands, bones, mouth, tongue, stomach, innards, belly, head (ראש poison), tongue; ch. 29: head, hand, mouth, tongue, roof of the mouth, ear, heart, eyes, feet, fangs, teeth, face, mouth, head; ch. 33: mouth, tongue, palate, heart, lips, spirit, breath, soul, ears, feet, soul, bones, flesh, bones, face, man; ch. 40.9–41.16: arm, nose, faces, right hand, loins, power (און—i.e., virility), muscles, belly, tail, sinews, thighs, bones, limbs, eyes, nose, tongue, jaw, skin, head, hands, face, teeth, back, eye lashes, nostrils, soul, neck, flesh, heart.

iv. Marvels of nature: ch. 9.5-10: mountains, earth, pillars, sun, stars, heaven, waves of the sea, Bear, Orion, Pleiades, chambers of the south; ch. 26: shades, Sheol, Abaddon, north, void, nothing, waters, thick clouds, cloud, moon, face of the waters, light, darkness, pillars of heaven, sea, Rahab, heavens, fleeing serpent, thunder; ch. 39.1-15: stone, steppe, salt land, city, mountains, pasture, furrow, valleys, threshing floor, earth, ground.

v. Quarries and precious stones: ch. 28: silver, gold, iron, copper, ore, stones, sapphire, dust of gold, flinty rock, mountains, silver, gold of Ophir, onyx, sapphire, glass, fine gold, coral, crystal, pearls, topaz, fine gold.

vi. Sins and transgressions: ch. 22: great wickedness, iniquities, exacting pledges, stripping the naked, not giving water to the thirsty or bread to the hungry, seizing land from others, oppressing widows and orphans, imposing fear, making light of God's knowledge and power; ch. 24: removing landmarks, seizing flocks, driving away the flock of the orphans, taking pledges from widows, oppressing the poor and unfortunate, murder, robbing without shame, adultery, stealing in secret, cursing, iniquity; ch. 31: coveting women, iniquity, falsehood, deceit, turning aside from the way, coveting, bribery, adultery, lewdness, exploiting manservant and maidservant, oppressing the poor and widows, starving others, neglecting the needy, smiting the orphan, trusting in wealth, idolatrous customs, rejoicing in other's misfortune, oppressing the stranger, not welcoming the wayfarer, hiding evil, exploiting the land.

vii. Animals: ch. 38.6–41.26: rooster, lion, young lion, raven, mountain goats, hinds, wild ass, swift ass, wild ox, ostrich, wild beast, horse, locust, hawk, eagle, Behemoth, Leviathan, bird, fish, rams.

This division into seven types of catalogues is not the only possible one. Catalogues i, iv, v, and vii may be unified under one common heading—that is, the cosmos and its wonders. One thereby obtains four main types of catalogues: (i) the cosmos and its wonders; (ii) organs of the body; (iii) human types; (iv) sins and transgressions (see Appendix I, which classifies these catalogues according to their distribution in the speeches of the book). The most significant fact arising from this table is that most of the catalogues are concentrated in the words of Job, and not in those of his friends. This may be the result of a certain constraint originating in the structure of the book, which required the author to place more material in Job's mouth than he does in the mouth of all the other friends. The catalogue is a convenient vehicle upon which to construct any sort of verbiage; by elaborating the items in the catalogue, one may expand at length even in those places where, from a substantive-theoretical viewpoint, or even in terms of the moulding of the character, one could have cut short. If this understanding is correct, it also illuminates the nature of the speeches of Elihu. They are almost as long as the speeches of all the friends, and therefore contain extensive catalogue elements which, as we have noted, encourage an abundance of verbiage. Their relatively large number indicates their clear stylistic relation to the rest of the book. This in itself does not indicate anything about their author: he could be the author of the entire book, but it is also possible that their author adapted them especially to the character of the book which he had in front of him.

Another interesting detail follows from this table: Job (unlike Elihu and God) does not necessarily relate to the subject of the cosmos and its wonders within a hymnic context, although this is its natural and common literary *Sitz im Leben*. On the other hand, the subject of the organs of the body is expounded in relation to a dirge, in conformity with the accepted tradition of lamentation literature, as we shall see below. Comparison of the three catalogues of sins reveals an interesting relation among them; this too shall be discussed below.

I shall note several methods used by the author of Job to rework these catalogues, all of them 'concealed', as indicated above. I do not intend to analyse them fully, but merely to note certain interesting representative phenomena. In such matters, one must avoid 'discovering' hidden exegetical meanings in every application of the model and finding hidden messages in every variation or uniformity. It is better to say less than to exaggerate. It nevertheless seems that examination of the catalogues belonging to the type of 'God's wonders in the cosmos' indicates that, even though they belong to the category of 'concealed catalogues', the author does not really bother to conceal them. On the contrary, the reader receives the distinct feeling that there is here a catalogue which the author has succeeded in diversifying, thereby overcoming the generic limitations of monotony, but nevertheless clearly preserving the characteristics of the model. By this, the author indirectly informs us that the marvels of God are so numerous that the most appropriate model for relating them is the catalogue. Such is the case in the following catalogues: 9.5-10; 24.14-19; 26; 37 (the catalogues of sins—22, 24, 31—will be discussed in the next chapter).

A striking example of literary sophistication appears in the speech by God (chs. 38–41). The openly catalogic framework of this speech is suitable to its intention—the detailing of the manifold wonders of God—but raises several problems of composition that require solution. First of all, the author needed to create a speech which would be explicitly different from the earlier speeches of the friends, in order to stress that God himself is now speaking. However, the fact of its being based upon the catalogue model, which had been previously used on more than one occasion, runs contrary to this intention. This difficulty could be overcome by the creation of a particularly detailed catalogue, with a great many items, creating a feeling that the author of this catalogue (i.e., God) has a far more comprehensive vision than those of the previous catalogues. But exaggerated use of a multi-itemed catalogue confronts the author with the limitation of this genre in all its severity—namely, its simple monotony, stemming both from the basic nature of the catalogue style and from the lack of inner development among its elements. This problem is particularly severe in the speech of God, which is intended as the climax of the book. Moreover, the rhetoric used in the speech of God[24] is of the greatest importance because in a sense it needs to compensate for the absence of a direct reply to Job's arguments against God, as we shall see below.

Looked at from the perspective of the catalogue genre, the speech of God is divided into three sections: 38.4-38; 38.39–39.30; 40.15–41.26. In terms of the explicitness of their characterization as catalogues, these three sections are arranged in descending order. In the first passage mentioned, the distance between the items of the catalogue is very short: its 35 verses incorporate no less than 43 items (foundation of the earth, morning stars, the sons of God, sea, clouds, thick darkness, waves, morning, dawn, skirts of the earth, light, springs of the sea, deep, gates of death, deep darkness, expanse of the earth, light, darkness, snow, hail, east wind, torrents, channel, rain, thunderbolt, desert, grass, drops of dew, ice, hoarfrost, heavens, stone, face of the deep, Pleiades, Orion, Mazzaroth, Bear, lightnings, skies, mists, waterskins, dust, clods; items that repeat themselves are mentioned here only once). The second section, which is primarily a catalogue of animals spread over 33 verses, contains only 15 items—about one third the number of elements in the first section (lion, young lion, raven, mountain goats, hinds, wild ass, swift ass, wild ox, ostrich, wild beast, horse, locust, hawk, eagle, chicks). In the third section the catalogue of animals is only discernible because it comes in the wake of the previous catalogue: here (40.14–41.26) there are only eight elements (Behemoth, ox, wild beasts, Leviathan, bird, fish, deer, lions [בני שחץ]) spread over 43 verses.

We thus find that, as God's speech progresses, the non-catalogue elements between one item and the next become predominant; however, due to the density of the first section, the sense of reading a catalogue is

---

24. See on this matter Fox (1981: 75), who discusses the rhetoric of God's speech 'in the classical sense, the art of influencing the audience'. He relates primarily to the rhetorical nature of the questions in the speech. His conclusion (p. 60) is that God essentially says to Job: you know very well that I alone created the world and sustain its arrangements, 'and I know that you know and you know that I know that you know'—meaning, that the rhetoric is an inseparable part of the answer itself.

preserved until the end of the entire speech. Moreover, in the third section the author turns from a catalogue of the wonders of God to one of the parts of the body. By doing so, he preserves the catalogic model on the one hand, and on the other somewhat limits the excessive monotony of a catalogue on one subject. In the first section, which is most subject to the danger of monotony due to its density and the large number of items, one may not yet feel this 'weakness', as this is only the beginning of the speech and the reader has not become tired. Nevertheless, the author requires an additional, non-catalogic means in order to overcome the monotony—namely, a developmental connection among the items, creating the expectation of a climax. The author begins with an enumeration of the invisible 'foundations' of the earth, goes on to speak of visible phenomena of nature, such as stars and the sea, and then goes on to come closer to those things with which humans have daily contact, and are able to feel with their own hands. The anticipation (unrealized—this too being a rhetorical tactic) is that at the end of the catalogue he will mention humanity, and there will even be a response to the problems raised by Job himself. But the important thing here is not in fact the development, but rather the catalogue model itself, which by its very nature is indifferent to the arrangement of its items according to any particular 'logic', for which reason it also jumps about from subject to subject, and there is no insistence upon avoiding repetitions of items.[25]

25. The basic catalogue nature of God's speech and the structure we have seen are a partial answer to the doubts raised by several scholars regarding the authenticity of this speech. There are those who wish to alter the order of the verses, while others propose deleting several passages which are in their opinion not authentic. Thus, for example, Fohrer (1963), in interpreting ch. 38, suggested that verses 18, and 19-20 are glosses, because they involve repetitions or variations of what has already been said in the chapter. But we have already seen how characteristic this is of the catalogue genre. Similarly, Tur-Sinai (1972: 323) suggests that 38.36 is misplaced because it speaks of animals, according to his interpretation of the word טחות, and thus belongs as it were to ch. 39. Pope (1973) resolves this by interpreting טחות (RSV: clouds) as 'Thot', the Egyptian god of justice, while שכוי (RSV: mists) is seen as a (Coptic) term for the planet Mercury. For a comprehensive exegetical discussion of v. 7, see Dhorm 1926: 591-93. However, there is in fact no need for these emendations. The structure of the verse, '...מי' ('Who has...'), appears earlier (vv. 2, 5, 25) as well as later on (37.41; 39.5). As for the contents, sometimes the author goes from one catalogue to another, and there is not necessarily a sharp transition. On the contrary, he incorporates one catalogue within another, creating a chain of catalogues. This is the case in ch. 3, which will be discussed below, and thus also in the transition from the catalogue of animals to that of parts of the body in ch. 40. But it may be that the author here

The gradual reduction of the density of items in the catalogue which characterizes God's answer is parallel to a gradual reduction of the density of rhetorical questions. The feeling is thereby created that God apparently wants to help Job to answer his questions. However, this is in fact a technique of intimidation, which is part of the very answer of God.

Another example of sophisticated use of the catalogue model may be found in ch. 3. The compositional status of Job's lament is here extremely important, serving as it does as a transition from the prose narrative to the poetic speeches; from the plot to the reflections concerning the basic subject of the book. Here the author needs to set forth a possible direction of development for the continuation of the work. Indeed, this chapter seems to serve as a mirror of one of the main artistic characteristics of the book, upon which I shall elaborate further on. I refer to the tension between structural schematism, which goes hand in hand with adherence to traditional models—in our case, the catalogue model—and the mimetic dimension, which can alone create an emotional connection to the work on the part of the reader, in addition to the intellectual interest in the problems which the work raises. This seems to be one of the main differences between the book of Job and 'I Will Praise the Lord of Wisdom' and 'The Babylonian Theodicy'; in the latter two, there is hardly any mimetic dimension, and hence the reader's emotional involvement is also very limited.

The status of ch. 3 as a bridge between the 'biographical' narrative and theoretical discussions concerning the issue of divine recompense demands solutions to two main difficulties, if one wishes to see it serving as a mimetic bridge and not as a purely technical one: namely, how to justify the philosophical and theoretical nature of what follows, and how to create a suitable background for the words of Eliphaz, which move from empathetic silence ('and no one spoke a word to him, for they saw that his suffering was very great'—2.13) to theories of recompense. The solution to both these difficulties lies in the creation of a mimesis of a person who undergoes a process of sublimation during which he directs his physical suffering to channels of intellectual suffering. The first part of Job's words is an outburst of curses lacking rhyme or reason (see below) whose subject—as opposed to the substance of the curse—is the

anticipates an item from the catalogue of animals, which he incorporates here prior to the end of the previous catalogue in order to preserve the continuity of catalogues. The strategy of anticipation in the book has been discussed *in extenso* by Alter (1985: 85-110); see below, p. 132.

events of the past (Job's birth), and not the future. This is the outburst of a person who has lost all logical connection with reality, a known side effect of shock occurring in the wake of a personal catastrophe. Only in v. 10, with the words 'because it did not shut...', does he begin to draw a distinction between past, present and future. This becomes clearer further on, as there gradually emerges from Job's words the understanding that the past cannot be corrected ('why did I not die in the womb...why did knees receive me...for now I would lie...', etc.— vv. 11-19). This process of sobering and intellectual refinement is intensified in v. 20. The question, 'Why is light given to him that is in misery, and life to the bitter in soul', creates a clear mimesis of a person who begins to feel that, so long as his pain is not perceived as a 'phenomenon', as an event that ought to arouse the concern of every person, it will be unable to transcend the narrow limits of purely personal interest. The generalized formulation of this question in turn invites the principled-theoretical response of Eliphaz, and it is this which determines the character of the book from then on. The end of the chapter ('For the thing that I fear comes upon me, and what I dread befalls me', v. 25) marks the height of Job's disillusionment, and opens the possibility for the author to place in Eliphaz's mouth words concerning his friend's past, such as, 'Behold, you have chastised many' (4.3), etc. Parallel to this, ch. 3 serves as a bridge between the frame-story and the speeches on the level of plot as well. Its opening—'After this Job opened his mouth and cursed the day of his birth...'—the stream of curses that comes in its wake, and the references to God, both explicit (vv. 4, 23) and implicit (v. 10), are all directly connected to the central riddle of the plot presented in ch. 2, which is meant to be resolved in the course of the book: namely, whether Job would 'bless' God to his face? The impression created by the chapter is that Job is coming closer and closer to the moment when he will curse God; the anticipation of the realization of this expectation (which is, of course, proven wrong) draws a kind of dramatic line of tension throughout the speeches by Job.[26]

26. This analysis seems sufficient to refute the view of Maag (1982: 99-107) that the chapter does not belong to the original work, but to one of its redactions, because it does not at all relate to the subject of theodicy, while the speaker therein is not a person who suffered physically but psychologically, because of his lack of understanding of the ways of God. Fishbane (1971) emphasized the relations of 3.3-13 (and Jer. 4.23-26) to the creation tradition. Genesis 1 is also a kind of a catalogue, and thus its relation to Job 3 also refers to the genre, and not only to the motif of creation.

JKM LIBRARY
1100 E. 55th Street, Chicago, IL 60615

Date Due Slip

Please keep this receipt with this
item and do not lend this item to
anyone else. Return or renew item by
due date noted below. Item may be
renewed online at www.jkmlibrary.org
(click "My Account" tab and enter
14-digit library card barcode number,
with no spaces), in person, by phone
(773-256-0739), by fax (773-256-0737)
or by e-mail (circdesk@lstc.edu)

ransaction Date: 04/15/05 03:55PM
****

ue Date: 04/15/06
 em Barcode: 39967000260385
 isdom, you are my sister : studies in ho
 of Roland E. Murphy, O. Carm., on
 l. No.: BS1455 .W564 1997

 ron Barcode: 29967000005071

These structural solutions are, as mentioned, interwoven through three catalogues—that of the wonders of God, of the organs of the body, and of human types. The latter stretches in effect over the entire chapter, constituting the framework for the other two catalogues. The catalogue of 'wonders of God' fills the opening verses (vv. 1-9), and immediately in its wake comes the catalogue of parts of the body. As in the speech of God, here too there is no separation between the beginning of the second catalogue and the conclusion of the first catalogue: the metaphorical organ, 'the eyelids of the morning' (v. 9) is composed of one element that belongs in its substance to the first catalogue (morning) and another that belongs to the second (eyelids). In fact, in terms of content vv. 1-9 may be read as a catalogue of curses (the perishing of the day and the night; let it be darkness; nor light shine upon it; let gloom and deep darkness claim it; etc.—all told, a catalogue with 17 items). However, comparison of the curses found here with those known to us from the literature of curses in the Bible or the international curse literature reveals two distinct differences: the traditional curses pertain to the future, and are based upon a catalogue of mishaps—human disease, natural disasters, social dangers—that is, catalogues which may be defined as 'negative' in their very essence.[27] By contrast, the curses of Job in ch. 3 pertain to the past, as part of the previously noted mimesis, and not to the future, and are based upon a catalogue of the wonders of God characteristic of the hymnic literature. We thus have here an ironic use of a catalogue that is also characteristic of the catalogues of the greatness of God in the speeches of Job further along in the book, as we have seen above.

Furthermore, regarding the nature of the catalogue in ch. 3, its framework is a list of human types, thereby making humanity the primary subject of Job's dirge. This is opposed to the catalogue in the speech of

27. Compare, for example: 'I will appoint over you sudden terror, consumption and fever that waste the eyes and cause life to pine away...and you shall be smitten before your enemies; those which hate you shall rule over you...And I will let loose the wild beasts among you...', etc. (Lev. 26.16ff.); and also in Deuteronomy: 'then all these curses shall come upon you...Cursed shall you be in the city, and cursed shall you be in the field... The Lord will send upon you curses, confusion, and frustration...until you are destroyed and perish quickly...The Lord will make the pestilence cleave to you...The Lord will smite you with consumption, and with fever, inflammation, and fiery heat...' (28.16ff.). The relation of ancient Near Eastern vassal treaty curses to the Bible has been discussed by Hillers (1964). A discussion of the biblical lists of curses appears in his book, pp. 30-42.

God with which the book concludes, which completely ignores humanity. In retrospect, this may be seen as alluding to the moving of the centre of gravity from the anthropocentric position of Job to the opposite position presented in the speech of God, which represents humanity in all its objective smallness contrasted with the cosmos as a whole.

Chapter 12 is yet another example of the sophisticated manner in which the author reworks the catalogue model. The following are the elements of the catalogue in the chapter: people, friends, just, blameless man, laughing stock, one who is at ease, those whose feet slip, robbers, those who provoke God, aged, length of days, deceived, deceiver, counsellors, judges, fools, kings, priests, mighty, those who are trusted, elders, princes, strong, nations, chiefs of the people of the earth, drunken man. The outstanding means used to conceal the catalogue framework of this chapter is the variety of syntactical forms of its components: single and plural, separate and conjunctive. Nevertheless, towards the end (vv. 17ff.) the use of a uniform formula becomes stronger, as does the awareness of the catalogue framework, and the claim that there are many proofs for the arbitrary rule of God becomes more firmly grounded.[28]

The book of Job's unique way of making artistic use of 'concealed catalogues' stands out particularly in comparison with the simple incorporation of catalogues in 'I Will Praise the Lord of Wisdom' and 'The Babylonian Theodicy'. In these works there is at least one explicit catalogue—that of the gates of Babylon, at the end of 'I Will Praise the Lord of Wisdom'. This is an expanded catalogue, with no attempt made to conceal it: all of its components share identical syntactic form, as place

---

28. Verses 16-25 are reminiscent of the catalogue of God's wonders in Psalm 107. This psalm is built around a framework of a catalogue of human types; each one of the first four strophes (vv. 1-9, 10-16, 17-22, 23-31) notes at its beginning those types of which it speaks: 'the redeemed of the Lord' (v. 2); 'Some who sat in darkness and gloom, prisoners in affliction and in irons' (v. 10); 'who were sick through their sinful ways' (v. 17); 'who went down to the sea in ships' (v. 23). It may be that this passage in Job bears a conscious ironic relation to the concluding strophe of Psalm 107 (vv. 32-43); whereas the psalm emphasizes the wisdom in God's mercies and the ethical purposiveness of his deeds, Job emphasizes more the absolute arbitrariness of his actions, whether for good ('He uncovers the deeps out of darkness, and brings deep darkness to light. He makes nations great...he enlarges nations, and leads them away', 12.22), or whether, and primarily, for evil. As against that, Segal (1949: 43) thinks that the passage in Job preceded Psalms and influenced the author of the psalm.

descriptions in the singular, and each one of them is preceded by the same preposition: *ina* (= Hebrew ב).[29] The catalogue of parts of the body (enumerated in relation to pathological symptoms) is likewise not concealed. The repetition of this catalogue at the end of the work, in the course of a detailed enumeration of the symptoms from which the poet was healed, leaves room for the possible conjecture that this catalogue had an independent existence, possibly for an apothropaeic-magical purpose.[30] The other catalogues, even though they are concealed, do not exhibit excessive sophistication either: they do not contribute to the shaping of any of the characters, nor to the characterization of the situation or the presentation of any problem in the work. It would therefore seem to be correct to say that in the book of Job the catalogues are reworked to become an integral part of the work. Thus, unlike the Mesopotamian works, the traditional model finds expression even in non-traditional forms. It is difficult to separate this aesthetic evaluation from the intellectual aspect as, unlike 'I Will Praise' or the 'Theodicy', the message of the book of Job is not a conservative one (a detailed discussion of this point appears in Chapter 7)

4. *The Catalogue and the Anthology*

We have already noted the fundamental similarity between the catalogue and the anthology, in that both are collections of units having a common denominator. However, whereas in a regular catalogue the units are items, each one of which constitutes a brief syntactic unit, in an anthology the elements are more complex units—proverbs, hymns, and the like. Nevertheless, this does not negate the substantive similarity between the two. Hence, several characteristics of the catalogue may be noted in an anthology as well, such as an emphasis upon the resemblance among the elements, and not only their substantive relation to a common denominator; the purely secondary importance of the order of elements; the foregoing of developmental continuity in the order of elements; and

29. One may assume that the lists of parts of the body were also catalogic by nature. Lambert (1960: 23) notes that the list of diseases in Tablet II is influenced by the incantation literature, but is fundamentally based upon the accepted listing of parts of the body from the head down.

30. Weimer (1974: 12) cites the view that 'I Will Praise the Lord of Wisdom' was a ritual text—the supplication of a sick king, composed by a priestly school for reading on the 'day of rest of the heart' (*um nuh libbi*).

so on. Thus, the same poetic problems which confront the author of a catalogue who is dissatisfied with the simple, monotonous model likewise confront the compiler of the anthology, albeit with lesser severity. And indeed, in biblical Wisdom literature one finds confrontation primarily with the poetic problematic of the catalogue, but also with that of the anthology.

The first example of this is the book of Proverbs, whose structure is catalogic-hierarchical, on the level of words, proverbs, and collections. Within this hierarchy, there is a consistent tendency to conceal its catalogic character on the level of words; this tendency is less striking in the succession of proverbs, and hardly exists at all on the level of collections.

The introduction to the book (1.2-7) is constructed as one unit, containing an approbation of the book and the importance of its study. Its structure obscures the fact that it is based upon a catalogue of praiseworthy spiritual characteristics, which according to the philosophy of the book are synonyms for the various shades of wisdom: wisdom, understanding, insight, righteousnss, justice, equity, prudence, knowledge, discretion, learning, skill, the fear of the Lord. Chapter 8 is likewise based upon an explicit catalogic framework. There is a catalogue of human types (men, sons of men, simple ones, foolish, noble, wicked, righteous, crooked, twisted, he who understands, he who finds knowledge, evil, pride, arrogance, king, rulers, princes, governors, judges); a catalogue of attributes (wisdom, crookedness, straightness, truth, prudence, knowledge, discretion, fear of God, hatred of evil, the way of evil, perverted speech, counsel, sound wisdom, insight, strength, righteousness); and a catalogue of the creation and its mighty things (depths, springs, water, mountains, hills, fields, dust of the world, heavens, skies, fountains of the deep, sea, foundations of the earth). This catalogue framework is organized around proverbs, each one of which might stand in its own right: vv. 1, 5, 7, 11, 13—as might, in practice, almost every verse in the chapter. However, just as the proverbs conceal the catalogues of terms, so does the editing of the proverbs as an 'autobiographical' speech of Wisdom praising itself conceal its catalogue character. Further examples of the concealing of lists of proverbs by their editing as speeches (of wisdom; the strange woman; parents to children) can be cited from chs. 1–8 in the first collection of the book of Proverbs.

A collection of proverbs is likewise a catalogue; hence, one may see the differences among the various collections in the book of Proverbs as reflecting different methods of obscuring their catalogue nature. Thus, for example, in Prov. 10–22.16 ('The proverbs of Solomon'), no attempt is made to conceal the catalogue-anthological model of the collection of sayings, and their brevity—each one consisting of a single isolated verse—emphasizes that they are items in a catalogue. The same is not true for Prov. 31.10-31, which is essentially a collection of sayings based upon a catalogue of praiseworthy characteristics of women. The author uses two methods to obscure its catalogic framework. First, he organizes the sayings in an alphabetical acrostic sequence. This is anti-catalogic by nature: in a catalogue the order of elements is not important, while in an acrostic the model forces a certain order. Secondly, he creates a seemingly dramatic framework, also anti-catalogic in terms of genre, in which all these attributes are ascribed to one figure—the woman of valour. Similarly, the initial question, 'A woman of valour who can find?' alludes to its contents, but obscures its catalogic nature. The latter would call for a heading such as 'a list of good characteristics of women'.

As opposed to the literary tendency to conceal catalogues insofar as this applies to isolated terms or proverbs, no such attempt is made to obscure the anthological character of the book as a whole. This is made clear by the headings of the various collections, which could easily have been removed at the time of editing. The fact that the order of collections in the translation of the Septuagint differs from that of the Masoretic text indicates the secondary importance given to their sequence, a characteristic typical of the catalogue genre.[31]

We have thus seen that, as one ascends the hierarchic scale and the elements of the catalogue are expanded, the need to conceal their catalogic nature correspondingly diminishes—and this is hardly surprising. As a poetic problem, the monotony and sporadicity attached to a catalogue of words, whose items are extremely short, is a great disincentive to its use. Due to its low level of sophistication, there is perhaps a certain reluctance to use a catalogue openly in a work of art. The weight of

31. According to the Masoretic tradition, the headings of the collections within the book are: 'The Proverbs of Solomon, son of David, king of Israel' (1.1); 'The proverbs of Solomon' (10.1); 'Incline your ear, and hear the words of the wise' (22.17); 'These also are sayings of the wise' (24.23); 'These also are proverbs of Solomon which the men of Hezekiah king of Judah copied' (25.1); 'The words of Agur son of Jakeh of Massa' (30.1); 'The leech...' (30.15); 'The words of Lemuel, the oracle...' (31.1). As is known, the sequence of the collections differs in the LXX, as follows: 1.1–24.22; 24.23–34; 25.1–29.27; 30.1-14; 15–33; 31.1-9; 10–31. The identical opening and closing in both versions indicates that there were also common considerations of redaction—but this is not the place to enlarge upon this point.

these restrictions lessens as the elements of the catalogue become more complex and diverse—for example, entire proverbs—and disappears when the elements themselves are extensive collections.

This awareness of the limitations of the catalogue is also evident in the editing of the books of Ecclesiastes and Song of Songs, whose catalogic framework has already been noted. The book of Ecclesiastes, besides being a catalogue of dozens of proverbs, each one of which has an independent standing, is an anthology of separate collections, albeit evidently the work of one author. The debate between those who see the book as a collection of sayings with a weak connection between them, and those who find therein a certain developmental-dramatic order,[32] indicates the true character of the work: like the book of Proverbs, it is fundamentally a hierarchic catalogue, which on each level confronts the segmentation of the catalogue model. However, unlike the book of Proverbs, it does not contain headings distinguishing one collection from another. On the contrary, there is a clear tendency to give the anthology an 'autobiographical' character; the isolated sayings are organized into a whole unit, creating a uniformly gloomy atmosphere. All these factors conceal the catalogue framework, creating the impression that all, and not only the majority, of the sayings in the book lie on the border between existentialism and nihilism.

A similar phenomenon also exists in the Song of Songs, as Fox has rightly emphasized.[33] We previously discussed its catalogue elements on the level of isolated words. These elements are concealed by being worked into poems whose subject is the various expressions and manifestations of love. But rather than being satisfied with a catalogic editing, and thus presenting an anthology of 'songs of love', the author edited these into a kind of drama, thereby lending the work a more sophisticated literary dimension. There is thus created a coherent framework for the different songs which seems to allude to a plot, even if this escapes a

32. See Fox, *EncBib*, VII, pp. 73-77; he rejects the views of those scholars who think that the book consists of 'scores of short sayings without any substantive connection among them'. On the unity and shaping of the book, see also Fox 1977 and 1987: 155-62.

33. Fox 1985. On pp. 202-22, he discusses the question of the unity of Song of Songs in comparison to Egyptian love poetry. Unlike those who see this scroll as a collection of separate love songs and who downplay the importance of the elements uniting it, he states (p. 220) that the scroll, at least in its original version, was composed by one author as a unified work. Similarly, Mays (1987: 6) defines Psalm 119 as a work which is not a mere anthology but a 'combination into a unity'.

reader who tries to follow the progress of its development closely.

One may therefore observe a continuing process, extending over hundreds of years, in the tradition of biblical-catalogic literature: struggle with the basic model, its elaboration, its assimilation within pseudo-catalogue models such as sayings, and the creation of greater units, including attempts to give coherence to the anthology in terms of subject matter and plot.

Let us now examine the book of Job in terms of this general framework of the process of 'liberation' from the catalogue model. I have already quoted Haezrachi's claim that every artistic work is essentially the 'solution of an aesthetic problem'. In the light of this, I posed the question as to the nature of the aesthetic problem which the book of Job sets out to solve. I now wish to propose a provisional answer to this question, which has emerged from our discussion thus far: the aesthetic problem which confronted the author of the book of Job was how to create a collection of various doctrines of recompense and of viewpoints concerning divine justice, in a framework of greater interest and significance than a mere anthology. The solution which took shape was that of a work with a dramatic framework based upon an ancient story, and the development of that story through speeches raising various aspects of theodicy: human suffering, the success of evil-doers, the greatness of the creator, solutions to the problems of the suffering of the righteous and the success of evil-doers, and so on. Hence, the main literary aim of the book of Job was not to provide a clear-cut solution to the problem of divine justice. For this reason, any criticism of the book which claims that it does not resolve this problem misses its main purpose.

Several side conclusions follow from this thesis. In accepting that the book of Job is essentially an anthology on the subject of recompense, and not an attempt to convince one of the rightness of any particular view, the view of the author becomes of secondary importance. From this, the question of the original text and the additions to the book also acquires a different perspective: it becomes secondary from an exegetical viewpoint, as the meaning of the term 'addition' in an anthology is completely different from its meaning in a non-anthological work. If we may assume that the catalogue nature of the book was not unknown to its various redactors, this would allow them to add new 'items', whether individual sayings or entire speeches, without worrying that these would not fit well into its dramatic framework. I will enlarge upon this matter below, in Chapter 8.

The perception of the book as an anthology also explains another characteristic phenomenon—the frequent repetition of similar ideas. This feature seems to involve an explicit wisdom element: the presentation of one matter in several formulae, at times even in variations of the same formula, as is also done, for example, in the book of Proverbs (e.g., 10.6 vs. 10.11; 10.7 vs. 10.30; 11.5 vs. 11.16; and many others). The extensive verbiage uttered both by Job and the friends concerning matters that neither advance the plot nor contribute to the emotional intensification of the reader's position, such as fragments of hymn, is among other things the result of the catalogic framework of the work.

The fashioning of the anthology within a dramatic framework presented the author with several structural problems which necessarily influenced its contents. One of these is the creation of a tension capable of carrying the weak plot of the cycles of dialogues, from which there follows another problem—that of moving towards some sort of climax. How can one reach a climax in an anthology? The solution to this would seem to be the placing of the final speech in the mouth of God himself, rather than in that of one of the friends. But by this a new poetic problem is created: the reader expects God's words to represent a climax in terms of their contribution to the solution of the problem presented throughout the length of the work. In other words, one anticipates a much higher level of argument, a speech that will instantaneously cut through the theoretical confusion that has been created. Opinions differ as to whether this hope is in fact realized, a point to which I shall return later.

To summarize this chapter: to distinguish the catalogic elements in the book of Job means to shed new light upon the understanding of several of its most important characteristics and to contribute to a more accurate evaluation of the exigencies confronting the author. His lack of ease with traditional literary forms, in which he was unable to find appropriate vehicles for expressing what he wished to say, becomes clearer; there follows from this the need to shape a new literary model, which would better resolve his aesthetic difficulty. He created this model from available types of materials: the hymn, the lamentation, the catalogue, the proverb literature, the speech, and the narrative. The need to express non-conventional ideas in the realm of faith could not be realized in a conventional literary framework. As a result, the new literary framework that took shape and the problem of faith (see on this Chapter 7) with which he came to grapple were combined with one another.

Chapter 5

HARMONIZING MIMETIC DEVICES

There is an inevitable gap between the strict structural and literary expectations aroused by the book of Job and its catalogue nature. This is translated into an aesthetic tension, without which it is doubtful whether any artistic creation could exist. The catalogue element dictates a certain indifference towards the sequence of its components and a sacrifice of any developmental movement, while the structure of the book requires a systematic organization of its various units. The catalogue-anthological element tends to underline the independent status of the various statements and speeches, while the structural rigidity of the book binds them together. However, these ties are merely formal and external, and from this point of view may even be defined as artificial or, to formualte it somewhat differently, an inadequate answer to the aesthetic problem which seeks its solution in the book. Having in the previous chapter stressed the catalogue elements, in this chapter we shall discuss the opposite pole of the artistic field within which the work exists—namely, those factors that unify the speeches into a significant continuity beyond the purely structural bonds.

In the background of our remarks lie such questions as: Does such a continuity exist? Does it exist to the same extent throughout the entire book? Through what means was it created? In the course of seeking appropriate answers to these questions, other related matters will be raised for discussion. In addition, I shall examine whether one may rely upon these conclusions in order to distinguish between the original stratum and the additions to the book.

Our discussion will revolve around three axes: (a) the nature of the dialogic continuity between the speeches; (b) the shaping of the characters; (c) the motif of the trial. All three of these axes share a common denominator: mimesis—mimesis of a debate, of 'group dynamics', of changing moods under changing circumstances. In those areas in which a partial overlap of subject matter is brought about among the three axes, the subject will be discussed *in extenso* only in terms of one of them, while regarding the others I will only touch the matter briefly, so as to preserve the flow of the argument.

The conclusions we will reach are meant to clarify certain questions of background and to illuminate the nature of the work from various other aspects. These issues will be elucidated separately with regard to the speech of Elihu, which constitutes an additional layer in our examination of the status of the speech in the book. It will be summarized in Chapter 8.

1. *Dialogic Continuity among the Speeches*

As we have seen, the book's structure elicits clear expectations as to the connection among the words of the participants in the debate in all three cycles: one anticipates dialogic connections and development in the relations between Job and his friends, and perhaps also among the friends themselves. To what extent and in what manner are these expectations realized? In order to focus our discussion, I shall examine two hypotheses regarding these matters: (a) that there is a discernible tendency towards exacerbation in the words of the friends to Job, that is to say, the debate becomes sharper and more polarized; (b) that there are definite connections among the speeches, as might be expected from the mimesis of a debate. The decision to examine these specific theses is not arbitrary, but is based upon valid reasons and methodological integrity: namely, that they are more likely to be proven than any other hypothesis concerning the existence of dialogic continuity; and that, if proven to be correct, this will be sufficient to prove the existence of such continuity.

While one must examine the hypothesis that there is a marked tendency toward exacerbation in the friends' remarks towards Job, one need not examine the question as to whether there is a similar tendency in Job's remarks towards the friends, as such a theory may easily be refuted, even without detailed discussion. Already in his initial reaction to the words of Eliphaz, Job accuses his friends of treachery and disloyalty— 'My brethren are treacherous as a torrent-bed, as freshets that pass away' (6.15); and of cowardice—'you see my calamity, and are afraid' (v. 21). In a tone of sharp irony, he observes their hypocrisy and arrogance—'How forceful are honest words...For you think that you can reprove words, when the speech of a despairing man is wind?' (vv. 25-

26); their willingness to sacrifice every social and ethical value—'You would even cast lots over the fatherless, and bargain over your friend' (v. 27). In none of his subsequent speeches do we find such extreme remarks addressed towards the friends. True, he does repeat similar accusations in the following speeches (12.2; 13.4-8; 16.1-4; 19.1-3; 21.3), but in none of these do they appear in such highly concentrated form or in such sharp formulations as in Chapter 6. Offhand, one might even see in this an expression of a tendency on Job's part to seek reconciliation, but in fact things are not thus, because he does not retract his accusations, but simply becomes less and less concerned with the friends. One gains the impression that he ignores them, an impression that is not altered by his one-time supplication towards them (19.21-22). Instead, he appeals to God, thereby illustrating one of the most significant differences between his own speeches and those of the friends: the latter do not address God directly even once throughout the course of the entire book. They thereby confirm, so-to-speak, that which is implied by Job's rhetorical question: 'Will you speak falsely for God, and speak deceitfully for him? Will you show partiality toward him...' (13.6-7). Thus, throughout the course of Job's replies to his friends, there is a tendency neither towards exacerbation nor towards moderation or reconciliation.

In the speeches of the friends, the picture is more complex. Eliphaz's first speech, in chs. 4–5, is composed of three parts—a model which is common to the speeches of all three friends in the first cycle of debates. This consists of an introduction, posing a rhetorical question towards Job, in principle unrelated to the problem of recompense (4.2-7);[1] a conclusion, likewise addressed directly to Job (5.17b-27);[2] and, in the middle, the body of the speech, which is general and theoretical. A comparison of each of these three components of the speeches may serve as a suitable test for our hypothesis concerning the gradual and continuous exacerbation of the debate.

i. The introduction to Eliphaz's speech is characterized by ambiguity,[3]

1. See 8.2-7; 11.2-6.
2. See 8.21-22; 11.12-20.
3. See on this Fullerton 1930; Hoffman 1980. On ambiguity as a deliberate poetic tactic in the Psalms, see Rabbe 1991. He observes the presence of ambiguity on different levels—lexicographical, phonetic, syntactical—and states that these are indicative both of the artistic level of the authors of the Psalms, as well as of their purpose—'such multivalence functions to engage the hearers/readers, to cause them to interact with the psalms...' (p. 227).

a kind of cautious groping in the light of the prolonged silence following Job's harsh words in ch. 3. His opening question, 'If one ventures a word with you, will you be offended?' (4.2) contains no real censure of Job, even if we do interpret it as an indirect criticism;[4] all the more so if we see it as a conciliatory sentence, as an attempt to open with encouraging words.[5] On the contrary, the opening question demonstrates a certain lenient consideration. Similarly further on: even if we assume that the description of Job as one who knew how to help others to overcome crises ('your words have upheld him who was stumbling', etc.—4.4) is only meant as an introduction, by way of contrast, to a criticism of his behaviour at the time of test ('but now it has come to you, and you are impatient'—4.5), this fails to cancel the positive image of his character prior to the catastrophe. The possibility that vv. 6-7 imply a concealed criticism (had you been God-fearing and walked with integrity; had you been innocent of sin, disaster would not have come upon you[6]) does not refute the opposite interpretation, which sees in these verses an expression of absolute faith in Job's righteousness (behold you are God-fearing and walk with integrity; therefore be not afraid, for you shall not be lost!).

On the other hand, there is no room for ambiguity in the opening words of the second friend, Bildad: 'How long will you say these things, and the words of your mouth be a great wind?' (8.2). This caustic remark is tantamount to an open declaration: I have come to insult you

4.   S.D. Luzzatto: 'If some trouble comes to you, will you immediately be offended?' Likewise Rashi: 'A language of astonishment...In the one test with which your Creator tested you and visited upon you, you are offended?'

5.   Thus Ibn Ezra: 'The letter *nun* indicates the plural, and the *samekh* is in place of the *shin*, and the *heh* in place of the *alef* [i.e., as if the word were נשא]..."and one who is of limited words cannot bear it"'. Dhorm (1926) and others have interpreted the verse similarly. Driver and Gray (1921) and others translate 'If one attempt a word with thee...'

6.   Dhorm (1926) sees here Eliphaz's sharp irony. Rashi interpreted it more severely: 'Now your end proves your initial intention, that the fear with which you were God-fearing was in fact foolishness, for it comes from foolishness and not from fulness of knowledge, and similarly your hope and your ways are all foolishness'. Likewise R. Joseph Kara in his commentary to Job; see Arend's edition (1989). On the relation between Kara's commentary and that of Rashi, see Arend 1989: 23-44. Similar to them is R. Levi Gersonides (Ralbag): 'That you were God-fearing was only because of your hope that He would protect your possessions, but when you lost these possessions, your fear of God left you'. I believe that these interpretations should be rejected.

for the things you said. The opening words of the third friend, Zophar, are even sharper—'Should a multitude of words go unanswered, and a man full of talk be vindicated? Should your babble silence men, and when you mock, shall no one shame you. For you say, "My doctrine is pure, and I am clean in God's eyes"' (11.2-4). He does not satisfy himself with censuring Job's words, as does Bildad, but attaches a shameful label to Job himself—'a man full of talk' (אִישׁ שְׂפָתַיִם, lit, 'man of lips'), that is, a hypocrite and demagogue (see Isa. 29.13). The extended sarcasm of his introduction, as against that of Bildad, also contributes to this exacerbation.

This clear tendency towards exacerbation is not expressed in the opening speeches of the friends in the second and third cycles, with the exception of the speeches of Eliphaz, to be discussed separately (below, pp. 133-40). The opening words of Bildad's second speech, in ch. 18, are harsh,[7] but do not entail actual insulting remarks, as does his first speech. He only addresses Job directly with one question ('shall the earth be forsaken for you?'—v. 4), which does not open the speech; thus the hurtful and insulting polemic element is weakened. Zophar's second speech likewise does not begin with words addressed to Job; it does not include insults, and his later appeal to Job ('Do you not know this from old...'—20.4) is to the point and not personal, relating to the actual contents of the debate in principle—the punishment of the wicked.

Bildad's brief words in the third cycle, ch. 25, are likewise not

---

7.   קִנְצֵי לְמִלִּין (18.2; translated by RSV as 'hunt for words') is interpreted by Driver and Gray, Kahana, Pope, and others as a muzzle to his words, derived from the Arabic *QN* to hunt, to place a trap. Tur-Sinai (1941) interprets it, 'For how long will you silence such words, as if with a whip or a cattle prod', based on a derivation from the Akkadian *qinnazu*, which according to him means 'cattle prod'. The LXX (παύσῃ) and the Vulgate (*finem*) derive קֵץ from קֵץ ('end')—i.e., the end of words—as does Ibn Janah. Driver (1960: 79) proposes the reading צִינַק לְמִלִּים, based upon the Syriac and Arabic *zanaqa*, meaning 'reins'. As for the phrasing of the appeal in the plural עַד אָנָה תְּשִׂימוּן...תָּבִינוּ ('How long...consider'): the LXX reads both verbs in the singular, as do Dhorm, Driver and Gray, and others. Others say that Bildad here addresses the friends rather than Job. Thus R. Joseph Kara: 'Till when? Put an end to your words! Job speaks and you answer him; hence there is no end to our words. But let him say all he has to say and understand them, and thereafter we shall speak and answer him'. Similarly Dhorm. S.D. Luzzatto took the opposite tack. Bildad chastizes him—'How long will you cause Job to say to you, "Put an end to words!"'. Tur-Sinai (1972) follows an intermediate path, arguing that this is 'the summary of Job's words to his friends, which the speaker merely quotes in order to answer them'. For a discussion of the verse and its versions, see Orlinsky 1958: 232-34.

addressed to Job, and certainly do not include words of insult. Given this, can one say that the line of development is in the opposite direction—namely, that following the first cycle the friends gradually moderate their words? Examination of the speeches in their entirety suggests that this is not the case: they convey a harsh and hostile reaction to Job. We therefore find that the exacerbation in the introductions to the speeches is characteristic of the first cycle alone. Moreover, in the second and third cycles the unified model of the friends' speeches starts to come apart, and the opening words addressing a rhetorical question to Job are more or less preserved in the speeches of Eliphaz alone (chs. 15, 22) to which we shall address ourselves below.

ii. In the remarks of all three friends in the first cycle, the speeches conclude with words of comfort and hope addressed to Job; nevertheless, there are certain differences among them in terms of their character and the resoluteness of their comforting. Eliphaz concludes his first speech with a series of eleven verses (5.17-27) giving an absolute and unequivocal statement that Job's good end is assured, being an inseparable part of an entire divine course, whose first stage is his suffering— 'You shall know that your tent is safe...You shall know also that your descendants shall be many...For, this we have searched out; it is true. Hear, and know it for your good' (5.24-27). By contrast, the words of encouragement at the end of Bildad's speech are not only far shorter (8.19-22)—something possibly appropriate to the brevity of the speech as a whole—but also ambiguous and conditional. This ambiguity is expressed in the fact that Bildad does not content himself with saying, 'He will yet fill your mouth with laughter and your lips with shouting' (v. 21), but adds to this the words, 'Behold, God will not reject a blameless man, nor take the hand of evil-doers' (v. 20), whose encouragement also involves a certain concealed threat. Moreover, the three concluding words of the speech do not deal at all with Job's good end. Even though they are seemingly mingled with words of encouragement—'Those who hate you will be clothed with shame'—they in fact contain a thinly-veiled warning to Job himself—'but the tent of the wicked will be no more'. The tendency to make the happy end conditional and qualified becomes more pronounced in the first speech of Zophar. Here the condition is explicitly presented in conjunction with the promise—'If you set your heart aright...If iniquity is in your hand, put it far away...Surely then you will lift up your face without blemish...' (11.13-15). Moreover, whereas in Bildad's speech only the last three words allude to the opposite side of the coin of divine recompense, here the entire final verse speaks of the end of evil-doers—'But the eyes of the wicked will fail; all way of escape will be lost to them, and their hope is to breathe their last' (11.20). Albeit from a syntactic viewpoint this merely complements the encouraging remarks found in the previous verse, the strategic location of this statement—at the very end of the speech—emphasizes its threatening element. The message of encouragement is thus confounded even more in the words of Zophar, and the feeling is created that his main intention is to frighten, rather than to calm.

In the second cycle of debates, the conclusions of the speeches do not include any words of encouragement to Job, nor indeed any reference at all in principle to the righteous man, but only to the wicked. Thus in the speech of Eliphaz—'They conceive mischief and bring forth evil and their heart prepares deceit' (15.35); in that of Bildad—'Surely such are the dwellings of the ungodly, such is the place of him who knows not God' (18.21); or that of Zophar—'This is the wicked man's portion from God...' (20.29). The nature of these conclusions is consistent with the overall picture of the friends' speeches in the second cycle, which deal primarily with evil-doers and their lot. We therefore find a certain exacerbation in the conclusions of all the speeches of the friends in the second cycle, as against their parallels in the previous cycle of debates. They are nevertheless far less sophisticated, being all of a piece, without any internal gradation such as that which characterizes the first cycle.

The truncation of the third cycle does not allow us properly to examine the conclusions of its speeches, with the exception of that of Eliphaz (ch. 22). His speech contains words of comfort whose conditional nature is strongly emphasized, similar to that found in the words of Bildad and Zophar in the first cycle. It is difficult to discern any clear-cut 'conclusion' in the brief speech of Bildad (ch. 25); in any event, it does not contain words of comfort.

iii. A thorough-going examination of the bodies of the speeches would require precise exegetical study, which is beyond the scope of the present work. Nevertheless, we may trace here one central motif—namely, the concept of recompense and its direct meaning with regard to Job.

In his first speech, Eliphaz presents a sophisticated concept of recompense, based upon a linear, rather than a dichotomic, understanding of the righteous man and the evil one: the righteous is one who sins little and whose transgressions are not serious. However, this does not imply that he does not sin at all, as man by his very nature is 'born to sin' (5.7)[8] and can never be found innocent in his judgment before God. The evil-doer, by contrast, sins a great deal. Hence, both of them are deserving of punishment, but the suffering of the righteous is only temporary, and he will in the end receive a good reward for his righteousness; for that reason, he is fortunate to have been chastened (5.17).[9] It follows from this doctrine of recompense that Job is righteous, as he has not been destroyed, from which it follows that his good future is guaranteed. Eliphaz thus succeeds in reconciling three seemingly contradictory facts: the reality of Job's suffering; the faith in God's justice; the knowledge that Job is righteous.

In his speech in ch. 8, Bildad proposes a simpler understanding of recompense: namely, that there is a direct relation between disaster and sin, and not every person necessarily sins. By stating this, and by presenting Job's righteousness as an alternative to divine righteousness ('Does God pervert justice?'—v. 3), he portrays Job as a sinner, whose good future depends upon his making supplication to God ('If you will seek God and make supplication to the Almighty'—v. 5) and is not automatically guaranteed him by virtue of his righteousness, as he is not truly righteous. Bildad's words indirectly imply that Job's suffering is an appropriate punishment for his sins, and that the magnitude of his disaster

---

8.   לעמל, as interpreted by Ibn Ezra, Kahana, and others. Even if we interpret עמל as pain and suffering (Driver and Gray, Pope, and others), this refers to the suffering which comes about because of human sin; as Rashi puts it, 'It is impossible that he not sin and undergo suffering for his sin and to incur disaster'. See Hoffman 1980: 116.

9.   It is in this light that one should understand 4.17: 'Can mortal man be righteous before God?'. See the interpretations of Kahana, Driver and Gray, Dhorm, and see the discussion Weiss (1984: 108-109). By contrast, Rashi reads, 'And may a man be more pure than his maker?' The argument of Tur-Sinai (1972)—that these are not the words of Eliphaz, but the words of Job which were erroneously placed here, seeing that they express the idea that the wicked and the just enjoy the same recompense—is incorrect. This interpretation forces Tur-Sinai to argue that Eliphaz's words in 15.14-15, which are very similar to his words here, are a quotation of Job's words. A detailed discussion of 4.12-21, summarizing the views of different scholars, is given by Smith (1990). He argues that Eliphaz is not the author of the vision (4.12-21), since it follows from it that Job is not wicked, whereas in ch. 22 Eliphaz claims that Job is definitely wicked. Smith here ignores the possibility that a development takes place in the figure of Eliphaz and that his words become more extreme. See a detailed discussion on this below.

is no more than testimony to the true measure of his 'righteousness'.[10]

The doctrine of retribution articulated by Zophar may be summarized in one verse: 'know then that God exacts of you less than your guilt deserves'—11.6. We may interpret this verse (as do Rashi and others) in the sense of: God is like a creditor towards you (compare the usage of the verb יׁשה in Deut. 15.2: 'what he has lent to his neighbor' אׁשר יׁשה ברעהו), because you have not 'paid' for the debt of your sins with an appropriate punishment, having been punished for only some of them; or we may read it (as do Ibn Ezra and others): God has so to speak agreed to forget (understanding יׁשה as in Deut. 32.18: 'You were unmindful [תׁשי] of the Rock that begot you, and you forgot the God who gave you birth') part of your sins and has punished you for only some of them. In either event, it follows that Job's sins were even more grave than might have been concluded from his punishment. This is, in short, an extremely negative perception of Job's character.

Thus, the increasing severity of the friends' understanding of recompense in the first cycle of debates corresponds to the tendency toward exacerbation which characterizes the openings and conclusions of the speeches.

A different picture emerges from the second cycle, and even more so from the third. The doctrine of recompense articulated by Eliphaz in ch. 15 is similar to that presented in his first speech, but its formulation is sharper and more caustic (compare, 'What is man, that he can be clean? Or he that is born of woman, that he can be righteous?...How much less one who is abominable and corrupt, a man who drinks iniquity like water!' [15.14-16] with 'Can mortal man be righteous before God...how much more those who dwell in houses of clay, whose foundation is in the dust...' [4.17-19]). However, there is not only a sharpening of the formulation here, but also the concealment, to the point of negation, of an important element: the need to promise a good future to the righteous man who is being punished. Since Eliphaz does not speak at all in ch. 15 of the goodness set aside for the righteous man or for Job, but concentrates upon the destiny of the wicked alone, one

10. Irwin wishes to conclude from his analysis of the plant imagery in this chapter (in the course of which he suggests certain textual emendations) that Bildad does not think that 'misfortune is *ipso facto* proof of ungodliness' (1933: 216). In his opinion, Bildad, like Eliphaz, accepts the theory that the righteous may suffer, but that in the final analysis his suffering ceases. I demur from this interpretation, both with regard to Eliphaz and Bildad.

receives the impression that Job's good end is not at all certain. As we shall yet see, the doctrine of retribution is further intensified by Eliphaz in the third cycle, in a manner approaching that of Zophar in his first speech.

On the other hand, in the speeches of Bildad (chs. 18, 25) and Zophar (ch. 20) there is no fully developed doctrine of recompense or retribution, but only descriptions of the suffering of the wicked. Thus, the intensification is reflected in the fact that the righteous are not spoken of at all, but the development is by no means sophisticated. The fine nuances that characterized the presentation of each of the friends' approaches towards retribution are here blurred and disappear.

It follows from our examination that our working hypothesis—namely, that there is a gradual and constant intensification in the words of the friends towards Job—is only partially confirmed. It clearly exists in the first cycle of debates, but is present in all three cycles only in the speeches of Eliphaz but not the speeches of Bildad and Zophar. While these are no less severe than Zophar's words in the first cycle, nor are they more so; there is no internal development; they do not preserve the structure of the speeches in the first cycle (there is not always an introduction with a direct address to Job, nor is there always a doctrine of retribution). Thus, it is not always possible to carry out a clear comparison in every section. They are not addressed directly to Job, but speak largely in general terms, and in this sense are less 'dialogic'; their general remarks concerning the lot of the wicked are at most an alllusion to Job, but they lack the biting directness which is so characteristic of the first cycle.

The main features of these findings are clarified in the summarizing table (Appendix II): systematic exacerbation in the speeches of all three friends only exists in the first cycle of debates, albeit the second cycle as a whole is more outspoken than the preceding one. It is only in the speeches by Eliphaz that the tendency towards exacerbation develops throughout the three cycles.

The obvious question is, How ought one to relate to this picture? Should one conclude that the structure of the book is confused, and that in the original version the intensification was more systematic and could be observed in all the speeches? May one interpret it as a sophisticated means of expressing indirect messages—for example, that Bildad and Zophar were less inclined than Eliphaz to react sharply to the words of Job? I shall return to these questions at the end of the present chapter.

Let us now turn to an examination of the nature of the connection between the speeches.[11] This is established in two ways: one, by the direct form of address of the speaker (Job or one of the friends) to his predecessor (one of the friends or Job). This is a simple, technical means of strengthening the dialogic facade of the speeches, but does not create a continuity of subject matter between them based upon any necessary order. The second means is by a direct response to what has been stated in the previous speech, which argues against the claims put forward there. This method gives the speeches a certain necessary order, and is thus likely to contribute more significantly to the shaping of the book.

Direct, simple phrases of address appear in the following verses: 4.2; 8.2; 11.2-3; 12.2; 13.1-2; 15.2-5; 16.2-4; 18.2;[12] 19.2-5, 21-22; 21.2-5, 27-29, 34; 22.2; 26.2-3; 27.5, 11-12. In examining the substantive connections between the speeches, I shall not take into account the indirect relations connected with the motif of the trial, as these will be discussed and summarized separately further on.

Substantive relation to the previous speech appears in the first speech of Eliphaz, chs. 4–5, in which he criticizes Job for his curses in ch. 3 (4.2-7) and for refraining from calling directly upon God's help (5.1). Job's reaction in chs. 6–7 is divided in two. In the first part, he responds directly to the words of Eliphaz, while the second part, ch. 7, is directed towards God, who is here addressed directly for the first time in the book (7.7-8). From here on, Job's words are sometimes addressed to the friends—in 12.1-9; 13.1-13; 16.1-5; 19.1-6, 21-29; 21.1-4, 27-34; 26.1-4; 27.1-12; sometimes directly to God—7.12-21; 9.26-31; 10.2-22; 13.20–14.22; while at yet other times they are not directed to any obvious listener, but seem to be primarily addressed indirectly towards God—thus 9.10-25, 32-35; 12.10-25; chs. 16–17 (although 17.3-4 may be addressed directly to God); 19.7-20; 21.6-26; chs. 23–24; 27.13-23; chs. 29–31.[13]

11. Some issues concerning this matter will be considered below, in the course of our discussion of the trial motif and the figure of Eliphaz.

12. On the use of the plural in 18.2, see above, n. 7.

13. The distribution of these three different addresses, the manner and circumstances in which the author moves from one to the other, and the ambiguity which he introduces on occasion regarding who it is that is actually being addressed—all these are part of his literary tactics. However, I will not discuss these here as such. Some of what needs to be said concerning this matter will appear further on, during the course of our discussions of the different matters in the book.

In the first part of the speech in chs. 6–7, one may identify the follow-ing reactions to Eliphaz's previous words.[14] (a) The claim 'O that my vexation were weighed', etc. (6.2-3)[15] is directed against that element in Eliphaz's theory of retribution which states that every person is deserving of punishment, since we are sinners by our very nature. As this axiomatic statement does not distinguish between severe punishment and light punishment, its ethical nature, Job hints, is negated from the very outset. (b) The rhetorical question, 'Does the wild ass bray when he has grass', etc. (6.5-6) relates to the principle of causality raised by Eliphaz ('for affliction does not come from the dust'—5.6-7). This implies criticism of Eliphaz's accusation 'But now it has come to you, and you are impatient' (4.5), as if Job's reaction to the disaster in ch. 3 were too severe. (c) Job's wish to die ('O that I might have my request, and that God would grant my desire; that it would please God to crush me, that he would let loose his hand and cut me off!'—6.8-9) is an indirect polemic refutation of one of the elements of Eliphaz's doctrine of retribution, namely, the argument that the righteous man who sins is punished lightly, while the punishment of the wicked is severe, that is, destruction. See, says Job, my so-called light punishment is more severe than the punishment of the wicked; the proof being that I wish to die. (d) 'What is my strength, that I should wait? And what is my end, that I should be patient?', etc. (6.11-12) is an ironic response to Eliphaz's so-called comfort, and to his advice to Job that one bear patiently 'for he wounds, but he but binds up; he smites, but his hands heal' (5.18). (e) The cry, 'Teach me, and I will be silent; make me understand how I have erred' (6.24), is a response to the accusation that Job has sinned.

---

14. On the relation of Eliphaz's speech to Job's words in ch. 3, see below.

15. See also the literal context of Eliphaz's words, 'Surely vexation (כעש) kills the fool' (5.2). The image of the scales in this chapter is clear and suits Job's main argument—the disproportionate nature of his punishment. However, the details of the image are not unambiguous. One may interpret it as, 'If one puts on one side of the scales my sin (כעש being read as a synonym for חטאי; see 5.2) and on the other, my being (Rashi—my disaster; see, for example, Ps 91.3, 'from the snare of the fowler, and from the disastrous pestilence' [מדבר הוות]) the side of the breaking, the disaster, will weigh more than all the sand in the seas'. Thus, for example, Dhorm. It may also be read as, if on one side you place my anger, and on the other my disaster, then the latter will be heavier than all the sands of the sea (thus Driver and Gray, and others). Again, one may interpret: 'If they place on one side my disaster (הוותי, כעש) and on the other side the sand of the seas—the former will be heavier' (thus Rashi, Kahana [1924] and others).

This claim is based upon the assumption that every person sins, which Job sees as hypocrisy, because it does not explicitly cite even a single sin that he has committed.

Bildad's speech in ch. 8 does not give any direct response to the words of Job. The sharply polemic note of his opening words may indeed be interpreted as a reaction to the fact that Job rejected Eliphaz's gentle reproof; but this connection is so indirect and doubtful that there are those who conclude from Bildad's opening words that the speech is not in its proper place.[16]

The connection between Job's words in chs. 9–10 and Bildad's preceding speech is somewhat stronger, but weak in comparison to that between the words of Job and those of Eliphaz. (a) The opening sentence, 'Truly I know that it is so; but how can a man be just before God?', etc. (9.2-3) may be seen in relation to the words of Bildad, 'or does the Almighty pervert the right?' (8.3), but also as a 'delayed' reaction to the words of Eliphaz, 'Can mortal man be righteous before God?' (4.17). (b) There is both a linguistic and substantive relation between Job's cry, 'I am blameless' (9.21) and the declaration by Bildad, 'Behold, God will not reject a blameless man' (8.20)—with a double meaning: if you are blameless, he will not reject you; but if, as you say, he has rejected you, then you are not blameless.

Even weaker are the connections between Zophar's speech (ch. 11) and the preceding one of Job. Zophar's accusation, 'and when you mock, shall no one shame you?' (11.3) has no basis in Job's speech in chs. 9–10. In these chapters, Job does not address the friends at all, and hence cannot have mocked them. One may, by stretching the point, see here Zophar's response to Job's accusations against the friends in ch. 6, which were not answered in the words of Bildad. As for a substantive connection between Job's speech in chs. 12–14 and the speech of Zophar, the motif of wisdom, which appears both in the words of Job (12.2, 12-13) and in those of Zophar (11.6-8, 11-12), may be seen as a link of an indirect connection.

---

16. The argument is that Bildad's words, 'Does God pervert justice' (8.3), imply that in the previous speech Job had accused God of perverting justice, an accusation not in fact found in chs. 6–7. Thus, Tur-Sinai (1941) relates these words to 19.6-7: 'Know then that God has put me in the wrong', or the like. But in fact what we have here is only a mimesis of debate: the sharper it becomes, the more each side cites the words of the other in distorted fashion, because it is easier to argue with absurd propositions.

In the second cycle of debates, the connections among the speeches are weaker and very general, and it seems doubtful whether one can identify any clear-cut relation between any given speech and the preceding one. For example, when Eliphaz changes his attitude towards Job in ch. 15, Job does not react to this. Job's comment, 'miserable comforters are you all' (16.2) has no connection to the speech by Eliphaz in ch. 15, containing as it does no words of comfort whatsoever. Job's accusations, 'These ten times you cast reproach upon me; are you not ashamed to wrong me?' (19.3) do not bear any clear connection to Bildad's previous speech, as the latter does not contain any accusations or insults towards Job. However, the severe condemnation therein against evil-doers is certainly not intended as a compliment to Job. The same is true of the connection between the speech of Zophar (ch. 20) and that of Job (ch. 21): while it is true that Job also speaks here a good deal about the wicked, and one can see the influence of Zophar's speech, the connection is an extremely general one. Even the technical means used to connect this speech to its predecessor, by phrases of address used in the openings of the speeches, only appears in some of them, as I have shown above.

Due to the truncated nature of the third cycle, it is impossible to speak of the connections between its speeches at all. Apart from chs. 22 and 26, there are not even phrases of address at the beginnings of the speeches.

In sum, it is clear that the links between the speeches become progressively weaker: in the first cycle, they are quite explicit in the speech of Eliphaz, somewhat less in the speech of Bildad, and even less so in the speech of Zophar. In the subsequent cycles, there is no definite connection at all between the speeches.

Appendix III clearly shows that the connection between the speeches becomes weaker from cycle to cycle. This follows, not only from the last column, but also, and primarily, from the second column, which demonstrates that there are only superficial formal connections between the speeches of the second cycle. In the first cycle, on the other hand, most of the interconnections are substantive. The impression created is that the author took the easiest path (formal connections) in order to sustain the appearance of at least some sort of connection between the speeches. Moreover, most of the connections appear in the speeches of Job and Eliphaz. This is consistent with the previous conclusions concerning the tendency towards exacerbation.

Unlike the speeches of the other friends, which are spread throughout the length of the book, Elihu's words appear in concentrated form. In the light of this fact, one needs to examine the assumptions concerning the continuity of the dialogue there in a different way than one does with regard to the other speeches. 'Continuity' here refers to the totality of everything that preceded the speech of Elihu and, according to his declaration (32.10-22), even that which should have been said but was not. The passage used to explain Elihu's entering into the circle of debates—'He was angry at Job becuse he justified himself rather than God...And when Elihu saw that there was no answer in the mouth of these three men...' (32.2-5)—specifically alludes to this continuity.

The connections between the speech of Elihu and the words pre-viously spoken are very close. Elihu addresses his words explicitly to Job's complaints, and at times even opens with a formula of quotation, such as 'Surely you have spoken...' (33.8, introducing his 'quotation' of the words of Job in vv. 9-11); 'For Job has said...' (34.5, preceding the quotation, '"I am innocent, and God has taken away my right"'); 'Do you say, "It is my right before God"' (35.2); 'that you ask, "What advantage have I?"' (35.3). Extensive use is also made therein of expressions taken from the speeches of the friends, even though he does not mention them by name.

The following are the most striking examples of things said by Elihu which relate to Job's earlier words: 32.6-9: 'you are aged...It is not the many that are wise, nor the aged that understand what is right', cf. 12.12: 'Wisdom is with the aged, and understanding in length of days'; 33.7: 'Behold, no fear of me need terrify you', cf. 9.34: 'and let not dread of him terrify me'; 33.10: 'he counts me as his enemy', cf. 13.24: 'and count me as thy enemy?'; 33.13: 'Why do you contend against him, saying, "he will answer none of his words"', cf. 9.3: 'If one wished to contend with him, one could not answer him...'; 33.11: 'He puts my feet in the stocks, and watches all my paths', cf. 13.27: 'Thou puttest my feet in the stocks, and watchest all my paths'; 33.12: 'Behold in this you are not right, I will answer you...', cf. 9.15: 'Though I am innocent, I cannot answer him...'; 33.23: 'an angel, a mediator, one of the thousand', cf. 9.3: 'one could not answer him once in a thousand [times]'; 33.31: 'Give heed, O Job, listen to me: be silent, and I will speak', cf. 13.5: 'Oh that you would keep silent, and it would be your wisdom!'; 34.3: 'for the ear tests words, as the palate tastes food', cf. 12.11: 'Does not the ear try words as the palate tastes food?'; 34.5: 'For Job has said, "I am innocent, and God has taken away my right"', cf. 27.2: 'As God lives, who has taken away my right'; 35.6: 'If you have sinned, what have you accomplished against him?', cf. 7.20: 'If I sin, what do I do to thee'; 36.6: 'He does not keep the wicked alive', cf. 21.7: 'Why do the wicked live, reach old age...'; 36.11: 'they complete their days in prosperity...', cf. 21.13: 'They spend their days in prosperity'.

The following phrases relate to the words of Eliphaz: 33.15-16: 'In a dream, in a vision of the night, when deep sleep falls upon men...then he opens the ears of men', cf. 4.12-13: 'my ear received...And thought from visions of the night, when deep sleep falls on man'; 33.19: 'and with continual strife in his bones', cf. 4.14: 'which made all my bones shake'; 34.7: 'What man is like Job, who drinks up scoffing like water', cf. 15.16: 'how much less one who is abominable and corrupt, a man who drinks iniquity like water!'; 34.9: 'For he has said, "It profiteth a man nothing..." ', cf. 22.2: 'Can a man be profitable to God?'; 35.2: 'Do you say, "I am right [RSV: it is my right] before God?"', cf. 4.17: '"Can mortal man be righteous before God?"' (cf. Job's words in 9.2).

Bildad's words are alluded to in the following: 36.26: 'Then man prays to God, and he accepts him, he comes into his presence with joy', cf. 8.21: 'He will yet fill your mouth with laughter, and your lips with shouting'; 34.12: 'Of a truth, God will not do wickedly, and the Almighty will not pervert justice', cf. 8.3: 'Does God pervert justice? Or does the Almighty pervert the right?'; 35.16: 'Job opens his mouth in empty talk, he multiplies words without knowledge', cf. 8.2: 'How long will you say these things, and the words of your mouth be a great wind?'

Phrases relating to the words of Zophar include 35.5: 'Look at the heavens, and see; and behold the clouds, which are higher than you', cf. 11.8: 'It is higher than heaven—what can you do? Deeper than Sheol—what can you know?'

These allusions to the preceding part of the book (21 in all, an average of 3.5 per chapter) reflect one of the decisive differences between Elihu's speech and the rest of the book (Dhorm 1926: ci). In the latter, we have found (see Appendix III) no more than 22 substantive references to that which was said previously (an average of 0.78 per chapter), and even those do not, generally speaking, explicitly quote the things to which the response relates. This relative abundance of allusions creates an explicit connection between the words of Elihu and the previous speeches, and even contributes to their presentation as one unit. One might say that Elihu strengthens the anti-catalogic tendency in the book by adding links which tighten the isolated speeches into one unified work.

Is there a tendency towards exacerbation in the speech of Elihu? This question has two aspects: is there a gradual escalation within it, and is the speech as a whole sharper and more caustic than those of the friends? It seems to me that both of these questions need to be answered in the negative. His polemic does not contain insult or cynical mockery, such as is found in some of the words of the friends addressed towards Job. True, in one verse he does accuse Job of keeping company with evil-doers ('What man is like Job, who drinks up scoffing like water, who goes in company with evil-doers and walks with wicked men?'— 34.7-8), but as these remarks are not addressed directly to Job, this somewhat softens matters. In terms of their content, they are less severe than the words of Eliphaz in his last speech, ch. 22. The outlook on retribution expressed in the speech of Elihu is essentially the same as that of the friends: namely, that Job's punishment is a sign of sin. Like them, he states that there is hope for one who sins, who was punished, and who seeks God's forgiveness ('Then man prays to God, and he accepts him, he comes into his presence with joy...He has redeemed his soul from going down into the Pit, and his life shall see the light'— 33.26-28). There is no clear internal tendency towards either exacerbation or moderation. Even at the end of his speech, ch. 37, in which he speaks of the greatness of God, there is no unequivocal message concerning the destiny of Job, but only a statement of Job's desire to understand the ways of God.

For a further examination of Elihu's speech and the conclusions to be derived from the data presented here regarding its authenticity, see below, Chapter 8.

2. *The Moulding of the Characters*

Three figures are posed over against Job. This multi-sided structure clearly serves as a counter-balance against the catalogic elements in the book, which would have been more striking had everything been placed in the mouth of one (as in 'I Will Praise the Lord of Wisdom') or two speakers (as in 'The Babylonian Theodicy'). This structure also makes things easier for the author in other respects. (a) It facilitates the repetition of those things which had already been stated earlier in other words, without damaging the mimesis (since it is reasonable that, during the course of debate, the protagonists would return to those ideas which had been expressed differently by their antagonists), but also without the clumsy exaggerated style in which the speaker repeats the same thing too many times, such as we find in 'The Babylonian Theodicy'. (b) It brings out the deviations between Job's view and that of the majority, which expresses the accepted, normative opinions. (c) It facilitates the presentation of a variety of views concerning the problem of the wicked and the righteous without 'forcing' one figure to alter his opinion from one speech to another.

This structure also arouses the expectation that we will discover at least something of the personality of each one of the speakers. These expectations were already aroused in the prologue, which shed light upon the figure of Job from a number of perspectives apart from that of his righteousness—his wealth, his family situation, his way of life, his fears (1.5). As we progress in the book, the anticipation of getting to know the friends better is strengthened, alongside our becoming better acquainted with Job through new data which is brought to our attention, and through the strengthening of certain details which are only alluded to in the prologue. For example, Job himself confirms that he had always feared that his happiness would only be temporary ('For the thing that I fear comes upon me, and what I dread befalls me'—3.25); in 19.13-21, light is shed on the everyday life of Job before and after his tragedy, in anticipation of more extensive treatment of the subject in chs. 29–31; Job's relation to others is illuminated from a different perspective in the opening words of Eliphaz ('and you have strengthened the weak hands. Your words have upheld him who was stumbling...'— 4.3-4); above all else, we come to know the stubborn honesty of Job, who is unwilling to buttress his faith by denying his own truth, notwithstanding the assurances of his friends that he can thereby attain contentment. The narrator gives explicit expression to the inner truth that guides Job by presenting him as the only one who dares turn directly to God, while the friends address Job alone, speaking about God but not to him. Another character trait that typifies Job is his great sensitivity, despite the harsh words which he directs towards God. This is expressed in the lament which he utters following his harsh criticism against God (see chs. 10, 14), indicating that his crisis was emotional and not only intellectual. Job's sensitivity is likewise expressed in the appeals to the friends. His reaction to Eliphaz's remarks reflects the astonishment of a person for whom friendship is a concept of profound emotional depth. Even after uttering the harshest things to his friends, Job tries to hold fast to their friendship, appealing to them—'Have pity on me, have pity on me, O you my friends, for the hand of God has touched me! Why do you, like God, pursue me?' (19.21-22). These words represent Job's emotional crisis in its full severity, adding to his image as an honest, sensitive person who, despite the deep crisis in which he finds himself, refuses to surrender and holds fast to his own truth. The image of Job is thus shaped from several different components. Even though it is doubtful whether one could say that he is known to us from all sides,[17] there is no doubt that we do have here a living figure. One can garnish information that helps in forming his image from nearly every chapter of Job's speeches. The exceptions to this rule are chs. 24, 26, and 28, which are totally free of any emotional reference pertaining to Job's debates with God or with the friends.

As it becomes clearer that the friends are the antithesis of Job, and as we come better to understand his character, we also expect to become better acquainted with his friends. To what extent are these anticipations realized?

There is one personal detail, cited in several places in the book, that pertains to all three of the friends: they are presented as elders, as older than Job. Job alludes to this when he asks ironically, 'Is wisdom with the aged, and understanding in length of days?' (12.12).[18] Eliphaz repeats that, 'Both the grey-haired and the aged are among us, older than your father' (15.10), while only Elihu may possibly be younger than him, as he comments, 'I am young in years, and you are aged...' (32.6).[19] Since Eliphaz was the first one to speak, we may take this as a hint that he is the oldest one among the group .

---

17. See Forster (1927: 103ff.), who developed this idea. I do not intend to deal here in depth with the theoretical issue involved here. For criticism of Forster's classification and suggestions for alternative terminology, see Even (1980: 33-44), who suggests three 'scales' for ranking the types of images in the short story: the scale of development, the scale of complexity, and the mimetic and symbolic scale.

18. R. Joseph Kara, Pope, Dhorm, and others interpreted this verse thus, as a question. As against them, others interpreted it as a statement: indeed, the elderly have wisdom, but 'with him are wisdom and might'—which is the decisive difference between God and the sage. Thus Kahana, Driver and Gray, and others.

19. Regarding this matter it makes no difference whether this speech is part of the original book or not. If the speech is not original, one may conclude that the author of the speech of Elihu understood that the book presented the friends as elders, and continued along that line. For a summary regarding the issue of the authenticity of Elihu's speech, see below, pp. 289-93.

Beyond allusions to their age, it is doubtful whether one can learn anything about the personalities of Bildad and Zophar from what is written here, apart from the stereotype of routine believers who accept religious conventions concerning the unquestioned absolute righteousness of God. The very general nature of the speeches of Bildad and Zophar, which does not allow the shaping of their images at all, clearly follows from the previously cited data (see the summarizing data in Appendixes II, III). They are thus presented as secondary figures who, as well as serving 'to make the hero speak, contribute to clarifying the situation by serving for it as background'.[20]

Such is not the case with Eliphaz. In him we find a well-defined, major character, who from both the artistic and the ideological aspect fulfils the role of constituting a clear antithesis to Job. Eliphaz's first speech occupies a place of strategic centrality in the book, because it introduces us for the first time to the friends of Job mentioned at the end of ch. 2. This role is strengthened by the anticipations aroused on reading the friends' impassioned reaction to Job's disaster ('and they raised their voices and wept...'—2.12-13) accompanied by a discreet and justified silence in the light of the circumstances ('and none spoke a word to him, for they saw that his suffering was very great'—2.13). The expectations connected with the words of the first friend are heightened in the light of Job cursing his day in ch. 3 (see on this above, Chapter 4): he who had previously been silent, through deep understanding of the poverty of words under such circumstances—what can he say now?

Indeed, from Eliphaz's hesitant beginning, one gains the impression of a sensitive and honest person, who feels his way cautiously before attempting to find his way to Job's troubled heart. Hence, there is also a tendency to judge favourably the ambiguous tenor of his words.[21] But this ambiguity hones our senses to grasp hints and hidden messages in every word of Eliphaz. Under these circumstance the question inevitably arises: For what reason does the author, who fashioned the image of Eliphaz as one who came to commiserate with Job and to comfort him, place in his mouth a theory of retribution, rather than presenting him as one who responded to the emotional need of the suffering Job by encouraging and strengthening him? Eliphaz's words are not elicited by

---

20. Simon 1969: 31-36. For more on the moulding of the secondary characters and their function in the biblical narrative, see Bar-Efrat 1979: 107-12.

21. See above, p. 118 n. 3 there. The following remarks are based on my paper concerning the image of the believer in the book of Job (Hoffman 1979b).

Job's dirge in ch. 3, in which the theoretical aspects of retribution are not mentioned at all. At most, one finds there astonishment as to 'Why is light given to him that is in misery...' (3.20), without any distinction being drawn between the righteous and the wicked. The fact that the author chose Eliphaz, rather than Job, to introduce the theoretical aspect of the problem of retribution, which is the central theme of the book, cannot be a matter of chance, and requires explanation.

And indeed, if the theory of retribution cannot be seen as a suitable response to the words of Job, one can only see it as Eliphaz's means of confronting his own problem in the light of what happened to Job. Eliphaz's attempt to find a doctrine of retribution that will be consistent both with the righteousness of the sufferer and with the righteousness of God (see above, pp. 121-22) is intended to strengthen Eliphaz's 'faith' in the bonds of a well-formulated theory; his 'faith' in quotation marks, because perfect faith and logical demonstration are mutually contradictory. That which is proven stands firm even without faith, while faith becomes emptied of its content if one adds to it the adjective, 'proven'. It follows from this that the book presents Eliphaz as one who finds his own faith, with which he had until now felt comfortable, put to the test by the catastrophe which befell Job, and he is now forced to buttress it up with a coherent doctrine of retribution.

Notwithstanding the ambiguity that characterizes the first part of his speech, it seems doubtful whether one would arrive at this evaluation of the figure of Eliphaz after an initial reading of his doctrine of retribution. Even his harsh outburst upon presenting his doctrine of retribution— 'Call now; is there any one who will answer you?...Surely vexation kills the fool, and jealousy slays the simple' (5.1-2)—surprising as it may be, may not be clearly understood upon first reading, because Eliphaz's deepest and truest (albeit perhaps hidden) motive is not his desire to encourage Job, but his need to strengthen himself. In any event, various doubts and hesitancies are presented, and with them the reader arrives at the second speech of Eliphaz in ch. 15.

We have already seen that the beginning of this speech is sharper than its counterpart in the first speech. Instead of the sympathetic stammering, 'If one ventures a word with you, will you be offended?', etc. (4.2), there are ironic words of criticism, accompanied by insults and accusations. Thus, in 15.2-6: 'Should a wise man answer with windy knowledge, and fill himself with the east wind?...For your iniquity teaches your mouth, and you choose the tongue of the crafty', etc. The change in Eliphaz's tone is no less recognizable in the coarse formulation of the doctrine of retribution which he presents, and in the absence of any assurance of a good end for Job. Hence the harsh tone of the second speech encourages the reader to return to the first speech, to see if he or she can find there the seeds which grew in this way. What had previously been a vague, amorphous suspicion now takes shape in the recognition that the ambiguity of Eliphaz's words was not mere chance; inevitably, the question emerges as to what led him to change his attitude towards Job in such a crude and harsh manner. Our attention is thus shifted in part from the content of the words to the personality of the speaker: Who is he? What were his motivations? How is it that he came to console, and even found a sophisticated formula upon which to base his consolation, and in the end said such sharp things, containing neither comfort nor calming?

At this stage, there is not yet any unequivocal answer to these questions, and one may suggest two contradictory conjectures regarding this matter. (a) Eliphaz is presented as a loyal and devoted friend who believes in divine justice. Even at the beginning he thought that Job's sufferings were a punishment for serious sins, and not for trivial matters. However, due to his own sensitivity, and hoping thereby to lighten Job's sufferings, to encourage him, and to awaken his desire to continue living, he refrained from any explicit statement of his own truth, mitigating it to the point where Job was represented as a righteous man, whose just reward was assured. However, once Job refused to accept his comforting and even accused him of hypocrisy and disloyalty (6.14-27), he was no longer able to conceal his true view of his suffering friend. (b) As I explained above, Eliphaz's motivations were egocentric. His anger and wrath stemmed from the rejection of his doctrine by Job, thereby upsetting his faith by denying him its rational facade. In response, he alters his own doctrine of retribution somewhat so that, rather than emphasizing that every person is subject to punishment by virtue of being sinful, he speaks of 'one who is abominable and corrupt, a man who drinks iniquity like water' (15.16), alluding to the idea that only one whose sins are particularly grave may anticipate severe punishment. By the very existence of these two alternative explanations for the image of Eliphaz, the reader is increasingly directed towards a personal context. They have another important function: to return the reader from Eliphaz's second speech to his first one, making it clear that, in order to decide between the two possibilities, one also needs to read the third speech. In other words, Eliphaz's speeches serve as a central axis for all the speeches, while simultaneously focusing the reader's attention upon the personality of the speaker.

Eliphaz's third speech, in ch. 22, differs substantially from all of the other words of the friends, as well as from his own two previous speeches. Rather than the general remarks concerning the recompense due to the righteous or the wicked, Job is addressed directly with unequivocal accusations concerning, not his reaction to the disaster, but his previous behaviour: 'Is not your wickedness great? There is no end to your iniquities. For you have exacted pledges of your brother for nothing, and stripped the naked of their clothing. You have given no water to the weary to drink, and you have withheld bread from the hungry' (22.5-7). At this point, we are left with no alternative but to interpret the general remarks uttered by Eliphaz earlier on the subject of evil-doers (5.1-5; 15.20-35) as in fact alluding to Job himself. For who is an evil-doer, if not one who performs such wicked deeds as these? Moreover, even the words of comfort at the end of the speech, whose conditional nature is strongly emphasized ('If you return to the Almighty and humble yourself...then you will delight yourself in the Almighty...'—22.23-26; compare the words of Zophar: 'If iniquity is in your hand, put it far away...Surely then you will lift up your face without blemish...'—11.14-15), appearing as they do after the accusations, indirectly suggest that Eliphaz's approach here is similar to that expressed by Zophar in his first speech: namely, that Job is being punished for only some of his sins, and hence total punishment may only be avoided by complete and perfect repentance.[22]

But even this does not yet adequately explain the figure of Eliphaz, and we cannot yet decide between the two possibilities suggested above: is Eliphaz being presented as one who has decided to thrust aside every inhibition of refinement and to say what he knew from the beginning, namely, that Job was wicked; or is his lack of honesty no more than a general formulation for a disproven theory, which reaches here the height of making false accusations? In the light of these explicit accusations, a third possibility also emerges: through the exacerbation of the debate, as it becomes clear even to Eliphaz that Job's punishment is indeed extremely harsh, there begins to emerge within him the realization that, if so, certainly 'there is no end to his wickedness'. He thus

22. This is the reason for the degree of severity given to these words of Eliphaz as seen in Appendix VII.

cites here, by way of illustration and conjecture, a series of severe sins, which presumably brought Job's disaster upon him.

An unambiguous determination among these three possibilities can only be made on the basis of analysis of the accusations directed against Job by Eliphaz: clear and publicly known sins of oppression, exploitation, and terrorizing others.

What I shall say below is based upon the assumption, noted previously, that the prose frame-story was an inseparable part of the original work. Hence, Job's righteousness prior to his catastrophe has an axiomatic status throughout the course of the book. This being so, the reader must reject out of hand the possibility that Job behaved as Eliphaz claimed. There can be no doubt that the accusations brought against Job by the latter are false. Is Eliphaz being presented then as one who deliberately lied? It seems to me that one cannot escape a positive answer to this question. Had he accused Job of hidden sins, such as theft, of whose existence no one could know for sure, there would be room for giving Eliphaz the benefit of the doubt. One might say that, due to his certainty of God's righteousness, he concluded (admittedly erroneously, but with the innocence of a believer) that Job had committed grave sins, but that these were hidden to all, and therefore Eliphaz too had previously erred in considering him a righteous man. However, such a theory is inconsistent with the public sins which Eliphaz attributes to Job, as Job was a righteous man, and widely known as such. Hence, he had no grounds for suspecting him guilty of any known sins. Eliphaz is thus presented as one who brazenly lies in his accusations against Job: as if to say, indeed, it is clear to both of us that I am deliberately lying, but what answer can you give me? There is a kind of final closing of the door against any further dialogue. And indeed, after this Job no longer relates at all to the words of the friends, albeit Eliphaz's slander does not remain unanswered, if indirectly.[23]

Thus, in the light of Eliphaz's last speech and the retrospective re-evaluation of his earlier words which it prompted, the riddle of Eliphaz's character is resolved in an unequivocal way. It becomes clear that he was portrayed as the archetype of a dogmatic, doctrinal believer, who is unable to sustain his faith without rationalistic support. During the

---

23. See below, in our discussion of the trial motif, where it will also become apparent that the author was aware of the distinction between revealed sins and concealed ones. One must therefore take exception to the formula of Dhorm (1926: xlv), that in ch. 22 Eliphaz presented 'a list of crimes which Job might have committed'.

course of his speeches, his own inner self is revealed. It gradually becomes clear that the mask of the loyal friend is too thin to conceal his true image. Once he began to engage in sophisticated formulations of discredited theories, he was in the final analysis forced to distort and falsify reality, to lie to himself and to others—all so that his 'faith' need not stand the test of truth—as such a test would reveal that it stood in contradiction to known, visible facts. His is the exact antithesis of the figure of Job, who is unwilling to blur facts, and certainly not to distort them, and who maintains his faith in God despite the uncertainties and questions for which he cannot find any answers. God's words to Eliphaz at the end of the book ('for you have not spoken of me what is right, as my servant Job has'—42.7) leave no room for doubt as to the author's stance regarding the question of the nature of the true believer: one who, like Job, is unwilling to ignore the dilemmas raised by his or her faith, does not reconcile her or himself with their existence, yet nevertheless continues in faith, albeit with certain doubts, pain and suffering.

The graduated and sophisticated fashioning of the figure of Eliphaz, not merely as background to the figure of Job but as his antithesis, is an exception to the usually accepted norm in the biblical story—namely, to present one principal hero, and against him pale secondary figures (see Simon 1969). While Job is clearly the dominant figure in the book, this does not justify the definition of Eliphaz as a merely secondary figure. It is more correct to see him as one of two poles, the other of which, Job, is more important than him. The aesthetic motivations noted above led to the decision to set around these two central axes two secondary figures—Zophar and Bildad.[24] The author was thereby confronted with a poetic difficulty. The structure of the book required him to place in their mouths a considerable quantity of rhetoric, which would ordinarily contradict the concept of a 'secondary figure'. Nevertheless, their fashioning as independent personalities was problematic: the crystallization of a narrative work around four central figures was beyond the realm of the literary conventions known to the author. Their fashioning as compromise figures between Job and Eliphaz would obscure the message rather than bringing it out, as the main purpose of the book is not to present different types of believers, but to sharpen a certain theo-

---

24. An allusion to this status of the figures of Bildad and Zophar in relation to Eliphaz may be found in the words placed in the mouth of God by the author: 'The Lord said to Eliphaz the Temanite: "my wrath is kindled against you and your two friends"' (42.7).

retical problem. Indeed, even the figures of Job and Eliphaz were only intended to further this tendency within the framework of a coherent work. The solution found (of necessity problematic) was to place in the mouths of the secondary characters certain words which repeat themselves, which are inadequate to fashion a character. Such a method also suits a catalogue whose subject is 'different aspects of the problem of retribution'.

This solution has no bearing upon the truncated nature of the speeches of Bildad and Zophar in the third cycle. The breaking of the structure established in the first two cycles is in contradiction to the tendency to shape the two as background figures, achieving as it does the opposite result: the explicit nature of the exceptions arouses maximum attention, which is in absolute contradiction to the very nature of a secondary background figure.

Is Elihu fashioned as a definite character, like Eliphaz and Job, or as a background figure, like Bildad and Zophar? Had his words been spread throughout the entire length of the book, his character could have been built up in a gradual way, but as his words are all concentrated in one place, he cannot be said to be an 'axial character' like Eliphaz. Nevertheless, the unusual location of his speech from the structural viewpoint—following the conclusion of the words of Job and his friends and before the speech of God—gives it a certain strategic status, focusing attention upon it and arousing curiosity concerning this figure. Whoever chose to offer the opinions in chs. 32–37 in the name of Elihu, rather than in that of one of the friends, and whoever chose to concentrate them in one sequence, clearly did so with the intention of presenting a new figure, and it is therefore likely that he would attempt to give him characteristic features of his own. And indeed, this intention is realized in the speech of Elihu. We find there the figure of a young man who knows that his age places him at a disadvantage against those older than himself ('I am young in years, and you are aged; therefore I was timid and afraid to declare my opinion to you'—32.6), but who feels that he has something to contribute to the debate so as to set Job right of his error, and that hence he is obliged to speak out. Unlike the other friends, he speaks at length about himself (32.10-11, 16-22; 33.2-7; 31–33, 35.4; 36.3-4) while his protestations of modesty (such as, 'Behold, I am toward God as you are; I too was formed from a piece of clay'—33.6) only serve to emphasize the arrogance that emerges from his other words. Of all the friends, he alone refers to Job by name several times

(33.1, 32; cf. 32.13; 34.5, 35, 37), thereby creating the impression that he is very enthusiastic to engage in debate, even if the actual content of his remarks is not particularly sharp. As Job's speeches are already concluded, these complaints are left unanswered, thereby strengthening their polemical character. Once it becomes clear that, notwithstanding his arrogant declarations (such as 'My words declare the uprightness of my heart, and what my lips know they speak sincerely'—33.3), Elihu has no new ideas to articulate;[25] he appears as a contentious loudmouth, who attempts to conceal the lack of originality of his ideas with high words and rhetoric that have no substance.[26]

Were Elihu's words merely intended to present yet another figure of an enthusiastic 'believer' in a ridiculous light? I am doubtful. While it is true that there are grotesque features of his speech, these are not sufficiently severe to justify this assumption. It would appear that the author intended to extend the catalogue concerning the subject of divine retribution (i.e., the book of Job), not necessarily because he had far-reaching innovations in this matter, but because he thought it suitable to present new formulae for stances which had been previously raised. Indeed, even the earlier speeches are not free of repetition of ideas. He preferred to do this by creating a new character, in order to achieve yet another end: a better meshing of the speeches into one integral whole, and the correction of one of the 'faults' of the book by the fashioning a figure who would answer Job's arguments one by one, thereby creating yet another connecting link among the disparate speeches. By doing this, the author revealed an awareness (or perhaps only an intuitive sense) of

25. Thus do Dhorm (1926: xcviii-cii) and Kahana (1924: 14—'Elihu does not do anything but give a kind of presentation of everything that has already been said by the previous speakers') evaluate the words of Elihu. On the other hand, Maimonides states that, while it is true that, at first sight, 'If someone considers his discourse, he wonders and thinks that he does not in any respect make an addition to what was said by Eliphaz, Bildad, and Zophar, but merely repeats in different terms and with amplifications…However, when you consider the matter, the additional matter that he introduced will become clear to you…' (*Guide for the Perplexed*, III.23; Pines 1963: 494-95). For more on Maimonides' interpretation of Elihu's words, see below.

26. Dhorm 1926: civ. It is not for naught that the exegetes likewise disagree concerning Elihu's basic position. There are those who argue that he sees in Job a righteous man (Kahana) while others think that he sees in him an evil-doer; thus, for example, Driver and Gray 1921: 278; Westermann 1956: 107-15. Kraeling (1938: 127) thinks that Elihu's contentious image emerges primarily in the additions to the original speech. For more on this, see below, Chapter 8.

one of the fundamental problems in the structure of the book of Job.

However, the creation of this figure is inconsistent with the overall tendency of the book: contradicting as it does the sharply drawn dichotomy between Job and Eliphaz, it can only come to blur the message that follows from this polarization. Thus, the development of the character of Elihu over and above that of the background figures reveals a misguided intuition as to what the book truly demands; it reflects inadequate sensitivity to the need for hazy background figures so as to emphasize the Job–Eliphaz axis, or lack of consideration of this need. Westermann (1956: 107-15) was likewise correct in observing that Elihu's orderly treatment of Job's arguments, making use of his own words, is too 'literary', and inconsistent with the previous nature of the debate. These conclusions need to be taken into consideration when one sets out to examine the question of the composition of the speeches of Elihu. On these points, see below, pp. 289-93.

3. *The Trial Motif*

We have thus far observed two content elements which contribute to the shaping of the book, the threads, so to speak, upon which the beads are strung: the tendency towards exacerbation in the first cycle of the debate, and the gradual formation of the figure of Eliphaz through the three cycles of debates. The following chapters thus combine into a series with a coherent logic: 4–15, 22. The logical continuity is somewhat harmed in the second cycle of debates, and completely disintegrates in the third cycle, in which the order of speeches is no more logical than any other possible order, exactly like the elements in a catalogue. Our examination of the trial motif will reveal it to be a further unifying factor in the book, another thread of the same necklace. Among other issues, I will examine the theory that all those chapters that did not find their place on one of the other threads mentioned were related to the whole by means of the trial motif. In other words, I will test whether this motif organizes all of the chapters of the book into one sequence with development and significance. Our examination will thus illuminate another aspect of the generic nature of the book of Job, which makes unique and novel use of characteristic elements from various different genres of biblical and ancient Near Eastern literature. In this case, our attention will be directed towards the individual supplication psalms.

During the course of his attempt at generic classification of the book of Job, Westermann examined its relation to the psalm literature, concluding that it is far closer to the lamentation literature than it is to Wisdom literature.[27] Bentzen went so far as to classify the entire book as a dramatization of a lament, seeking a cultic context which would suit this classification.[28] And indeed, one cannot help but notice the large number of lamentation elements in the book, as well as the function which they fulfil in its general structure: melancholy adagio movements appearing between the outbursts of pain, thereby creating the rhythm of all of Job's words, which contain heights and depths, rebellion and submission. However, this in no way confirms Baumgartel's view[29] that most of the lamentation passages in the book are late additions.

The trial constitutes one of the major motifs in the biblical supplication psalms. This motif plays an important structural role therein, providing the literary and logical justification required by the literary convention of the supplication model for a transition from the description of the poet's distress to an expression of confidence in God's help.[30] Surely, once his innocence, or at least his relative righteousness in comparison with his enemies, comes to light through the trial, God will save him.[31]

However, in the book of Job the trial is not specifically related to supplication. Thus, of the 27 occurrences of the root שׁפט ('to judge') found in the book of Job (see Appendix IV), only 11 appear in passages that are classified by Westermann as supplications. This would suggest

27. Westermann 1956: 107-15. On p. 25, he points out the following passages of lament that appear in Job's words: chs. 3; 29–31 in their entirety; 6.4-20; 7.1-21; 9.17-31; 10.1-22; 12.13-15; 13.20–14.22; 16.6–17.16; 19.7–20.23, 27. It seems that the terms 'Klage' or 'lament' are not suitable to the passages referred to by the scholars. I have therefore used the term 'supplication', which indicates both the element of dirge or lament as well as its purpose—i.e., the petition for salvation and trust in God's help.

28. See Bentzen 1959: 182. From the relation between the book of Job and 'I Will Praise the Lord of Wisdom', Bentzen concludes that both works were used in the cult.

29. See in greater detail below, Chapter 8.

30. See on this Hoffman 1986. For a theoretical discussion of the understanding of the motif in folk literature generally, see Ben-Amos (1980). For a discussion of the function of these motifs in the Bible in order to express abstract ideas, see Talmon (1988).

31. Compare the use of the root שׁפט in the following supplication psalms: Pss. 7.9; 9.5, 8, 9, 17, 20; 10.5, 18; 17.2; 35.23; 43.1.

that the appearance of the motif in this book differs from the conventions of the psalms, even if it may have derived from them.[32] In order to clarify their function in the shaping of the book, I shall deal below with the different manifestations of the trial motif.

The trial motif does not appear in the opening narrative, as everyone acknowledges Job's righteousness; even Satan questions only his motivations, but does not deny his righteous conduct. Nor do there appear any words from the fields of justice and trials, such as the roots שפט ('to judge'), צדק ('to justify'), ריב ('to dispute'), and the like. Even in ch. 3, where Job curses the day he was born, there is no clear expression of that motif. The wicked are mentioned in v. 17, but this term is too common in wisdom and hymnic literature for it to elicit any specific associations of a trial.

The trial motif first receives clear expression in the opening speech of Eliphaz, chs. 4–5, albeit there it is not yet particularly emphatic. For the first time, there are used here verbs which are clearly connected to judgment, such as נקה ('to acquit/find innocent', 4.7) and צדק ('to be righteous', v. 17). Eliphaz's comment, 'Can mortal man be righteous before God?' (4.17), alludes to a trial situation. Yet notwithstanding this, the motif is vague: there is no use made of the root שפט; the argument itself is theoretical and not substantive; and the thing as a whole is lost within the overall thrust of the speech. This tendency to touch upon a theme without making it central continues in Job's response to Eliphaz, chs. 6–7, which begins with a metaphor from the realm of commerce that appears on more than one occasion in the context of a trial—the act of weighing on scales.[33] Thereafter, no further use is made of words from the juridical realm, and only towards the end of the speech does one once more hear an echo—'pardon my transgression and take away my iniquity' (7.21).

---

32. Gemser (1955: 134-35) particularly emphasized the relation of the book of Job to juridical matters: 'The book not only abounds in judicial phraseology, but formally it cannot be better understood than as a record of the proceedings between Job and God Almighty...' A summation of the legal aspects of the book of Job appears in H.P. Muller 1978: 94-98. See also Huberman-Scholnick 1982, a paper devoted to the use of the word משפט (judgment/trial) in the book of Job.

33. The root שקל ('weighed') and the term מאזנים ('scales') appear on more than one occasion in a clearly legal framework. See Isa. 28.17; Hos. 12.8; Amos 8.5; Mic. 6.11; Prov. 16.11; etc. See also Job 31.6. The image also appears in the 'Protest of the Eloquent Peasant' within the context of doing righteousness in judgment. See, e.g., *ANET*, p. 409.

The verb שׁפט appears for the first time in the speech of Bildad, in a statement explicitly referring to legal procedure: 'Does God pervert justice? Or does the Almighty pervert the right?' (8.3). Further on there appear the words 'sinned', 'transgression' (v. 4); 'pure and upright', 'your righteousness' (v. 6). This concentration of phrases taken from the legal realm at the beginning of the speech gives the motif an important status for the first time. Moreover, these remarks focus one's attention due to their severity and inexactness, for Job has thus far refrained from accusing God of perverting justice. On the contrary, at least on the face of it he admits 'I have sinned' (7.20), and even seeks pardon—'Why dost thou not pardon my transgression and take away my iniquity' (v. 21).[34] Nevertheless, Bildad's words are not completely false . While Job takes care not to accuse God explicitly of perverting justice,[35] he is not far from doing so in his argument that there is no human sin that can justify such a severe punishment as that which has befallen him ('Am I the sea, or a sea monster...'—7.12). In any event, these words of Bildad focus the trial motif by making Job's righteousness a substitute for that of God and standing in contradiction to it, something which Eliphaz managed to avoid in his own doctrine of retribution. By presenting Job as one who has denied divine justice, through distorted 'quotation' ('How long will you say these things...Does God pervert justice?...'—8.2-3) of his words, the trial motif is added to the mimesis of a progressively intensifying polemic,[36] some expressions of which we have already noted.

It is interesting to observe the placing of the trial motif within the development of the debate as a whole: namely, in the transition from the description of Job's suffering (ch. 7) to the promise of his salvation (8.20ff.)—that is to say, within its traditional context in the supplication of the individual. One thereby finds an ironic outcome: whereas the author of the supplication psalm calls upon God to judge him in confidence of God being a righteous judge, Bildad invokes the same motif to attack Job, who had declared that God, as it were, perverts justice. By following the conventional pattern of the structure of indi-

---

34. Driver and Gray correctly translate v. 20: 'if I have sin'; and similarly Dhorm. One should understand v. 21 not as a concrete admission of sin, but as an assumption for polemical purposes—i.e., even if I had sinned, you would need to pass over my transgression, because I am unable to cause you any harm.

35. Unlike the view of Gordis 1965: 85.

36. Hence there is no basis for Tur-Sinai's objection to the incorporation of the verse in this context. See above, n. 16.

vidual supplications, the author emphasizes his deviation from convention: it is not the supplicant (Job) who raises the trial motif, but his opponent. One finds here an ironic allusion to Job's lack of faith in his chances of being saved by the divine judge; one may also see this as an attempt to avoid a direct confrontation with God for, if he demands a trial, such a confrontation will be unavoidable.

In any event, after being presented with the motif by Bildad in such a strident manner, Job can no longer ignore the trial motif, and he in turn places it in the centre of his speech in chs. 9–10. This is easily noticeable, if only by the extensive use of terms taken from the semantic field of judgment, such as שפט ('to judge': 9.15, 19, 24, 32); ריב ('to dispute': 9.3; 10.2); צדק ('to justify': 9.2, 15, 20); רשע ('to be wicked': 9.20, 22, 24, 29; 10.2, 3, 7, 15); עוד ('to testify/give witness': 9.19; 10.16).

The opening words, 'Truly I know that it is so; But how can a man be just before God?' (9.2) allude to Eliphaz's words, 'Can mortal man be righteous before God?' (4.17). However, it is only after Bildad has stated that there is a contradiction between Job's righteousness and God's righteousness does Job comprehend the full relevance of these words regarding himself; hence, his delayed reaction is readily understandable.[37] He expresses agreement on the face of it with Eliphaz's statement, but justifies it for the opposite reason, combined with the (ironic) conclusion, as if it were an inseparable part of Eliphaz's doctrine: namely, that humanity cannot be found righteous before God, not because every person is necessarily sinful, but because 'If one wished to contend with him, one could not answer him once in a thousand times' (9.3). This is one of the most interesting formulations in the book, and the wide variety of exegetical options, stemming from the use of the verb ריב ('quarrel', 'contend') and its unusual syntax, calls attention to it and gives it a central place in the development of the motif of judgment.

In most occurrences in the Bible, the verb ריב ('dispute') is used as a technical term for a legal procedure.[38] In some passages its significance is less technical—an exchange of words expressing non-agreement.[39] In

---

37. Here, too, one cannot concur with Tur-Sinai in his interpretation of 9.2. In his opinion, this verse belongs to the dream mentioned in 4.12ff.; this dream, which the redactor mistakenly attributed to Eliphaz, was originally part of a long speech by Job which preceded the words of the friends (Tur-Sinai 1972: 52-53, 113-14).

38. Exod. 23.3, 6; Isa. 1.17, 23; 3.13; 50.8; Mic. 6.1, 2; 7.9 etc. And in Job: 29.16; 31.13. See also what Gemser (1955) has written on this.

39. Thus, e.g., in Deut. 25.1; Job 33.13; Neh. 5.7; 13.11; 17, 25.

a small number of passages, it is concerned with an actual struggle or war,[40] or with vengeance.[41] In quite a few passages, its use is not confined only to one of these limited meanings, but is associated with the broad semantic field that came into existence among them.[42] In more than one case, including the verse at hand, the author of Job relates to the full range of meanings of this verb, no one of which openly contradicts the other, making it difficult at times to decide to which one of them a particular passage refers.

Regarding the syntax of the verse: the sentence is a conditional one, in which the conditional clause is composed of a subject, an expanded predicate ('If one wished to contend') and an indirect object ('with him'), while the main clause consists of a subject, a predicate, a direct object ('cannot answer him') and a reference to time ('one time out of a thousand'). The large number of syntactic possibilities derives from the unqualified nature of most parts of the sentence. Hence, from a purely syntactical viewpoint there are four exegetical possibilities:

If he/He wished to contend with him/Him, he/He cannot answer him/Him

אם יחפוץ לריב		עמו		לא יעננו
1.	Man	with God	God	to man
2.	Man	with God	man	to God
3.	God	with man	man	to God
4.	God	with man	God	to man

At first glance, this seems to be a purely theoretical syntactical speculation. However, further examination reveals that the various semantic meanings of ריב enable us to accept all of these as plausible interpretations. And indeed, each one of them is expressed during the course of the book.

Options 1 and 2 assume Job's willingness to enter into a dispute with God. This is articulated throughout the course of the speech—in vv. 4, 16, 20, 35—as well as in his subsequent speeches (see, for example, 13.3, 15, etc.). Options 3 and 4 assume God's initiative to quarrel with Job. This, too, is alluded to more than once, first and foremost in the frame story: it was God who caused the disasters that befell Job (the figure of Satan does not alter this statement); see likewise 9.12, 23; 10.2,

40. Gen. 26.20, 21; Judg. 11.25; Hab. 1.3; Ps. 35.1.
41. 1 Sam. 25.39; Jer. 50.34; 51.36; Lam. 3.58.
42. Jer. 12.1; Ps. 43.1; 74.22.

5-7; etc. On Job's inability to dispute properly with God (options 2 and 3), see 9.12, 15; 13.22; etc. The assumption that God will not at all answer those who argue with him (options 1 and 4) is mentioned in 10.2; 11.5; 13.19; 19.7; etc. Thus, the large number of syntactic possibilities for this saying is not accidental, and the possible interpretations are not mutually exclusive alternatives; rather, all of them are correct and complement one another.[43] It must nevertheless be emphasized that the idea that man is able to emerge victorious in his dispute with God will always turn out, in any way that it is examined, as absurd.

Hence, this verse gives a key role to the dispute with God. This subject achieved its central position by degrees, thereby also shedding light upon the status of the trial references in previous passages: these are not random, but fulfil a function as anticipatory hints in the construction of a major motif. We will only succeed in ascertaining their degree of centrality after its function has been examined throughout the course of the book as a whole. But at this point it is worthwhile to formulate the argument that I shall attempt to establish further on: the trial motif serves the book by providing it with a 'main theme', in the sense in which this term is used in the realm of music. One may turn it about from every side, reworking it within itself, making it easy to detect, as well as combining it with other themes, where it is more difficult to distinguish. At times one may only hear a few notes of it in the background, while at others it dominates the entire speech, echoes of it being heard even in the following speech.

Further on in this speech, Job toys with the idea of the trial, attempting to determine whether he nevertheless erred in his pessimistic declaration, 'how can a man be just before God' (9.2).[44] The more he mulls things over, the clearer it becomes to him that he has arrived at the truth, and how absurd was the idea (traditionally accepted in individual supplications) that a trial with God could extract him from his distress. The discussion is carried on through the formulation of possibilities, their dismissal and

---

43. It therefore seems that each one of the following commentators was partially right in interpreting this verse according to one of the options: option (1) was chosen by Gordis (1978), Dhorm (1926), and Kahana (1924). Driver and Gray (1921), Tur-Sinai (1972), and Ewald (1854) followed option (2). Option (3) was chosen by Duhm (1897) and R. Moses Kimhi (according to Schwartz 1969: 85); I have not found anyone who adopted option (4).

44. Kahana (1924) interpreted this verse 'and what (מה) and if not...', following the Arabic (*ma* = not)—a view that is not necessary.

the use of the dismissed possibility as a basis for further examination: our experience teaches us that no man can emerge victorious in a confrontation with God (9.4), and therefore there is no point in entering into judgment with him. Even if one ignores this decisive argument, no one will dare to criticize God, whatever he may do (v. 12).[45] Even if it becomes clear to God that he erred, he will not renege on his anger (v. 13). Moreover, even if we disregard this obstacle, one must forego the idea of a trial; because of the fear imposed upon me by God's presence, I certainly cannot tell him the truth and I will be forced to beseech him (v. 15). But in truth, I cannot speak with him at all, for even should he turn to me, I would not believe my own ears (v. 16).

The most succinct and harsh formulation of the dilemma with which the idea of the trial confronts Job is 'Though I am innocent, my own mouth would condemn me; though I am blameless, he would prove me perverse' (9.20). One needs to distinguish here between two different levels: (a) the earlier verses, describing the fear which God places upon Job, lead to the interpretation of this formulation given in v. 15: because of his great fear, he will speak in a confused and unconvincing manner, which will necessarily convict him. But in the light of the difficult conclusion that follows this statement, it seems proper to me to interpret it on an additional level, in relation to the words of Bildad, namely: (b) if I justify myself, this will necessarily be an indirect declaration of God's wickedness; yet there can be no clearer proof of man's wickedness than his claim that God is wicked![46] It is this bind that brings Job to say 'I am blameless; I am confused; I loathe my life' (9.21). This is a declaration of absolute innocence that nevertheless refuses to accept the unavoidable conclusions that follow from it regarding God's qualities ('I am confused'); hence, it inevitably leads Job to the conclusion that is the ultimate escape from every personal conflict—death. Along with this, there is an attempt to confront the theoretical side of the dilemma—'It is

45. יחתף is interpreted either as a parallel to יחטף (thus in Ben Sira 15.17)—that is, if God will snatch away a person (namely, cause him to die); or according to the Aramaic, in the sense of 'to break' (Driver and Gray 1921: II, 56); or from the root חפף—to surround, encompass, encircle (Dahood 1973: 55). See the discussion on this in Grabbe 1977: 60-63.

46. It follows from this that one ought to reject the proposed emendation, פיו ירשיעני ('his mouth would condemn me...'), suggested by Holscher (1952), Pope (1973), and Fohrer (1963). There is likewise no need to turn to the Ugaritic, as suggested by Dahood (1957: 311), in order to read פי as 'and for then', a suggestion also adopted by Cox (1978: 64).

all one; therefore I say, he destroys both the blameless and the wicked'
(v. 22)—that is, there is no correlation between a person's lot and their
degree of righteousness. It follows from this that my suffering is no
proof of my wickedness, but to the same extent my declaration of
innocence lends no support to my challenge against God that he violates
the rules of justice, because in this matter there are in fact no rules at all!

The obvious conclusion from Job's words is that he ought to abandon
the idea of the trial entirely. Indeed, he returns to this conclusion in
vv. 28-33: whatever may be, God will not find me innocent, but will
condemn me in his judgment (vv. 28-29); even if I am pure and clean as
snow (vv. 30-31); even if the trial does in fact take place, Job cannot
answer God (v. 32). An important development within the motif appears
in this connection: thus far, Job has considered the idea of being judged
before God; it now becomes increasingly clear to him that this is liable to
be a trial against God, where the chances are even slimmer, as God will
function simultaneously both as one of the litigating sides and as judge
(v. 33). Yet despite all this, Job declares his readiness to stand in judgment, and asks only that God cease to place fear and terror upon him (v.
34) so that he may speak freely before him (v. 35). This is a logically
absurd declaration, but one that is very understandable from the psychological viewpoint, serving as one of the details building the mimesis of a
person who seeks to assuage his physical suffering through intellectual
analysis of the options available to him. Moreover, the immediate significance of Job's request, 'Let him take his rod away from me' (v. 34) is
first and foremost let God stop my physical suffering! This is the
intellectual wrapping for the simple human longing that his suffering
shall cease. Thus, the motif of the trial is established as an axis linking
together the two aspects which create the coherency of the book—the
principled-theoretical aspect and the existential-personal aspect.

The tendency to present Job's holding fast to the idea of the trial as an
obsession is also implied by the second half of this speech, ch. 10. This is
mostly a dirge by Job over his bitter fate (see Westermann 1956: 25),
combined with the prayer that he be allowed to live out the rest of his
days without further suffering. But here too the motif of the trial recurs
repeatedly, breaking the continuity of the petition (vv. 2-7, 13-17) both
in terms of the motifs and the atmosphere, because it is brought within
the framework of sharp words directed against God, inconsistent with
the traditional manner of supplication. We therefore find that a motif
which, in the conventional supplication, only served as a transition here

becomes a primary motif, disintegrating Job's supplication from within. This stands out particularly from v. 8 on. The language of address, 'remember' (זכור—'Remember that thou hast made me of clay'— v. 10) is routinely used in traditional supplications in the framework of a submissive appeal for God's mercies and fatherly compassion.[47] Upon reading vv. 8-12, one receives the impression that this is the case here as well; hence, in the wake of the description of the kindnesses God has performed for Job since the day of his birth, one anticipates the traditional sort of petition—therefore have mercy on me. Instead, the petition develops in the opposite direction: the motif of the trial re-emerges ('If I sin...dost not acquit me if my iniquity. If I am wicked...'—14-15), coupled with a most severe accusation against God—torture. For there is no other definition (unless one compares it to an experiment upon a laboratory animal) for God's programme to cultivate Job, to raise him in wealth, to do kindness to him—all so that his suffering will be even harder when God decides to strike him, so as to see whether he will sin or not.[48]

In the following speech, that of Zophar (ch. 11), the trial motif is only alluded to indirectly (for example: 'But oh, that God would speak'— v. 5), as it is also in the first half of Job's reply to Zophar (the reference to the judges in 12.17). However, on the basis of the continuation of the speech, one may see this as an intermezzo preparing the background for the concluding formulation, the most decisive and clearest statement of Job's position concerning this matter, in 13.7-23. Judgment with God is presented here as a principled demand, lacking in any practical purpose, possibly even dangerous: 'Though he will slay me, yet I trust in him; I will defend my ways to his face' (v. 15). What is important is not the result of the trial, but the very fact of its taking place—'Who is there that will contend with me? For then I would be silent and die' (v. 19). To the preconditions which Job had presented for the trial to take place ('Withdraw thy hand far from me, and let not dread of thee terrify me. Then call, and I will answer; or let me speak, and do thou reply to me'—vv. 21-22; compare 9.34-35), there is added now another request—

47. See Exod. 23.13; Deut. 9.27; Jer. 14.21; Ps. 25.6, 7; 74.2, 18, 22; 132.1; Lam. 3.19; etc., and see also the words of Job himself, 7.7.
48. The idea that the happiness of the righteous is imaginary is an ironic turnabout of the approach expressed in Ps. 73.18, 'Truly thou dost set them in slippery places; thou dost make them fall to ruin', which presents the success of the wicked as imaginary. See on this below, Chapter 7.

that God present an indictment: 'How many are my iniquities and my sins? Make me know my transgressions and my sin' (v. 23). This wish was already covertly implied earlier on ('let me know why thou dost contend against me'—10.2), but from this point until the end of the book it becomes stronger, pushing aside the general-principled aspects of the trial motif, which have already been played out. It thereby gives new vitality to this theme, opening to the author another possibility, fully concretized in chs. 29–31: involvement in the 'biography' of Job.

The trial motif reaches a high point in 13.12-23 by means of its isolation within its overall context, in which it only appears vaguely and allusively, between ch. 11, 12.1–13.6, and chs. 14–18. However, the vague expression of the motif after Job has clearly formulated his request for a definite accusation serves an additional structural function. It creates the impression that God is avoiding a reply, thereby preparing the ground for the continuation, as we shall see. Eliphaz (ch. 15) and Bildad (ch. 18), who represent themselves as God's spokesmen, hide behind conventional rhetoric ('Your own mouth condemns you, and not I...'—15.6; compare 9.20 and the rhetorical portrayal of the destiny of the wicked in ch. 18). Eliphaz repeats his old argument that every man is sinful (15.14-16; compare 4.17-21), which in this context seems like a substitute-excuse for an indictment. The motif is further weakened in Job's words in chs. 16–17, and even more so in the words of Bildad (ch. 18), where one can perhaps find only a verbal echo, in such words as 'although there is no violence in my hands' (16.17); 'O earth, cover not my blood' (v. 18).

In ch. 19, Job explicitly returns to the trial motif when he says, 'Know then that God has put me in the wrong...Behold, I cry out, "Violence!" but I am not answered; I call aloud, but there is no justice' (vv. 6-7). The descriptions of Job's isolation and humiliation in the following verses, which also anticipate that stated *in extenso* in ch. 29, are in this context an indication of punishment without trial.

In general, throughout the block of chs. 14–21 there is barely a hint of the trial motif. The impression is created that the author has reached a dead end in its development: if God will answer Job's requests to be judged with him, the book will necessarily come to an end; if he continues to ignore these demands, and the author places the same arguments in Job's mouth over and over again—which cannot sound new, as his arguments had already been exhausted earlier—this would be an unjustified excess. Because the motif fades away, it seems likely to disappear entirely before the end of the book—in itself hardly surprising, given that there is also room in an artistic work for motifs which are not continued throughout its entire length. However, in the light of the conceptual importance given to the motif thus far, its disappearance at this stage, before being substantively completed, is likely to seem forced. And indeed, it is not truncated, but continued, even undergoing a major turning point in ch. 22. After reading this chapter, one may speculate that the low level on which the motif was kept in chs. 14–21 served a double structural function: on the one hand, to bring out the climax in 13.12-23 (see above) and, on the other, to stress the special importance of the motif on its appearance in ch. 22. However, it is questionable whether, from the artistic viewpoint, the almost complete disappearance of such a central motif for eight consecutive chapters is an appropriate means to accomplish this end. I tend to think that this is not the case. A dirge in ch. 14 would have sufficed as an 'anti-climax' to emphasize the climax in ch. 13, while the absence of the motif from ch. 21 would have been sufficient preparation for the new climax in ch. 22. By this evaluation, I open the way to one of two conclusions, or perhaps to some combination of the two: either the author made a mistake here, as in my judgment he violated the immanent compositional norms of the work, or else this is an indication of the corruption of the extant text. My own view on this question will appear in the summarizing discussion in Chapter 8, based as it must be upon other data besides the issue of the trial motif.

We have already observed the critical function played by ch. 22 in shaping the image of Eliphaz. The importance of this chapter in developing the trial motif as well renders it an important crossroads in the structure of the book as a whole.

Chapter 22 contains the first and only response of one of the friends to Job's extremely important demand in the realm of justice—'How many are my iniquities and my sins? Make me know my transgressions and my sin' (13.23). This call was addressed as a challenge towards God, after it had previously been directed towards the friends ('make me understand how I have erred'—6.24). The fact that Eliphaz is the one to react to it contributes to the reader's feeling of a polarization between two camps: Job against God and the friends. With the definite, unambiguous and harsh accusations directed against Job by Eliphaz, and with the creation of a clear trial situation, the trial motif is rescued from the dead end to which it had been confined, without God himself needing to speak. This poetic solution is not artificial, but derives its logic from the content and the course of the debates. The status of prosecutor assumed by Eliphaz is made possible by the kind of accusations which he hurls against Job—accusations belonging to the realm of visible social transgressions, of the type for which human beings are wont to sue their fellows and against which, should the transgressors claim innocence, they need to defend themselves. Some of these accusations may even contain some hint concerning Job's behaviour as judge,[49] thereby adding an ironic dimension to the polemic, of the order of 'Take out the beam from your own eyes'; as if to say he who has trespassed against his task as judge should not accuse God of wrongdoing in this area. The justification given by Eliphaz is that he, and not God, is reading his own indictment to Job, as if to say, God is not afraid of you, so why should he trouble himself on your account when your crimes are visible to all, so that even a human being like myself can accuse you?[50] By the logic of this argument, it is only natural that Eliphaz should 'volunteer' to help God, as by doing so he is in fact coming to the defence of himself and his own faith, as I suggested above.

With Eliphaz's indictment, the trial motif undergoes a sharp turn: Job is turned from accuser to accused, from the one who demands answers to one from whom answers are expected. In cognisance of this, the

49. 'The man with power possessed the land, and the favoured man sat in it [i.e., to judgment]' (22.8). Indeed, Job responds to these things further on in the words, 'the fatherless who had none to help him…and I caused the widow's heart to sing for joy. I put on righteousness, and it clothed me; my justice was like a robe and a turban' (29.12-14, and see below). A hint of activity contrary to the law is implied in the words, 'for you have exacted pledges of your brother for nothing' (22.6). A similar accusation is brought by the worker against the foreman, Hoshayah ben Shevi, in the Yavneh-Yam inscription: 'And he took the garment of your servant when I completed this harvest…My brothers will testify that I have been free of guilt, return my garment…' (Donner and Röllig 1964: I, inscription 200).

50. These things are implied by vv. 2-4, even though they are not completely clear to me. The word יִסְכָּן (also used by Eliphaz in 15.3) is obscure. It is conventionally interpreted in the sense of יוֹעִיל ('to help/be useful')—that is, 'Can I be of use to God?' (thus in Driver and Gray, Kahana, and others). But it may also be understood in the opposite sense, as danger: 'Why should God trouble himself to answer your request? Can you endanger his position?' Similar ambiguity is also found in the phrases תִּצְדָּק (v. 3: that is, either: 'you shall emerge righteous in judgment'; or: 'change your ways and behave with righteousness'); הֲמִיָּרְאָתְךָ יֹכִיחֶךָ (v. 4: i.e., 'does he need to present you with an indictment because he is afraid of you?'; or 'does he chastise you despite your being God-fearing?').

reader's expectations are henceforth altered: from Job, one awaits an appropriate response; from Bildad and Zophar, one expects an effort that will not allow Job to escape giving such a response. These expectations are not at all realized in chs. 23–28, and only in ch. 29 does Job respond to Eliphaz's accusations, albeit indirectly.

In chs. 23, 24, and 27, which are attributed to Job, the trial motif does indeed appear, but without any explicit connection to Eliphaz's accusations. In ch. 23 Job again expresses his wish to be judged with God ('Oh, that I knew where I might find him...I would lay my case before him...Would he contend with me in the greatness of his power?...—vv. 3-7), but nevertheless explains why this is neither possible nor beneficial ('But he is unchangeable and who can turn him?...Therefore I am terrified at his presence...'—vv. 13-15).[51] This entails the repetition of arguments which have already been articulated; however, the rebellious excitement and direct appeal to God which characterized his earlier formualations (9.29–10.2; 13.20-24) are here replaced by a gentler, more allusive style of thought, suggesting that Job has in truth already relinquished any hope that his appeal to be judged with God will be answered. Appearing as they do after the speech by Eliphaz, one may evaluate them thus: it was precisely the fulfilment of Job's demand for an indictment, even if Eliphaz, and not God, was the one doing the accusing, that removed the sting from Job's legal claim, and made it clear to him that he has lost any chance that God himself will tell him his sin.

In ch. 24 the trial motif only appears indirectly. There are various thoughts concerning the crimes of the wicked, a kind of theoretical catalogue of accusations. It is as if Job says I too, like Eliphaz, can enumerate social crimes, but I will enumerate them out of shock and surprise at God, who fails to prevent such injustices (vv. 1, 12).[52] However, the

51. A discussion of the phrase מי יתן ('O, that I knew...'; 23.3) appears in Cox 1978: 33-35. In his opinion, the words מי יתן in the book of Job are to be seen as a wish in whose realization the speaker does not believe. However, the lack of exact tenses and of a modal system in Biblical Hebrew not only render it more difficult to understand, but also place in doubt the possibility that the author clarified for himself exactly what kind of wish his words referred to. It is therefore difficult to determine whether these words are meant to imply that Job did not believe in this possibility. For an examination of the idiom מי יתן in the Bible, see Jongeling (1974), who translates 23.3 as, 'Ah! si je savais ou je pourrais le trouver...'

52. Driver and Gray, in their commentary, rightly point to these verses as a proof that the chapter is not a cold and apathetic description of the facts of life, but a

essence of the chapter is not protest against God—neither in terms of its power, nor in term of its scope, nor in terms of the function it plays in the development of the trial motif. The essential element of the chapter is the list of crimes, fulfilling a double structural purpose: an echo of the words of Eliphaz, keeping us aware of his accusations, and preparation for Job's words in ch. 29. The speech fulfils this task whether we ascribe it to Job, or whether we ascribe it to Bildad or Zophar.

The same holds true with regard to ch. 27. Here, too, the trial motif appears without any clear relation to Eliphaz's indictment. This is expressed in three ways: by Job's declaration that God has removed his judgment, ('taken away my right', v. 2); his insistence upon his own claim of righteousness (v. 6); and allusions to the wickedness of the friends (vv. 5, 7ff.).[53] On the whole, in chs. 23, 24, and 27 the motif of the judgment fulfils the function of a kind of echo chamber allowing Eliphaz's accusation to go beyond ch. 22, yet nevertheless to dissipate gradually in the intermezzo preceding chs. 29–31. Moreover, in this way the feeling is gradually developed that Job is afraid of confrontation with the accusations, circling around them in order to avoid a substantive reaction to them—in this way too preparing the ground for chs. 29–31. In other words, throughout these chapters the trial motif fulfils a struc-

---

contribution to the difficulties raised by Job in his speeches concerning the ethical judgment of God. Against them, there are those who think that this chapter is part of a truncated speech of Bildad or of Zophar. Fohrer (1963, following Duhm 1897) sees in the chapter four wisdom poems which are not authentic. Dhorm proposes altering the order of several verses, to place vv. 14-18 after 27.13. For a comprehensive discussion of the chapter, see Gordis 1978: 531-34, in which the different views are elaborated.

53. Verses 8ff. express the idea that God repays the evil and the righteous according to their deserts. There are those who conclude from this that these words were not said by Job, as they are inconsistent with his arguments in other speeches. Thus, for example Driver and Gray (1921: 225), who state that vv. 7-10, 13-23, and possibly also 11-12 were taken from one of the speeches of the friends, evidently the missing speech of Zophar. I do not wish to consider this question here. In any event, one can also understand the words as being said by Job, to wit: it is not possible that I acted wickedly, knowing that God punishes the wicked; and also: I do not understand how you can behave towards me wickedly, for you know that God punishes the wicked. Gordis (1965: 253) argues that the remarks concerning the punishment of the wicked are a quotation by Job from the words of one of the friends. Hence, one could state that the trial motif indeed appears in a coherent order, but this is insufficient to prove that this is their original place. Dhorm combines 27.13, 24.18-24, and 27.14-23 together into one speech, which he attributes to Zophar.

tural function and does not introduce anything new in terms of ideas.

At first glance, one might argue that even Bildad's fragmentary speech in ch. 25 fulfils a similar structural function. It revolves entirely around the trial motif, expressed in the words 'How then can man be righteous before God?' (25.4), which is no more than a variation upon what Eliphaz said in his first (4.17-21) and second (15.14-17) speeches. These words do not introduce anything with respect to the earlier formulae, nor do they contribute any new ideas in terms of the development of the trial motif. But whereas in chs. 23, 24, and 27 there is a correspondence between the structural function of the motif and its content—namely, Job's understandable avoidance of Eliphaz's accusations—this is not the case in ch. 25. The total absence of any reference to Eliphaz's accusations in Bildad's words is so incomprehensible, and thus so astonishing from the aesthetic point of view, that it does not even fit among chs. 23, 24, and 27 from the structural viewpoint.

Even more surprising is the total absence of the motif in chs. 26 and 28, as that contradicts the structural status of the block as described above. Therefore, one may definitely state that chs. 25, 26, and 28 do not fit well into the general pattern of the trial motif in the book. This conclusion must be taken into consideration in determining one's position regarding the original location of these chapters, but this cannot stand by itself, being only one of a wide range of factors.

Chapters 29–31 have certain unique, explicit characteristics which set them apart as a well-fashioned literary unit able to stand in its own right. This is a speech of an explicitly autobiographical colour, and the difference between it and Job's other speeches has led quite a few scholars to discuss it independently or even to claim that it is a later addition to the book.[54] Others have argued that the original location of this block was

---

54. A number of studies have been specifically devoted to this block of chapters. One such is Ceresko (1980), who focuses primarily upon the linguistic aspect, emphasizing that it is an inseparable part of the book. Likewise Dick (1979; 1983), who notes especially its generic character, finding therein a combination of individual lamentation, declarations of innocence and wisdom sayings. By contrast, there are others who think that these chapters are a later addition. Kraeling (1938: 111-12) states that vv. 30.16-31; 31.35, 37, are authentic, but are mislocated. In his wake, Holbert (1983) argues that the lack of irony in these chapters distinguishes them from the rest of the book and proves that they are not authentic. In his opinion, they were introduced so that, in the final analysis, when Job will stand before God, he will be clean and purified.

following ch. 3, which likewise bears an autobiographical character.[55] And indeed, the difference between chs. 29–31 and the other speeches is striking. They turn the book from an ideological direction to an explicitly personal one; they are addressed neither to the friends nor to God (with the exception of 30.20-23); and it seems as if there is no connection between them and God's reply. However, examination of their position in relation to the trial motif reveals that they constitute an inseparable part of it. Indeed, they represent the climax of the motif, without which it would be truncated and nearly without significance. But since the motif of the trial is, in my opinion, an organizing tool of the first order in the book, its climax is automatically an integral part of its context, specifically in its present location.

The closed cyclical structure of this section is evident. It begins with a list of acts of kindness performed by Job (ch. 29) and concludes with an enumeration of injustices from which he has refrained. Thus, this constitutes an enumeration of his righteousness in both the positive and negative sense, similar to (albeit in the opposite order) the passage in Psalm 1: 'who walks not...nor stands...nor sits...but his delight is in the law of the Lord'. A similar means is used by Ezekiel when he sets out to exemplify who is the righteous person and who is the evil-doer, likewise combining positive features with negative ones:

> If a man is righteous and does what is lawful and right—if he does not eat upon the mountains...or lift up his eyes...does not defile...or approach... does not oppress anyone, but restores to the debtor his pledge, commits no robbery, gives his bread to the hungry and covers the naked with a garment, does not lend...or take...executes true justice...walks in my statutes and is careful to observe my ordinances... (Ezek. 18.5-9).

The portrayal of Job's difficult present situation in ch. 30 lends these descriptions a certain coloration of protest against God's justice. Hence, there is no reason to question the unity of the block, nor to break it down and scatter its components among other speeches.

One nevertheless needs to examine these chapters, not only as a block in its own right, but as part of the flow of the trial motif as a whole. We have already seen that the autobiographical element in ch. 23 (vv. 9-12),

---

55. Thus Kahana (1924) and Tur-Sinai (1972) and similarly Snaith (1968). In his opinion, the first edition (out of three, in his view) of the book of Job only included part of the frame-story (see on this in Chapter 8), ch. 3, and part of God's speech, chs. 29–31.

as well as the list of sins in ch. 24, prepare the ground for chs. 29–31 by providing a kind of anticipatory allusion to them. However, the main test of the status and the present location of chs. 29–31 relates to the question of whether they bear any relation to Eliphaz's indictment in ch. 22, echoes of which reverberate through chs. 23, 24, and 27, which remains unanswered by Job in any serious way. And indeed, ch. 29 clearly touches upon this accusation, dealing as it does with the selfsame issues: Job's functioning as a judge (29.7); his concern for widows and orphans (vv. 12-13); his struggle against the mighty (v. 17); the reverence (not fear) which everyone showed him (vv. 8-10). But even if there is a certain relationship here, there is no categorical denial of the accusations of Eliphaz. Yet from a legal viewpoint, the only suitable rebuttal of such an accusation is its outright denial; a declaration of good deeds, such as that recited in ch. 29, can only assist the accused after he has explicitly denied the accusation levelled against him. Job does not inform us that he denies Eliphaz's accusation (he does not say: 'I did not exact pledges from my brothers; I did not strip the clothes off the naked'; etc.), which is particularly striking in the light of his 'denials' in ch. 31, which do not pertain to Eliphaz's indictment. It therefore becomes clear that scripture deliberately draws our attention to the fact that Job does not deny Eliphaz's accusations, as would be required in a proper legal proceeding. If we did not know the utter baselessness of Eliphaz's accusations in the light of the axiomatic status of Job's righteousness in the book, we would be tempted to see simple evasiveness in the manner of Job's response. However, our knowledge of his innocence requires us to see his words in ch. 29 as a deliberate ignoring of Eliphaz's accusations, the true significance of which is a non-ignoring.[56] That is to say, everybody (Eliphaz, the friends, God, and, on another level, the reader) knows that these accusations are false, and hence their denial is superfluous, and even implies a certain insult towards Job. Nevertheless, to ignore them totally would be contrary to the mimesis of a heated debate and, from the structural viewpoint, would leave us uprooted from the context. There follows from this the solution whereby Job reacts to the accusations indirectly, through nostalgic thoughts concerning his past situation. These thoughts likewise serve as background to the antithesis

---

56. In the formula of Gordis (1965: 256): 'Job does not dignify Eliphaz's accusations with a direct denial'. Thompson (1960) formulated this (regarding Job's speech in ch. 6) with the term 'apparent irrelevance'.

in ch. 30—'But now they make sport of me', etc. (v. 1).[57]

Thus, chs. 29–30 combine into one unit, whose syntactic structural frame exists on two levels. On the more superficial level, it assumes the structure of a compound sentence—that is, in the past I was happy (ch. 29) and now I suffer (ch. 30). At this level it does not at all touch upon the trial motif. The deeper structure is that of a statement of renegement which pertains directly to the trial motif: despite my past righteousness (ch. 29) I suffer in the present (ch. 30). Perhaps one may also see on this level a sentence of cause and effect: in the past I judged righteously and punished evil-doers (ch. 29), therefore I now suffer from them (ch. 30). This is a heavily ironic statement directed against God.

The absence of the trial motif in ch. 30 on the overt level creates an ebb that serves to augment the peak of the motif in ch. 31; its presence on the deeper level of the chapter preserves the necessary connection between ch. 29 and ch. 31.

Some scholars wish to draw a comparison between ch. 31 and the 'negative confession', known to us from ancient Near Eastern literature, in which the worshipper presents his innocence by enumerating those sins and transgressions which he has not performed. The closest example is taken from the Egyptian texts gathered under the title, 'The Book of the Dead', which show the prayer of the dying person when he presents his soul before the throne of judgment. Here is a representative passage:[58]

> What is said on reaching the Broad-Hall of the two Justices [the place of the next world judgment]
> …I have come to thee, my Lord…Lord of Justice…
> I have not committed evil against men.
> I have not mistreated cattle.
> I have not committed sin in the place of truth.
> I have not known that which is not.
> I have not seen evil…
> I have not blasphemed a god.

---

57. Gray (1970) compared 29.7-17 to 'I Will Praise the God of Wisdom', Tablet II.23-32, in which the worshipper recounts his pious behaviour in the past. However, the differences are significant. From a literary viewpoint, the Mesopotamian work does not contain any reflective-nostalgic element; from a substantive viewpoint, all of the declarations there pertain to the realm between man and his god: prayer (ll. 21-24, 27); cult (ll. 25-26); preserving the existence of the cult among the people of the worshipper (ll. 29-30); education to fear of god and king (ll. 30-32). As against that, Job's words pertain largely to the interpersonal realm.

58. *ANET*, pp. 34-35.

I have not done violence to a poor man.
I have not done that which the gods abominate.
I have not defamed a slave to his superior.
I have not made (anyone) sick.
I have not made (anyone) weep.
I have not killed.
I have given no order to a killer.
I have not caused anyone suffering.
I have not cut down on the food (income) in the temples.
I have not damaged the bread of the gods.
I have not taken the loaves of the blessed (dead).
I have not had sexual relations with a boy.
I have not defiled (polluted) myself.
I have neither increased or diminished the grain measure.
I have not diminished the *aroura* [a measure of land area]
I have not falsified a half *aroura* of land.
I have not added to the weight of the balance.
I have not weakened the plummet of the scales.
I have not taken milk from the mouth of children...
I am pure! [to be repeated four times].

Indeed, the resemblance to ch. 31 is noticeable. First and foremost, the basic situation is similar: a person standing in judgment before his god presents a list of accusations, so that God may clear him of them. There is also considerable similarity of subject matter: the relation of man and God (compare 'If I have looked at light when it shone, or the moon moving in splendour, and my heart has been secretly enticed, and my mouth has kissed my hand; this also would be an iniquity to be punished by the judges, for I would have been false to God above'—vv. 26-28); the relation to the servant ('If I have rejected the cause of my manservant', v. 13); sexual purity ('If my heart has been enticed to a woman', v. 9); food for children ('or have eaten my morsel alone, and the fatherless has not eaten of it', v. 17); the motif of just weights and measure ('Let me be weighed in a just balance', v. 6. In Egypt, this motif also appears in drawings in which the virtues and shortcomings of the human soul are weighed before the decision concerning his final lot after death.)

In the light of these points of similarity, one may assume that the author of the book of Job knew similar texts, making it appropriate to evaluate the uniqueness of ch. 31 against this background. There are a number of explicit differences between this chapter and the Egyptian negative confession. The most striking of these is that in ch. 31 there is no declaration of absolute innocence; as noted above, nowhere does Job declare 'I have not done...'[59] Further differences pertain to the nature of the accusations (see Gordis 1978: 546): Job does not even mention such a severe accusation as murder, while most of his remarks pertain to matters between man and his fellow rather than to ritual matters. Conspicuous by its absence from Job is a general declaration of his righteousness, albeit this is indirectly implied in vv. 35-36: 'Let the Almighty answer me! Oh, that I had the indictment written by my adversary! Surely I would carry it on my shoulder; would bind it on me as a crown.'

It is instructive to examine ch. 31 and to note its uniqueness against the background of related biblical texts. אם ('if'), a key word in the chapter, is repeated here no less than 18 times, and determines its basic character: a series of conditional sentences, similar to the casuistic formulae of the law, rather than a 'negative confession' based upon statements of absolute denial, nor a series of positive declarations of innocence. The reason for this does not lie in the absence of models of such declarations in Israelite literature, as one can note any number of passages which demonstrate the opposite. An example of negatively phrased declarations of innocence may be cited from Ps. 26.1-5: 'Vindicate me, O Lord, for I have walked in my integrity...Prove me, O Lord, and try me...I do not sit with false men, nor do I consort with dissemblers. I hate the company of evildoers, and I will not sit with the wicked'. It would seem that the description of the archetype of the righteous person in Ezekiel 18 ('he does not eat upon the mountains or lift up his eyes to the idols of the house of Israel, does not defile his neighbour's wife or approach a woman in her time of impurity, does not oppress any one'—vv. 5-7) is likewise based upon this traditional model. Positive declarations of innocence generally appear as part of the negative model. Thus, for example, in Psalm 15, while it is true that the formulation is phrased in the third person, in principle it is a declaration of innocence by one entering the Temple: 'He who walks blamelessly, and does what is right, and speaks truth from his heart; who does not slander with his tongue, and does no evil to his friend, nor takes up a reproach against his neighbour' (vv. 2-3).

---

59. There are those who explain the verse, 'how (ומה) then could I look upon a virgin' (v. 1) in the sense of 'I will not', etc. based upon the Arabic *ma* (not). Thus in the LXX, Peshitta, Vulgate; and also in the interpretations of Kahana, Dhorm, and others. However, this does not fit the rest of the chapter. Tur-Sinai (1972) interpreted this as a language of oath, similar to, 'I adjure you...that you stir not up (מה תעירו) love' (Cant. 8.4).

See also Pss. 1.1-2, 24.2, and elsewhere. One may therefore state that in Job 31 we find the casuistic model, rather than the apodictic model of absolute declaration of innocence, notwithstanding the widespread dissemination of the latter in the Bible.

For variety, the conditional model appears in several different forms in the chapter, for which parallels may also be found in other scriptural passages. (a) Condition followed by punishment—31.7-8, 9-10, 39-40. This basic model is based upon the casuistic formulation of the law, in which the punishment is combined with the sin (such as: 'If the ox gores a slave, male or female, the owner shall give to their master thirty shekels of silver, and the ox shall be stoned'—Exod. 21.32). (b) A series of conditional statements of transgressions concluding with a punishment, as in 31.19-22—'If I have seen any one perish...if his loins have not blessed me...If I have raised my hand against the fatherless...then let my shoulder blade fall from my shoulder'. Cf. Ps. 7.4-6: 'O Lord my God, if I have done this, if there is wrong in my hands, if I have requited my friend with evil or plundered my enemy without cause, let the enemy pursue me...' (c) In vv. 5-6, the condition is not complemented by a punishment, but by an expression of confidence that God will recognize Job's righteousness: 'If I have walked with falsehood, and my foot has hastened to deceit; Let me be weighed in a just balance, and let God know my integrity'—31.5-6. Cf. Ps. 44.18-22 in which a negative apodictic formula is combined with a conditional formula): 'We have not forgotten thee, or been false to thy covenant. Our heart has not turned back...If we had forgotten the name of our God, or spread forth our hands to a strange god, would not God discover this? For he knows the secret of the heart'. In addition to these three types, ch. 31 also contains conditional sins which are completed, not by punishment, but by the explanation that the very theoretical possibility that Job sinned is absurd (vv. 1-4, 13-18), as well as conditional sins that are listed without any complement (vv. 24-34). The completions of the conditions are also formulated in different ways, such as הלא ('did it not', vv. 3, 4, 15); ומה ('and what', vv. 2, 14); כי ('because', 'that', vv. 11, 12, 18, 23). This tendency towards variation is even more noticeable in ch. 31, as the complete absence of declarations of innocence is not accidental but deliberate: it is intended to emphasize that Job's words are not meant to be understood as a traditional declaration of innocence,[60] because such a

60. A different view is articulated by Dick (1979; 1983). In his opinion, the chapter is constructed according to accepted models of declarations of innocence,

thing is superfluous. Job never ceases to declare his innocence throughout the length of the book (cf. 9.20; 10.7; 13.18; etc.). In fact, Job's
words are presented as an indictment which he formulates against himself, one not anchored in any legal reality, either in terms of content or
structure, and which may only be understood in terms of the development of the trial motif within the book.

As for its content, what is unique about the indictment is not the light-
ness of the sins[61] but their hidden nature, which makes them difficult to
prove and obviates the possibility of presenting them within the framework of an indictment that would be brought by other people: coveting
women (v. 1), taking bribes (v. 7), adultery (v. 9), exaggerated trust in
wealth (vv. 24-25), secret practice of pagan customs (v. 27),[62] rejoicing in
the misfortunes of others (v. 29), cursing an enemy (v. 30), inappropriate
exploitation of land (vv. 38, 39).[63] This list seems to counter the list of

which were part of a legal proceeding in which the accused turns to a civil suit after, in
his opinion, justice has miscarried. In this proceeding, the accused would bring his
adversary before a 'listener' (31.35), who was meant to determine that the accusation
was in fact no more than libel. Dick's position is problematic in several respects: he
has not proven the existence of such a procedure within Israel; there is no evidence
that שומע ('listener') is a technical term; God is not presented in this chapter as a
litigant, but as a judge, as I shall clarify below. Dick offered evidence for a procedure
of appeal before a 'hearer' from the Yavneh-Yam inscription. However, there the
complainant addressed the appointed official, and not a 'listener'. There is also no
resemblance between the formula of the complaint and ch. 31. For more about the
cultic usage of declarations of innocence (*Tempeleinlassliturgen*), see Reventlow
1969: 328-34 and the bibliography there.

61. Unlike Gordis (1978: 542: 'sins of the spirit committed within the law'),
Fohrer (1983: 78-93) argues that the chapter is based upon stereotypical lists of sins.
He enumerates there twelve sins; vv. 1-4, 38-40 are a later addition of the author himself, from which it follows that the chapter is composed of two lists containing ten
sins each. Fohrer's arithmetical arguments are not convincing, and the attempt to
isolate expansions by the author himself seem to be refuted *ab initio*.

62. Unlike the opinion of Driver and Gray (1921: 269), who argued that this verse
does not speak of hidden idolatry, but of a specific pagan custom which was punish-
able (Deut. 17.2), deriving this from the phrase, עָוֹן פְּלִילִי (31.28). However, one
cannot infer from this any sin for which one may be tried. See, for example,
וְאֹיְבֵינוּ פְּלִילִים, Deut. 32.31.

63. The location of vv. 38-39 at the end of the speech is difficult, and many place
them somewhere between vv. 5-35 (see details in Driver and Gray 1921: 261). Their
meaning is likewise unclear. Duhm thinks that they allude to violations of the laws of
the sabbatical year or of mixing of kinds; Tur-Sinai, Dhorm and others interpret them
as theft of land from the lawful owners; R. Joseph Kimhi interprets, in the wake of

known, severe sins of which Eliphaz accuses Job in ch. 22. It is as if Job were to say everybody knows that Eliphaz's accusations are palpably untrue, but should there be anyone who thinks that my suffering is retribution for hidden sins known only to God and myself—here is my reaction, which totally refutes such suspicions as well.

In terms of structure, too, this accusation is not anchored in concrete legal reality. The conditional sentences, and the punishments which Job imposes upon himself in their wake, following the model of self-adjuration,[64] present him at one and the same time as accused, accuser, and sentencing judge. There is missing here only the decision as to whether Job is guilty or innocent. He imposes this decision upon God, as it were, by forcing him to reveal his stance unequivocally, and to cease to avoid the issue: if he will bring upon Job the punishments appropriate to these conditional sins, that will be a sign of Job's guilt; but if these punishments are not brought upon him, that must necessarily prove a divine recognition of his innocence, and then God (in accordance with legal principles) will be forced to remove Job's unjustified suffering. The result of Job's self-adjuration is thus two-fold. First, it turns the tables on his original remarks regarding the trial: the paradox of God being at once the accuser (without presenting the accusation), the judge, and the one sentencing is reversed: now Job is at once the accused, the accuser, and the one passing verdict. The circle is thereby closed on the trial motif in the book. Second, since God is now being forced to articulate his stance by taking concrete steps regarding Job, the book automatically returns to its narrative starting point, whose subject is the ill brought by God upon Job (chs. 1–2). The way is open for the epilogue in ch. 42— returning from the realm of words to that of deeds. In this way the

Rashi, 'If he who works my land cries out against me that I have exploited his wages'; and similarly Driver and Gray in their interpretation of the verse. In any event, it would appear that the words, 'If my land has cried out against me, and its furrows have wept together', allude to a hidden sin, and therefore it is impossible to try him for it. Likewise unclear is v. 21, 'If I have raised my hand against the fatherless, because I saw help in the gate'. Driver and Gray, Dhorm, and others interpret this as an abnegation of the use of force, despite the fact that Job's high position permitted this.

64. Compare 'I have sworn to the Lord...that I would not take a thread or a sandal-thong, or anything that is yours' (Gen. 14.22-23); 'The Lord has sworn by his right hand and by his mighty arm: "I will not again give your grain to be food for your enemies...but those who garner it shall eat it"' (Isa. 62.8); 'If I forget you, O Jerusalem, let my right hand wither!' (Ps. 137.6); etc.

restoration of Job's fortunes is connected to the central motif of the book.

The circle of the trial motif has now been closed, and the background prepared for God's non-verbal response. This illuminates the unique situation of the speeches of Elihu and the answer of God.

In Elihu's first speech, ch. 32, the trial motif appears immediately in the heading that explains his very entering into the circle of the debate: 'He was angry at Job because he justified himself rather than God; he was angry also at Job's three friends because they had found no answer, although they had declared Job to be in the wrong' (32.2-3). Further along as well, Elihu makes considerable use of words from the semantic field of law and judgment (see below, Appendixes IV, V, VI), even addressing Job with words relating directly to his arguments concerning this matter:

> Answer me, if you can; set your words in order before me; take your stand…Behold, no fear of me need terrify you…Surely, you have spoken… 'I am clean, without transgression; I am pure, and there is no iniquity in me…he counts me as his enemy; he puts my feet in the stocks, and watches all my paths', etc. (33.5-11).

The centrality of the trial motif in Elihu's speech stands out, because (following the initial heading in the formula, 'And Elihu continued, and said') every paragraph therein begins by mentioning it. Thus 34.3-4: 'Let us choose what is right…for Job has said, "I am innocent, and God has taken away my right"', etc.; 35.2: 'Do you think this to be just? Do you say, "It is my right before God"'; 36.6: 'He does not keep the wicked alive, but gives the afflicted their right'.

But despite all this, Elihu's words do not contribute to the development of the motif. They do not contain any new ideas, nor do they provide any response either to Eliphaz's accusations in ch. 22 or to the decisive speech by Job in chs. 29–31. Moreover, from a structural viewpoint the taking root of the motif of the trial is a kind of remnant of the cycle of the motif which was closed in ch. 31. Just as, from the stylistic viewpoint, one finds in this speech a tendency to give a kind of summary of all of the previous speeches in the book, so it is regarding the trial motif: the awareness of the axial role which the motif plays in the book caused it to be presented as a central axis in the words of Elihu as well. Thus, this motif contributes to the setting up of Elihu's speech as a miniature sample of the book as a whole. For the conclusions which follow from this regarding the original relation of Elihu's speech to the book, see below, Chapter 8.

If ch. 31 indeed closes the verbal cycle of the trial motif, moving it into the realm of God's acting (or failure to act), and if Elihu's speech is indeed a kind of remnant, then the appearance of this motif in God's speech is even more astonishing—namely, in his 'proposal' that, if God's ways do not please him, Job should take upon himself the running of the world: 'Will you even put me in the wrong? Will you condemn me that you may be justified? Have you an arm like God...Hide them all in the dust together; bind their faces in the hidden place' (40.8-13). This statement is one of the threads connecting the cycle of the debates with the speech of God,[65] the most striking feature of which is its blatant ignoring of the words said by Job and the friends throughout the course of the debates. This connection is striking because in it alone one hears a sharp and harsh tone, mocking the very idea that one might criticize God by analogy to legal procedures. These verses deal with the trial motif in the same manner as does Elihu's speech: they weave the thread of the trial motif all the way through to the end of the book in a most emphatic style. As for what this implies regarding their authenticity, see below, Chapter 8.

Let me now summarize the conclusions to be drawn from our discussion of the trial motif.

i. The position of the motif within the book is to be examined from two points of view. The one, which might be called that of 'first reading', even though it is not necessarily such, is the point of view of the reader who approaches the text free of any *a priori* assumptions regarding the presence of such a motif within the book, and certainly with regard to its status. The second is that of the reader who, having reached the end of the book, weighs and evaluates anew various details to which he or she had not previously paid attention. In the 'first reading', we find the first hint of the trial motif in the opening speech of

---

65. Alter has noted the technique of creating a relation between the speech and the debates (1985: 94-109). Some of his analysis seems forced, but the argument itself, namely, that the speech contains elements connecting it with the book as a whole, seems to me to be correct. Huberman-Scholnick (1982: 529) argues that the Hebrew root שפט also has the meaning of rule, and thus God's speech connects with the trial motif: in the wake of God's speech, Job understands that the משפט for which he has been hoping also entails the acceptance of God's yoke as the ruler of the world, and that this is the lesson of the book. For a fuller discussion of God's speech and its relation to the book as a whole, see also Huberman-Scholnick 1987. Her approach implies that the entire book of Job is no more than an exercise in the semantics of the word משפט, an argument which seems to me rather doubtful.

Eliphaz (4.7); thereafter, it gradually grows, until it acquires a central position in Job's responses to Bildad (chs. 9–10) and to Zophar (ch. 13). In chs. 14–21, it is incorporated in a less prominent manner, reaching a new peak in ch. 22, which determines the nature of the motif and its centrality in Job's final speech, chs. 29–31.[66] In ch. 31 the motif sets the scene for the epilogue in ch. 42, in which the restoration of Job's fortunes 'twice as much' (42.10) serves as a non-verbal confirmation of his righteousness, as does the conclusion of the self-adjuration/accusation in ch. 31. In the light of this, one needs to re-evaluate the status of the trial motif in the prose prologue. Viewed retrospectively, it would seem that the framework for this motif is already established there in the axiomatic statement, repeated several times, of the absolute righteousness of Job. It is only the reader's constant awareness of this statement that gives the trial motif the status which it enjoys in the book. Without it, misgivings would arise concerning Job's righteousness, which would make shallower the questions of principle which the motif is used to emphasize. In brief, the definition of the trial motif as a central axis applies, not only to the speeches, but to the prose framework of the book.

On the other hand, there are several chapters which, in my judgment, do not fit smoothly into the developmental line of this motif, either because they contain only a faint echo of it (chs. 15–20, 25), because it is completely missing from them (chs. 26, 28), or because its appearance is excessively prominent and therefore seems artificial (chs. 32–37). Precisely because of the key position held by this motif within the book, these exceptions stand out and require that we see this as a problem requiring solution. This matter too will be discussed below, in Chapter 8.

ii. The trial motif includes a quasi-dramatic element because it arouses a certain expectation, which is indeed realized in ch. 22, when Eliphaz presents his indictment pertaining to Job's past activities. Hence the weaving of the motif throughout the entire book constitutes a counter-

66. See the summarizing graph on p. 316. Regarding the status of the reader in a literary text, the distinction between the 'real reader' and 'theoretic reader', the dynamic of reading and the two-directional understanding of the text, as well as other issues pertaining to the theoretical aspect of our discussion of the trial motif, see *Semeia* 48 (1989). Together with the theoretical discussions, one will also find there extensive important bibliography, as well as literary analyses of chapters from the New Testament, in the centre of which there stands the question of the relation between the reader and the written word. The theoretical articles are concentrated on pp. 3-80. For more on these questions, see Perry 1979.

balance to its non-dramatic, theoretical elements. This may be understood because, given the absence of a tradition of abstract philosophical discussion in biblical literature, the author needed dramatic elements within which to weave the theoretical elements. The introduction of the motif at the beginning of the book, when there is not yet any poetic necessity for it, allows it to be developed gradually and naturally, so that at the crucial moment, once the attempts to explain what befell Job in terms of the various doctrines of retribution have been played out, it can serve as a life-belt to hold on to. And indeed, this possibility is realized in chs. 29–31, in which the theoretical aspects of the book are completely supplanted, and it is turned in an existential 'dramatic' direction. In this respect, chs. 29–31 constitute a suitable preparation for the speech of God (albeit not for the speech of Elihu), which likewise rejects the possibility of a theoretical explanation for Job's catastrophe, as I shall explain below in Chapter 7. This literary move also has a psychological justification, namely mimesis: it is convenient for Job to adhere to hard facts—his righteousness in practice—rather than to struggle with theological speculations. If, immediately following the disaster, his involvement in theoretical doctrines of retribution helped Job by creating an intellectual sublimation, during the course of the book this same intellectual involvement became intolerable, and the trial motif comes to save Job from this confusion. It also saves the author from the same difficulty, because the final stage of the motif in ch. 31 opens for him a convenient literary option by which to conclude the work, without needing to resolve the theological issues in principle.

iii. There is no doubt that the trial motif may properly be described as a structural element belonging to the framework of the book. In this respect, the book of Job resembles the psalmic supplications of individuals, in which the trial motif sometimes fulfils a similar function, and differs from the Mesopotamian works, 'I Will Praise the Lord of Wisdom' and 'The Babylonian Theodicy', whose numerous points of similarity to the book of Job have been noted above. In the latter two works, there is not so much as an echo of the trial motif. Hence, notwithstanding the perplexity they do express regarding God's manner of rulership, their submissive, non-rebellious character is emphatically felt in contrast to the book of Job. In this respect, they follow in the path of Mesopotamian supplication literature. There, too, the trial motif is either not mentioned at all[67] or fulfils a purely marginal role, and is not an integral part of the

---

67. See, for example, the supplication to Nargel, given in Koch 1969: 179.

framework of the work. It is thus, for example, in the Supplication to
Ishtar (see Weiss 1967: 169-73); within the framework of the praises to
the goddess, the poet says: 'For you are great and you are supreme...
you judge the people with truth and righteousness' (ll. 23-25), and no
more than that. His hopes for Ishtar's assistance depend upon her
mercies: 'Mercy upon my miserable body...Mercy upon my sick heart...
mercy on my spirit...', etc. (ll. 46-50), and so on.

There is thus a substantial difference between the position of the trial
motif in biblical supplication literature and the book of Job, and its
marginal status in the Mesopotamian literature. Hence, an argument
such as that of Bentzen that the book of Job, like 'I Will Praise the Lord
of Wisdom', was intended for cultic use, is incorrect, even if such a
statement were proven regarding the Mesopotamian works. One must
similarly reject his suggestion that the book of Job be defined as a
'dramatization of a dirge' (see above, p. 36 n. 8). Moreover, notwithstanding my conjecture that the trial motif plays a structural role both in
biblical supplication literature and in the book of Job, the book of Job is
unique in its use of this motif. From a structural viewpoint, it serves here
as a central axis throughout the length of the book, whereas in the
supplicatory literature it merely serves to bridge two sections (namely,
the description of the poet's misfortune and the expression of his trust in
God's help). This characterization is connected with the unique role
played by the motif in the system of arguments in the book of Job: in
biblical supplication literature the idea of the trial frees the poet from his
own psychological suffering, whereas in the book of Job his distress
deepens the more the motif is developed, as it becomes increasingly
clear that God, who is meant to be a righteous judge, evades judgment.
We find here that the idea assumes a rebellious character, totally opposed
to the conventions of both biblical and Mesopotamian supplications.

From our examination of those matters that are connected both substantively and associatively with the trial motif, we find that the motif
develops in a series of peaks and troughs, whose zeniths are the
speeches by Job in chs. 9–10, 13, 29–31, and Eliphaz's speech in ch. 22.
By contrast, several chapters (15–20, 26, 28, 32–37) seem to deviate
from this pattern of development. We may arrive at similar conclusions
by examining the motif using another method: namely, through an
examination of the distribution of key words from the semantic field of
law and judgment: שפט (judge); עוד (witness); רין (quarrel/dispute); נקי
(clean/innocent); צדק (justice, righteousness); חטא (sin); פשע (transgression/

crime); עָוֹן (iniquity); עַוְּת (distortion/miscarriage of justice); רֶשַׁע (evil/ wicked). The details of this data are presented in Appendix IV and in the diagram that follows it. It becomes clear through this that the trial motii creates a graph which goes up and down throughout the length of the book, and that in a number of chapters there is no exact correlation between the substantive importance of the motif and the distribution of 'trial words'. We thus have the following models.

a. Full correspondence between the two systems (i.e., the semantic and the substantive) appears in chs. 9–10. The importance of these chapters for the development of the motif matches the abundance of trial words therein.

b. An opposite kind of correspondence appears in chs. 16–20, 25, 26, and 28. These do not contribute substantially to the development of the motif, as is expressed in the small number or total absence of trial words therein.

c. A less clear-cut correspondence is found in chs. 13, 22, and 31, where the number of trial words does not reflect the full importance of these chapters for the development of the motif.

d. There is no correspondence at all between the crucial importance of chs. 29–30 for the development of the motif, and the (limited) use of trial words therein.

It seems to me that groups (a) (c) and (d) indicate the varied ways in which this motif is developed. Had there been full correspondence between the concentration of trial words and their thematic importance in all of these chapters—that is, had all of them belonged to group (a)—there would have been a uniform abundance of such terminology, which would have been dull. Group (b) may create the impression that it does not fit in well with the course of development of the trial motif. Alongside it, one may distinguish another group (e), including such chapters as 11, 12, 14, and 23, in which there is likewise a correspondence between the absence of trial words and the lack of other expression of the trial motif, but which nevertheless fit into the development of the motif by the creation of a deliberate delay, which allows it to be spread through the entire length of the book. The distinction between this group and group (b) is subject to the judgment of the reader, and it is doubtful whether one may set forth objective standards regarding this matter. I will refer to this matter again in Chapter 8 when I shall examine the question of the original edition of the book. Chapters 32–37, the speeches of Elihu,

A Blemished Perfection

constitute a group unto themselves (group f), in which there is an inverse relation between the semantic and thematic aspect. We previously saw that the trial motif in Elihu's speech constitutes a kind of remnant, but from the lexicographical viewpoint represents a peak in the use of trial words. In this, we return to the same phenomenon which we observed in our analysis of the shaping of the characters: the author of the speeches of Elihu saw the entire book before his eyes, took note of several of its important characteristics, but used this insight in insensitive and exaggerated ways. This might be compared to someone who would add yellow paint to Van Gogh's well-known picture of a chair: while this colour is consistent with the general tone of the painting, it has inner tension as it stands precisely because the predominance of the yellow is muted despite its being the dominant colour; the addition of yellow would detract from this, by removing this tension. I shall discuss below the conclusions to be drawn with regard to the authenticity of these sections, and from the unusual appearance of the motif in the speech of God. However, it is important to reiterate that our classification is not intended to pigeonhole all of the chapters into one or another group, as if the motif was developed according to a precise plan. Such full response to a well-designed master plan is inconsistent with the literary conventions which we noted in the earlier chapters of this study, and it is doubtful whether they in fact correspond to the creation of any artistic work. Therefore, one should not attempt to 'explain' each and every phenomenon; at times, lack of explanation may be a more suitable response to one or another literary question.

4. *Summary*

The results of our examination of the unifying mimetic elements in the book appear below, in Appendix VII. The following are the most striking facts that emerge from it:

i.   The central unifying elements are the development of the central figures and the trial motif, which continue throughout the length of the book. However, whereas the trial motif appears in the speeches of all of the friends, characterization only pertains to Job and Eliphaz. We therefore find that the trial motif is the primary device uniting the book as a whole into one flowing continuity, with the characterization of Job and Eliphaz as a secondary device.

ii.   The first cycle of debates is more fully developed than the two cycles that follow.

iii.   The most fully crystallized of the four literary blocks examined is the speech of Elihu. This results from the fact that the tendency towards intensification, which can be presented in the speeches of the other friends through the three-fold cycle, cannot be expressed in a speech presented in one fell swoop.

The statistical mean of the unifying elements is as follows (see Appendix VII): first cycle—2.66; second cycle—1.71; third cycle—1.5; Elihu's speech—2.83.

iv.   The mean number of unifying elements classified by distribution among the speeches of the friends, is as follows: Job—2; Eliphaz—3.25; Bildad—0.66; Zophar—1.5; Elihu—2.83.

v.   In nearly every chapter one finds at least one unifying element. Exceptions to this rule are the following: chs. 18 (Bildad), 20 (Zophar), 24 (Job), 25 (Bildad), and 28 (Job). In two chapters one finds only one unifying element (chs. 17, 26), but with the following difference between them: in ch. 17 this element ('the moulding of the characters') extends over the entire chapter, whereas in ch. 26 the unifying element ('polemical connections') refers to a purely technical connective phrase in the first three verses alone.

The most striking conclusion to be derived from this chapter of our study pertains to the very nature of the book of Job. In the Chapter 3, I observed that two substantive literary features of the book, which are also authentic, are the tendency to emphasize structural and schematic lines, and the difficult language. It is now apparent that there are grounds for arguing that the tendency toward mimesis is also among the substantive features of the book.[68] The extension of mimesis throughout the speeches and its multi-faceted nature indicate that it is among the authentic characteristics of the work. At the end of Chapter 4, I suggested a partial answer to the question as to the nature of the aesthetic problem confronted by the author of Job. In the light of the conclusions which we have now reached, we may add the following: mimesis is the central factor (alongside structure and the dramatic framework) that

68. I take issue with the position of von Rad (1972: 209-10) that the polemical character of the book is entirely secondary, and that the book is entirely lacking in any tendency to portray personal or 'spiritual biography' features.

gives the book significance beyond that of an anthology. Its contribution lies in the creation of an emotional response on the part of the reader towards the figures and problems with which the book deals. Thus the reader is led to participate on an emotional level in the problem of divine justice, which by its very nature is intellectual. This factor has important implications for the reader's reaction to the various approaches presented concerning the subject of God's justice.

We have nevertheless seen that the unifying mimetic factors do not completely negate the catalogic-sporadic elements of the book, and that not all of those means which could have united it more tightly were utilized completely. In the first cycle, the unifying elements are stronger than the divisive ones, providing us with an orderly sequence of dialogues; however, in the following two cycles the independent elements are more powerful. The chapters in the second cycle are only unified by the figures of Job and Eliphaz and by the trial motif, but as these two elements do not appear in the speeches of Bildad (ch. 18) and Zophar (ch. 20), we find these speeches standing out awkwardly from the flow of the book. In the third cycle, not only does Bildad's speech seem unconnected (ch. 25), but so too do a number of chapters attributed to Job (chs. 24 and 28). If there is a literary defect here, one may attribute it in principle to the catalogue tradition of the wisdom and psalm literature. By this I do not mean to imply that the author wished to nullify the catalogic nature of the book completely, and refrained from doing so only because he yielded to certain literary conventions which, as it were, did not 'allow' him to do so. Nor do I claim that, even had this been his goal, he would have been unable to succeed in realizing this due to the absence of an appropriate literary tradition. My argument is rather that, because of the literary conventions, he was unable *ab initio* to set for himself such a goal, and it was only his artistic instinct, and not any theoretical knowledge, that led him to confront and modify the catalogic elements in the book. However, can one really consider this acrobatic balancing on the thin line between catalogue and coherent dramatic work as a literary fault? Indeed, it suits remarkably well the manner in which the author confronts his subject, enabling him to manoeuvre between a fixed position concerning the issue of divine justice, and the adoption of the posture of one who stands aside, as the editor of a catalogue. On a deeper level, it reflects the tortuous path which Job undergoes between 'He destroys both the blameless and the wicked' (9.22) and 'I know that my Redeemer lives' (19.25); between the wish to be judged by God and the fear of such a judgment. Hence, that which might be considered a fault, from a theoretical-abstract point of view in isolation from the work itself, in actuality contributes to its integrity. Without this 'fault' its artistic perfection would in fact be defective.

But it is doubtful whether this theoretical explanation of the disconnection of several chapters applies in equal measure to all of them. I would suggest applying it with greater force to chs. 24 (Job), 18, 25 (Bildad), and 20 (Zophar). The awkwardness of these latter chapters may also be explained against the background of the lack of a literary tradition of fashioning various additional figures apart from the main figure. This claim has less force with regard to ch. 28, and perhaps also with regard to ch. 26, which are attributed to Job, but these seem to be exceptions from the totality of the speeches attributed to him in the book, as I shall explain below.

Another example of the dialectic character of the data which we have gathered is the speech of Elihu. As we have seen, this is the most well-shaped speech in the book, with numerous unifying elements. This factor also stands out in the light of the relatively high concentration of trial words in this speech (Appendix VII). Nevertheless, I do not find this a proof of its authenticity because of the possibility that a later author wished to further crystallize the book, and therefore deliberately made extensive use of unifying elements of the type found in the rest of the book. One therefore needs to devote a separate discussion to the distinction between original text and additions, taking into consideration other factors apart from the existence or absence of unifying elements. A summarizing discussion of these questions will appear in Chapter 8.

Chapter 6

ON THE DIFFICULT LANGUAGE OF THE BOOK OF JOB

We have noted, during the course of this attempt to examine the book of Job in terms of the aesthetic criteria which it fixed for itself, that one of its major characteristics—together with its tendency toward schematism, its emphasis upon structural elements, and its mimetic tendencies—is its difficult language. In the present chapter I shall elucidate various issues pertaining to the difficult language of the book.

The phrase 'difficult text' is not a scientific definition, but an empirical-subjective description. What is difficult for one reader may be transparent to another; at other times, a given literary text may seem to be readily understood because one has not fully delved into its true meaning. Should such a text be described as 'difficult'? How numerous do the difficulties need to be in order to 'entitle' a given text to be described as 'difficult', and what is their nature? Or is the true measure perhaps the level of the difficulties and not their quantity? It is clear that we are not dealing with a scientific term; nevertheless, the characterization of the book of Job as a 'difficult book' is not a subjective one, being universally accepted, even if scholars may disagree as to the theoretical definition of a 'difficult text'. Tur-Sinai, for example, opens his commentary on the book of Job with a motto from Isa. 29.11 and the words: 'Indeed, a sealed book is the biblical Book of Job'. Virtually all of the exegetes of the book concur in this opinion, each one observing in his or her own way that its language is more abstruse than most, if not all, of the other books of the Bible. For that reason, I cannot avoid a discussion of certain general questions pertaining to this feature of the book, even if I will refrain from systematic exegesis, which is not our concern here. The basic question to be resolved is the source of the difficulties in the understanding of the book. Are they accidental? Do they originate in various peregrinations in the original text? Or are they to be perceived as an inseparable part of its poetic norms, similar to the other characteristics discussed in the previous chapters? The basic assumption of our discussion is that knowledge of the linguistic characteristics of a literary work will enable us better to understand the exigencies which determine its nature. Language, with all its possibilities and limitations, decisively determines the ability of an author to express himself.

1. *The Data*

The difficulties involved in understanding a text written in natural language may be the result of any one of several factors: complicated or unusual syntax—whether standard but idiosyncratic, or non-standard—either on the level of the individual sentence or that of the paragaraph; use of vocabulary that is unfamiliar to the reader; extensive use of unusual metaphors; an unusually high level of abstraction; highly personal associations between phrases, sentences or paragraphs.

In attempting to explain why a given text is not clear to the reader, one first needs to determine the nature of the difficulty encountered. In the case of a biblical book, it seems rather unlikely that the latter two factors would apply: the Bible is bereft of texts written on a highly abstract level, and the literary practice of extremely personal-associative connections is likewise alien to biblical literature, as it is to ancient literature generally. As for the syntactic aspect, the poetics of Job does not deviate from that of biblical poetry generally. Like the latter, it is dominated by various kinds of parallelism, which also serve the reader as an explicit exegetic tool.[1] It may indeed be that there are more syntactic problems in the book of Job than in other biblical books, as there are indeed verses which present syntactic riddles. Thus it would seem appropriate within this framework to dwell also upon the syntactic aspect. I do not do so because I have not found any means of classifying syntactic difficulties into groups to facilitate the discussion of their nature and the unravelling of the causes of their syntactic difficulties. Moreover, it

---

1.   Kugel (1981) denies that one may speak of poetry in the Bible at all, and even attempts to show that it is lacking in real parallelism, in the sense of 'doubling of the subject in different words'. He places strict technical limitations on the concept of poetry; his opinion that there is no parallelism in the Bible is based upon the assumption that no language has true synonyms, and that hence any given thing can be said in only one manner. Yet even if we accept these arguments in principle, they do not refute the existence of the phenomenon of parallelism in a certain limited and well-defined portion of the biblical writings, and at most one may perhaps seek other definitions for it.

rapidly became clear to me that a large number of those difficulties which appear to be syntactical originate in fact in difficult words rather than in departures from accepted sentence structure.[2] Under such circumstances, an examination of the syntactical aspects would require exegetical involvement in a considerable number of verses of obscure syntax, which would in turn require a complete departure from the framework of the present work.

I therefore saw fit to concentrate primarily upon the lexicographical aspect of the difficult language of the book. Indeed, many scholars who turned their attention to this problem have seen it as primarily dependent upon the vocabulary of the book, the solutions which they proposed relating to this aspect. My own focus upon the lexicographical aspect likewise stems from my wish to test these solutions. I shall begin by examining the data concerning *hapax legomena*, and thereafter turn to the data pertaining to the presence of foreign words in the book. I shall also give a statistical sample of the distribution of metaphors, which also constitutes an important lexicographical element.

A non-conventional lexicon, such as that creating a 'difficult text', is characterized by the extensive use of unusual words. Since their rarity is primarily expressed through *hapax legomena*,[3] our discussion shall concentrate upon them at this stage. True, the uniqueness of a word within a given corpus does not necessarily indicate its rarity (and hence its 'difficulty') within the overall context of that language. Thus, for example, the word מעצד ('plane'[?]) appears only once in the entire Bible (Isa. 44.12), but the verb appears in the Gezer inscription, from which we may conclude that it was reasonably common and well understood. The word זדה ('breach'[?]) does not appear in the Bible at all, but is found in the Shiloah inscription, for which reason one may assume that it was common and understood. Nevertheless, if one is not speaking of any one specific *hapax legomenon*, but of a high concentration of *hapax legomena* within a given corpus, such a concentration does in fact

---

2.   In a study devoted to the syntax of biblical poetry, Sapan did not find any unique features of the poetry of the book of Job. In an appendix, he takes note of the syntactic characteristics of the books of Psalms, Proverbs and Job, among which he finds only one marginal detail unique to the book of Job—the use of לא rather than אין in one type of sentence (1981: 156-58, 174).

3.   From both a substantive and a statistical viewpoint. Thus, for example, Rabin (*EncBib*, IV, pp. 1066-1070) notes that the number of ('isolated') *hapax legomena* in the Bible reaches some 2,440 (out of an overall lexicon of some 7,000-8,000 words), while the number of words that appear twice is no more than 500-600.

constitute a definite stylistic feature, and it is reasonable to associate it with the term 'difficult language'. Hence, one needs to ascertain whether the concentration of *hapax legomena* in the book of Job is greater than in other books of the Bible, to the degree that we may see it as a characteristic of the book. But before undertaking the examination itself, it is worthwhile noting that, together with the recognition that every author does make use, among other things, of *hapax legomena*, at times it is possible that in the Bible these may be the result of a simple copyist's error.[4] Thus, upon encountering a rare word in the Bible, the exegete first needs to decide whether to assume that the text is corrupted, correct it according to his or her best judgment, and then interpret it; or whether to accept the reading as it is, and then, notwithstanding its rarity or uniqueness, attempt to interpret it on the basis of its context, etymology, relation to other Semitic languages, and the like. However, unlike the exegete, someone who sets out to discuss the lexicographical composition of the book of Job need only be disturbed by this problem if they assume that here, in this book, errors resulting from the process of copying are quantitatively greater, in a striking manner, than in any other biblical book. In such a case, it might be considered sufficient to state that the difficult language of the book stems from particularly poor transmission of the text. By contrast, the exegetical stage meant to follow in the wake of this statement involves the correction of the errors; however, it seems doubtful to me whether there would be any justification for discussing the overall linguistic nature of the original book on the basis of such a conjectured reconstruction of the text. In any event, if such is indeed the case, proper methodology would require us, at the outset of our discussion, to answer the question as to whether the lexicographical difficulties of the book ought to be resolved on the assumption

4.   However, an examination of *hapax legomena* in the Bible reveals that their relative distribution, in comparison with other literary works, falls below what one would expect statistically. That is to say, the uniqueness of a word alone is unable to justify its 'correction'. See Greenspahn 1977: 24-74. He was also surprised at the small number of *hapax legomena* in the Bible. A partial reason for this phenomenon may relate to the protracted process of transmission of the biblical text, during which copyists tended to 'correct' unclear words, reducing the number of *hapax legomena* over the course of time. This explanation is the opposite of that of Rabin (though it perhaps does not entirely contradict it), namely, that even though isolated words 'are a perfectly natural phenomenon and there is no basis for the opinion that they are corrupt', nevertheless 'an isolated word is less protected from scribal error than a common word'.

that its text is more corrupt than any other biblical book, and that hence comes unique linguistic coloration. Such a question must be answered with a resounding no—but not because it is theoretically impossible to assume that the text of a given biblical book is more corrupted than that of other books. While such a thing may be possible, we can only accept such an assumption if we have clear evidence, apart from the difficult language itself, to prove the large number of corruptions during the process of shaping and copying of the text. Even so, we would need to establish that this is not the result of the particularly difficult language of the original version, which engendered misunderstandings on the part of the copyists, and hence corruptions in their copies. Under such circumstances, it would be correct to say that the numerous corruptions were caused by the difficult original version, and not by carelessness on the part of the copyists. In any event, there is no evidence to indicate that the text of the book of Job underwent substantially different kinds of metamorphoses than the text of the other biblical books; hence, its difficult language cannot be attributed to the history of its transmission.[5]

The seemingly simple concept of *hapax legomena* in fact combines several different meanings: unique forms, unique verbal roots, or a unique meaning of forms or roots which are not in themselves unique (i.e., 'homonyms' or 'homographs'). But even this secondary classification is not unequivocal. The term 'unique forms' might include all the minor variations listed in the *Masorah Parva*, differences between plene and defective spellings, and the like; or it might be used without including such minor differences. If one is dealing with unique roots, one needs to decide how one is to deal with 'variant' roots (i.e., variant spellings of common roots due to transposition of consonants, such as כבש and כשב; שמלה and שלמה, and the like), or with consonants having dual forms (such as כעס and כעש; גרש and גרש.) Similarly, the different definitions of

---

5.   Beyond the theoretical aspect, Dhorm's statement (1926: cxcvi) that, relative to the number of verses in the book (1,069, according to Ginzberg's count), there are not many scribal errors therein, seems to be correct. Likewise, comparison between the Masoretic Text and the LXX does not indicate any unusual textual history of the book of Job. The particularly free nature of the Greek translation of the book of Job ('far from being a translation in the strict sense of the term', Orlinsky 1958: 229) indicates that already the Greek translator had encountered a difficult text. See on this Driver and Gray 1921: lxxi-lxxvi. Between the MT and the LXX there are a number of additions and lacunae, and all told the latter is one-sixth shorter than the MT, as noted by Origen. But this is not substantively different from what is found in other books. See on this also Jellicoe 1968: 136-37.

the term[6] present difficulties for anyone who sets out to examine the uniqueness of the book of Job from this respect, as it is impossible to place the numerical data provided by the various different studies under one rubric. This difficulty is further exacerbated by the fact that the uniqueness of a word is determined on more than one occasion only after a scholar has corrected a word which in their opinion was corrupted, and hence was added to or removed from the list of *hapax legomena*. Nor is there always common agreement as to whether a given word is a proper noun, in which case it is not considered a *hapax legomenon*, or whether it is some other part of speech, and is considered to be one. This situation finds statistical expression in the different numbers of *hapax legomena* given by different scholars.[7]

As in this context it suffices that we describe the situation of the *hapax legomena* in the book of Job relative to the other biblical books, and not in an absolute sense, I would propose the following method by which to overcome the problem of different criteria for defining *hapax legomena* in different studies: namely, that one examine each study in its own right and thereafter compare the data. We may thereby obviate the error of mingling together different criteria in one examination. A similar solution will be applied to the examination of foreign words in the book, further on in this chapter.

From our comparison of the distribution of words defined as *hapax*

---

6. The mediaeval Hebrew grammarians used such terms as 'it has no like' (אין לו אח/רע/דומה/דמיון) but inconsistently and without any clearcut definition. See Greenspahn 1977: 4-5. The study by Cohen is based upon the following definition of *hapax legomena*: 'Any biblical word whose root occurs in but one context' (1978: 7). Greenspahn mostly discusses 'absolute *hapax legomena*', defined as 'Any word other than a proper noun which is the only exemplification of its root within the Hebrew sections of the received text as represented in the BHK' (1977: 48). However, in the comparative tables he also relates to 'non-absolute Hapax Legomena', consistent with a broader definition, such as that given in the OED: 'A word or form of which only one instance is recorded in a literature or author'. See Greenspahn 1977: 24. For a theoretical discussion of the question of definition, see pp. 24-41.

7. I mentioned above Rabin's enumeration (based upon Kohler—2,440 *hapax legomena*); according to Cohen's definition, their number reaches 258 (as far as I could tell from the various lists in his book, which include words that he corrected). According to the lists of the mediaeval grammarians, they number 152. I refer to the works of Judah Hayyuj, Ibn Quraysh, Ben Saruq, R. Saadya Gaon, and the anonymous author of *She'elot 'Atiqot*. See Cohen 1978: 1-4, 101-105. According to the count of Greenspahn (1977: 46) the overall number of *hapax legomena* in the Bible is 1,501, while the number of 'absolute' ones is 289 (plus another 33 doubtful cases).

legomena by various scholars and exegetes (Appendix VIII), we learn that the relative number of *hapax legomena* in the book of Job is far greater than that of other books in the Bible, but that it is not statistically significant. The only exception to this is the Song of Songs, which has a disproportionately large number of *hapax legomena*. This may be explained both in the light of the special subject of the book, and by the fact of its being a later work: the gap in time between the date of its composition and that of the majority of the other biblical books may be measured in centuries. To this one may perhaps also add a third reason—its close relation to Egyptian literary sources.[8] Another method of examination,[9] given in Appendix IX, yields similar, if not identical, results:[10] a relatively large but not deviant number of *hapax legomena* in the book of Job relative to other biblical books. How is one to explain this fact? I shall postpone the answer to this question to a later stage, after other linguistic characteristics of the book become clear to us, as the phenomenon of *hapax legomena* cannot be isolated from the other phenomena to be examined.

The discussion of *hapax legomena* will be incomplete without a discussion of the related phenomenon of homonyms: roots that occur in the Bible more than once, but which appear only once in a given meaning (such as מכרתיהם [RSV: 'their swords'; Gen. 49.5], which is certainly not to be interpreted on the basis of the commonly used root מכר, 'to sell'). There can be no doubt that extensive use of homonyms, perhaps even more so than the large number of *hapax legomena* as such, may be an important factor in the creation of a difficult text. But if, as we have seen, scholars disagree as to the number of *hapax legomena*, there certainly is not and cannot be any consensus regarding homonyms. This

8. Concerning the late date of the book (the Hellenistic period) and its close relationship to ancient Egyptian literature, see Fox 1985.

9. 'It is based on a comparison of the actual number of a particular phenomenon per unit of text with that which would result from a perfectly even distribution; this difference is squared and divided by the number one would have expected in an even distribution' (Greenspahn 1977: 49-50, where there is a more detailed explanation). Not all those who deal with this subject are in full agreement regarding the theoretical aspect involved in examining the distribution of words in the text. I shall refrain from taking a position here on the subject. See on this Yule 1944; C. Muller 1969.

10. Indeed, incomplete correspondences between the deviations of *hapax legomena* of both kinds, and comparison of the conclusions of Appendix IX with those of Appendix VIII, suggest the degree of caution which ought to be taken towards statistical examinations of this type.

is so because of the considerable subjective element involved in determining that a given well-known word has a unique meaning in a given
context. For this reason, there is no point in compiling a comparative list
of homonyms in the books of the Bible or deriving conclusions on its
basis. The subjective nature of the definition of words as 'homonyms'
may be illustrated from Tur-Sinai, who tends to argue for the presence
of a large number of homonyms in the book of Job, and interprets many
common words as having unique meanings. The following are several
examples of words which he sees as homonyms:

שחק (35.5; 36.28; 37.18, 21; 38.37) is not the heavens, as is usual, but
clouds which have worn away and broken up; קץ (6.11; 16.3), usually
translated 'end', is 'purpose'; רוח (19.17), usually 'spirit', becomes a
'sigh'; קשח (39.16), usually 'hard', is 'distanced' or 'abandoned'; בד
(usually 'branch') is an olive or wine press in 9.8, and also 'strap' in
18.13; ברח (usually 'flee' or 'run away') is a flower (14.2), and a bird
(27.22); חדוד (usually 'sharp') is the iron blade of a plough in 41.22; חדל
(usually 'stop' or 'cease') is 'to fall behind in one's work' in 14.6; חסידה
(usually 'stork') is 'beloved', 'cherished' in 39.13; כחש (usually 'deny')
is 'to hide' in 38.2. These are but a few of the 300 words cited by Tur-
Sinai whose meaning, according to him, is unique.[11] But not only is
there no need for us to accept these specific interpretations in every
case; even if we accept them and their like, there remains some doubt as
to whether it is correct to define all of them as 'homonyms'. Most seem
to be words used in their regular, basic meaning, which the poet has
coloured with a slightly different shade of meaning; such, after all, is the
way of every poet. In fact, it is doubtful whether, in any serious literary
text, there are many words whose meaning in context is not in some
sense 'unique'.

If the book of Job indeed makes considerable idiosyncratic use of
words which take on a unique coloration—and the impression (only!) is
that such is indeed the case—this constitutes a stylistic characteristic, for
which it is worth seeking an explanation. But even if there is no proof
that the number of homonyms is in fact greater than in any other book,
there is still insufficient ground for the statement that the large number

---

11. For purposes of comparison, it should be noted that Cohen (1978: 140-43)
counts only 21 homonyms in the book of Job. On the methodological aspect relating
to the identification of homonyms, see Grabbe 1977: 136-38. On pp. 138-44, he
relates in principle to the semantic and lexicographical aspects of comparative philology as raised to him in the course of his study of the book of Job.

of homonyms is additional proof that the book of Job is a translation from the Aramaic,[12] a claim which we shall examine below.

I shall now turn to examine the presence of foreign words in the book of Job in order to determine whether its difficult language stems from their unusually widespread presence. This examination, summarized in Appendix X, is based upon Barr's book on comparative philology, in which he brings a random sampling of 334 words from the Bible that are discussed and interpreted on the basis of foreign languages. On the basis of this list, which is presumably also representative, I would like to examine the distribution of foreign words in the book of Job as compared to their distribution in other books of the Bible.[13]

The table suffers from a number of limitations, which should not be ignored: the corpuses examined are not uniform, either in terms of period or authors; the words were counted on the basis of a random sample, as mentioned, and hence one must refrain from overly hasty conclusions. Barr emphasizes that he did not examine in a fundamental way every one of the words whose etymology he gave, and hence he is unable to state with certainty that every such etymology is established beyond all doubt; nevertheless, he believes that he has reached the truth. For our purposes, the methodological advantage of such a list is that its words were gathered from the various sources by a philologist, who weighed each suggestion substantively and was not guided by any *a priori* assumption concerning the presence of foreign words in one or another biblical book. Hence, even if there are differences of opinion concerning one or another specific statement of Barr's, one may assume that the statistical picture, which is what is significant in this matter, is substantially correct.

It clearly follows from this table that the book of Job is characterized by the extensive use of words that can be explained on the basis of their sense in languages other than Hebrew. The average numerical expression of 'foreign words' in all of the books of the Bible (with the exception of the book of Job) is 165.88, while the average for the book

---

12. 'The entire picture given above concerning the language and style of the book of Job, with all their characteristics and with all the difficulties they imply for the understanding of the book, is changed and corrected by our awareness of the fact that the main part of the poetry in the book, in its extant form, is a translation from an Aramaic source' (Tur-Sinai 1972: 367).

13. Barr 1968: 320-37. On the problematics involved in the identification of foreign words and the definition of the term, see Rabin, *EncBib*, IV, pp. 1070-1080.

of Job is 3.95 times greater than that for the Bible as a whole; 1.81 times greater than for the book of Proverbs; 2.38 times greater than for Isaiah 40–66; and 2.43 times greater than for Isaiah 1–39, which are the closest to Job in this respect.

Thus, if this table faithfully represents the distribution of foreign words in the Bible, one may state with some confidence that the use of foreign words is a definite stylistic feature of the book of Job.[14]

Another linguistic factor that may present difficulty for the understanding of a literary work is the excessive use of metaphor, which is a characteristic sign of a poetic text. However, it is difficult to conduct a precise comparative examination of the concentration of metaphors in a literary text. First, there exists a problem in the definition of 'metaphor':[15] it is not always possible to decide whether a particular idiom is metaphorical in the full sense of the term,[16] and at times it is even difficult to distinguish between a true metaphor and a 'frozen' metaphor. This distinction is very important for our examination, because a frozen metaphor does not necessarily create difficulty in the understanding of the text as does a regular metaphor. Second, one encounters the problem of

---

14. Another list of 150 foreign words in the Bible is given by Ellenbogen (1962). However, we cannot utilize it, because it only includes words from the realm of realia: raw materials, articles produced by artisans, army, agriculture, public administration, and the like—but roots or verbal forms. He identified only six foreign words in Job: אד (36.27)—from Akkadian; אשפה (39.23)—from Akkadian; גמא (8.11)—from Egyptian; כתם (28.16, 19)—from Akkadian or Egyptian; ספיר (28.6, 16)—from Sanskrit (?); פטדה (28.19)—from an unknown source. If there is anything to be learned from such an examination for our subject, it is that, in comparison with other biblical books, Job does not make extensive use of foreign words from the realm of realia. Lists of a similar nature are given by Rabin, but they are not classified by book.

15. According to Aristotle (*Poetics*, ch. 21, 1457b8-10), a metaphor is a 'the application of an alien name by transference, either from genus to species, or from species to genus, or from species to species, or by analogy'. This definition is extremely broad. Today, the term 'metaphor' customarily refers only to 'transfer' 'by analogy of image' alone, and I used it here in this sense.

16. According to Richards (1936: 96), 'A word may be simultaneously both literal and metaphoric'. Much has been written concerning the theoretical aspects of metaphor, and I will not enlarge upon this point. See, for example: Beardsley 1958: 134-47; Black 1962: 28. Perdue (1991: 22-72) enlarged upon the theoretical aspects of metaphor in the realm of religion, analysing a number of basic metaphors through an anthropological approach. His study deals primarily with transformations of metaphors and paradigms in the book of Job. Extensive and up-to-date bibliographical references to the literature on the theory of metaphor is given there, p. 22, n. 1.

counting metaphors which are combined into one picture, such as 'who walks not in the counsel of the wicked, nor stands in the way of sinners, nor sits in the seat of scoffers' (Ps. 1.1). Should this be counted as one metaphor or as three, or perhaps even as five (walks in the counsel; way of sinners; stands; sits; seat of scoffers). Notwithstanding these reservations, I conducted a comparative sampling of the distribution of metaphors in the book of Job as opposed to another poetic text, the results of which are given in Appendixes XI-XII. I chose the Psalms, as they are more similar to the book of Job than are the prophetic books or the poems incorporated in the Pentateuch. I examined two blocks of the same size, Job 3–14 and Psalms 1–22. In order to minimize the seriousness of the above-mentioned methodological problems, uniform criteria were applied throughout the sample: frozen metaphors were not taken into account, because they do not constitute a linguistic problem, while complete pictures were not divided into isolated metaphors, for a similar reason. The purpose of the examination was to determine whether the number of metaphors in the book of Job is unusually large in comparison to that in Psalms. A positive answer to this question would indicate that this is another stylistic characteristic, which may also relate to the difficult language of the book.

And indeed, from my examination it became evident that the number of metaphors identified in the book of Job was 17 per cent higher than their number in the corresponding block in Psalms. Moreover, in the Psalms a larger proportion of the metaphors are stereotyped images, characteristic of the hymnic language (even if not frozen), their context known, and hence easier to understand. Thus, for example: to walk in a good / bad path (Ps. 1.1); 'many are rising against me' (3.2): 'thou didst smite...the cheek' (3.8); 'sinking' as an image for trouble and distress (9.16); hiding of the face (10.11); 'boasting tongue' (12.4); and so forth. However, one must emphasize, in addition to the reservations already offered above, that this examination does not enjoy adequate theoretical support, especially in the light of the limited size of the corpuses examined which hence may not present a representative sample. The conclusions given in the table ought to be weighed in accordance with this. Nevertheless, this seems adequate ground on which to base the impression that the large number of metaphors is one of the factors which contribute to the difficulty of the book of Job—a claim which I shall examine further on.

Before we begin to discuss the explanations offered for the unique language of the book, it should be re-emphasized that the data presented above are characteristic of the book as a whole, and not only of a portion of it. Quite a few studies have been devoted to the question as to whether one may distinguish linguistic blocks within the book which are exceptions to the rule. It would seem that a positive, unequivocal answer to this question may only be given with regard to the difference between the language of the prose frame-story and the poetic language in the body of the book.[17] Within the poetic sections, with which this chapter is exclusively concerned, I have not found substantial differences between the various literary units. *Hapax legomena*, homonyms, unique metaphors—all these are scattered throughout the length of the poems, and small differences of distribution do not diminish the linguistic uniformity of the book. The only literary block in which some scholars have found a stylistic uniqueness is that of the speeches of Elihu, chs. 32–37. Thus, Driver and Gray state that the language of these speeches is sufficiently distinctive so as to support the theory that they were not written by the author of the other speeches. The following are their principal findings: Elihu makes more extensive use of the divine name אל than do the other friends (19 times as against 36 times in the entire balance of the book); he reveals a definite preference for the first-person pronoun אני (9 times) as against אנכי (twice), unlike the friends (אני—15 times; אנכי—11 times); unlike the rest of the book, he only makes occasional use of such phrases as עלי, כמו, מני, למו, עלימו; he uses certain phrases which are not found in the dialogues, such as אנשי רשע (34.8, 10, 34, 36) as against מתי רשע ('people of evil') in the dialogues (11.11; 19.19; 22.15; 31.31); he seems to use slightly more Aramaisms, albeit they claim that this is not a clear-cut finding (Driver and Gray 1921: xlii-xlvii).

In any event, data such as these do not negate the uniform linguistic character of the book as regards its difficult language. They may perhaps contribute to the conjecture that the speeches of Elihu were not written by the author of the rest of the book, although even regarding this point there is no agreement among scholars.[18]

17. In the spirit of the Wellhausean documentary hypothesis, the use of the divine names יהוה, האלהים, אלהים, שדי, אלוה, אל, throughout the book is examined. Driver and Gray noted the uniqueness of the prose frame-story in its use of the Tetragrammaton, but correctly observed that this is not to be attributed to its having a different author, but to the unique nature of the frame-story. See Driver and Gray 1921: xxxv-xxxvi; Dhorm 1926: lxv-lxx.

18. See on this Chapter 8. Dhorm (1926: ciii) suggests that one exercise great

2. *Previously Suggested Solutions*

Against the background of the above data, I shall now test two conjectures concerning the composition of the book of Job which some scholars have proposed to explain its difficult language. The first is that the book was originally written in a different Hebrew dialect than the Judaean dialect common in the Bible; the second, that it is a translation into Hebrew from some foreign language. The distance between these two conjectures is not great, as the difficulty entailed in drawing a sharp and clear boundary line between dialect and language is well known. Hence, both of these conjectures relate to the same range of languages, which includes 'standard Biblical Hebrew', 'Northern Hebrew', Moabite, Ugaritic, Edomite, Aramaic, and Arabic. As the method of testing and proving applies equally to both these conjectures from a methodological viewpoint, the only distinction being among the various languages to which the language of the book of Job is compared, they shall be presented and examined together.

The conjecture that the book was composed in a different Hebrew dialect than that widespread in the Bible is directed in two separate geographical directions: northward and southward. In the northern group one may include, notwithstanding the differences in details among them, Freedman, Ceresko, Pope, Blummerde, Michel, Andersen, and others.

On the basis of the orthography of the book, Freedman stated that the book was originally northern and was written at an early date: it was composed among the exiles from Samaria in the seventh or early sixth century BCE (1969: 43). He did not present the basis for his statement that the book was only composed after the destruction of the northern kingdom, a point which does not necessarily follow from his explanation of the orthographic findings. Andersen, in his commentary, follows Freedman's linguistic claim, stating on its basis that the book took initial shape mostly in Gilead prior to the Assyrian conquest, and thereafter assumed final shape in Judah, during the reign of Josiah (1976: 63-64).[19]

---

caution in using stylistic tests to examine the authenticity of Elihu's speeches, but is convinced that they do have a certain uniqueness, though not overly definite. By contrast, Snaith (1968: 72-85) denies the assumption that the language used in the speeches of Elihu proves that they were not written by the author of the rest of the book. He rejects the datum that the distribution of Aramaisms and *hapax legomena* in the speech of Elihu is high relative to the rest of the book.

19. I do not intend to consider here the question of the date of the work, but only

Ceresko likewise follows in Freedman's wake, claiming that his own research confirms the theory of the latter as to the northern background of the book and its relation to the literatures of Canaan and Phoenicia.[20] Blummerde, Michel and Pope followed a similar direction. They all stressed the Phoenician and Ugaritic elements in the book, albeit they took care not to state on their basis the dialect in which it was composed.[21]

In the 'southern' group may be included such scholars as Kahana and Guillaume. In his commentary, Kahana stated that the author

> makes use of many phrases and expressions which can only be interpreted in light of the Arabic lexicon. He was clearly influenced by the Arabic language, which was dominant in those places that were in the environs of Arabia and Edom...Certainly the book also reflects influences and elements from the Idumean language, but these cannot be determined, because there are no remaining remnants of this language.

He likewise mentions the remarks of R. Zerahiah of Barcelona, who notes in his commentary on the book, *Tiqvat Enosh*, that, 'This book contains numerous foreign words, whose like do not appear in the Bible, but in the Arabic language' (16.16). Guillaume devotes a monograph to this subject, in which he concludes that the unusual language of the book of Job indicates that it was written among the Jews of Tema (in the area of the contemporary Hejaz) by an Arabic-speaking author.[22]

the question of the dialect supposedly reflected in the current text. Recently, Rendsburg (1990: 10-11) also expressed support for Freedman's view, despite the fact that he objects to several of his conclusions. He supports the opinion of Kaufmann (1988: 55) that the northern dialect of the book of Job is the result of a deliberate attempt to give the book a 'Trans-Jordanian' flavour.

20. Ceresko 1980: 196. On pp. 7-8 he declares his intention to seek additional evidence to strengthen Freedman's theory.

21. Michel (1987: 5) declares that he follows Dahood. He attempts to preserve the consonantal text while interpreting it according to the Ugaritic, on the assumption that the Ugaritic and Hebrew were in practice closest to one another in every possible respect. Similarly also Blummerde and Ceresko, as well as Pope, particularly in the third edition of his commentary. In the earlier editions he stressed the Aramaic elements in the book, reaching the conclusion that it was written after the Exile by an author who had visited the Aramaic-speaking community of Alexandria (1973: clxxvii). Pope wished by this means to explain passages which indicate (indeed?) that the author knew Egypt, such as 28.10—יאורים ('channels' or 'Niles'); 8.11—אגמון— which is none other than papyrus; 9.26—אניות אבה ('skiffs of reed'); 40.15-32— בהמות (hippopotamus); 7.1-2; 14.14—an allusion to Jewish soldiers of fortune.

22. Kahana 1924: 22-23; Guillaume 1968: 1. See Guillaume 1964, where he expresses this claim and attempts to show that there are no Aramaisms whatever in the

A sharper and more unequivocal theory holds that the book was not originally written in Hebrew, but that its Hebrew version is a translation, hence its difficult language. This theory was proposed by Ibn Ezra, who in his commentary to 2.11 writes:

> Our Sages, of blessed memory, said that Moses wrote the Book of Job, but it seems to me most likely that the book was translated. It is therefore difficult to interpret, as is the case of every translated book.

Concerning these remarks, Spinoza wrote:

> I wish he could have demonstrated this more convincingly, for we might therefore conclude that the Gentiles, too, possessed sacred books…And here I am also inclined to agree with Ibn Ezra that this book is a translation from another language, for its poetic style seems to be characteristic of the Gentiles…But these are mere conjectures, and not firmly founded.[23]

From his time down to our own day, various scholars have attempted to prove that the book was translated from some other Semitic language, thereby explaining its difficult language. In 1932 Fosster also suggested that the book was translated from Arabic.[24] Pfeiffer (1926) stated that it

book, apart from one word. However, he does not argue that this is a dialect, but a patois, characteristic of a bilingual society; however, for our purposes there is no significant difference between them. Most of Guillaume's proofs come from the realm of language, while others are invoked from realia and from the world of flora and fauna portrayed, in his opinion, in the book. He also finds the Babylonian conquest of the region of Tema reflected in the disasters depicted in ch. 1. In the words 'who bring their god in their hand' (12.6) he finds an allusion to Nebunaid. From the language of the prophet of consolation, 'that her time of [military] service is ended' (Isa. 40.2), he finds proof that Jews served in the army of Nebunaid. For more arguments of this sort, see Guillaume 1964: 1-15.

23. Spinoza, *Tractatus Theologico-Politicus* (Shirley 1989: 189).

24. Fosster observes the Arabian social and geographical background of the book. However, his main proofs are from the realm of language. He compares passages in the book to Arabic (especially to the Koran), arguing that only thus can they be understood. Thus, for example, the phrase ואחרון על עפר יקום ('and at last he will stand upon the dust', 19.25) is interpreted by him according to the passage in the Koran (9.85), *wa-la yaqum 'la qibri*, meaning, 'he shall not pray on my grave' (1932: 28). The word יראתך ('your fear'; 4.6; 22.4; and also 15.4), referring to the fear of God, is seen as taken from the Arabic, in which the root *tqwy* ('he shall fear') appears in this sense without being placed in conjunction with the noun 'God' or the like (p. 32). His proofs are generally unconvincing, and he even admits that they ought to be seen as material for thought rather than as proven conclusions which are beyond challenge.

was originally written in Edomite, but his impression is based upon the picture of society, the flora and fauna, and the world-view which he finds expressed in the book, and not upon any linguistic considerations (there being no extant data concerning the Edomite language): hence, this is not the appropriate forum in which to discuss his approach. Tur-Sinai argues that 'The Book of Job in its authentic poetical passages, in the words of Job and his friends, and in the speech by God, is translated from Aramaic', and was written by 'one of the Judaean exiles at the beginning of the Babylonian exile', and translated into Hebrew 'when the Babylonian exiles returned to Zion' (1972: 367, 371, 372).

Most of the proofs for the various opinions cited came from the realm of lexicography, which shall be discussed below. The argument of Freedman (1969) is unique in that it is based upon an orthographic examination of the book of Job. On the basis of his examination of the Masoretic Text (BHK edition, based upon MS Leningrad), he argues that, relative to the other biblical books, one may identify in the book of Job a large number of words from the weak verbs פ"י and פ"ו that are written defectively. This spelling reflects, in his opinion, a type of pro-nunciation in which the diphthongs *aw/ay* had already been contracted into the long vowels *e, o*. Since the process of contraction of the diph-thongs took place in northern Israel before it did in Judah, one may conclude from this datum that the book of Job is a northern Israelite work.

However, these conclusions must be rejected on both the methodolo-gical and the logical level. The statement that the contraction of the diph-thongs in the northern dialects of Canaanite preceded the same process in the south is widely accepted, being based *inter alia* upon a compari-son of northern Hebrew inscriptions with southern inscriptions from the same period. However, the data which he invokes to demonstrate that the book of Job follows a different system of spelling from the rest of the Bible with regard to פ"י and פ"ו verbs is not statistically convincing. See, for example, the table of data which he offers regarding the writing of the verb יסף in the active causative (*hif'il*) and the conclusions which he derives from it (Appendix XIII).

Regarding these data, Freedman comments that only in the book of Job and in the Pentateuch are the occurrences of יסף in plene few and far between in a definite way, as the Torah reflects an ancient spelling. But even if we assume that this is not accidental, what can we conclude from this? Certainly not that the Torah is a 'northern' work. Why then should we conclude such a thing regarding the book of Job? In fact, if one wishes to conclude anything from the data presented in the table, one needs to provide a coherent explanation regarding all of the data, and not just part of them. Yet in the block of the Former Prophets we find almost compete equivalence between plene and deficient spellings (see the two left-hand columns), while in the literary prophets the relation between them is 3 : 24. We can learn nothing from this fact, from which it follows that the method as a whole is incorrect.

The concluding datum of Freedman is that the sixteen פ"י and פ"ו[25] verbs in Job are written 64 times in plene and 38 times in defective, as opposed to the other books of the Bible, where they are written 1,667 times in plene and 159 times in defective. While this finding seems to be quite definite statistically, it does not necessarily lead to the conclusion suggested by Freedman.

The assumption that the method of writing the פ"י and פ"ו verbs in the Masoretic text indicates a northern origin for any biblical text needs to be examined in an entirely different manner: namely, to begin with known facts and to draw conclusions from them concerning that which is unknown. For our purposes, we may refer to those texts whose northern origin is generally accepted, such as the book of Hosea and certain of the Psalms. If it can be proven that there is a clear difference among these works in the spelling of פ"י and פ"ו verbs, we would be justified in making this datum a criterion for the examination of other texts. An examination which I conducted in the book of Hosea and in Psalms 77, 80, 81, which are generally accepted as northern,[26] reveals

---

25. For some reason, Freedman's study does not touch upon verbs from the roots ירש (והורישני), 9.19); יעד (יועדני), 38.28); הוליד (ילד, 40.14); אורך (ידה) ירש (תוגיון, 19.2); ינה 13.26; יורשו, 20.15) which might change the statistical picture somewhat.

26. Regarding the northern origin of these psalms, see Hoffman 1983: 102-105, 113. Various speculations concerning the northern origin of various biblical texts and the nature of the 'northern dialect' in the Bible have been suggested by Rabin, *EncBib*, VI, p. 65-66, following Albright, who was Freedman's teacher regarding this issue. One is permitted some scepticism concerning our ability to distinguish the niceties of the dialects through the text of the Masorah. In any event, Rabin does not propose that the orthography of one or another biblical book is likely to teach anything as to its place and date of composition. Rendsburg (1990) recently attempted to establish linguistic criteria for identifying the northern provenance of Psalms, according to which Psalms 77, 80, and 81 (among the 'Psalms of Assaf') are northern as well. However, the methodology he used is extremely faulty, a point on which I cannot elaborate here. I will only state that he accepts the northernness of the book of Job as

that they do not display any unique characteristics regarding this point. Thus, for example, in Hosea, we find the plene spellings הושע (1.1); אוסיף (1.6); אושיעם, והושעתים (1.7); במועדו (2.11); מועדה (2.13); etc.

This should not be surprising. The gradual and unsystematic manner in which vowel letters were added (or sometimes omitted) during the numerous copyings of the biblical text led to random occurrences of the distribution of vowel letters in different books, and hence there is no way to conclude on the basis of its orthography anything regarding the time or place of composition of one or another book—including the 'northern' source of the book of Job; certainly, this cannot provide an explanation for its difficult language. What is implied in principle by Freedman's argument? That before the diphthongs were contracted the פ"י and פ"ו verbs were written plene; once the diphthongs were contracted, they came to be written in a defective manner (i.e., as in the Samaritan writing or in Job). Thereafter, as their spelling was filled out with vowel letters, the letters *vav* and *yod* were reintroduced into these verbs, albeit not in a consistent manner—for if not, why are they so ubiquitous in 'late' writings, from the period in which diphthongs were already contracted? I am extremely doubtful as to whether there is any epigraphic evidence for such a process. Moreover, are we indeed allowed, as seems to be suggested by the data given by Freedman, to push the date of composition of the book of Job into that same brief period of time between Stage 1 and Stage 3 in the orthography of the פ"י verbs (and specifically in the Assyrian exile)? It seems to me that we may best conclude this brief discussion with the words of Barr: 'The spelling of the MT of Job...may well have nothing to do with the origins and provenance of the book, and give no evidence about them. The spelling does not, or may not, belong to the beginning of the book'.[27]

axiomatic, basing the 'northernness' of the Psalms in question upon it, among other factors. But this is no more than a castle built on sand. One may especially doubt the methodological validity of his claim that Aramaisms are indicative of northern origins, particularly when one is speaking of a book from the period following the destruction of the Temple, such as the book of Job (according to the accepted view), when the Aramaic influence upon biblical language was already very great.

27. Barr 1985: 32. This article is entirely devoted to an examination of Freedman's arguments concerning the conclusions to be reached from the writing of vowel letters generally, and פ"י verbs in particular, in the book of Job, all of which he rejects. See Barr 1986: 91. A discussion of vowel letters in the Masorah appears in Andersen and Forbes 1986: 33-81. I reject the critique of Andersen (1991), who sees in Barr's remarks purely impressionistic claims (p. 122).

Let us now turn to the various proofs based upon examination of the vocabulary and style of the book, intended to establish a certain dependency of the book of Job (either dialectic or translational) upon some Semitic language other than Hebrew. All the scholars who attempt this use a similar method: a list is prepared containing lexicographical data from the book of Job (roots, parallels, etc.), meant to be interpreted according to the other language, or by whose means one can point directly to some special relation to that language. The longer the list, the more convincing the proof is meant to be. This method suffers from two major drawbacks: (i) objective limitations which it is impossible to overcome; (ii) a methodological fault, which can and ought to be corrected.

i. The most difficult objective limitation, requiring us to relate with considerable hesitation and caution to the comparisons invoked, is the great similarity among the system of roots of the various Semitic languages. Due to this similarity, it seems doubtful whether there are many words that can be conclusively derived from one specific language. Numerous examples may be brought to demonstrate this point, but these are superfluous, as my claim is not based on statistics but on a principle. Hence, the following examples are only illustrative:

כחול ארבה ימים ('I shall multiply my days in the sand', 29.18) is interpreted by many commentators as alluding to the legend of the phoenix (i.e., reading כחול as 'like the phoenix' rather than 'like sand'), who returns to life after dying. Guillaume (1968: 112) derives חול from the Arabic *jaylan*; Ceresko (1980: 22-23) derives it from the Ugaritic *ḥl*; but already in *Gen. R.* 19.9 we find, 'Apart from one bird, whose name is *hol*, as is written, "I shall multiply my days like the phoenix"...which lives for a thousand years...' etc. I would be rather surprised if Rabbi Yannai, the author of this midrashic saying, knew either Ugaritic or Arabic! It is true that he may have known the word from Hebrew or Aramaic, but one may also simply interpret the verse 'as the sands of the sea'—that is, as a metaphor (and double entendre on *yamim* as 'seas' and as 'days') for long life (thus, for example, Tur-Sinai in his commentary [1972]).

מן גו יגורשו ('They are driven out from among men', 30.5) is derived by Guillaume (1968: 113) from the Arabic (meaning, 'congregation', or, in southern Arabic, 'low land', hence, a desert oasis); Ceresko (1980: 52-53) derives it from the Canaanite in the sense of 'congregation'; Kahana in his commentary cites both the Arabic ('land', 'field') and the Phoenician; Tur-Sinai combines מן and גו to derive it from the Targumic

Aramaic *nagwa*, in the sense of 'land', 'scenery'. However, he himself notes that the word already appears in Akkadian (*nagu*) and in Arabic (*naga*—hill).

These examples, and a host of others one could give, indicate how fragile is the argument concerning the derivation of a particular word from one cr another Semitic language, and the caution one needs to exercise regarding the claim that the book contains a collection of 'Ugaritic', 'Aramaic', or 'Arabic' words, etc., as these could to the same extent also be 'Hebrew'—albeit, at times, *hapax legomena*. Since the Bible necessarily contains only a fragmentary documentation of the language of the period, that which seems to be 'Aramaic' may in fact be an authentic Hebrew root not otherwise known to us from the extant writings. One can only prove unequivocally that a given word is Aramaic if there are clear phonological signs indicating a non-Hebrew root (e.g נטר–נצר).[28]

Another objective limitation of this system is the very definition of a given verse or phrase based upon Biblical Hebrew as being 'difficult', and on this basis its relation to a word from the lexicon of some other Semitic language. There are numerous examples of this as well, and I will give only two.

(a) Concerning כי לפני לחמי אנחתי תבוא ('for my sighing comes before my bread', 3.24), Tur-Sinai notes that one cannot interpret לחם literally as bread, but as 'disaster', 'fear'—לוחמא in Aramaic.[29] But is it indeed

28. This, of course, does not mean that one need object in principle to the interpretation of biblical words on the basis of other Semitic languages. On the contrary. However, there is a great difference between that and the claim that one or another word is not proper Hebrew. On the problems involved in defining 'Aramaisms' in biblical literature, see Driver 1953. Concerning the present issue, his statement (following Kautzsch 1902) that 'Aramaisms' are characteristic of biblical poetry in general is particularly important. It is also worth citing his following remarks, from which one may infer the caution that needs to be taken in defining the Aramaic origin of a given word: 'Many if not most of the supposed Aramaisms, though now found only in Aramaic dialects, might be proven *gemeinsemitisch* if the sources were available for tracking them down' (1953: 36). For more on the problem of defining 'Aramaism', see Guillaume (1968: 27-28) according to whom there is only one Aramaism in the entire book of Job. See below on his approach.

29. See Tur-Sinai 1972: 367. Moreover, the accepted root used in biblical Aramaic to mean 'fear' is דחל (as in Dan. 4.2); thus also in the Aramaic Targumim (for example, *Targ. Onq.* Gen. 19.30). The root לחם in the sense of fear is only documented for late Aramaic, some thousand years after the composition of the book of Job, according to Tur-Sinai. Even if we assume, then, that לחמי is to be interpreted

'impossible'? Perhaps this is no more than a metaphor? לחם serves in quite a few places in metaphors, as in כי לחמינו הם ('for they are bread for us', Num. 14.9), as well as to indicate a fixed and important custom—'My tears have been my food [לחם] day and night'—Ps. 42.4. Similarly, there is no difficulty in the phrase נדד הוא ללחם ('He wanders abroad for bread', 15.23) and hence no necessity to interpret it as 'he wanders about against fear'. Compare, for example, 'the righteous forsaken or his children begging bread' (לחם, Ps 37.25) for the expression of a similar idea.

(b) ואקוב נוהו פתאום ('but suddenly I cursed his dwelling', 5.3). Even though these three words are well known to us from Biblical Hebrew, Guillaume nevertheless suggests (1968: 81) that one interprets them as being derived, not from the roots קבב or קבה (see Num. 23.8: מה אקב לא קבה אל—'How can I curse whom God has not cursed?'), but from another root, close to the Arabic *wqb*, meaning *rot*. As a result, the word נוה cannot be understood as 'home', and hence Guillaume derives it from the Arabic root *nwh*, meaning a plant at the beginning of its growth. Again, I wonder whether the difficulty existing in this verse justifies the statement that we have here two words which need to be interpreted specifically by means of the Arabic, especially given that the verse is a metaphor which may be interpreted in a number of other ways (see Weiss 1984: 185-87).

It is sometimes difficult to escape the impression that those who advocate the use of accumulated proofs in order to demonstrate that the book was written in a foreign language or dialect forget that a collection of many very weak proofs does not add up to one decisive proof. True, not all of the arguments offered in proof of the relation of the book of Job to some foreign Semitic language belong to this type; hence, I do not suggest that one completely rule out such arguments, but merely that one recognize their limitations and weigh them accordingly.

ii. The methodological fault in this system of proof is rooted in the focusing of each of the various scholars upon only one foreign language, namely, that one whose relation to the book of Job they wish to prove. In so doing, they ignore a fundamental principle of research—namely, that every claim of a special relationship between two things must be based upon a broader and more comprehensive field of comparison. The

in our verse as 'my fear', whence does he derive the assumption that this word, which is not documented in early Aramaic, did not also serve in the Hebrew of our author in the same sense?

special relationship of the book of Job to Arabic or Ugaritic or Aramaic cannot be proven without simultaneously examining with the same tools the possibility of its relationship to other languages, as well as the data from other books. It is self-evident that anyone who wishes to prove a relation to a particular language while ignoring the data likely to indicate a relation to another language has thereby prejudiced the result of the examination; therefore, the findings must be approached with a great deal of scepticism.

We find in the above-mentioned studies the following data. Guillaume (1964) gives a list of 330 Arabic words which in his opinion bear relation to passages throughout the book of Job; Ceresko (1980: 229-32) offers a list of 48 Ugaritic word-pairs which he finds in chs. 29–31 alone; and although Tur-Sinai does not give a list of Aramaic words in Job, one may extract from his commentary some 200 words which he interprets on the basis of the Aramaic, and which serve him as proof for the Aramaic origin of the book.

Each of these systems of data is extremely impressive, and each one taken by itself seemingly confirms the theory which it sets out to prove. Once one sets them alongside one another, this is no longer the case: they then cancel each other out, and it becomes clear that these impressive data were chosen to fit a pre-determined theory.[30]

Indeed, by a comparative examination of foreign words in the book of Job, not intended to prove a particular theory connected with any particular foreign language, a completely different picture emerges. We shall need to turn our attention to this when we examine the proofs offered for the claim that the book was translated from a foreign language or written in an unusual dialect.

From an examination of the distribution of foreign Semitic words in

---

30. An explicit example of this is the comment by Tur-Sinai (1972: 370) that, while for several words we find only Ugaritic, Akkadian or Arabic parallels, we may presume that these words also served in early Aramaic (or even in Hebrew), even if we do not have any data to that effect. Another example of the impressionistic nature of several of his linguistic arguments may be cited from his comment (p. 372) that only the speech of Elihu was originally written in Hebrew, by a Jew who was zealous for his God, but that it is late and the few Aramaic influences therein are to be attributed to Aramaic being the spoken language in Palestine at the time. By contrast, Dhorm argues (1926: clxxv) that Elihu's speech has a stronger Aramaic coloration than the rest of the book. (And in fact Tur-Sinai himself wrote elsewhere that Elihu's words are also translated from Aramaic, and that the chapter 'is the product of the spirit of the prophet Ezekiel'—*EncBib*, I, p. 254).

the Bible (Appendix XIV) based upon Barr's research, we arrive at the following conclusions:

i. On the basis of the table, the distribution of 'Arabic' words in the book of Job is 65.4 per cent of the total distribution of foreign Semitic words in the book of Job. The deviation of 7.9 per cent from the average overall distribution of 'Arabic' words in the Bible as a whole is not sufficiently significant to justify the argument that the book was written in an Arabic-Hebrew patois, as claimed by Guillaume, or in Arabic, as suggested by Fosster.

ii. According to the table, the distribution of 'Aramaic' words in Job is 14.5 per cent, a deviation of 3 per cent from the distribution of such words in the other biblical books. This slight deviation is insufficient to justify the conclusion drawn by Tur-Sinai.

iii. The same holds true regarding Ugaritic: the distribution of 'Ugaritic' words in the book of Job according to the table is exactly equal to their average distribution in the other biblical books (16.3 per cent).

Thus, if Appendix XIV properly represents the distribution of Semitic words in the Bible and in the book of Job, it does not confirm any of the theories concerning the foreign origin of the book of Job.

Likewise, the concluding data offered by Pope in his commentary as to the existence of a special relation between Job and any foreign language is unconvincing. This is so notwithstanding his declared intention to establish the relation of the book of Job to Ugaritic literature.[31] According to his data, the book of Job contains 68 Arabic, 5 Ugaritic, 44 Akkadian, and 20 Aramaic words. However, we should not be surprised by the large number of Arabic words that also follow from Barr's analysis. This derives, not only from the richness of the Arabic language, but primarily from the tremendous number of Arabic words to be found in the lexicon of the different periods and dialects of Arabic. Given this, the chances of finding a root in Arabic for nearly every biblical word are far

---

31. Pope 1973: 369-75. Alongside the foreign words whose parallels are found in the book of Job, he also enumerates a few foreign words which do not appear in Job (such as words from 'I Will Praise the Lord of Wisdom'). Nevertheless, the lists do reflect the lexicon of foreign words which he used to interpret difficult wordings in the book of Job.

greater than for almost any other Semitic language. Hence, one may not draw any conclusions from this regarding the origin of the biblical text under discussion.

The data concerning the distribution among the various biblical books of word-pairs that have been defined as 'Ugaritic' is given in Appendix XV, based upon data from Fisher's book, *Ras-Shamra Parallels*.[32] It should be noted that Fisher stresses the relation of the Bible as a whole to Ugaritic literature without any intention of stressing the special status of the book of Job in this respect. A two-fold conclusion emerges from the data in this table. First, that there is no clear difference between the concentration of Ugaritic word-pairs in the book of Job and their concentration in the books of Joel and Psalms, at least. Second, there is no correspondence between the distribution of Ugaritic pairs and the accepted scholarly theories regarding the original language of the biblical books, their cultural background, or the dates of their composition. Hence, even if the findings with regard to Job were more definitive, they would not suffice to prove that the book was not originally written in Hebrew.

The theory that the language of Job is difficult because it was originally written in a foreign language (Tur-Sinai, Fosster) or in a mixed dialect (Guillaume) may also be confuted by theoretical considerations. There are no grounds for the assumption that a translation from a foreign language results in a more difficult text than the original. On the contrary, generally speaking the opposite is the case: the translator also interprets difficult passages, so that anyone reading the translation without knowing the source will not even notice the difficulty in the original source. Examples of this abound in nearly every ancient translation of biblical poetry. Thus Orlinsky, in his study of the Septuagint to Job (1958), classifies those cases in which the translator deviated from the Hebrew text. He notes various kinds of passages which the translator altered with the aim of simplification and clarification. Thus, the translator frequently exchanged an obscure expression for a more lucid Greek one (1958:

---

32. Fisher 1972: 455-77. There is no need to give here the data from the entire Bible, but only from those books in which a relatively large number of parallel word-pairs was located. Barr (1974) devoted a sharply polemical paper to the approach of the 'Roman School'—that of Dahood and his disciples—which attempted to obscure the boundaries between Hebrew and Ugaritic, and find an abundance of 'Ugaritisms' throughout the Bible. See Grabbe 1977: 21, 175-77; Craigie 1979; Aufrecht 1985: 29-30.

248-52); on occasion, he replaced words that were too abstract for his liking with clearer Greek ones (pp. 256-58); in yet other cases, he altered the meaning of the Hebrew text because it seemed to him illogical or inappropriate to the context (pp. 258-60); while in some cases he added words for the sake of clarification (pp. 265-69). The same is true of the Aramaic translations, such as those of Onqelos and Jonathan. Notwithstanding the differences among them, one may definitely state that they shared one common tendency: to clarify the ambiguities of the poetry, even at the expense of literal precision, for which they generally strive in their translations. True, one may not derive any conclusive logical inferences regarding the method taken by the 'Hebrew translator' of the book of Job several hundred years earlier. It nevertheless seems logical to assume that he would have adopted a similar method, and not preferred an unclear translation over a clear and coherent text.

This principle is generally speaking true of modern translations as well: all of them are far easier and infinitely more comprehensible than the Hebrew text. A good example of this is the book of Job itself: anyone reading the book in one of its modern translations cannot realize how difficult the Hebrew *Vorlage* is. An exception to this rule may be found in one case: when the source is particularly obscure, and the translator is interested in preserving this linguistic feature because it is seen as a literary characteristic which must not be lost in translation. Examples of this approach may be found, for example, in the Hebrew translations of James Joyce's *Ulysses* and of Nabokov's *Lolita*.[33]

But if such is the case in the book of Job (and I have my doubts as to this, as I do not know any ancient example of such poetics in translation), then even were the book of Job translated from a foreign language, this would not be the reason for its difficult language, as the source itself would already have been difficult. We are therefore left, as before, with the need to explain the difficult linguistic character of the book of Job.

Tur-Sinai's claim that the translator did not quite understand the Aramaic source and therefore translated it into difficult language, to a

---

33. See Yael Renen's Hebrew translation of James Joyce's *Ulysses* (Tel-Aviv, 1985), and Devorah Steinhart's Hebrew translation of Nabokov's *Lolita* (Tel-Aviv, 1986). The latter contains an afterword by the translator entitled 'How Does One Translate a Crossword Puzzle?' (pp. 317-32), in which she shares with the reader the problems of translation of a work the outstanding feature of whose poetics is its enigmatic language.

sort of 'non-language', is to be rejected out of hand.[34] Is it conceivable that 'the greatest poetic work of biblical literature', as Tur-Sinai himself calls the book of Job (1972: 354), was translated by someone who did not understand what he was reading? Nor does it make sense that a translator among those who returned to Zion in the days of Ezra would not have had proper knowledge of Babylonian Aramaic, which was written in the exile where he had lived. The linguistic similarity between Aramaic and Hebrew provides extremely easy conditions for translation, allowing for translation on the same linguistic level and without syntactic difficulties (unlike, for example, translation from Hebrew to Greek or vice versa). Likewise, the cultural background of the Aramaic-speaking exiles and of the allegedly Hebrew-speaking translator were too similar for us to imagine that he would have been unable to translate properly due to cultural differences.[35] Even if the translator encountered a word that he did not understand, it seems reasonable that he would interpret

---

34. See the formulae of Tur-Sinai (1972: 367, 368): 'In several places the translator was imprecise'; 'The translator of the book did not understand this word'; 'This is simply a misunderstanding of the Aramaic'; 'Had the translator known this, he would have used a comprehensible Hebrew word instead of this'; 'But it was incorrectly translated'; 'Since the things were not understood'; etc. One may also disagree regarding the actual identification of these 'imprecisions'. But there is no reason to polemicize over details; let us present only one of the many surprising statements of Tur-Sinai, which formed the basis for his general statement as to the lack of precision of the translator. The verse, חצי שדי עמדי ('For the arrows of the Almighty are in me'; 6.4) is to be interpreted in his opinion as 'visions of the Almighty', based upon the Aramaic חזוי, which may be interpreted either as 'half' or as 'vision'. But what is faulty or not understood in the comparison of the divine wrath to arrows being fired? Compare, for example, 'But God will shoot his arrow (חץ) at them suddenly', Ps. 64.8; 'He has set me as a mark for his arrow' (לחץ), Lam. 3.12.

35. On the limitations of translation, see Catford 1965: 93-103. Among other things, he states that: 'Translation fails—untranslatability occurs—when it is impossible to build functionally relevant features of the situation into the contextual meaning of the TL (Target Language) text. Broadly speaking the cases where this happens fall into two categories. Those where the difficulty is linguistic and those where it is cultural' (p. 94). On pp. 83-92, Catford touches upon the question of stylistic and dialectal registers in different languages, which do not always have an equivalent in the Target Language, thereby creating difficult problems in translation. It does not seem to me that this kind of problem would confront someone who set out to translate from Aramaic to Hebrew. For more on the question of 'translation equivalency', see Toury 1979.

it, rather than include words which were meaningless to him in his Hebrew text.[36]

Similarly, the assumption that the language of the book is a mixed patois of Hebrew and Arabic does not withstand theoretical examination, even if we accept Guillaume's claim regarding the unusual number of Arabic words in the text. True, the incorporation of foreign words in works which emerged in a bilingual society is a known phenomenon; thus, for example, we find Aramaic elements in early Hebrew poetry or Arabic words in that of R. Saadya Gaon.[37] However, in these cases the number of foreign words included is quite small, and all of them are taken from one foreign language, rather than there being a mixture of foreign languages, such as that portrayed in the studies of Job surveyed above.

In conclusion, there is no indication that the book of Job was written in a foreign language or in a different dialect from that accepted in the Bible. Even if one were to invoke a clear proof of this, it is doubtful whether one could thereby explain the difficult language of the book. The repeated attempts to establish a foreign linguistic background or to note the limited understanding of the 'translator' not only involve seeking a solution to the linguistic difficulties of the book in the wrong direction, but at times even harm its understanding as a poetic work. I will invoke only one example to clarify this point, even though one could offer many such. Tur-Sinai cites a series of passages which indicate, in his opinion, the stylistic failures which must necessarily be attributed to the translator from Aramaic.

> It is difficult to assume that a fluent author, the composer of such sublime poetry, would forget the rules of the Hebrew language to such an extent as to write לֹא יֵשׁ (9.33) rather than אֵין, or to write לֹא עֵת (22.16) rather than אֵין עֵת (1972: 369).

---

36. Indeed, at times one can identify the original language behind the translated text through misunderstandings of the translator. See, for example, Kahana 1960: I, 148, sect. 5. However, such cases are extremely rare, and pertain to texts that were translated from Hebrew to Greek. In that case, there are far more serious problems of translation due to the reasons described by Catford (1965).

37. For example, in the *Seder 'Avodat Yom ha-Kippurim* of Yossi ben Yossi (Bradi-Wiener 1946: 13): חשרת פיר פלג מלא מים, where פיר is the Aramaic for digging; in the poetry of R. Saadya Gaon: אתכרית רוחי אם אביע מעלליו (ibid., p. 48; אתכרית is the Aramaic for 'was anxious'; see Dan. 7.15); זעו אבריו ממזיה (ibid., p. 51; ממזיה is Aramaic for 'to heat'; see Dan. 3.19).

To this, one can only ask for what reason he assumes that these things were written in this manner through lack of knowledge of the language, rather than for strictly literary reasons, which would dictate to the author, as much as to the translator, how to express himself?[38]

3. *The Proposed Solution*

From the above discussion it may be concluded that one must seek other reasons for the particularly difficult language of the book of Job. I believe that these are principally poetic, pertaining to the very fact of its being a work in which form and content are unified—that is, a work of art. These reasons will be classified below into two groups: literary and psycho-linguistic. However, it needs to be emphasized that this separation is not a substantive one, but a purely didactic one.

The reference to 'Noah, Daniel and Job' in Ezek. 14.14, 20 and the book of Job (on this see below, Chapter 8) indicates that the common denominator of these three figures, apart from their righteousness, is that they do not belong to the people of Israel. The choice of a righteous Gentile as the hero of the book of Job is not accidental, but follows from its wish to present the universal human problem of humanity confronting its God. Another possible reason for this choice is that it makes it easier for the author to place in Job's mouth certain extremely harsh statements about God. Had these been placed in the mouth of a well-known righteous Israelite, they would have diminished his status as 'blameless and upright, one who feared God and turned away from evil' (1.1), thereby removing the ground beneath the basic assumption of the book. In the final analysis, critical words are more easily accepted from the mouth of a Gentile, because they enable us to assume that the Israelite, who knows God, would not express himself so sharply. Hence,

---

38. For example, the idiom לא עת in ch. 9: the entire chapter is filled with words that are partly based upon the components of the word אל, the consonants א and ל (v. 2—אל; vv. 3, 12—אליו; v. 13—אלה; compare the negative, אל, in v. 34), giving the negative לא a central role in the chapter (vv. 3, 5, 7, 11, 13, 15, 16, 18, 21, 24, 25, 28, 32, 33, 35a, 35b). The same holds true with regard to לא עת in 22.16; הלאל—v. 2; אלמנות—v. 9; אל אלוה—vv. 12, 13, 17, 26; אליו—v. 27; לא—vv. 5, 7, 11, 12, 14, 16, 20. In both chapters, the combination of both words appears in the middle: אלוה לא in 9.13; הלא אלה in 22.12. One could go so far as to find hidden allusions in this, but I prefer to limit myself to noting the data and defining them as 'literary means', without engaging in excessive exegesis. On the use of לא instead of אין in the book of Job, see above, n. 2.

the creation of a non-Israelite background for the plot is called for, and the systematic avoidance of any allusions to Israel—such as scenery of the land of Israel, typically Hebrew names, or Israelite historical background—is a substantial component of the artistic mimesis. For the very same reason, the book does not attempt to portray any particular ethnic-geographic environment, so as not to circumscribe the things said in principle within a narrow and exclusive realm. Thus, alongside one another there appear descriptions of wilderness, of desert tribes, of nomadic society, of urban society, scenery of rivers, snow, animals from different geographical regions, and other details that contribute to the universal coloration of this work.

It is against this background that one should also understand the large number of foreign words in the book of Job which, as we have seen, do not originate in any specific Semitic language. This is the most explicit mimetic device used by the author for the ongoing artistic moulding of the non-Israelite reality of the book. The use of rare words (this term is not synonymous with *hapax legomena*, although some of the latter are certainly rare), and of foreign words from various Semitic tongues, creates a feeling of distance and strangeness which accompanies the reader throughout the length of the book. Even though we are unable to measure the likely influence of this style upon the author's contemporary readers, it nevertheless seems reasonable to assume that they felt its strangeness and uniqueness even more than the modern reader, because they were more sensitive than ourselves to the distance between it and the 'normative' style of poetry in their day. Hence, the argument that the author made deliberate mimetic use of unfamiliar language and idiom which did not belong from the poetic viewpoint to the period in which the book was written need not strike us as improbable. The use of special language as an explicit literary device in other biblical books strengthens this claim. An example of the deliberate use of foreign words (in this case, Aramaic) for the creation of a mimesis of a Gentile milieu may perhaps be seen in Isa. 21.12: אם תבעיון בעיו שבו אתיו ('If you will inquire, inquire; come back again'). Similarly the Aramaic phrase in Jer. 10.11 (כדנה תאמרון להום, 'Thus shall you say to them'), addressed towards non-Israelites. The prophecy over Tyre in Ezekiel 27 contains extensive mention of the names of peoples and lands in order to exemplify Tyre's status as an economic power. Elsewhere, language is used to create other kinds of mimesis, as in צו לצו צו לצו קו לקו קו לקו ('precept upon precept, precept upon precept, line upon line, line upon line', Isa. 28.10, 13), intended to exemplify the 'strange lips and alien tongue' of the 'scoffers' (vv. 11, 14). Another well-known example is 1 Sam. 9.12—the mimetic presentation of the water-drawers who are fascinated by the figure of Saul ('He is; behold, he is just ahead of you. Make haste'). A well-known example of a unique style being placed by the author in the mouth of one of his heroes to create mimesis is that of the demogogic manner used by Hushai in speaking to Absalom, in order to play upon the nerves in the soul of the glory-seeking rebellious son (2 Sam. 17.7-13).[39]

Nevertheless, the manner in which style is used to shape mimesis in the book of Job is a definite innovation within biblical literature, for two reasons: the choice of difficult and unusual language, and the use of this method throughout the entire length of the book, rather than in selected passages alone. The use of a unique style to create a mimesis of a foreign society would seem to be the result of a deliberate choice on the part of the author, because this style is required by the plot and ideational framework of the book. If the book of Job was indeed written during the period of the Exile, its author's use of foreign words also reflects the linguistic reality of the Israelite community in the place of composition of the book. For example, the author did not need to trouble himself overly much in order to find suitable Aramaic words, as these were in any event commonly used among the exiles (and afterwards among those who returned to Zion). It was easy to weave the rare Hebrew words upon the warp of the foreign words so as to obtain an idiosyncratic, obscure linguistic fabric.

The second possible reason for this style lies in the realm of literary exigencies. Due to the structure of the book—which requires numerous speeches by Job and his friends on an identical subject—a gap is created between the sparse amount of new content and the large quantity of speech lacking in any substantive novelty (albeit it does fulfil other poetic functions in the book, such as strengthening the mimesis of an increasingly sharp debate). This gap necessarily forces the author to stretch the limits of his vocabulary in search of increasingly rare words: the more the gap grows, the greater the use of rare words to be anticipated, whether their source is Hebrew or otherwise. This theoretical explanation is strengthened when we examine the distribution of *hapax legomena* among the different literary blocks of the book of Job: the prose frame—chs 1–2 and 42; the speeches of Job; those of Eliphaz; of

---

39. For other examples and a general discussion of style as an indirect means of shaping the figures, see Bar-Efrat 1979: 89-99.

Bildad; of Zophar; of Elihu; of God. Such an examination (Appendix XVI)[40] indicates the great gap between the number of *hapax legomena* in the different components of the book, making it more likely that this is not an accidental occurrence. It should be noted that there is no correspondence between these data and accepted theories concerning the identity of the original material and additions to the book of Job. There are those who argue that God's speech is a later addition to the book, and hence contains a particularly large number of *hapax legomena*, a fact that on casual inspection would seem to support this claim; however, it is matched in this respect by the speeches of Job and of Eliphaz, and not by those of Elihu, whose authenticity is more doubtful than that of any other block of material in the book. Thus, the explanation for this fact must be sought elsewhere. The data in the table pertaining to the other blocks in the book are not particularly conclusive, and it seems doubtful whether there is any need to seek an 'explanation' for them. However, it does seem to me that they may serve to confirm our claim concerning a direct, non-random relationship between the length of the block and the distribution therein of *hapax legomena*—and this over and above the considerations already mentioned. One may understand this in terms of the formula for deviation from the expected, namely, the shorter the text placed by the author in the mouth of one of his participants, the less need to innovate in terms of contents, and accordingly the less pressure there is to extend its vocabulary beyond the norm. However, this is only a partial explanation, one which will be completed in the next section.

There is thus a direct correspondence between the length of the unit and the number of excess *hapax legomena* therein, with the single exception of the speeches of God. In the latter case, one may offer a double explanation for the abundance of *hapax legomena*: the length of the speech in comparison to the limited scope of the subject matter treated therein; and the literary need to emphasize the uniqueness of the word of God. For our author here dares to quote God, not on the basis of tradition (as in the case of the narrator of the account of the Sinaitic revelation, who quoted the words 'I am the Lord your God', and so on

---

40. Greenspahn 1977: 253. See also the diagram under the heading, 'Deviation from expected distribution', p. 52. The speeches of God and the speeches of Job head the list, also in comparison with other units elsewhere in the Bible. Following them come, in order, the following units: Isaiah 1–39; the speeches of Eliphaz; the 'Elohist' Psalms; Psalm 2; the speeches of Elihu; the speeches of Bildad; Trito-Isaiah (Isa. 56–66); Ezra; etc.—all of them above the anticipated mean for the Bible.

throughout the entire Torah and historiographic literature); nor by virtue of a personal experience of revelation, like the prophets; nor as an exegete of God's word to the prophets (as in the additions and expansions within the prophetic literature); nor even as a pseudepigraphic author. This daring almost forces him to use a unique style, expressed not only in its rhetoric, but also in the vocabulary of the speech.

A third literary explanation for the obscure language of the book pertains to its relation to the background literature of the ancient Near East. 'I Will Praise the Lord of Wisdom', 'The Babylonian Theodicy', and the poetic sections of 'The Eloquent Peasant' are written in difficult and obscure language, and it is not for naught that 'commentaries' were written on the first two in ancient times.[41] It would therefore not be rash to state that, by utilizing obscure language, the author of the book of Job adapted himself to an accepted norm of ancient Near Eastern literature, upon which he drew and to which he related, whether deliberately or unconsciously .

As an epigraph for the psycho-linguistic explanation, we may use the following words of the mediaeval exegete, R. Zerahiah ben Yitzhak ben Shealtiel of Barcelona:

> That this book was composed and arranged with the intention of hinting at secrets and advice...which the author intended to hide and to conceal, for two reasons. The one reason is...to conceal the divine secrets from the masses of people...and the second reason was that, if the author were to reveal all the matters of this book, in a transparent explanation, and say that it was truly a parable, most or all of the people would flee from it and would mock the intention of the book...And it would engender harm, in that the book would be forgotten and would no longer be extant today among people (Schwartz 1969: 170).

I do not fully agree with the reasons given by R. Zerahiah for the author's wish to hide his intentions—for example, his opinion that the primary reason was a deliberate and planned attempt[42] to obscure things,

---

41. See Lambert (1960: 26), who writes that in 'I Will Praise the Lord of Wisdom' there are many *hapax legomena* and homonyms, and a far broader lexicon of words than that commonly accepted in other Mesopotamian religious texts. The difficulty of the 'Theodicy', according to Lambert (pp. 65-66) stems primarily from the epigrammatic nature of the lines (each one having four primary accents) which obscures their meaning.

42. It would seem that R. Zerahiah derived his theory from Maimonides' approach toward obscuring his intentions, knowing that his words would be read by people of different levels. See *Guide for the Perplexed*, 1.26, 33, etc.

as as we shall explain below. Nevertheless, R. Zerahiah was in principle correct in stating that the obscure language of the book is not the result of external factors, but is an immanent part of the work.

I believe that the author was led to write in an obscure manner by the exigencies of the expected norms of religious thought. However, this obscurity was not a tactical means of hiding his intentions from the readers, or exposing them only to select individuals who were cognizant of the divine secrets, but an expression of the psychological state of an individual who was reluctant to admit the full force of the inner truth at which he has arrived even to himself. More than a means of expression, this obfuscation is an expression of the author's stance towards his own words. Thus, the difficult language of the book becomes the most suitable tool for expressing Job's own hesitations, even when he says harsh things which seem certain beyond all doubt.

The following statement by the renowned Hebrew poet, Hayyim Nahman Bialik, taken from his well-known essay, 'Revealment and Concealment in Language', articulates the view that known and routinely used words may be unsuitable to an artist because of their clarity, while non-routine words may serve his or her goals precisely because of their obscurity:

> No word contains the complete dissolution of any question. What does it contain? The question's concealment. It makes no difference what the particular word is—you can exchange it for another—just so long as it contains the power momentarily to serve as concealment and barrier....
>
> A word or system declines and yields to another, not because it has lost the power to reveal, to enlighten, to invalidate the 'stet', either totally or in part, but for the very opposite reason—because the word or system has been worn out by being manipulated and used, it is no longer able to conceal and hide adequately, and can, of course, no longer divert mankind momentarily. Man, gazing for a moment through the open crack, finding to his terror that awesome 'void' before him again, hurries to close the crack for a time—with a new word. That is to say, he seizes the new 'talisman', like its predecessor a proven momentary diversion—and is saved from the terror (Bialik 1966: 130-31, 133).

Without taking a stand as to the theoretical applicability of these remarks, one may appreciate them as the testimony of a great poet. They express the hesitation—and thus inability—of artists to say certain things which they themselves are reluctant to admit even to themselves in full clarity, in writing. How much more so when such doubts exist regarding challenges presented to Heaven, even if the author hides beyond the fictitious image of Job. St Jerome well illustrated the unique difficulty involved in understanding the book of Job when he used the image of the eel, which I quoted in the preface to this study. We find here not only a description of the situation, but also a recommendation: do not attempt to understand the book fully, because it will 'slip out' beneath your hands. This recommendation reflects both the reluctance of Jerome—for reasons of faith—to delve excessively into the problems of the book, as well as the posture of the author of Job himself towards his work.

At this point I would like to add something on the nature of metaphors and their use in difficult texts. The relation between the two is not at all simple, but dialectic. On the one hand, one may justly argue that an author uses metaphor in order to clarify something which he or she could not succeed in expressing properly without it—from which it follows that metaphor is used to enhance the reader's understanding. On the other hand, it is nearly impossible to understand fully the 'intention' of a metaphor—not only because we cannot fully share the associative world of the author or fully understand his or her motivations in choosing this specific metaphor, but because there is serious doubt as to whether the author was fully aware of what it conceals. For this reason, metaphor always remains something of a riddle combining things that are impossible in ordinary speech,[43] making it impossible for us to be certain of its correct explanation. In brief, the extensive use of metaphor contributes to the obscurity and difficulty of understanding what is written. At times, this obscurity may reflect the author's quest for greater precision than possible through the use of 'regular speech', while at others it may express his or her reluctance to say certain things directly and unequivocally. Yet these are in fact no more than two sides of the same coin, indicative of the difficulty the author feels in fully expressing their thoughts. Hence, if the comparative examination cited above indeed accurately reflects the abundance of metaphor in the book of Job, this is yet another indication of the dialectical stance of the author towards his words.

Further confirmation of the contention that the obscure nature of the language of the book of Job is immanent to the work and does not derive from any external motivation may be seen in the work of Ludwig Wittgenstein. His remarks concerning language and its exigencies, involving both philosophical and psycho-linguistic aspects, are of import-

43. Aristotle, *Poetics*, 85a.

ance in their own right; but for our purposes, they are to be considered as a 'confession of an interested party', as he too writes in an obscure and unclear manner:

> Much is latent and implicit and it becomes the task of the reader to enter into the idea and bring it fully to light within his own understanding. This is not always easy, particularly because one can never be sure that what one understands is what the writer intended to say.

These things were written, not about the book of Job, but about Wittgenstein's own manner of expression (Morrison 1968: 9). On the interrelationship between ideas and language, between the wish to express something in a precise manner and the ability of language to express it, Wittgenstein writes : 'Man has the impulse to run up against the limits of language', on which Brand comments: 'and philosophy stems from that. Man wants constantly to say what cannot be said.'[44] Applying this approach to the book of Job, we will find that the author, in challenging the limitations of language, expresses a quest for truths which are beyond his comprehension. In *Tractatus* 4.114-115, Wittgenstein writes: 'Philosophy is concerned with tracing the limits of language and therefore of thought from within'. Brand observes here that philosophy 'must set limits to what can be thought. It must set limits to what cannot be thought...It will signify what cannot be said by presenting what can be said.' And further on, in *Tractatus* 5.6-62, Wittgenstein adds:

> The limits of my language mean the limits of my world. We cannot think what we cannot think. So what we cannot think we cannot say either.
>   The world is my world: this is manifest in the fact that the limits of language (of that language which alone I can understand), mean limits of my world.

The limit of thought is the limit of the ability of expression, and vice versa; hence, as the author of Job attempts to stretch the limits of thought to the almost-impossible (his approach leading to logical contradictions with his faith axioms), language too is *ipso facto* stretched almost beyond the limits of its capacity for clear expression.

One may object to these psycho-linguistic explanations of the obscure style of the book of Job by responding that they are only valid with regard to the speeches of Job, as all the other speakers say things that are normative, and hence there is no reason to obfuscate. The answer to

---

44. Brand 1979: 167. The clauses from the *Tractatus* are quoted according to this book.

this objection is two-fold. First of all, as we have seen, the relative distribution of *hapax legomena* in the speeches of Job is indeed greater than in other parts of the book, apart from the speech by God. Second, since Job's claims constitute the main bulk of the book both intellectually and in terms of its emotional burden, they in turn determined the linguistic norm for the entire work.

I would suggest a similar explanation for the phenomenon of obscure language in writings of an entirely different genre: namely, the eschatological prophecies, on the border-line of apocalypse, both in the Bible and in post-biblical literature. Examples of this are the book of Daniel, and the eschatological chapters in Isaiah (24–27) and Zechariah (9–14), which are among the most difficult and obscure passages in prophetic literature. Here, too, we find expression of the authors' reluctance to make explicit and unequivocal statements concerning the nature of the final redemption and the stages that will precede it. The enigmatic language of such writings is not necessarily the result of the authors' 'sophistry', that is, that they present themselves, without any real basis, as so-to-speak visionaries who know the future. In many cases, this is doubtless a consequence of the confusion in which the author finds himself, due to the gap between his own feeling that he 'knows' the future, which may perhaps be an ecstastic feeling, and his innate fear to define things too explicitly. Again, this is not out of fear that he will be branded an impostor by others, but rather because of his own reluctance to see in such explicit terms the things that he has written concerning esoteric matters. This feeling is expressed in the Rabbinic dictum explaining why Jonathan ben Uziel was not allowed to translate the Hagiographa: 'because it contains the Messianic End' (*b. Meg.* 3a). This saying evidently refers to the book of Daniel, and its sense is roughly as follows: it is fitting (also in the aesthetic sense, that is, in terms of balance of form and contents) that things should remain as they are written—obscure, enveloped in mist.

The two systems of explanation which I have proposed for explaining the style of the book of Job, the literary and the psycho-linguistic, do not contradict one another. In fact, any separation between them is artificial and purely didactic, as noted above. At first glance, the need to create a similitude of Gentile society led the author to a deliberate decision concerning its style, while both his reluctance and his inability to say explicit things are not the result of any conscious judgment. But one cannot really separate these two factors, because one system of considerations derives from the other, and it is impossible to determine (and not only due to lack of suitable information) which preceded the other, or which reason is predominant. Indeed, one may speculate that the phenomenon of foreign words is more connected to literary considerations, while the large number of metaphors and *hapax legomena* is more closely associated with the author's mental attitude towards what he has written. But even on this count it would be better not to adopt any firm conclusions whose validity it is impossible to check.

4. *Irony*

My contention that the obscure nature of the book of Job is substantive to the work and an authentic part thereof, and that it is one of the most important components of its poetics, may be confirmed by another stylistic characteristic—irony. More than any other biblical book, the book of Job is constructed on all levels upon a basis of irony. Hence, if we ignore this feature or view it as somehow marginal, a kind of literary embellishment, this will cause us severely to misunderstand the book.

I would accept Kierkegaard's concept of irony as a statement in which the true intention of the one making it is the opposite of that conveyed by its literal meaning.[45] It follows from this that by its very nature irony tends to obscure the written word and make it difficult, to the extent that it may be understood in the opposite sense from that intended by the author. Since it is often difficult to discern whether the intention of the written word is its literal meaning or the opposite, irony serves as

---

45. An important discussion of irony appears in Kierkegaard, who defines it as a form of speech in which 'The phenomenon is not the essence but the opposite of the essence' (1989: 247). On irony in the Bible generally, see Good 1965. On irony in the book of Job, see Hoffman 1983a; what follows is based upon that article. For the sake of brevity, I have not repeated here all the examples which I gave there. See also Janzen (1987: 528-31), who sees irony as the most important literary tool for 'transformations' in the Israelite tradition (in relation to the Creation, the Garden of Eden narrative, the tradition of the Exodus, etc.), which also characterize the book of Job. I share his appreciaton in principle of the important task of irony in the book of Job, but it is difficult to escape the feeling that at times his reading of the book borders upon mere homiletics. An example of this, in my opinion, is the claim that Job 24.1-12 'may challenge Exod. 2.23-25 the way Job 7.17-18 challenges Psalm 8' (p. 529). The linguistic relation between Job 7 and Psalm 8 is insufficient proof of an ironic dialogue between the two, and it is certainly difficult to see in Job 24.10-12 any allusion to the Exodus tradition.

an obscuring factor. Hence, Kierkegaard was right in saying that at times the author uses ironic language in order to hide his or her true intention:

> Irony is the process of isolating itself, for it does not generally wish to be understood…the more the ironist succeeds in deceiving and the better his falsification progresses, so much the greater is his satisfaction (1989: 249).

Irony is manifested on several levels in the book of Job. In some cases it is on the surface and one cannot help but see it. It thereby guides the consciousness of the reader to more obscure levels of irony, legitimizing the interpretation even of those things which could be understood literally in opposition to their literal meaning. Hence, the implied permission to interpret a considerable number of things in ambivalent ways is a definite cause of perplexity, contributing decisively to the obscure nature of the book.

The following are the levels which I found in the book, in the order of transparency of their irony:

i.   Ironic statements, directed by the speakers against one another, which are evident to all: to Job, to his friends and to his readers.

ii.   Irony of the author towards his characters. This level is understood to the readers, but (according to the conventions of writing) not to Job or to his friends.

iii.   Irony (through either a statement or a situation) of the author towards his readers.

iv.   Irony of the author towards his work, that is, towards himself.

i. Statements on the first level are spread throughout the entire book; they are easily identified, and a few examples will suffice. (a) In Job's words to his friends: 'How forceful are honest words' (6.25); in the designation of God as 'watcher of men' (7.20; Dhorm in his commentary notes that the irony is detectable here through comparison with v. 12: 'that thou settest a guard over me'[46]); 'Truly I know that it is so;

---

46. The verb שמר seems to be spread throughout the length of the book, and is accompanied by more than a hint of irony. The first hint of its ironic nature appears in God's charge to Satan, 'only spare (שמר) his life' (2.6), intended as it were to place a limit upon Job's disaster, while further on it becomes clear that this limitation is to his detriment, as he would prefer to die. See also 10.12-14: 'thy care has preserved (שמרה) my spirit…If I sin, thou dost mark me (ושמרתני)'; 13.27: 'Thou puttest my feet in the stocks, and watchest (ותשמור) all my paths' (compare 33.11); 14.16: 'thou wouldest not keep watch (תשמור) over my sin'; 23.11: 'I have kept (שמרתי) his way and have not turned aside'; 24.15: 'The eye of the adulterer also waits for the twilight

but how can a man be just before God?' (9.2)—he seemingly agrees
with their assertion that man cannot emerge righteous before God, but
makes this dependent upon the power of God, rather than on man's
righteousness; 'No doubt you are the people, and wisdom will die with
you' (12.2), and further on: 'But ask the beasts, and they will teach
you...Who among all these does not know...' (12.7-9); 'Oh that you
would keep silent, and it would be your wisdom!' (13.5; this in contrast
with the Wisdom saying: 'Even a fool who keeps silent is considered
wise'—Prov. 17.28); 'I also could speak as you do, if you were in my
place; I could join words together against you, and shake my head at
you' (16.4); 'As God lives, who has taken away my right' (27.2)—an
oath taken in the name of the God of injustice. (b) In the words of the
friends to Job: 'Behold, you have instructed many' (4.3); 'Is not your
fear of God your confidence' [or 'your foolishness'—כסלתך, 4.6]; 'Call
now; is there any one who will answer you?' (5.1); 'Should a wise man
answer with windy knowledge, and fill himself with the east wind?'
(15.2); 'Are you the first man that was born? Or were you brought
forth before the hills?' (15.7); 'Beware lest you say, "We have found
wisdom"' (32.13); 'Behold, no fear of me need terrify you' (33.7;
against Job's words in 13.21). (c) The rhetorical questions which God
poses to Job all have an ironic nature. Their literal meaning is that God
does not know where Job was at the time of the creation, but their
intention is to say the exact opposite: I know as well as you where you
were at the time of creation. The irony stands out in particular in God's
suggestion that Job run the world in his stead: 'Have you an arm like
God?...Deck yourself with majesty and dignity...Then will I also
acknowledge to you' (40.9-14; see on this below, Chapter 8).

 ii. It is more difficult to pinpoint the second level, that of the irony
shared by the author and readers. Job and his friends are not meant to
understand the irony on this level, because the readers here need to
remove themselves from the imaginative world of the work. The basis
for this type of irony is already laid in the prologue. While the dialogues
are presented as a report of what is said among the friends, which is
presumably equally well known to Job, to his friends and to the readers,
in the prologue the author assumes a posture of omniscience, sharing
information hidden from Job and his friends with the reader. By so

(שמרה נשף). Thus, through the accumulation of an ironic burden, the verb receives
such a coloration also in the words of God, who praises himself in his relation to
animals—'Do you observe (תשמור) the calving of the hinds?', 39.1.

doing, the author places us on a higher level of knowledge than that of his heroes, an awareness that accompanies us, like it or not, throughout the length of the book. This position is an alienating factor of the first order, preventing the readers from feeling simple identification and empathy with Job, and requiring that they constantly examine what is being said on two different levels: that known to Job and his friends, and that which is hidden from them. Almost of necessity, such a presentation imposes a certain ironic viewpoint, forcing us to examine everything from an additional level of perception which cannot be shared with that of Job and his friends. It is thus, for example, regarding the basic axiom of the book, according to which Job's wealth is evidence of God's kindness to him. Yet we know that, were it not for this wealth, Satan would not have been spurred to bring upon Job all those disasters so as to place him to the test. The irony is that a reality in which Job sees divine blessing turns out to be the exact opposite. Moreover, from the prologue the reader (alone) learns that Job suffers, not despite his right-eousness, but precisely because of it; in its absence, there would have been no reason to put him to the test. What could be more ironic than that? Similarly, Bildad's words, 'Does God pervert justice?' (8.3) are a rhetorical question based upon the axiom that God does not pervert justice. Yet the reader, knowing why Job suffers, cannot but detect the author's ironic wink. The same holds true of the verse, 'Behold, God will not reject a blameless man' (8.20), formulated as an axiom. Yet we know that Job was visited by catastrophe specifically because he is 'innocent and upright', and because he held fast to his innocence (see 2.9) despite the disaster which befell him.

iii. The author's irony towards the reader is even more concealed. I have only found it with regard to what is seemingly only a single tangential matter, albeit one that is related to the essence of the book: its stance toward the philosophy of retribution represented by the friends.

Anyone reading the prologue is seemingly immune to the errors of judgment into which Job and his friends are 'allowed' to fall. We are meant to know that the various theories of retribution propounded by the friends are incorrect, being based as they are upon the (erroneous) assumption that Job sinned. We are thus meant to be freed from the temptation to provide rational-ethical justifications for Job's catastrophe. But are we indeed immune? With respect to at least one matter it seems to me that the author lays a trap, meant to teach us that even we, the supposedly wise, are no less caught up in conventions than are the friends of Job, and that notwithstanding our greater knowledge we too are prey to routine thought and the convenience of dogmatism. I refer to a statement made concerning the sons of Job. In two different places the friends allude to the fact that they died in punishment for their sins. Eliphaz says, 'His sons are far from safety, they are crushed in the gate, and there is no one to deliver them' (5.4), while Bildad states 'If your children have sinned against him, he has delivered them into the power of their transgression' (8.4). Our author seems to have deliberately presented things in the prologue in such a manner as to lead even the 'wise' reader to the conclusion that the sons suffered death as punishment for their sins. The description of their self-indulgent way of life, the feasts they held, Job's own fears that perhaps they 'cursed God in their hearts' (1.5)—all these tempt us to accept the theory of the friends. And indeed, there are some commentators who accept this approach, such as R. David Kimhi, who in his commentary *Mezudat David* (8.4) states: 'For when your sons sinned by making constant feasts, which lead to frivolity, I banished them from the world, the place of their transgression...' We find that, through a sophisticated trick, the book leads the reader too to be trapped in conventional thinking. There is a certain irony here directed towards those who see themselves as protected against superficial and disproven solutions.[47]

iv. The subtlest level of irony is that entailed in the ambivalent view of the author towards himself and his entire work. This perspective is manifested throughout the book behind the various other levels of irony, but reaches its height in the speech of God, in which we would expect to find an answer to the questions that have been raised thus far. There is considerable controversy concerning the nature of the answer provided by this speech, a difficulty that deeply disturbs the scholars.

What is the nature of the solution proposed in the speech of God? For

---

47. The arguments raised in this regard are based upon the assumption that the statement by the omniscient narrator in the prologue concerning Job's righteousness is meant to be taken as axiomatic by the reader, who is used to the norms of the biblical narrative. As against that, Sternberg (1985: 345-46) states that the reader is meant to question the narrator's statement, which only acquires unequivocal status in the epilogue, from the moment that God confirms Job's righteousness. But this is not true, as already in the prologue God took a clear-cut stance on the subject. Sternberg's remarks are made in the course of his arguments concerning 'the poetics of ambiguity' in the biblical narrative. But as in other issues of his system, here too it is doubtful whether one may speak of an inviolable poetic 'law' in the biblical story.

purposes of clarity, the answers given to this question by scholars and exegetes may in principle be classified into three:

a.   The speech provides a coherent answer to Job's arguments.
b.   There is no convincing answer given, and the author deliberately places evasive words in God's mouth.
c.   There is no convincing answer, even though the author intended to give such an answer; that is, the author failed in his task.

In examining the various solutions, the third possibility, that assuming failure on the part of the author, ought to be pushed to last place, as the position of last resort. Before expressing lack of confidence in his ability, one needs to consider the possibility that here too, as throughout the work, he indeed succeeded in expressing what he wished. As for the first two possibilities, divergent as they may be, they share the supposition that the author did not explicitly state his primary intention. This point is self-evident with regard to option (b). An examination of option (a) will indicate that here too the situation is similar: any claim that God's speech contains a convincing answer to Job's difficulties is not based upon what is explicitly stated in the speech, but upon the assumption that the answer is indirect, alluded to, or even hidden.[48]

The following are the primary solutions that have been proposed from this group:[49]

i.   The very fact of divine revelation is the answer. God thereby proved to Job that the suffering person is not forgotten nor abandoned.[50] However, his speech does not contain even one

48. Licht (*EncBib*, VIII, p. 299) quite rightly wrote the following: 'And God, in answering Job out of the whirlwind, does not refute Job's arguments or answer his protest; in any event not explicitly…for nearly every deep reader learned something slightly different from the text'.

49. God's answer will also be discussed in the next chapter, where I will enumerate further solutions. On 40.10-14, in which God relates to the issues explicitly, see below, Chapter 8.

50. Thus Y. Kaufmann 1960: II, 614; Rowley 1970: 18-21; MacKenzie 1959; Eichrodt 1964: II, 491; similarly also Driver and Gray 1921: lx. It seems that Maimonides also alluded to this approach in *Guide for the Perplexed*, 3.23: Job expressed incorrect views because of his suffering, 'as long as he had no true knowledge and knew the deity only because of his acceptance of authority…But when he knew God with a certain knowledge, he admitted that true happiness, which is the knowledge of the deity, is guaranteed to all who know Him' (Pines 1963: 492).

word in which this is explicitly stated. Hence, anyone claiming that this is in fact the solution must rely upon implication.[51]

ii. The creation is depicted as a complete and beautiful whole, without blemish. One is meant to conclude from this that all of God's deeds and his behaviour towards human beings, including Job, are perfect. When humanity includes itself within the beauty of nature its sufferings wither away, and nature becomes a key to the truth.[52] Again, these things are not stated explicitly, but are at most implied between the lines.

iii. Similar to this is the view that the description of the creation comes to teach that divine justice is greater and more sublime than human justice.[53]

iv. Another accepted explanation is that, through the detailed description of the creation, God proves to Job that 'Thou canst not understand the secret of any thing or being in the world, how much less the secret of man's fate'.[54] Here too, the principle is not stated explicitly, but inferred by logical deduction .

v.   Another sort of interpretation is that proposed by Tzevat. According to him, God's answer is intended to imply that he is not limited by the fetters of the 'ethical' law which humanity has imposed upon him. Ethics is an autonomous human social

51. One should note that this approach would only require a brief speech, as the very act of revelation, and not its contents, are important. Indeed, there are a few who argued thus; see the discussion in Chapter 8.

52. Thus Gordis 1965: 134. He also favours solution (iv), below. Similarly, with minor differences of emphasis, von Rad 1972: 220: once he was convinced that God alone protects and sustains the world, Job nullified his complaint, through the awareness that his lot too is protected by the secrets of God.

53. Buber 1960: 195: 'Designedly man is lacking in this presentation of heaven and earth, in which man is shown the justice that is greater than his'.

54. The formula of Buber (1960: 194), who sees in this a part of the solution. Kahana advocates a similar opinion in his commentary (1924). In this he is close to Maimonides, *Guide for the Perplexed*, 3.23: 'The purpose of all these things is to show that our intellects do not reach the point of apprehending how these natural things that exist in the world of generation and corruption are produced in time and of conceiving how the existence of the natural force within them has originated them...How then can we wish that His governance of, and providence for, them, may He be exalted, should resemble our governance of, and providence for, the things we do govern and provide for?' Williams likewise emphasizes that, in the final analysis, the most important lesson of the book is the acquisition of 'not-knowing knowledge' (1971: 251).

ideal, and as such one may not make the manner of conduct of the world dependent upon it: 'The God who speaks to man in the Book of Job is neither just nor unjust. He is God.' Tzevat admits that these things are not stated explicitly, which he explains by the fact that they contradict the conventions of the period so sharply that the author refrained from formulating them explicitly.[55]

If all of these solutions are in fact based upon the assumption that God's speech omits the essential point, one must ask what answer is most suitably conveyed in such an indirect and non-explicit manner. Why did the author of the book of Job, who knew how to address harsh words against the creator and his conduct of the world openly and in sharp language, see fit to bring the solution to the problem in an indirect and allusive manner? Presumably he thought that he would thereby express his position most suitably. In other words, we need to determine the substance of that selfsame message, whose concealment is the best method of its revealing. However, it seems to me that, at least in the four former solutions, it would have been more appropriate had the above messages been conveyed directly rather than obliquely. As for Tzevat's solution: the assumption that the author of Job was reluctant to say unconventional things is inconsistent with his daring to rebel against convention during the course of the book.

From this we must turn to examining option (b), according to which the author intended to put an unconvincing answer in God's mouth. I would claim that, ironically, he thereby presented himself as having answers to the problems raised—but only ironically. The real meaning of the passage (which seems to say: here you have an orderly and convincing answer) is in fact the exact opposite. In God's speech the author is in fact telling us: I do not know how to answer the severe questions which you have raised, and they remain in all their severity. This is self-irony, as throughout the length of the book the author creates the impression that in the end we will receive a proper answer. By presenting himself as one who has the answers at hand, the author is

---

55. Tzevat 1966: 105. See also Good 1965: 239, and the previous note concerning Williams's view. Similarly Jacobsen's words (1976: 163): 'The personal, egocentric view of the sufferer—however righteous—is rejected. The self-importance which demands that the universe adjust to his needs...is cast aside...an individual has no rights, not even to justice.'

allowed the freedom to seek a path, both while presenting the various problems and when he attempts to find solutions to them. God's 'answer' presents a kind of 'solution' which destroys itself during the course of its own presentation, thereby constituting a kind of indirect confession of the author: throughout the length of the book I have attempted to find various human solutions propounded to the problem of divine justice; now I have attempted a 'divine' solution, and this is all I have been able to manage. This is an ironic admission of failure to resolve the problem, and perhaps even more so: it is an ironic admission that the problem itself has no solution whatsoever.[56] In this, we are very close to the nihilism of the book of Ecclesiastes. Here too, Kierkegaard is correct in claiming that the first potency of irony is in the creation of a self-destructive theory of knowledge. And:

> When an ironist exhibits himself as other than he actually is, it might seem that his purpose were to include others to believe this. His actual purpose however is merely to feel free, and this is through irony.[57]

The assessment of God's speech as an ironic 'solution' may seem to contradict the suggestion made earlier in Chapter 3, which sees in the book of Job a catalogue of writings concerning the subject of divine recompense, and not necessarily one which attempts to present a definitive solution to this problem. But this is not the case. The perception of the book as a catalogue does not contradict, but only weakens, the anticipation of an absolute solution; it gives the answer—any answer— a less committal, less important, less conclusive nature. The catalogic nature of the book, like its irony, somewhat removes the author's personal responsibility for providing a 'true' answer to the problem he has presented and, exactly like irony, its catalogic nature gives him greater freedom to say what is in his heart without being totally committed to it.

---

56. Fullerton (1924) explains the speech of God in a similar vein. However, in my opinion, he gave too much weight to the tactical tendency of the author to deliberately present a double message: one to the dogmatic believer—behold, there is a solution to the problem; and the second, to the 'thinking' believer—there is no solution to the problem of suffering. Williams also suggested irony as one of the possible interpretations of the speech of God, but admits that 'I have a problem with this reading of Job', and it would appear that he prefers the position of Tzevat (1971: 250).

57. Kierkegaard 1989: 256. Similarly, see the words of Booth (1974: 41): 'having decided for myself that the ostensible judgment (based on the apparent meaning of the text) must somehow be combatted, I make the new position mine with all the force that is conferred by my sense of being judged independently'.

To the common denominator of irony and the catalogic form, one may also add the other stylistic features discussed in this chapter—the foreign words, the *hapax legomena*, the homonyms and the relative abundance of metaphor—all of which give the author freedom from full and unequivocal responsibility for the things which are said. However, the dramatic nature of the work *per se* already gives him this freedom— it consists entirely of the words of others, while his own view is not expressed at all. It is nevertheless possible to understand his need for other means of attaining this freedom. While its dramatic form and catalogic nature free the author of commitment to the things are said, not by himself, but by 'others' (Job, the friends, God), its obscure style gives him freedom towards himself to say those things which he perhaps would have been unable to say—that is, to think—in another manner.

One could have proposed independent explanations for each of the phenomena discussed in this chapter. The advantage of the explanation offered here, among other things, is that it provides a single answer to all of the phenomena discussed, as well as bringing out the coherence of the book. In the wake of this, I may introduce a minor correction to the earlier formulation of the aesthetic problem which the book of Job sets out to solve, and reformulate it as follows: to create a collection of different doctrines of recompense, of varied outlooks concerning divine righteousness, within a framework more interesting and significant than that of an anthology, one allowing its author complete freedom of expression while properly reflecting his dialectic position on the subject.

Chapter 7

ON GOD'S JUSTICE IN THE BOOK OF JOB

In the course of the previous chapters, we have discussed various aspects of two interrelated claims:

a. That the book of Job was created as a kind of sophisticated anthology of writings concerning the subject of divine retribution.

b. That the viewpoints expressed on this subject in the book were so radical, even provocative, in relation to what was generally accepted in the cultural environment of the author that conventional literary and linguistic tools were unsuitable to express them. Hence, he was forced to create innovative means of expression suitable to the nature of the positions which he expressed.

This chapter will be devoted to an examination of these claims in relation to the central subject of the book—the problem of divine recompense or, as it often called, the issue of theodicy or divine justice.[1] Regarding the former claim, we will need to examine whether the majority of passages in the book do in fact relate to the issue of divine recompense, and to what extent it mirrors a variety of approaches to this issue in the Bible. The latter claim will require a comparison between the view of recompense implied by the book of Job and other views concerning this matter in the Bible and the ancient Near East.

---

1. The term was originally coined by Leibniz to refer to involvement in the question as to how the existence of evil in the world may be reconciled with the goodness of God (A. Weinrib, *EncHeb*, XXXII, p. 446). I use this term or the phrase 'the problem of recompense' below in the sense of the contradiction between the belief that God is a righteous judge, and the existence of righteous men who live poorly and wicked who live well. An important summary of this matter was written by Licht, s.v. 'Reward and Punishment', *EncBib*, VIII, pp. 287-306.

These issues dictated the structure of the present chapter and fixed the parameters of the discussion therein. In point of fact, elucidation of the views expressed in the book in isolation from other aspects is incompatible with the overall approach of this work, which asserts that one cannot separate 'literary' and 'content' aspects of a work of art. Hence, this distinction—which is not absolute, as shall become clear during the course of the chapter—should be seen as essentially didactic (which is one of the considerations distinguishing works of art from works that discuss them).

The following are the principal components of the subject of divine recompense—the sides of the equation, so to speak: (a) the righteous, the wicked; (b) happiness, suffering; (c) the nature of the relations between the former two groups. In other words: What is a righteous person? What is a wicked one? What is happiness and what is suffering? Is the relation between (a) and (b) accidental or causal? If causal, is the causality systematic? And if so, can one discover the underlying system? Is it ethical? Can each and every manifestation of human suffering and happiness be explained in terms of reward and punishment? If the book of Job is indeed a sophisticated anthology on the subject of retribution, one would expect it to deal with each of these elements, and one might expect its innovativeness to be expressed thereby.

In order to clarify these matters, our discussion will be divided into three parts. In Part 1, I will present those passages from the book of Job pertaining to theodicy, and the ways in which it uses a gamut of terms connected to the subject. In Part 2, I shall examine the various approaches to recompense in the book of Job and in the Bible. In Part 3, I shall inspect certain texts from ancient Near Eastern literature pertaining to the question of recompense, so as to elucidate the nature of the intellectual innovation of the book of Job in comparison with this literature as well.

As for the parameters of the discussion, a comprehensive examination of the biblical view of recompense would require us to elucidate such issues as personal, familial, group, and national recompense; the belief in divine recompense in relation to other central concepts, such as that of the covenant between God and his people; the redemption of Israel; personal ethical choice vs. predetermined divine decree; etc. However, a proper examination of all these aspects would require a separate study, beyond the purview of the present work, these subjects not being directly treated in the book of Job. The theory that the book is to be

read as a national allegory[2] is to be rejected totally. As for familial retribution, there is indeed passing allusion to this idea, as the death of Job's
sons was part of the disaster which Satan visited upon their father, and
this could be read as implying a certain outlook regarding mutual
responsibility within the family vis-à-vis the subject of retribution; however, this is a purely secondary matter, and clearly not the central concern of the book. On the contrary, the book completely ignores numerous
marginal questions which would be likely to blunt the edge of the main
subject, namely, how to explain the suffering of the righteous. Even the
problem of the success of the wicked—which cannot be completely
ignored, being as it is the other side of the coin of divine justice—is
marginal to the book as a whole, albeit it does contain more than a few
depictions of the wicked.

1. The Reward Equation of the Book of Job:
Terminology and Distribution

In Appendix XVII, I classify those passages in the book of Job concerned
with the main elements of the equation of divine recompense. My purpose
there is to determine whether their distribution supports the view which
sees the book as a kind of anthology on this subject. It clearly follows
from the table that the vast majority of passages in the book are indeed
devoted to the subject of recompense. Only in chs. 37–41 are there no
motifs related to this subject (with the exception of 40.1-14, 28). There is
hence no doubt that, at least in this respect, there is support for the
statement that the book as a whole is devoted to the issue of divine
recompense, even though these data do not necessarily indicate that the
book ought to be seen as an 'anthology'. However, in Chapter 4 I
offered a justification for the use of this generic terminology regarding
Job.

The extensive and variegated involvement of the Bible with the subject of recompense quite naturally created a need for suitable terminology, and indeed there are certain clearly defined terms that are set
aside, facilitating clearer involvement in the complex subjects of theodicy.

---

2.   Thus recently Wolfers (1990). In his opinion the Leviathan (40.25–41.26)
and 'the river' (40.23) in God's reply are an allegory for the rule of Assyria in the
world, while the Behemoth (40.15-24) and the Jordan (40.24) symbolize both Judah
and Job. All this is allegedly in the spirit of Isaiah's outlook concerning the faithful
remnant, which is so to speak represented by Job.

Two of the terms that took shape for this purpose are צדיק ('righteous')
and רשע ('wicked')—the principal components in group (a) of the
equation of recompense. Although we are unable to identify the stages
of semantic development with certainty, it would appear that these terms
developed in parallel, as two opposites, through a process that shaped
and strengthened their status as distinctive terms. From the manner in
which the Bible tends to portray divine characteristics in human terms,
one may conclude that the term 'righteous'[3] referred primarily to human
beings, and only secondarily became one of the attributes of God. This
theory is strengthened by the fact that in only a few, mostly late, writings
is the term applied to God.[4] As a descriptive adjective used to refer
to a person, the word is sometimes used to designate an ethical status
(such as: 'You are more righteous than I', 1 Sam 24.17) or judgment
('acquitting the innocent', Deut. 25.1) of a person with regard to a
specific matter; while at other times, the adjective appears as an absolute
definition of a personality. However, only one concrete figure is designated in the Bible as 'righteous' in the second sense of the term: Noah is
'a righteous man, blameless in his generation' (Gen. 6.9; compare 7.1—
'righteous before me in this generation').[5] Ezekiel mentions 'Noah,
Daniel and Job', noting their 'righteousness', but they are not explicit
designated as 'righteous men' (צדיקים, Ezek. 14.12-20). Similarly
Abraham: it is related of him, 'And he believed the Lord, and He [he
(?)] reckoned it to him [himself (?)] as righteousness' (צדקה, Gen. 15.6),
but he is not designated 'righteous' as such. Thus, the primary meaning
of צדיק is first and foremost as a theoretical term, used primarily in the

---

3.   It appears in the Bible in its various forms 202 times, as follows: 65 times in
Proverbs, 50 in Psalms, 40 in the Latter Prophets (primarily Ezekiel), 17 in the Torah,
8 in Ecclesiastes, 7 in Job, and 5 in the other books. Fullerton (1930: 244-45) counted
194 occurrences of צדיק. See his semantic discussion there of the root צדק in the
Bible. For more on this, see Koch 1953.
4.   Exod. 9.27; Deut. 32.4; Isa. 45.21; Jer. 12.1; Zeph. 3.5; Pss. 11.7; 14.5; 116.5;
119.137; 145.17; Lam. 1.18; Dan. 9.14; Ezra 9.15; Neh. 9.8, 33; 2 Chron. 12.6.
5.   There is a well-known discussion among the Sages (*b. Sanh.* 108a; cited in
Rashi's commentary on this verse) concerning the question as to whether the word
דרתיו ('his generations') is intended to diminish from [Noah's] righteousness ('in
his generation he was righteous, had he lived in the generation of Abraham he would
not have been considered as anything'), or to augment it ('how much more so had he
lived in a generation of righteous men, he would have been an even greater righteous
man'). The word תמים ('blameless' or 'pure'), which implies wholeness, seems to
support the second interpretation.

wisdom and psalm literatures, to refer to a person deserving of God's
goodness. There are cases of description of the behaviour of the righteous,
such as Ezek. 18.5-9, in which positive imperatives and negative injunc-
tions in the realm of ethics, divine worship, and ritual purity and impurity,
combine into something approximating a definition of the term.[6]
However, it would appear that the nature of the 'righteous' is most
commonly defined in the Bible by means of negative analogy: righteous
is the opposite of wicked. Thus Abraham protests to God, 'Wilt thou
indeed destroy the righteous with the wicked?' (Gen. 18.23; compare v.
25). According to the Psalmist, God's righteousness necessarily implies
that he hates the wicked (11.5-6); there is a constant war between the
wicked and the righteous (37.12; 58). The Psalmist generally refrains
from declaring himself to be righteous, but this is indirectly implied by
the representation of his enemies and pursuers as wicked (17; 31.15-18).
In the book of Proverbs, the righteous and the wicked appear regularly
as an opposed parallel pair (10.3, 6, 7). This approach is exemplified,
more than any other text, by Psalm 1, whose central theme is that the
righteous and wicked are diametrically opposed in every conceivable
respect, leaving no possible doubt as to their identification.[7] The extensive use of the terms 'righteous' and 'wicked' in the psalm and wisdom
literature creates a dichotomous world-view, without any intermediate
people. Indeed, this is a further expression of the semantic nature of
these words—terms that were, so to speak, created to present a
theological-theoretical approach or to place it to the test.

In addition, the Bible utilizes other words to designate the righteous
and the wicked, such as נָקִי ('innocent') תָּם ('quiet', 'whole'), יָשָׁר
('straight', 'upright')—as opposed to עֲוֵל ('crooked'), פּוֹעֵל-אָוֶן ('doer of
evil'), and the like. These words evidently did not acquire the semantic
status of recognized terms, and it is hence doubtful as to whether there
is any justification for exegetical attempts to draw clear boundaries

---

6.   See Licht, 'Righteous, Righteousness', *EncBib*, VI, 1971, pp. 678-79. When
speaking of words that were smelted into idioms, attempts at exact definition would
seem to be a later stage in the semantic process. Such is the case of 'righteous' and
'wicked'. The opposite is obviously the case regarding words which were initially
coined as terms, particularly in the various sciences.

7.   See on this below. The distribution of רשע in the Bible, like that of צדיק
expresses the close relation between the two terms. The word appears altogether 263
times in the Bible, as follows: 81 times in Psalms, 78 in Proverbs, 26 in Job, 29 in
Ezekiel, 20 in the other latter Prophets, and the rest in the other books.

among them;[8] they ought, rather, to be seen as synonyms. The differences among them are of nuance alone, stemming more from context than from the use of the word itself. Despite the extensive use of these synonyms, their overall occurrence in the Bible is less than one-third that of the terms צדיק and רשע, justifying our perception of them as 'substitutes' for the usual terms. This formulation does not require us to assume that they were only created after the words צדיק and רשע had already become standard terms, but it does express the assumption that their use was the result of a deliberate stylistic preference on the part of the majority of the biblical authors, whereas the use of 'righteous' and 'wicked' was routine and more spontaneous.

Against this background, it is interesting to test the manner in which the book of Job relates to the words 'righteous' and 'wicked' and their substitutes. First of all, one may note that the principal adjectives used throughout biblical literature as synonyms for צדיק and רשע likewise appear in the book of Job. This datum should not be surprising in the context of a book which is a kind of anthology on the subject of retribution; as may be seen from Appendix XVIII, the same holds true to a large extent regarding the anthologies of Psalm and Proverbs. However, there is a clear distinction between the book of Job and these other books: whereas the numerical ratio between the term 'righteous' and the totality of its synonyms in Psalms is 50 : 31, and in the book of Proverbs the ratio is similar, 65 : 27, the ratio in the book of Job is 7 : 30. In other words, the authors of Proverbs and Psalms use a substitute word for צדיק only half as often as they use the word צדיק itself; by contrast the author of Job uses an 'alternative' word four times as often as he uses the word צדיק itself.

Is there any particular significance to these data, or are they merely

8.   See, e.g. Weiss 1984: 182-84. In n. 39 he notes the distinctions between נקי ('blameless' or 'innocent') and צדיק drawn by the Talmud, Rashi and Fullerton. But in fact the term נקי like צדיק is also used in a comprehensive and absolute sense (for example: 'in hiding places he murders the innocent' [נקי], Ps. 10.8); in a relative sense (e.g., 'let the king and his throne be guiltless [נקי]', 2 Sam. 14.9; 'who does not take a bribe against the innocent', Ps. 15.5); and in a legal context with regard to a specific matter ('but the owner of the ox shall be clear [נקי]', Exod. 21.28; 'and do not slay the innocent [נקי] and righteous', Exod. 23.7). Indeed, unlike the adjective צדיק the Bible never applies the term נקי to God. The reason for this seems to be that the frozen metaphor נקי never completely lost its connection to the non-metaphoric use of the word connected with filth and dirt, and that it is clearly inappropriate to use it to describe a divine quality.

random? While it is difficult to give a definite answer to this question, I will nevertheless risk a conjecture consistent with the nature of the book: that in this way the semantic status of 'righteous' as a definite term becomes blurred, making it equivalent to its synonyms. The existential problem of the suffering righteous is thereby sharpened: in the absence of a special status for the conventional term צדיק, which is loaded with theoretical weight and hence possibly hackneyed and lacking in emotional impact, the words צדיק, נקי, ישר, תם, ירא-אלהים, סר מרע, and נדיב all come to enjoy equal status. All of them describe human beings, and in effect nullify the tendency towards precision in the theoretical aspects of the term צדיק. Hence, צדיק is no longer a term requiring definition. The 'righteous' is Job: he is the one whom everyone knows is innocent, upright, God-fearing, and shunning evil; who is innocent, pure and upright; who behaves as described in chs. 29 and 31; whose behaviour is the opposite of that described in chs. 21 and 24—in brief, the opposite of the 'wicked' (I will return to this subject at greater length below).

Against the background of this explanation—and because in the centre of the book of Job stands the problem of the suffering of the righteous, rather than that of the prosperity of the wicked—one may also explain the use of the term רשע ('wicked') and its parallels. 'Wicked' likewise enjoys the status of a fixed term in the Bible, perhaps even more so than 'righteous'. We have already noted that the most common means of defining the 'righteous' in the Bible is to state that they are the opposite of the 'wicked', the latter, as a term which it is superfluous to define, being self-understood. Indeed, even though the word 'wicked' has many parallels in the book of Job, these do not disturb its status as an explicit term. In this respect, the book of Job reflects the situation throughout the Bible, particularly in the Psalms and Wisdom literature: 'wicked' is a primary term while the others are explicitly substitutes, which serve as literary variations and bring out fine nuances. Details of this picture appear in Appendix XIX. Against this background, the approach of the book of Job becomes clearer. First, as an anthology on the subject of recompense, it is only natural that it makes maximal use of terms to designate the righteous and wicked. Secondly, its particular use of the word 'righteous' stands out against the background of the routine use made of the term 'wicked' and its parallels, thereby illuminating the problem which lies in the centre of the book—not the success of the wicked, but the meaning of the sufferings of those who do good. This sophisticated use of the accepted biblical lexicon for dealing with the problem of recompense suits a book whose main subject is the engagement with this subject of a particular unique individual.

The book follows a different approach regarding the components of pair (b) in the equation of recompense—that of happiness and suffering. As in numerous psalms and in the book of Proverbs, so too the book of Job contains metaphorical descriptions of happiness (such as 5.21-24; 8.7, 21; 11.19) and especially of suffering (such as 4.8-11; 6.4; 7.1-3; 8.14-19; 16.8-9, 12-15; 18.5-21). However, these are entirely secondary to those sections which explicitly describe the nature of happiness and of suffering. The descriptions of Job's felicity in chs. 1, 29, and 42 are the primary resource upon which the reader relies for a concept of the nature of true happiness; against them are placed the stories of the loss of Job's property, the death of his sons, his painful illness (chs. 1–2), and other explicit descriptions (such as 7.3-6, 13-15; 15.20-23; 16.10-11; 19.13-20; 21.10-12; 27.14-18; 30) which elaborate upon the nature of suffering. That is to say, the book, not on the basis of generalized and colourless definitions nor by theoretical terms, but through concrete descriptions, establishes the nature of the components in group (b). I shall claim below that this method serves the message of the book regarding the relationship between groups (a) and (b)—that is, its doctrine of recompense.

2. *The Problem of Recompense in the Book of Job and in the Bible*

Where else and in what manner is the problem of the justice of God's behaviour toward the individual presented in the Bible? In the book of Proverbs, God's righteousness is presented as an axiom rather than as a problem requiring solution. The advice given there is based upon the assumption that one who behaves wisely will always emerge rewarded. Given that wisdom and the fear of God are synonymous—'The fear of the Lord is the beginning of knowledge' (1.7; compare 'The fear of the Lord is the beginning of wisdom', Ps. 111.10)—*ipso facto* there cannot be any problem. Even when the book advises one not to rely upon wisdom but upon the fear of God ('Be not wise in your own eyes; fear the Lord, and turn away from evil', 3.7), it simply means to warn that, if at times it appears that human 'wisdom' contradicts the fear of God, it is clear that this is not true wisdom, and one should not act according to it. The wise man knows how to distinguish between what appears to be wisdom but is not really so, being opposed to the fear of God, and that which is true wisdom, and hence cannot be contrary to the fear of God.

Similarly, in biblical historiography, including that of the Torah, there is no clear presentation of the problem of divine justice towards the individual, nor is any attempt made to resolve it. Here and there the subject is touched upon, as in Abraham's pleading with God concerning the people of Sodom ('Wilt thou indeed destroy the righteous with the wicked?', Gen. 18.23; and v. 25), but the assumption of the story is that there were in fact no righteous people to be found in Sodom,[9] and hence no problem of the righteous suffering. In the story concerning the census conducted by David (2 Sam. 24), he turns to God and says, 'But these sheep, what have they done? Let thy hand, I pray thee, be against me and against my father's house' (v. 17). However, not only is no attempt made here to resolve the problem of the suffering righteous when he has done no evil, but the problem is not even alluded to; the subject under consideration is rather that of collective retribution.[10]

On more than one occasion the prophets touch upon the problem of recompense, but primarily in its national aspect (as in Isa. 10.5-15; on Hab. 1.2-4, 13-17, see below, n. 20) which, as mentioned, will not be discussed here.[11] Only in the prophecies of Ezekiel is there extensive involvement with the subject of personal recompense, but there too it is not presented as a problem relating to theodicy as such. In the background of that prophet's words (Ezek. 3.17-21; 33.1-20) stands the

9.   The question as to whether Lot was saved by virtue of his own righteousness or that of Abraham does not arise in the book. Ezek. 14.12-20 seems to make one polemical reference to this story. The statement that the righteous of the earth, Noah, Daniel and Job, 'would deliver neither sons nor daughters, but they alone would be delivered' (v. 18) evidently reflects the interpretation of the tradition according to which Lot was saved by virtue of Abraham, and not because of his own righteousness.

10.   Consciousness of one or another aspect of the problem of individual recompense is also expressed in such passages as Gen. 20.4-18; 21.11-13; Judg. 9.59; 2 Sam. 1.14 (in relation to 1 Sam. 24.10); 12.11-12; 24.17; 26.11; 1 Kgs 11.12, 34; 2 Chron. 33.12-13; 35.22; etc. However in all of these the problem of recompense is marginal and hence we do not discuss it here.

11.   Indeed, there is a close connection between theodicy in the realm of the individual and in that of the nation. However, in the realm of the nation the solutions may be entirely different, and indeed they are so. The lifetime of a nation is not necessarily limited, and its definition as righteous or wicked is never exact—all of which allows for greater flexibility in the solution of the problem of divine recompense. Similarly, the theology of the covenant between God and his people, which does not exist in the realm of the individual, is an important component in the equation of national recompense.

question of the recompense due to a wicked person who repents of his wickedness and, on the other hand, of the reward of a righteous person who ceases to be righteous. This of course relates to the problem of theodicy, but only indirectly; one may only derive conclusions regarding the solution to this problem by implication, and by methods of philosophical discussion which are alien to the Bible.[12] Thus, apart from the books of Job and Ecclesiastes, the problem of individual recompense[13] as an issue pertaining to God's justice only arises in the Psalm literature,[14] whether in its largest collection, the book of Psalms, or in those psalms that are incorporated within other books.

A central generic convention of the psalms literature is that the authors of the psalms are not wicked. Even if the poet admits at times that he has sinned (as in Pss. 38; 51; 69.6), the very fact of his confession and contrition are taken as expressions of his righteousness. There is not even one psalm in which the poet is represented as wicked, for self-evident reasons: he is engaged in prayer to God, which is not the way of

12. For a summary discussion of the understanding of recompense in Ezekiel, see Brin 1975: 80-105.

13. So as not to over-extend our discussion, I shall concentrate here upon those psalms that seem personal. This, despite the fact that there is no sharp distinction between personal and national in the Psalms. See, for example, Psalm 102: 'A prayer of one afflicted, when he is faint and pours out his complaint before the Lord...For my days pass away like smoke, and my bones burn like a furnace.. My heart is smitten like grass, and withered; I forget to eat my bread' (vv. 1-6); but further on: 'Thou wilt arouse and have pity on Zion...to hear the groans of the prisoners...that men may declare in Zion the name of the Lord' (vv. 14-22). Similarly, in Psalm 94: 'How long shall the wicked exult...They crush thy people, O Lord, and afflict thy heritage' (vv. 2-4); but then: 'Blessed is the man whom thou dost chasten, O Lord, and whom thou dost teach out of thy law' (v. 12). Moreover, some scholars challenge the very distinction between individual and communal psalms, assuming that the individual is no more than a personification of the nation as a whole. Thus Mowinckel (1962: 76) states that 'There is no sharp distinction between public and private psalms'. For more on this subject see Robinson 1936; Porter 1965. Against the idea that a lack of distinction between the individual and the public is a sign of primitive, pre-logical thinking, see Rogerson 1985.

14. For this reason, I will not discuss here those psalms which do not involve some challenge to God's righteousness, such as 15, 24, 34, 37, 112, etc. Particularly outstanding in this regard is Psalm 119, which consists entirely of the celebration of divine justice. However, between the lines of these psalms one can occasionally discern a certain awareness of the problem of theodicy, which I shall discuss where necessary.

the wicked. True, on more than one occasion the psalms 'quote' the wicked, but this is only a literary device to concretize his essence, in the sense of 'let his own mouth speak for him'. The wicked are thus represented as saying 'there is no God' (Ps. 15.2); 'God has forgotten, he has hidden his face, he will never see it' (Ps. 10.11); 'who is our master?' (Ps. 12.5). Even in those psalms which praise the greatness of God's works in the cosmos ('When I look at the heavens, the work of thy fingers...'—8.4; 'Bless the Lord, O my soul! O Lord my God, thou art very great! Thou art clothed with honour and majesty'—Ps. 104.1) it is clear that the speaker fears God, for if not there would be no value to the praises of God which he utters. The same holds true even when the poet does not speak in the first person. Here too, the generic assumption is that the author is not wicked, for if he were, he certainly would not claim that God does good to the righteous and punishes the wicked (Ps. 1), or that only the righteous 'shall never be moved' (Ps. 15.5). A wicked person would not invoke the praises of God (Pss. 146–150) nor call to relate his wondrous deeds to Israel (Ps. 114). This convention was well understood by the various redactors, and hence they only ascribed the psalms to unimpeachable figures, such as David, Solomon, Hannah the mother of Samuel (1 Sam. 2), Jeremiah (Jer. 17.5-13), Isaiah (Isa. 12), Hezekiah (Isa. 38.9-20), and the like. Even the hymn of Jonah in ch. 2 of that book is no exception to this rule, as the prophet says there that he admits his error.

This being so, even when the psalm presents the problem of recompense there is a definite assumption that the psalmist is God-fearing, whether he presents one side of the coin—the success of the wicked (as in Ps. 73)—or both—the success of the wicked and the suffering of the righteous (as in Ps. 10); whether the psalm has a lyric quality, written in the first person, or whether the image of the poet is not present there at all, and is of a reflective-Wisdom nature.

I shall now examine separately the manner in which both aspects of the problem of recompense is raised in these types of psalms. Two characteristics of the lyric type of psalm bearing upon the issue of recompense are relevant to our theme: the psalmist never explicitly describes himself as 'righteous', and in no psalm is the problem of the righteous suffering presented as such, but only alongside the other side of the problem of theodicy—namely, the successful wicked.[15] Both of these characteristics

---

15. Exceptions to this rule are those psalms in which the suffering poet appeals to God's mercy rather than to his justice, as in Psalm 88. The generic assumption that

may be combined in one claim: namely, that in all of those lyric psalms touching upon the problem of divine retribution, the terms 'righteous' or its parallels are relative: the poet's righteousness, known to us from the generic convention, is interpreted and emphasized in comparison to the wicked. By saying 'Many are rising against me' (Ps. 3.2) and by seeking the help of God, he hints that those rising against him are wicked (v. 8); he finds them to be bloodthirsty and deceitful men (5.5-7); the good qualities of the unfortunate and afflicted person (6.2-8) are referred to in the designation of those who seek his misfortune as 'workers of evil' (v. 9); he is confident that God will save him from his pursuers (7.2). And, from the positive viewpoint: he relates that he comes to the house of the Lord to worship (5.8), he prays to his God (5.3), he swears that there is no wrong in his hands (7.4-5), he asks to be judged 'according to my righteousness and the integrity that is in me' (7.9), but never actually states that he is righteous. His righteousness is only alluded to indirectly, as when he prays for the end of the 'wicked' (7.10) or in general statements such as 'establish thou the righteous' (7.10). The presentation of the wicked as the personal pursuers of the one praying emphasizes even more the relative nature of the psalmist's righteousness. See, for example, Ps. 10.1-2: 'Why dost thou stand afar off, O Lord? Why dost thou hide thyself in times of trouble? In arrogance the wicked hotly pursue the poor'; 'By the noise of the enemy, because of the oppression of the wicked. For they bring trouble upon me, and in anger they cherish enmity against me' (Ps. 55.4).

The significance of these characteristics to the problem of recompense is clear: the very fact that the suffering author does not describe himself as righteous, but makes do with presenting himself as a victim of the wicked, greatly blunts the edge of the theological problem concerning the justification of the suffering of the righteous. The answer to the problem is implied in the very manner in which it is presented: the poet does not claim for himself absolute righteousness; rather, his hope for God's help is based upon his appeal for mercy (as in 6.3; 41.5; 56.2), from which it follows that his suffering as such does not contradict God's righteousness.[16] Against this background, it is easier to accept the

---

the one appealing is not wicked suffices here to give weight to the plea for the mercies of God.

16. In a number of hymns containing confession and justification of the divine edict, the suffering of the worshipper is not presented outright as a theological problem. Thus, for example, he says 'For I know my transgressions, and my sin is ever

answer implied by these psalms as the solution to the problem of the
suffering of the righteous: namely, that suffering is only temporary. In
the final analysis, God will answer the sufferer's plea and remove his
travail. This solution could not be an acceptable one were the psalmist to
insist upon his own absolute righteousness, for in that case there would
be no justification for even temporary suffering. The manner in which
the righteousness of the lyric psalmists is presented *ab initio* suggests
the transient nature of their suffering as a suitable solution.

The idea that the suffering of the righteous does not contradict God's
righteousness is elegantly expressed in the saying, 'Remember not the
sins of my youth, or my transgressions' (Ps. 25.7). This is based upon
the principle that God does not always react immediately to man's acts,
making it possible for the innocent righteous man to be punished in the
present for the sins of his youth, which he presumably committed, even
if he no longer remembers them. Thus, the suffering of the righteous is a
legitimate punishment, making the prayer to ignore the sins of his youth
not an appeal to God's justice, which is the basis for his punishment, but
to his mercy. Note that I do not claim that the personal psalms do not
raise the suffering of the righteous as a theological problem, but that
they present it from the beginning as somewhat softened, making its
solution understood by the very manner of its presentation. An outstanding example of this is Psalm 22. The author provides an extensive,
moving description of his difficult situation: 'But I am a worm, and no
man; scorned by men, and despised by the people. All who see me
mock at me...Many bulls encompass me...They open wide their mouths
at me, like a ravening and roaring lion. I am poured out like water, and
all my bones are out of joint...Yea, dogs are round about me; a company of evildoers encircle me...They divide my garments among them,
and for my raiment they cast lots' (vv. 7-19). He nevertheless does not
claim that he is righteous, but instead bases his request for help upon
God's mercies ('For he has not despised nor abhorred the affliction of
the afflicted', v. 25), and concerning the good lesson that all will learn
from his success ('I will tell of thy name to my brethren', v. 23; 'All the
ends of the earth shall remember and turn to the Lord', v. 28). Similarly

before me' (Ps. 51.5). More than acceptance of God's judgment, this implies an
admission by the poet that he is being punished even less than he deserves according
to his acts—'He does not deal with us according to our sin, nor requite us according
to our iniquities' (103.10). In psalms of this type, the problem of theodicy does not
exist at all, and all suffering is seen as justifiable punishment that befalls a person.

in Psalm 69: the acute theological dilemma which would be raised by a reading of the harsh descriptions of the author's suffering at the hand of his wicked enemies (vv. 2-5, 8-13, 20-22) is blunted by such remarks as, 'O God, thou knowest my folly; the wrongs I have done are not hidden from thee' (v. 6), which balance such strong claims as, 'For it is for thy sake that I have borne reproach' (v. 7). Likewise, Jeremiah's severe complaint (Jer. 15.15-18), presenting the prophet as one who has suffered because of his righteousness—'Know that for thy sake I bear reproach'—is softened by the same means as those generally accepted in the psalm literature: Jeremiah does not describe himself as 'righteous', and himself moderates the problem by alluding to his vengeance upon his enemies (Jer. 15.15). The issue is further softened by the immediate context of the psalm and the general context of the book. In the immediate context, the proximity of God's answer somewhat obscures the problem—'If you return, I will restore you, and you shall stand before me...I will deliver you out of the hand of the wicked' (vv. 19-21). As for the overall context, the knowledge that one is speaking of a prophet, who consciously accepted upon himself a difficult mission, places Jeremiah's suffering in a unique light. He does not suffer for naught, but for an important national purpose.[17]

The literary power of the lyric psalms lies in the empathy which they create towards the psalmist, particularly if he is 'known' to us, as is Jeremiah. While this makes the emotional power of the problem of the suffering poet even deeper, the refusal explicitly to claim that he is righteous is, as mentioned, a mitigating factor with regard to the theoretical aspect of the problem of divine recompense. This balance is one of the characteristics of psalmic piety, which cannot by its very nature present the suffering of the righteous in overly sharp contradiction to divine justice. Another example of this tendency may be invoked from Psalm 23. It too is a personal psalm ('The Lord is my shepherd, I shall not want'), but unlike the other psalms mentioned it does not raise the issue of theodicy, but deals with it indirectly. The righteous (by convention)

---

17. The question as to whether Jeremiah is the author of the psalms appearing in the book bearing his name, or whether perhaps a later redactor incorporated them there for various reasons, is irrelevant in this context. See on this the recent commentaries to the book of Jeremiah, especially McKane 1986; Carroll 1986; and Holladay 1986. And see also the studies of Baumgartner (1971) and O'Connor (1988) devoted to the psalms of Jeremiah. The latter also contains up-to-date bibliography.

psalmist declares: 'Even though I walk through the valley of the shadow of death, I fear no evil; for thou art with me; thy rod and thy staff, they comfort me' (v. 4). The implication of this statement is that there is no 'suffering righteous', for according to his testimony even God's staff comforts him. By this means, the author approaches a solution of the problem of the suffering righteous by means of semantic sophistication, as I shall note further along.

As for the success of the wicked in the lyric psalms, this is present in the background of the suffering of the righteous in the wake of the designs of the wicked. Only occasionally is special emphasis given to the motif of the prosperity of the wicked, and not merely as a means of stressing the suffering of the righteous. The success of the wicked appears as a central problem in the following personal psalms: 10, 12, 14 (= 53), 58, 64, 73, 109; Jer. 12.1-3. In most of these, there is no clear-cut solution offered to the problem, but the conclusion of these psalms generally dims their severity by intimating the end of the wicked in a number of ways: calls of encouragement to God ('Arise, O Lord; O God, lift up they hand'—10.12; 'Break thou the arm of the wicked and evildoer'— v. 15); reports of God arising to perform salvation ('"I will now arise", says the Lord'—12.6; 'But God will shoot his arrows at them; they will be wounded suddenly'—64.8); and, towards the end of the psalm, expression of confidence ('O Lord, thou wilt hear the desire of the meek'—10.17; 'There they shall be in great terror, for God is with the generation of the righteous'—14.5; compare 64.11; 109.30-31). Indirectly, but more clearly, a solution parallel to that suggested with regard to the suffering of the righteous begins to emerge: that the success of the wicked is only temporary, until God will, as it were, turn his attention to this, perhaps in the wake of the psalmist's appeal. Its temporary nature is clearly articulated in Psalm 94, where it is applied to both sides of the problem of recompense: 'Blessed is the man whom thou dost chasten, O Lord, and whom thou dost teach out of thy law, to give him respite from days of trouble, until a pit is dug for the wicked' (vv. 12-13). In other words, the suffering of the righteous is only temporary, and has a practical aim—to educate humanity.[18] This is likewise the solution to the

---

18. This is the sense of most occurrences of the verb יסר. Compare 'Thou hast smitten them…but they refused to take correction' [מוסר], Jer. 5.3; 'Be warned (הוסרו) O rulers of the earth', Ps. 2.10; 'as a man disciplines (ייסר) his son, the Lord your God disciplines you (מיסרך)', Deut. 8.5; and many others. Compare 'It is good for me that I was afflicted (כי עניתי) that I might learn thy statutes', Ps. 119.71.

question asked at the beginning of the psalm, 'How long shall the wicked exult?' (v. 3).

In the majority of the personal psalms, no attempt is made to confront the theoretical aspect of the problem of theodicy systematically. An exception to this is Psalm 73. Notwithstanding its personal nature (the word 'I' appears there emphatically in vv. 2, 22, 23, and 28), the problem is presented there in the systematic manner appropriate to a principled examination; however, as becomes clear at its end, it is not written as a personal psalm for nothing. It opens with the presentation of the principle and its clash with the reality known to the poet: 'Truly God is good to the upright, to those who are pure in heart. But as for me, my feet had almost stumbled...For I was envious of the arrogant, when I saw the prosperity of the wicked' (vv. 1-3).[19] The poet argues that the opposition between the principle of divine justice and the reality which seems to contradict it constitutes a social problem, in that it encourages ethical degeneration—a tendency to adopt the way of the wicked. Hence, it is not merely a theoretical problem![20]

The solution to the problem is presented in two stages. First, it becomes clear to the poet that there is in fact no problem of the prosperity of the wicked, because the peace of the wicked is imaginary, no more than a stage in their ultimate downfall ('Truly thou dost set them in slippery places; thou dost make them fall to ruin', v. 18). In this, he propounds a more sophisticated version of the accepted solution of the temporary

19. The complaint in Jer. 12.1 has a similar structure. I do not find any justification for Briggs's claim in his commentary to Ps. 73 (1907) that vv. 1, 17-20, and 27-28 are glosses. In any event, this question will not be discussed here, as it makes no difference whether the one responsible for the final version of the psalm is the 'original' author or a later poet. I likewise find doubtful the claim of Kraus in his commentary to this psalm (1961) that the word לישראל ('to Israel') in the first verse is 'impossible', because it does not fit the chapter as a whole. He proposes correcting it to לישר אל ('God [is good] to the upright'). While it is true that the psalm does not deal with the nation, the relationship between personal and national psalms has already been noted (above, n. 13). In any event, this correction does not relate to the understanding of theodicy in this chapter.

20. Compare also 'Why dost thou make me see wrongs and look upon trouble?...So the law is slacked...For the wicked surround the righteous...', Hab. 1.3-4. The prophet's complaint is in clearly psalmic style. Despite the fact that it is focused upon the problem of the suffering of one nation at the hands of another, the point of departure is the recompense of the individual, from which an analogy is drawn to the national aspect.

nature of the wicked's success. In its wake, the poet states as it were that one needs to formulate anew the well-known problem: no longer 'Why does the way of the wicked prosper?' (Jer. 12.1), but rather, if there is no phenomenon of the wicked prospering, how then can we explain why people envy them? In other words, the problem of the success of the wicked is not theological and does not pertain to God, but is essentially psychological. The psalmist's answer is, 'I was stupid and ignorant, I was like a beast toward thee' (v. 22): man in his great foolishness mistakenly thinks that there are wicked who prosper. It is not by chance that this solution is proposed within a personal psalm, as it is not based here upon objective wisdom proofs, but upon personal-autobiographical experience—'until I went into the sanctuary of God; then I perceived their end' (v. 17): the psalmist came to a recognition of the truth, not by rational analysis, but by a religious experience.

A similar idea is offered in Psalm 92, also a lyric psalm, albeit one whose main subject is not divine recompense. In the course of praises of God, the poet says, 'The dull man cannot know, the stupid cannot understand this; that, though the wicked sprout like grass and all evildoers flourish, they are doomed to destruction for ever' (vv. 7-8), as against 'the righteous flourish like the palm tree' (v. 13). But this metaphor too implies that the prosperity of the wicked is imaginary: sometimes the farmer waters his field so that the weeds may grow, in order to make it possible to uproot them thereafter. The prepositional *lamed* in the word להשמדם ('that they may be destroyed') reinforces this interpretation. But at times, the author notes, the dull person is unable to understand this. Similarly, 'Because they [i.e., the wicked] do not regard the works of the Lord, or the work of his hands, he will break them down and build them up no more' (Ps. 28.5).

Parallel to the argument that the success of the wicked does not exist as a problem on the theological plane, Psalm 73 touches indirectly upon the subject of the suffering righteous. It hints that the true reward of human beings is in the feeling of closeness to God—'But for me it is good to be near God' (73.28). That is, there is no righteous person who does not receive his just reward, while the person who does not understand that nearness to God is the true reward is *ipso facto* not unqualifiedly righteous, and what right has he to complain? Psalm 23 expresses a position similar to this.

The subject of theodicy is not raised as a problem by even one among the non-personal wisdom psalms which touch upon it. Such psalms as 1,

15, 37 (which is not personal, despite the fact that two verses, 25 and 35, are formulated in first-person proverb-like sayings), 49 (again, notwithstanding the first-person introduction in vv. 4-6, this is not a personal psalm), and 58 affirm the righteousness of God, but do not question it. This should not be surprising, as these are wisdom psalms, whose stance is generally speaking in the spirit of the book of Proverbs. Nevertheless, they also include statements clearly connected with the solutions given to the problem of recompense, which were more fully formulated in the personal psalms discussed above: the temporary nature of the success of the wicked ('I have seen a wicked man overbearing, and towering like a cedar of Lebanon. Again I passed by, and lo, he was no more; though I sought him, he could not be found'—37.35-36); the argument that the success of the wicked is imaginary and that one ought not to be jealous of them ('Fret not yourself because of the wicked, be not envious of wrongdoers! For they will soon fade like the grass, and wither like the green herb'—37.1-2). Even a declaration such as, 'I have been young, and now I am old, yet I have not seen the righteous forsaken or his children begging bread' (v. 25) seems an indirect refutation of the problem of the suffering righteous.

Unique in this respect is Psalm 1, which the redactors did not place at the beginning of the book for naught. The belief in divine justice expressed by this wisdom psalm is seemingly free of any hint of the problem of theodicy. It nevertheless seems to me that it is in fact entirely devoted to an attempt to resolve the problem in an original and unique manner. Its structure seems to be intended to provide a definition of the term 'righteous': it opens with a description of the behaviour of the person, goes on to a description of his reward, and only towards the end does it propose the appropriate term for describing this person—'righteous' (vv. 5-6). On the face of it, the definition seems circular, because it is mostly a negative one ('who walk not in the counsel of the wicked, nor stands in the way of the sinners, nor sits in the seat of scoffers', v. 1), based upon another undefined term—wicked. The statement that 'a righteous is whoever is not wicked' is meaningless so long as neither of these two terms is defined in an independent manner. However, this circularity is broken at two points. (i) Two main claims follow from the psalm: (a) that the righteous and the wicked are two opposites; (b) that the righteous is like 'a tree planted by streams of water...' There follows from this the definition: the righteous is he who is not wicked, and is like a tree planted by streams of water. That which

is generally considered to be the reward of the righteous—that is, a tangential aspect, something which, while it is an anticipated consequence, is
not part of his essential nature—is here presented as an inseparable part
of the definition itself.[21] (ii) Another break in the circularity of the
definition appears in the description of the righteous as one whose
'delight is in the law of the Lord, and on his law he meditates day and
night' (v. 2). But since the wicked and the righteous are opposites, it is
clear that the wicked does not behave in this manner. Hence, the above
definition of the righteous is not circular. Thus, if you see a person who
is like a tree planted by streams of water, and is not wicked—then he is
righteous; whereas a person who is not like a tree, etc., even if he is not
wicked—is not righteous. In other words, it is logically impossible that a
righteous person suffer or a wicked one prosper; if such a problem
seems to exist, the source of the error in fact lies in the incorrect use of
the terms 'righteous' and 'wicked'. The manner in which the argument
is presented here may be misleading, as it seemingly implies that the
author of the psalm also arrived at his argument through means of
systematic philosophic analysis, which is not the case. The presentation is
presumably spontaneous, flowing from the axiomatic status enjoyed by
the righteousness of God in the faith of the author of the psalm. But
while the attempt to resolve a theological problem by means of appropriate semantics is rare in the Bible, it is not unique. We have already
observed a similar path in Psalm 23; see more on this in the discussion
of Job 28, below, pp. 278-85.

The solutions suggested for the problem of retribution are therefore
the following: the success of the wicked and the suffering of the righteous are temporary; the success of the wicked is only apparent, but the
stupid person does not understand this; true happiness is closeness to

---

21. According to this view והיה ('He shall be') in v. 3 is not in the future tense,
coming in the wake of a series of verbs expressing continued activity in the past (יהגה,
הלך, עמד, ישב) I would propose interpreting all of these verbs, including והיה, as
expressing a fixed standard state. The multitude of verbal forms—קטל, יקטל, וקטול, קטול—
are intended either for stylistic variation, or in order to express nuances of modality.
The system of tenses in Biblical Hebrew is still a mystery, and it is difficult to evoke
unequivocal linguistic arguments for the claim presented here, or indeed for any other
claim. Thus, for example, McFall writes (1989: xii): 'The central difficulty in the
verbal Hebrew system has been, and still is, the correct understanding of the two
principal verb forms, the Prefix and Suffix forms (i.e., *yqtl* and *qtl*) and their respective
waw consecutive constructions (i.e. *wayyqtl* and *wqtl*). For a detailed discussion of
metaphors in this psalm, see Weiss 1984: 135-63.

God, and hence the suffering of the righteous cannot exist in reality at all; suffering is always a punishment, even if only for the sins of youth; proper definition of the terms 'righteous' and 'wicked' would prevent error, and it becomes clear from them that the suffering righteous or the successful wicked are logical absurdities (oxymorons). In brief, the lyric psalms and the wisdom psalms do not differ greatly with regard to the proposed solutions to the problem of recompense. The main difference between them is that, whereas in the personal psalms the problem is articulated clearly, albeit in softened form (i.e., the suffering poet does not claim that he is a righteous man), in the wisdom psalms solutions are propounded, but only in the background, behind the declarations of faith, can one distinguish the problem.

In the light of this picture, one needs to examine the claim that the book of Job is an anthology of teachings on retribution whose innovation is to be found, not only in the literary-formal realm, as discussed in the previous chapters, but also in the theological realm. Drawing a parallel between the book of Job and the above-mentioned psalms, its similarity to the type of the personal psalms will become clear: like them, Job too presents his suffering in the first person, and even the friends speak in the first person. A further point of similarity is that, like the authors of the lyric psalms, Job too does not describe himself as a righteous person.[22] These points of contact create an appropriate framework for drawing a comparison between the manner in which the problem of theodicy is presented in the book of Job and in the Psalms, and will they assist us in distinguishing the uniqueness of the book of Job.

As we have seen, the suffering of the righteous is presented in the lyric psalms in a manner that does not sharply focus the problem of divine justice *ab initio*. In the book of Job, on the other hand, the picture is entirely different. The presentation of Job's absolute righteousness as axiomatic, and the phrase 'there is none like him on the earth' (1.8; 2.3)—as if to say, if there is anyone in the world who deserves to be considered as a perfectly righteous man it is Job—are initial data creating ideal 'laboratory conditions' within which to examine the problem of the suffering righteous in a way that does not allow for any obfuscation or

---

22. The phrase שחוק צדיק תמים ('a just and blameless man, am a laughing stock', 12.4) is the only one which is seemingly not consistent with this statement. However, the term צדיק in this verse may be interpreted as an ironic allusion to Zophar. Even if we do interpret it as applying to Job, it does not contain an explicit declaration by Job of his righteousness.

blurring. The righteousness of the psalmist is only relative, making it possible to explain away his suffering as punishment. This is not so with regard to the righteousness of Job. Hence, by the very manner in which they presented the problem, the authors of the Psalms left themselves a convenient escape route, whereas the author of the book of Job blocked this way of evading the issue from the very outset. It is as if he were to say: I set out upon the treacherous path of seeking an answer to the problem of the suffering of the righteous, consciously taking upon myself the danger that I will arrive at a dead end. In order to set out on this path, he is forced to invent the story of the argument with Satan, thereby explaining the disasters that will befall Job in a manner other than as punishment. We have already observed that the introductory frame-story hones the problem even more through its irony: Job suffers because of—and not despite—his absolute righteousness. Had he been a mediocre person, or even a righteous man of the order of the authors of the personal psalms, there would have been no point to the wager between God and Satan, because he would not have been able to serve as an example through which to examine the substance of his righteousness.

In the light of these factors, how are we to explain that Job nowhere describes himself as 'righteous'? Why, in the opening narrative, is he referred to as 'blameless and upright, one who feared God, and turned away from evil'—but not as 'righteous'? I have no definitive answer to this question but, continuing what was said above, must content myself with speculation alone.

We have seen that the author makes very sparing use of the term 'righteous', in contrast to the rest of the Bible. Of the seven occurrences of the term in the book, three occur in the speech of Elihu, which is of doubtful authenticity (see below, Chapter 8). This could be seen as a purely stylistic feature, but such an explanation is difficult to accept in a book whose very substance is the confrontation with a problem in the conventional formulation of which people make extensive use of the term 'righteous'. Moreover, the use of the opposite term, 'wicked', is extremely widespread in the book, as we have seen. For that reason, I suggest the following explanation: the author of the book of Job refrained from using the term 'righteous' so as to weaken the 'semantic' solution to the problem of the suffering righteous, which he refutes by means of argumentation. The problem is too serious and substantial, he says, to be dismissed by means of a semantic straw; therefore I present it in a new formula: what is the explanation for the suffering of one who is 'blameless and upright, one who feared God, and turned away from evil'? Thus, if in the Psalms the poet refrains from defining himself as 'righteous' in order to blunt the edge of the problem, in the book of Job its hero is not defined as such precisely in order to exacerbate the problem and to block the way against a facile solution which, while it may be faultless from the logical viewpoint, is from the theological point of view no more than an evasion of the heart of the problem.

All of those solutions to the problem of the suffering righteous which appeared in the book of Psalms may be found within the framework of the speeches in the book of Job. However, in striking contrast to the psalms, the solutions put forward here are not presented as final, but as a basis for further discussion and examination.

The solution of the transience of the suffering of the righteous is stated explicitly in the answers of all the friends. Thus, Eliphaz says, 'For he wounds, but he bind up; he smites, but his hands heal' (5.18); 'You shall come to your grave in ripe old age' (5.26); 'If you return to the Almighty you shall be built up...then you will delight yourself in the Almighty... and light will shine on your way' (22.23-28). Similarly, Bildad: 'And though your beginning was small, your latter days will be very great' (8.7), and Zophar: 'You will forget your misery; you will remember it as waters that have passed away. And your light will be brighter than the noonday; its darkness will be like the noonday' (11.16-17).

As mentioned, the prosperity of the wicked is of marginal importance in the book. Nevertheless, as an anthology, it is impossible for the book's author entirely to ignore this problem or its proposed solutions. Job argues: 'The earth is given into the hand of the wicked' (9.24); 'The tents of robbers are at peace, and those who provoke God are secure' (12.6); 'Why do the wicked live, reach old age, and grow mighty in power?' (21.7, and in the continuation); Chapter 24 is devoted entirely to depicting the wealth and the transgressions of the wicked. Chapter 30, as in the convention of the Psalms, portrays the peace of the wicked who mock the righteous (Job) and rejoice in his fall. These arguments too are answered in terms of their temporary nature. Eliphaz says, 'I have seen the fool taking root, but suddenly I cursed his dwelling. His sons are far from safety...' (5.3-4; compare Ps. 37.35-36);[23] and: 'The wicked man writhes in pain all his days, through all the years that are laid up for the ruthless. Terrifying sounds are in his ears; in prosperity the destroyer will come upon him' (Job 15.20-21). Zophar says, 'that

---

23. For a comparative discussion of this subject, see Weiss 1984: 164-65.

the exulting of the wicked is short, and the joy of the godless but for a moment' (20.5). In ch. 21 it would appear that Job himself states that the success of the wicked is only momentary: 'For the lamp of the wicked dies out, and their calamity comes upon them; he distributes pains in his anger. They are like straw before the wind, and like chaff that the storm carries away' (vv. 17-18).[24]

The book offers several arguments challenging the solution of transience, as applied in both directions. Its logic in the book of Psalms is compatible with the viewpoint of the friends, who are prepared, at most, to see Job as a 'righteous' person who has sinned, like the poets of the psalms. However, as we have already seen, the book from the very outset negates the ethical validity of this solution with regard to Job. The narrative through which the reader—but not Job—knows this allows the author to place in the mouth of his hero additional arguments against this solution which in its general aspects pertains to the 'ordinary suffering righteous', but not necessarily to the perfect righteous. The simplest argument is: 'What is my strength, that I should wait? And what is my end, that I should be patient? Is my strength the strength of stone, or is my flesh bronze?' (6.11-12), or, to express it in principled terms: at times the sufferings of the righteous are so harsh that he is unable to withstand them, and the suffering which was meant to be temporary becomes final. The second argument pertains to the very assumption that temporary suffering is a relatively easy punishment, and therefore suitable to one who is not truly wicked. Job himself refutes this by his wish to die ('O that I might have my request, and that God would grant my desire; that it would please God to crush me, that he would let loose his hand and cut me off!'—6.8-9). The general point of this argument is

---

24. The chapter is a difficult one. At the beginning (vv. 6-15) and towards the end (vv. 23-26) Job sharply formulates, in a manner similar to Psalm 73, the problem of the wicked who are successful in everything they do: 'They spend their days in prosperity' (v. 13); 'One dies in full prosperity, being wholly at ease and secure' (v. 23; compare Ps. 73.4, 'For they have no pangs; their bodies are sound and sleek'). However, in the middle (vv. 16-22) it is stated that the success of the wicked is temporary and does not contradict divine justice. Briggs (1907) resolved this by interpreting vv. 16-23 as a challenge: How often are the wicked really punished? Very little! Thus also Kahana 1924. Maimonides (*Guide for the Perplexed*, 3.23) interpreted: 'Even supposing matters are as you think and the children of the prosperous unbeliever perish after he is no more and their traces vanish, in what way is that prosperous man harmed by what happens to his family after he is no more?' (Pines 1963: 492).

that intense and continual suffering is sometimes more difficult than annihilation; this being so, punishing the righteous more severely than the wicked certainly contradicts justice. The third argument likewise pertains to the severity of suffering: 'Am I the sea, or a sea monster, that thou settest a guard over me' (7.12). That is, even if suffering is temporary, its parameters cannot be defined save in terms of the substantive limitations of a human being. In the light of these limitations, people are incapable of committing sins so great as to justify terrible punishments of the type that God sometimes brings upon them. This argument certainly negates the contention offered in the Psalms, that man is only punished for some of his sins, likewise echoed in the words of Zophar: 'Know then that God exacts of you less than your guilt deserves' (11.6).

The argument of the temporary nature of the prosperity of the wicked is not refuted in the book as such, but (according to the interpretation cited above) Job argues that it is only rarely activated in practice.

The more sophisticated version of the solution of transience—that is, that the success of the wicked and the suffering of the righteous are only apparent—is likewise alluded to in the book of Job. Zophar's words— 'because his greed knew no rest' (20.20)—imply that, even if to all appearances it seems that the wicked has prospered, he in truth knows no peace, and his 'prosperity' is illusory. An ironic polemic with this outlook is alluded to in the words of Job (10.8-17), which suggest that it is precisely the success of the righteous which is imaginary, as it is no more than a preparatory stage for the sufferings that God prepares to bring upon him, whether he commit evil or not.

Indirectly, there is also an ironic double refutation of the assertion that the true reward of the righteous is not material, but spiritual—that is, 'closeness to God'. (a) It clearly follows from both parts of the prose frame-story that flocks, cattle, camels, servants and honour are all the reward of the righteous man, just as in the conventional and unequivocal outlook of the book of Proverbs. (b) Job argues that he has lost 'closeness to God' precisely because there is no explanation for his suffering. His remarks concerning 'the months of old, as in the days when God watched over me, when his lamp shone upon my head, and by his light I walked through the darkness' (29.2-3) express his longings for the time when he was close to God. And from what did this closeness flow, if not from the correspondence between his righteousness and his material reward? We may conclude from this that gratuitous disasters simply push man away from God. Thus, the idea that one ought to be content with 'closeness to God' as an answer to the problem of the suffering of the righteous is absurd, if not downright cynical.

Similarly rejected is the solution implied by Psalm 23, according to which that which is perceived by an ordinary person as suffering is none other than consolation to the righteous. Yet does not Job, the perfect righteous man, explicitly testify of himself that he suffers severely? These are not the words of some 'third party' misinterpreting the feelings of the righteous man.

The book likewise mentions the solution of 'sins of youth'. This is evidently alluded to in the words of Elihu, 'Let his flesh become fresh with youth; let him return to the days of his youthful vigour' (33.25), and is explicit in the words of Job, 'For thou writest bitter things against me, and makest me inherit the iniquities of my youth' (13.26; and see Ps. 25.7). There is a certain readiness here to assume that his suffering is indeed a response to sins, even if these were sins of youth which he is unable even to remember. It follows from the context that he likewise agrees with the principle that it is not unjustified to punish a person for the sins of his youth. But this agreement is no more than a basis for the counter claim: that punishment for youthful sins ought by rights to be extremely mild, and hence his severe suffering cannot be justified by the sins of his youth.

In addition to the solutions to the problem of retribution found in the Psalms, the book of Job invokes other possible solutions, which were not formulated clearly or at all in the biblical writings prior to Job. These include the following.

'Can mortal man be righteous before God? Can a man be pure before his Maker?' (4.17) or, formulated differently: 'What is man, that he can be clean? Or he that is born of a woman, that he can be righteous?' (15.14). That is, man by his very nature is sinful, and therefore deserving of punishment.[25] This leaves no room for the argument that there are righteous people who suffer without being guilty; all suffering is

---

25. Smith (1990: 463) suggests interpreting this verse differently from others, finding therein two unique explanations for the problem of theodicy: (a) God has angels who at times err in executing his mission, and thereby mislead God. (b) Another reason for the injustice in the world is the behaviour of human beings: at times they kill one another like moths (Job 4.19), and thereby interfere in the rule of divine justice. This interpretation is to be rejected. It does not follow from the text, and it contradicts a fundamental assumption of the book, concerning which there is no dispute between Job and his friends—the omnipotence of God.

punishment. The view that humanity by its very nature is sinful is not unique to the book of Job. It is formulated explicitly in Solomon's prayer for the dedication of the Temple, 'for there is no man who does not sin' (1 Kgs 8.46), albeit not as a solution to the problem of the suffering of the righteous. In Psalm 51 the psalmist confesses: 'Behold, I was brought forth in iniquity, and in sin did my mother conceive me' (v. 7). If this is not intended merely as literary hyperbole to punctuate the greatness of his regret, here too there is an echo of the same view— but again, not in relation to the problem of the suffering righteous. The power of this solution lies in the simple truth underlying it, which cannot be denied. Hence, it is rejected in the book of Job primarily by means of the above-mentioned claim of Job, that his suffering does not suit any possible sin of a mortal human being. One may understand that the very assumptions of the opening frame-story do not allow one to enlist this solution in order to justify the suffering of Job.

This subject is also touched upon in the words of Elihu in 33.12-29. However, here too we do not find a solution to the problem of the suffering of the righteous, but rather a continuation and exacerbation of Eliphaz's argument that every person sins and is deserving of punishment. Indeed, as formulated, these things clearly allude to Eliphaz's vision, and like them are based upon a divine revelation ('in a dream, in a vision of the night', 33.15). The underlying question is: If every person sins, what chance have they to be saved from suffering and affliction? And if they have already been punished, have they any hope of being restored? Elihu's answer is, 'If there be for him an angel, a mediator, one out of a thousand, to declare to man what is right for him; and he is gracious to him, and says, "Deliver him from going down into the Pit, I have found a ransom"' (vv. 23-24).[26] Maimonides ascribed pivotal importance to this verse, claiming that Elihu's entire speech was only written by virtue of it:

> However, when you consider the matter, the additional notion that he introduced will become clear to you; this notion is the one that is intended... which he expresses parabolically when he speaks of the intercession of an angel. For he says that it is an attested and well-known thing that when a man is ill to the point of death and when he is despaired of, if an angel intercedes for him—regardless of what angel—his intercession is accepted

---

26. Thus Pope 1973: 219; see also Klein 1982, and below, n. 36. Some scholars find in this verse an echo of the belief in a personal god, who is able to redeem a person from death, found in the Sumerian religion.

and he is raised from his fall…However, this does not continue always,
there being no continuous intercession going on forever, for it only takes
place two or three times (*Guide for the Perplexed*, 3.23; Pines 1963: 495).

From God's response out of the whirlwind, one may draw further
solutions which are not clearly expressed in the other books, as follows.
In the discussion in the previous chapter we saw that God's answer was
fundamentally ironic, its conclusion being that God himself is unable to
give a suitable solution to the problem of the suffering of the righteous.
However, the claim that this is the final answer of the book does not
contradict the existence of other additional solutions, even if they are
ultimately rejected, just as various solutions were proposed and rejected
throughout the length of the book. The power of irony to propose a self-
destructive theory allows it to allude indirectly to a variety of solutions,
whose ultimate refutation is part of the ironic dimension of the answer as
a whole. I enumerated above five answers given by various exegetes to
the question of the meaning of God's answer, all of which I rejected. My
rejection of them does not mean that they are not in fact alluded to in
the answer of God, but merely that none of them corresponds to the
position of the author. In any event, these answers all constitute new
solutions to the problem of the suffering righteous. For the sake of
completeness, I shall once again enumerate them in brief, in continuation
of the previous answers.

   i.   God's appearance as such is the answer. The significance of
         this answer in a society that believes in prophecy, that is, in
         regular phenomena of divine revelation, is that God's very
         readiness to reveal himself to human beings is proof of his
         personal providence over them, and negates the possibility of
         injustice in the running of the world.
   ii.   The beauty and harmony of the creation refute the possibility
         that the creator does not judge his world justly.[27]

---

27. To a certain degree, one may see the speech of God as a kind of mirror image
of Psalm 104: the main part of the book of Job deals with the problem of theodicy,
whereas its end portrays the creation; the main body of Psalm 104 describes the
creation, while it ends with a comment about retribution: 'Let sinners be consumed
from the earth, and let the wicked be no more!' (v. 35). However, the conclusion
which follows from the final verse of Psalm 104 is that evil in the world is temporary,
and not that it is non-existent. The question as to whether the final verse is an integral
part of the psalm or a later addition is beyond our interest here. See on this Hoffman
1992.

iii.   Divine justice is greater and higher than human justice.

iv.   No person is capable of understanding the secrets of the creation, and the system of recompense is no more than a small part of them. This argument adds a principled dimension to the previously mentioned solution of 'human foolishness'. It does not imply that whoever thinks that the wicked prosper is actually stupid, only that the substantive limitations of human beings must lead them to abandon the pretence of understanding God's ways in the world. Another innovation is the manner of presentation of the argument regarding human foolishness: in the Psalms (73; 92) it is expressed by the believer and presented as a personal conclusion, which cannot be understood by one who has not merited to the experience of revelation. On the other hand, God's speech confirms the argument, as it were, by showing clearly that humans do not stand at a vantage point allowing them to perceive the entire world, either from the dimension of time or that of space.[28] How much more is it the case that no human is able to understand this complex system or to truly understand how it operates .

v.   God is not limited by the moral bonds imposed upon him, so to speak, by human 'wisdom'.

These solutions, detected in the speech of God by various scholars, are not necessarily mutually exclusive, and may be seen as one complex— and in this respect as well the book of Job is innovative.[29] God's speech performs the same function in the book of Job as the book as a whole does in relation to the Bible, namely: the presentation of a sophisticated anthology of various doctrines of retribution. The reader is not required to accept any one of the doctrines presented in the book. On the

28. See Fox 1981: 59: 'God is not quizzing Job, not trying to squelch him by stumping him with hard questions. God overwhelms Job by showing him the obvious, by opening his eyes to what he already knows. If the theophany had been a revelation of something new or hidden, the book would not be so relevant for people who do not receive such a revelation.'

29. Thus, for example, Greenberg (1969: 54-55): 'The fault in the moral order... is swallowed up in the totality of God's activity; as the phenomena of nature teach us, this does not imply that they are comprehensible or make sense'. And also: 'When Job comes to know in the God of Nature, with the totality of his qualities, the same God who is revealed to him in his personal fate, the storm within his soul calms down. He descends to the depths of truth by touching the qualities of God.'

contrary, from the very outset (in the opening frame-story) the author presents them as being refuted, thereby allowing the reader to reject them. In this way, precisely, the author guides the reader towards a critical evaluation of the doctrines of retribution presented in the speech of God, thereby advancing the ironic statement that even God himself is unable to provide a suitable answer to the problem.

The claim of an ironic solution is based above on the fact that, according to the exegesis, not even one of the answers brought in the speech of God is stated there explicitly. This is not precisely the case. One of the answers is indeed stated explicitly, or at any event more clearly than any other answer:

> Have you an arm like God,
> and can you thunder with a voice like his?
> Deck yourself with majesty and dignity;
> clothe yourself with glory and splendour.
> Pour forth the overflowings of your anger,
> and look on every one that is proud, and abase him.
> Look on every one that is proud, and bring him low;
> and tread down the wicked where they strand.
> Hide them all in the dust together;
> bind their faces in the hidden place.
> Then will I also acknowledge to you,
> that your own right hand can give you victory (40.9-14).

More than any other possible solution, this call of protest prepares the ground for the ironic solution, through its allusions to God's limitations in imposing justice upon his world. However, it is doubtful whether these words were originally intended in this sense.[30]

The daring required, against the background of the belief system inherent in the Bible, to suggest the possibility that even God has no suitable answer to the problem of the suffering of the righteous in the world, is clear. The implication is that Job's claim, 'he destroys both the blameless and the wicked' (9.22), may be correct, and that perhaps there is no ethical principle underlying the conduct of the world. The far-reaching revolutionary nature of this answer may best be understood in the light of the decisive importance given by the Bible, on all levels, to the view that human beings may indeed understand the principle of

---

30. This point depends upon whether these things are an authentic part of the speech or whether they are a late addition. My opinion on this matter will be elaborated in the next chapter.

God's activity in our world. This assumption forms the basis for the outlooks upon which are based the exhortations in the Torah and the prophetic literature, the historiographic thinking in the Bible, and the biblical eschatology.[31]

As we have noted, the author's ultimately sceptical conclusion is already implied in the fundamental assumptions of the opening story, which from this point of view is a summarizing 'conclusion' no less than it is an opening. This is so because the true reason for Job's suffering is not retribution but the 'wager' with Satan. Is there any ethical justification for bringing suffering upon a man simply in order to prove Satan wrong? God's response to the astonishment likely to be felt by the reader (but not by Job) upon arriving at this formulation of matters is that he, too, has nothing to say by way of reply except for several evasive answers, and to correct the injustice by restoring Job's fortunes.

Nevertheless, in presenting his answers to the problem of Job's suffering, the author seems to be walking upon a thin wire: despite their extreme formulation, his words are not the same as the mocking claims of the wicked. They ask: 'How can God know? Is there knowledge in the Most High?' (Ps. 73.11); they think in their heart that 'there is no God' (10.4); 'he will never see it' (v. 11); they pride themselves: 'Who is our master?' (12.5); 'The Lord does not see; the God of Jacob does not perceive' (84.7). They do not wish to know the ways of the Lord and refuse to serve him: 'They say to God: "depart from us! We do not desire the knowledge of thy ways. What is the Almighty, that we should serve him?"' (Job 21.14-15). Job, by contrast, rebels against injustice and refuses to compromise his own truth. But as bitter as may be his words, as difficult as may be the 'solution' that follows from God's answer, the author is determined not to cross the line dividing the scepticism of the suffering, afflicted believer from that of the wicked, who take pride in their heresy.

The unorthodox nature of the positions presented in the book of Job invite the question, how far may one go in assuming the revolutionary nature of the book? In other words: if the author was indeed a theological

---

31. I cannot elaborate upon this issue here. Koch (1983) argues that the Bible does not contain any view implying a moral system of recompense, and that those verses which seemingly express such a view in fact reflect the opinion that there are automatic connections between acts and their consequences, without any divine intervention. Such a position is unacceptable; see on this Licht, 'Reward and Punishment', *EncBib*, VIII, pp. 287-93.

revolutionary, can one ascribe to him any conceivable argument, so long as it has some basis, however weak, in the text? This question is elicited upon reading the suggestion of Zemach that this is another way to understand the speech of God. According to this suggestion, the author deliberately portrays, not only the beauty of the world, but also its cruelty. 'There are things that God does only because of their aesthetic beauty and grandeur'; 'The aesthetic value of the monsters is more important to Him than the ethical damage they cause'; 'Since the realm of aesthetic values is no less profound or serious in its demand for absoluteness than is the realm of ethical value...the choice between them is left to the divine will, which prefers the aesthetic consideration'.[32] The theoretical framework of the present work, as described above in the first chapter, forces us to reject this suggested interpretation utterly, because it goes far beyond the circle of historical exigencies within whose framework the work was written. There is no basis in the Bible either for the outlook that there is no beauty without evil, upon which Zemach bases his claim philosophically, or for the view that aesthetic considerations have an autonomous status in the eyes of the creator in isolation from wisdom, justice, or practicality. On the other hand, the claim that God himself is unable to resolve the problem of his justice, radical as it may be, is a natural continuation to reflections found elsewhere in the Bible regarding this matter. The anachronistic nature of Zemach's claim is shown by the total absence of any allusions to the outlook which he would find in the speech of God, either in later, post-Joban biblical literature or even in early post-biblical literature. By contrast, my claim that the message of the book of Job is that there is no solution to the problem of God's justice finds definite continuity, primarily in the book of Ecclesiastes. On this, see the concluding chapter.

On the basis of the premise that the book of Job ought to be interpreted in the light of the basic beliefs of the Bible, I reject Cross's view concerning the position of the book of Job (particularly with regard to the position of God's answer to Job in the history of biblical thought). In his opinion, God's appearance then expresses a certain reaction:

32. Zemach 1988: 16, 17. It may be that Zemach, whose discipline is philosophy and not biblical criticism, did not intend to argue that his suggestion in fact expresses the intention of the book, but rather to present a certain philosophical idea while in relation to a rather free exegesis of a biblical passage of aesthetic sublimity, to which it is easy to attach various interpretations.

> It repudiated the God of history whose realm is politics, law and justice...
> The God who called Israel out of Egypt, who spoke by prophet, the
> covenant God of Deuteronomy...The Lord of History failed to act...The
> transcendent creator spoke. Only he lived. Job saw him and bowed his
> knee (Cross 1973: 344).[33]

This conclusion is only valid if we assume that it is impossible for an
Israelite author to deal with the subject of personal recompense in isolation from the national realm or the national tradition. However, this
assumption is unjustified, as may be seen when the book is read against
the background of Wisdom literature generally. This literature does not
refer to the national traditions, yet there is no reason to see here a polemic
against them or disappointment with the values that they represent. It is
simply an independent phase.

3. *Theodicy in Mesopotamian Literature*

Our characterization of the presentation of the problem of theodicy in
the book of Job as 'revolutionary' was based on comparison with other
biblical writings. Is this conclusion also justified with respect to the literature of the ancient Near East? I shall examine this question primarily in
light of the two Mesopotamian works discussed above in Chapter 3, 'I
Will Praise the Lord of Wisdom' and 'The Babylonian Theodicy'. A
comparison with the Egyptian story, 'The Complaint of the Eloquent
Peasant', which likewise involves protest against the injustice in the
world, will not contribute towards understanding the innovation in the
book of Job, as the complaint is directed there against a human ruler
rather than against God.

Both Mesopotamian works mentioned present figures of sufferers and
afflicted people who, like Job, beg for their lives and wonder how they
will be saved. The following are the important, substantive points of
contact (as opposed to the literary ones, which were already noted in

---

33. By the same token, I also disagree with his statement further on that the book
of Job 'repudiated...a simple Deuteronomistic view of historical process in which the
mighty acts of God are transparent'. Indeed, by means of a theoretical-logical analysis it is possible to arrive at the conclusion that someone who denies a simplistic
understanding of recompense will necessarily demur from the illusion that it is
possible to understand the process of history. However, I do not think that such an
extrapolation from the destiny of the individual to history necessarily reflects the view
of the book's author.

earlier contexts) between these works and the book of Job.[34]

i. All three works present figures of sufferers and afflicted individuals, who describe their bitter lot *in extenso*. In 'I Will Praise', the sufferings are mostly severe illnesses, as in the following:

> My lofty stature they destroyed like a wall,
> My robust figure they laid down like a bulrush,
> I am thrown down like a bog plant and cast on my face.
> The *alu*-demon has clothed himself in my body as a garment.
> Sleep covers me like a net.
> My eyes stare, but do not see,
> My ears are open, but do not hear.
> Feebleness has seized my whole body,
> Concussion has fallen upon my flesh.
> Paralysis has grasped my arms...
>> (Ludlul Tablet II.68-77; compare the entire passage in this tablet,
>> lines 50-108).

The 'Theodicy' also depicts bodily sufferings (ll. 27-32), but there the main complaints are directed against changes in the order of society which reduce the mourner from a high status to a low and contemptible one:

> I will take the road and go to distant parts
> I will bore a well and let loose a flood,
> Like a robber I will roam over the vast open country.
> I will go from house to house and ward off hunger;
> Famished I will walk around and patrol the streets.
> like a beggar I will....
> Bliss is far away...
>> (ll. 137-143; see also ll. 181-184, 221-223, 243-253)

Both kinds of suffering are expressed throughout the book of Job, the social realm being stressed particularly in chs. 29–30.

ii. In the Mesopotamian works, as in Job, the sufferers wonder about the reason for their suffering and are unable to find it:

> I called to my god, but he did not show his face,
> I prayed to my goddess, but she did not raise her head.
> The diviner with his inspection has not got to the root of the matter,
> Nor has the dream priest with his libation elucidated my case,

---

34. The following quotations are only from the Mesopotamian works, because in the previous chapters I have already given sufficient examples concerning these matters from the book of Job.

> I sought the favour of the *zaqiqu*-spirit, but he did not enlighten me;
> And the incantation priest with his ritual did not appease the divine wrath
>   against me.
> What strange conditions everywhere!
>   (Ludlul Tablet II.4-10).

And also:

> My complaints have exposed the incantation priest,
> And my omens have confounded the diviner.
> The exorcist has not diagnosed the nature of my complaint,
> Nor has the diviner put a time limit on my illness.
>   (ll. 108-111)

Likewise in the 'Theodicy' the sufferer asks: 'How, if I had known, will my good day be restored me?' (l. 33)

iii. In all three works, the sufferers reject the possibility that their sufferings are the result of sins against God, emphasizing their own proper behaviour. In this context, they invoke lists of the worshipper's good deeds and declarations concerning sins that he has not done. The most striking example in the book of Job is chs. 29 and 31. Similar to them is the following:

> Like one who has not made libations to his god,
> Nor invoked his goddess at table...
> Does not engage in prostration, nor take cognizance of bowing down;
> From whose mouth supplication and prayer is lacking,
> Who has done nothing on holy days, and despised the gods' rites...
> And abandoned his goddess by not bringing a flour offering...
> For myself, I gave attention to supplication and prayer.
> To me prayer was discretion, sacrifice my rule.
> The day for reverencing the god was a joy to my heart...
> I instructed my land to keep the god's rites....
>   (Ludlul Tablet II.12-33)

And in the 'Theodicy':

> [Have I] held back offerings? I have prayed to my god,
> I have] pronounced the blessing over the goddess's regular sacrifices...
>   (ll. 54-55)

And:

> In my mouth I sought the will of my god;
> With prostration and prayer I followed my goddess.
> But I was bearing a profitless corvee as a yoke.
>   (ll. 72-74)

In the 'Theodicy', as in Job, the poet complains about the prosperity of the wicked:

> [   ] the nouveau riche who has multiplied his wealth,
> Did he weigh out precious gold for the goddess Mami?
>   (ll. 52-53)

> Those who neglect the god go the way of prosperity,
> while those who pray to the goddess are impoverished and dispossessed.
>   (ll. 70-72)

> My god decreed instead of wealth destitution.
>   (l. 75)

> People extol the word of a strong man who is trained in murder,
> But bring down the powerless who has done no wrong.
>   (ll. 267-268)

iv. From these texts, there emerges a picture of the cries of those who have felt themselves deceived by the code which was meant to assure a good life, which they find no longer serves them as a guide through the darkness. In the wake of their disaster, the illusion that one can know the way to enjoy the goodness of god has vanished:

> What is proper to oneself is an offence to one's god,
> What in one's own heart seems despicable is proper to one's god.
> Who knows the will of the gods in heaven?
> Who understands the plans of the underworld gods?
> Where have mortals learnt the way of a god?
> He who was alive yesterday is dead today.
> For a minute he was dejected, suddenly he is exuberant.
> One moment people are singing in exaltation
> Another they groan like professional mourners.
>   (Ludlul Tablet II.34-41)

That which was there formulated in rhetorical questions is presented in the 'Theodicy' in the framework of the answer of the friend to his suffering friend:

> The divine mind, like the centre of the heavens, is remote;
> Knowledge of it is difficult; the masses do not know it.
>   (ll. 256-257)

The claim that man can never understand the counsel of the gods, which is the only response given by the Mesopotamian works to the question of the cause of suffering, is also made in the book of Job, as we have seen.

v. Notwithstanding these arguments, the friend in the 'Theodicy', like the friends of Job, states that suffering flows from sins, and accordingly he gives advice:

> He who waits on his god has a protecting angel,
> The humble man who fears his goddess accumulates wealth.
> (ll. 21-22)

> You have forsaken right and blasphemed against your god's designs.
> In your mind you have an urge to disregard the divine ordinances.
> (ll. 79-80)

And hence the advice:

> Rather seek the lasting reward of (your) god.
> (l. 66)

And elsewhere:

> Unless you seek the will of the god, what luck have you?
> He that bears his god's yoke never lacks food, though it be sparse.
> Seek the kindly wind of the god,
> What you have lost over a year you will make up in a moment.
> (ll. 239-242)

vi. 'I Will Praise the Lord of Wisdom', like Job, concludes with the appearance of god or of his representatives, a kind of *deus ex machina*. In his dream, the poet sees a vision of a divine figure who saves him from all his illnesses:

> A bearded young man with his turban on his head.
> An incantation priest carrying a tablet,
> 'Marduk has sent me.
> To Subsi-meshre-Sakkan I have brought prosperity.
> From Marduk's pure hands I have brought prosperity'.
> (Ludlul Tablet III.40-44)

vii. In 'I Will Praise', as in Job, the end of the work parallels its beginning: against Job's past wealth, there is presented his new wealth; against the severe illnesses suffered by the poet in 'I Will Praise', there is a parallel detailing of the end of his illness:

> My illness was quickly over and [my fetters] were broken.
> (Ludlul Tablet III.49)

And:

> [He drove] away the Evil Wind to the horizon,
> To the surface of the underworld he took [the Headache].
> [He sent] down the Evil Cough to its *Apsu*,
> The Irresistible Ghost he returned [to] *Ekur*.
> He overthrew the *lamastu*-demon, dismissing it to the Mountain,
> He tore up the root of Importance like a plant.
>   (Si 55 [q], Reverse, lines 2-10; Lambert 1960: 53]

viii. 'I Will Praise' concludes with a hymn to Marduk, to Wisdom, which, like the speech of God in the book of Job, praises and extols the greatness of he who created so many creatures in the world:

> Wherever the earth is laid, and the heavens are stretched out,
> Wherever the sun god shines and the fire god blazes,
> Wherever water flows and wind blows,
> Creatures whose clay Aruru took in her fingers,
> Those endowed with life, who stride along,
> Mortals, as many as there are, give praise to Marduk
>   (Tablet IV.37-42; Lambert 1960: 59, 61)

Several of these points of similarity are also shared with another Mesopotamian work, known as 'Man and His God'.[35] This work deals with a man who presents himself as wealthy, of high rank, correct and righteous, who suddenly finds his entire world crumbling around him as he is plagued by illness, social humiliation, and suffering . He presents his suffering before god, and wishes that his mother, his sister, his wife, and the professional keener all say a dirge with him. Indeed, god answers him and he is restored to his previous condition.

Both the substantive points of similarity and the literary relationship among these works justify a comparison of their religious outlooks. The purpose of such a comparison is not only to bring out the uniqueness of the book of Job, but also to argue the possibility that it was composed in a dialogic relation to these Mesopotamian works, or to similar works which have not survived. There are nevertheless significant differences between the Mesopotamian works and the book of Job.

The poets in the Mesopotamian works declare that they always behaved properly but, unlike the book of Job, no objective confirmation is given of this. As a result, there is no sense of the reality of a suffering

---

35. Thus Kramer translated the heading of the Sumerian work which he published. In his opinion (1960: 170), the work was written at the time of the Third Ur Dynasty, ca. 2000 BCE.

righteous man but, at most, of one who claims that he behaved properly. As we are insufficiently familiar with the generic conventions of Mesopotamian hymn and wisdom literature, it is difficult to know whether or not these claims ought to be accepted. In either event, these works are without the tendency to emphasize the 'righteousness' of the worshipper. In 'Man and His God' this difference stands out even more markedly: towards the end, before his salvation, the mourner declares: 'O god, now that you have shown me my sins...' (l. 111)—implying that he sinned. Similarly, we find a declaration of joy by the author of 'I Will Praise' because Marduk has erased his transgressions (Tablet IV.55).

In 'I Will Praise' and 'Theodicy', the poet's complaint is not addressed to an ethical evil; rather, his ill fortune is brought about because he does not know the code by which to decipher God's acts and bring about changes. 'Man does not know what is good in the eyes of god; the will of the gods is hidden and difficult to fulfill'. Job, by contrast, knows what God's will is, at least according to the biblical view, in which 'it is self-evident that it is always possible to clarify the nature of righteousness, and the will of God as explicit in his commandments' (Licht, Reward and Punishment', *EncBib*, VIII, 1982: 304). Thus, the proper behaviour invoked by the Mesopotamian poet is entirely within the realm of ritual and cult. The divine service—prayer, sacrifices, and the like—is intended to protect man against catastrophe, and the poet is greatly confused because he feels himself helpless despite the ceremonies which were meant to grant him magical protection against harm issuing from the gods.

By contrast, in the book of Job the motif of ritual is marginal (for example 1.5; 31.26) and not only in Job's words. None of the friends seek the reason for Job's suffering in improper ritual behaviour (see on this Eliphaz's remarks in ch. 22, and those of Job in ch. 31), but in his ethical behaviour. In 'Man and His God', there is no perplexity expressed as to the reason for his suffering, because the poet knows that the reason is sin—'There was never born an infant to its mother who was free of sin, a fetus free of sin never existed' (ll. 102-103; he is, however, not disturbed by the question of the nature of this sin. Compare Eliphaz's, 'May mortal man be righteous before God?', etc.—4.17.)

Ipso facto, the Mesopotamian works do not relate to the question of theodicy, which is not mentioned there at all. The salvation of the sufferer in 'I Will Praise' is cultic-magical: the image that appears to him purifies him in a magical ceremony, thereby resolving the 'technical' question which the magicians and sorcerers did not know how to solve. Similarly, the sufferer in 'Theodicy', who towards the end—as in the individual supplications in Psalms—expresses the hope that the gods will help him ('that the goddess who has abandoned me shall have mercy on me; that the sun, who shepherds men as a god, shall guide me'—ll. 296-297), does not make this dependent upon his righteousness or repentance, in marked contrast both to the Psalms and the book of Job. According to Kramer, the lesson of 'Man and His God' is that in the event of suffering, even if it appears unjustified, the sufferer must praise and extol his gods, and he will in the end be answered.

Indeed, in the closing hymn of 'I Will Praise' Marduk is not necessarily presented as the god of justice, nor is this quality relevant to the dirge sung by the poet. This is also striking in its opening:

> I will praise the lord of wisdom, the [deliberative ?] god,
> Who lays hold on the night, but lets free the day,
> Marduk, the lord of wisdom, the [deliberative god]
> Who lays hold on the night, but lets free the day,
> Whose fury surrounds him like the blast of a tornado,
> Yet whose breeze is as pleasant as a morning sephyr.
>   (Lambert 1960: Addenda, p. 343)

The same holds true for the beginning of 'Man and His God': humankind is called upon to praise the god for his power and for sustaining the world, but not necessarily for his righteousness. As the subject of justice is outside the ken of these Mesopotamian works, they are certainly unable to present the problem of theodicy. They are thus lacking in the note of ethical pathos which accompanies Job's words. In 'I Will Praise' and 'Theodicy', suffering does not contradict any faith principle, but is simply a confusing and frightening state, and certainly not one creating any difficulty requiring solution in the philosophical realm.

There follows from this also the decisive difference between the conclusion of 'I Will Praise' and that of Job. Despite their similarity, there is no irony to be found in the conclusion of 'I Will Praise': the poet bemoans his suffering, and God brings him salvation, for which it is fitting that he praise his greatness and wisdom—which the poet indeed does. Not so in the case of Job. First, it is God who praises himself; second, God's self-praise does not relate to the main subject of the book—in any event not directly—the ethical injustice caused to Job.

It is thus clear why the Mesopotamian works do not contain a collection of solutions to a problem which is not raised there—namely, that of theodicy—and why there is no need for more than one reaction to the turnabouts in the destiny of man: to wit, 'Who knows the will of the gods?' In the absence of any ethical or philosophical overtone to the astonishment of the sufferer, and in the light of the statement that in any event we cannot understand the acts of the gods, the suggestion of the friend in 'Theodicy', like the lesson learned from 'I Will Praise' and 'Man and His Gods', namely, that one wait patiently until the wheel turns again, makes good sense. Not so in the book of Job, as the turning of the wheel in no way resolves the serious problems that have been raised.

If we assume that this latter position also follows from the speech of God in the book of Job, then it has a definite ironic dimension, because the reader is aware of the true reason for Job's suffering—the wager with Satan—and is unable to accept such an argument as a solution. The identification of the reader with Job, which grows steadily throughout the course of the book, contributes to the shaping of a somewhat reserved stance towards this answer and its perception as an evasion, not a solution. Furthermore, Job and his friends share a common point of departure: man's suffering is punishment, the result of God's ethical system. Job's words, 'the blameless and the wicked he destroys', are the result of a painful sobering which he refuses to accept; when he is forced to accept it, it removes the ground from underneath one of the foundations of his faith. Not so in the Mesopotamian works.

Thus, only in the book of Job is there a confrontation among central and powerful ideas presented by God and humanity, and only in it, and not in the Mesopotamian works, are the necessary conditions created for true tragedy. The rebellious nature of the book of Job, which is entirely different from the tone of elegiac submission in 'I Will Praise' and 'Theodicy', follows from this.

These differences between the book of Job and the Mesopotamian works derive to a not inconsiderable degree from the monotheistic approach of the Israelite author. The perception of the one God as the God of justice necessarily exacerbates both the theological crisis and the emotional crisis. This is particularly striking in comparison to 'Man and His God': there the lamenter turns to his personal god, who is meant to represent him before the heavenly pantheon and to intercede between him and them.[36] In 'I Will Praise' the understanding of god is also personal, and hence lacking in the sense of universal ethical injustice

---

36. Kramer 1960: 171. For more on the personal god in Sumerian belief, see Klein 1982.

manifested in the case of the suffering righteous. The suffering of the poet is his own personal problem, which must be resolved within the framework of the 'personal relations' between himself and his god, just as the son expects his father's ear to be attuned to his pleas. Not so in the book of Job. Nevertheless, the universal perception of God in the book of Job does not abnegate the personal nature of the conflict between him and God, but rather steers it in the direction of a principled ethical problem. Such sayings as: 'Will you speak falsely for God, and speak deceitfully for him?' (13.7), or 'Even though he slay me, I will hope in him; I will defend my ways to his face. This will be may salvation, that a godless man shall not come before him' (13.16-17), express the quintessence of the conflict involving both a theological and a personal side. These cannot be separated: in expressing the dual nature of Job's faith in God, he is both personal and universal-ethical.[37]

The intellectual daring of the book of Job is consistent with its literary innovativeness, and they are in fact two sides of the same coin. The basic structure of the book is singularly appropriate to the presentation of unconventional opinions and stances and for the testing of conventional outlooks. The initial refusal of the author to take an explicit stance (i.e., the dramatic character of the book) allows him to place whatever he wishes in the mouths of his speakers, whether this is a satirical presentation of normative positions or an outspoken presentation of unconventional ideas. This freedom is not only external, but also directed towards the author himself: the ability to say things without being 'responsible' for them. The participation of a number of different figures in the work facilitates exchanges which are somewhat reminiscent of the Socratic dialogues. Note the chronological sequence: 'I Will Praise the Lord of Wisdom'–'Babylonian Theodicy'–the book of Job–the Socratic dialogues. This sequence reflects stages both in the development of discursive thought and in its literary forms of expression, leading towards the genre

37. For a discussion of the nature of personal religion in Mesopotamia during the second millennium BCE as a stage towards the development of national religion in Israel, see Jacobsen 1976: 147-64. Among other things, he writes (pp. 162-63): 'The contradictions are indeed insoluble as long as the attitude of personal religion is allowed to reduce existence, the infinite universe, to the narrow compass of a personal world, and expect it to center in an individual and his personal needs'. For this reason, the only way out for the suffering Mesopotamian poet is 'that he can only escape in doubt about himself and his own powers of judgment'. On Jacobsen's opinion regarding the solution proposed by the book of Job to the question of human suffering (which I do not share), see above, Chapter 6, n. 55.

of pure philosophical reflection. Obviously, I do not wish to imply here that Plato was influenced by Job, but merely to point out the unique position of the book of Job within the framework of the development of a literary genre, and parallel to that of religious thought within biblical literature. It is in this context that one also needs to understand several of my arguments in this chapter. From some of them, one might gain the impression that I attribute greater philosophical sophistication to the author of the book of Job and to several of the Psalmists than they presumably had—that is, discriminating, careful use of terms and of their parallels, and the like. Therefore, allow me to clarify this point: the linguistic sophistication which I found in those writings concerned with the problem of divine justice is evidently more the result of their authors' intuition and linguistic sensitivity than it is of systematic philosophical thought. Nevertheless, one should see this as an important stage in the taking shape of reflective writing in Israelite culture, of which the book of Ecclesiastes is one of the later stages.

Did the author of the book of Job know the Mesopotamian works? One cannot reject this possibility out of hand. Whether the book was composed in the Babylonian exile or in the land of Israel, it was written during a period in which the influence of Babylonian culture upon Israel was unavoidable. Was Snaith correct in assuming that the first edition of the book of Job was directly influenced by 'I Will Praise'? While this may be so, it cannot be proven. What is more certain is that, even if the book of Job was not directly influenced by the Babylonian works mentioned above, it was certainly influenced by similar works that are as yet unknown to us. For this reason, its examination, not only against the background of biblical literature, but also against that of these works, and perhaps even as a reaction to them, sheds light upon and sharpens our awareness of its innovativeness.

Chapter 8

STRUCTURE AND MIMESIS

In this chapter I shall clarify certain questions pertaining to the original composition and structure of the book of Job. My having postponed these discussions to the end of this study may lead the reader to the mistaken impression that the main purpose of our work was to arrive at conclusions regarding these questions; such, however, is not the case. The location of this discussion derives rather from the opportunity this afforded of making use of certain peripheral conclusions arrived at thus far in the course of our discussion. From this point of view, the chapter is of the nature of a summary; yet it is not to be considered as the primary harvest, but more on the order of a collection of gleanings picked up on the way. I cannot attempt to summarize here all of the opinions ventured by scholars regarding this subject. The space available is inadequate to such a task, as there is hardly a verse in the book about whose authenticity or proper location one or another scholar has not cast doubt. We have already noted some of these things; a fuller picture may be gained from the various introductions to the book, and from those works whose main purpose is to address themselves to these issues.[1] It is my intention here merely to focus upon several conclusions at which we arrived earlier and to examine their consequences with regard to the subject at hand, while applying the underlying principle of our work that a work of art is to be evaluated in terms of the poetics that it establishes for itself. We have already seen several examples of doubtful conclusions derived from judgment of the book based upon criteria which are alien to it. The following are two more examples, intended to clarify by way of contrast the aim and theoretical basis of the present discussion.

Baumgartel set out various criteria for distinguishing between authentic material and additions to the book of Job, on whose basis he concluded

1. Such as Westermann 1956; Maag 1982; H.P. Muller 1978; Kuhl 1953; Kraeling 1938.

that the original book was constructed of only one cycle of debates and a concluding monologue by Job, and that it consisted of the following passages: 4.1–5.7; 5.27; 6.1-30; 8.10-11, 20-22; 9.1-3, 11-23, 32-35; 11.1-5, 10-20; 13.1-19; 16.6, 9, 12-17, 18-21; 19.2-29; 23.2-7, 10-17; 31.35, 37. The rule established by Baumgartel, whose application led to this extreme conclusion, was that the only authentic passages were those which satisfied the following criteria: clarity, simplicity, internal consistency of Job's words, and ascending order of development in the words of the friends.[2] However, we have already seen that there is no ground for the assumption that the original book met these criteria at all. Anyone attempting to impose upon it clarity of language ignores a basic immanent characteristic common to it and to the Near Eastern background literature; anticipation of a clear order of development is only possible by ignoring the literary milieu within which it was written; nor is simplicity precisely the most suitable quality for a work rooted entirely in difficulties, innovation, and rebellion against conventions, both intellectual and literary.

A second example of the imposition of purely subjective norms may be found in Tur-Sinai's claim that 'each one of the friends who participates in the debate speaks only once: thus, we have three speeches of the three friends, while Job, whose words opened the debate, answered them all in one reply; thereafter, God revealed Himself to Job' (1972: 385). Yet such works as 'The Babylonian Theodicy' and 'The Eloquent Peasant' are constructed on a far more complex pattern, completely refuting the theory that the original structure of the book of Job was necessarily so extremely simple.

The present chapter by contrast wishes to summarize the question of the original text on the basis of the standard of the book as we have come to know it thus far, its main features being, an emphasis upon structural and compositional features, linguistic sophistication, and the use of mimetic tactics during the course of the debates. Awareness of the immanent nature of these qualities of the book is also helpful for identifying the central aesthetic problem which the book sets out to

---

2.   Baumgartel (1971: 168) established the principle that the original dialogue was clear and simple, both in its structure and in the manner of expression of its ideas. During the course of the discussion, he states that the original text was characterized by other strict norms, such as the absence of any direct appeal of Job to God (pp. 77-84). On this basis, he also refutes the authenticity of such major passages as 7.1-10, 12-21; 9.25-31 and others. On pp. 158, 189 he gives tables summarizing the authentic sources.

resolve. The term 'aesthetic', as used here, is intended to cover both aesthetic and theological aspects, the separation between which is purely didactic, and is intended to determine the overall image of the work. If we have indeed taken its proper measure, then we may suggest the hypothesis that the original texts are only those which, within the framework of the poetic norms established for the work, either integrate themselves within the tendencies of structure and composition or contribute to mimesis. This formula implies that there is a certain opposition between adherence to a rigid, fixed structure and mimesis. And indeed, the introduction of tempestuous exchanges within the framework of a strict cyclical pattern is totally opposed to the mimesis of an argument. In other words, the strict structure is an expression of anti-mimetic tendencies within the book. However, this opposition is not one of contradiction between two mutually exclusive tendencies, but rather a contrapuntal tension: the two systems develop independently of one another, creating an aesthetic harmony. I will attempt to examine this tension, and will even argue that it itself served the author as a means of expression. It therefore needs to be added to the criteria on whose basis we shall examine the original composition and structure of the book, and we must reformulate our hypothesis as follows: the authentic writings in the book of Job are those which, in accordance with the aesthetic norms established therein, contribute to mimesis, serve the anti-mimetic tendencies, expressed primarily in structure and composition, or help to create the artistic counterpoint. The authenticity of the writings in the book shall be examined on the basis of this hypothesis. The linguistic standard is not expressed therein because, as we have already seen,[3] from this point of view the poetic layer, with the possible exception of the speeches of Elihu, is uniform. It is true that this is not in itself adequate evidence of there being only one author[4] (just as one would not argue, for example, that all of the psalms have one author or originated in one time period simply because their style is similar), but it certainly is not a counter-indication against that.

In the course of examining the book in the light of this hypothesis, we

3.   See Chapter 6. The tension which I have designated as 'artistic counterpoint' was defined by Licht (1976: 139) as a confrontation between a 'pure aesthetic tendency' of 'perfect formal fashioning', and mimesis.

4.   As against the view of Ceresko (1980: 199-200, following Andersen 1976: 55), who claims that linguistic criteria indicate the unity of the book as a whole, including the speech of Elihu.

must inevitably start from a certain prior assumption: namely, that the author of Job successfully met the literary criteria which he established for his work, and that he did not fail in any major ways which would undermine the foundations of the building which he constructed. This assumption is impossible to prove, as even a great artist may find his or her artistic powers waning at a certain stage. Nevertheless, this is a proper methodological assumption, deriving its legitimacy by analogy to the principle of the innocence of one whose guilt has not been proven. As for our issue: in the absence of any information whatsoever concerning the author, there is no reason to think that, at a particular stage of his life, a deterioration took place in his artistic talent. Therefore, as we are dealing with an ancient work, if there are any serious faults to be found which may be attributed to its peregrinations over the course of centuries, it is preferable to admit such a possibility rather than to blame them upon our author.

Having established these points of departure, we shall now examine the authenticity of the following literary units, which have been questioned by many scholars: the frame-story, the third cycle of debates, the speech of Elihu, and the answer by God.

1. *The Frame-Story*

It is generally accepted that the frame-story is based upon an early tradition concerning a certain 'Job', who was saved from great catastrophes by virtue of his righteousness. This is implied by Ezek. 14.12-20, which mentions Noah, Daniel and Job, who by virtue of their righteousness were alone saved from the disasters brought by God upon their sinful countries. From this passage, one may conclude that Ezekiel knew the tradition of the flood; perhaps he even engaged in polemics against the moral learned from it by the Bible, by stating that, as opposed to what is related there concerning the sons of Noah, sons may no longer be saved by virtue of their fathers' righteousness. It is difficult, however, to reconstruct exactly the folk tradition behind the story of Noah and Daniel, apart from their being 'righteous' and that their sons played an important role in their lives.[5] In any event, it is clear that the story of the

---

5.   The Daniel mentioned here (and in Ezek. 28.3, 'you are indeed wiser than Daniel') is of course connected to the Ugaritic story of Aqhat, concerning a Daniel who judged righteously the orphans and widows, but whose happiness was incomplete because he himself was childless, until the gods gave him Aqhat, who was sub-

righteous Job is based upon an earlier tradition known to the community who listened to the prophet. But this assumption does not necessarily imply the conclusion, held by quite a few scholars, that the present frame-story once existed as an independent work, and that a later poet took it as is and made secondary use of it for the purposes of his poetic work.[6] I have already argued my stance against this view in another context, where I demonstrated that the nature of the connections between the prologue and the dialogues is indicative of one author.[7] It

sequently killed by Anath. We thus find that Noah saved his children, while Daniel and Job did not save their sons from death, albeit Aqhat was perhaps resurrected (see Driver 1956: 8), while Job was given other sons. On the figure of Daniel in the Ugaritic epoch and its relation to the Bible, see recently Margalit 1989: 30-32, 67, 88, 489-490. Gordis (1965: 69) thinks that, on the basis of the tradition known to Ezekiel, Job and Daniel also saved their children like Noah. Gese (1958: 32) put forward the theory that there was a genre of Wisdom literature in the ancient Near East concerning the suffering righteous, on which the legend of Job was based. It consisted of three parts: the misfortune of the righteous, his dirge, and the restoration of his fortunes by the god. In the wake of Duhm (1897), Gese thought (p. 70) that the frame-story in principle stood in its own right, and that the dialogues were only added to it later.

6.   According to H.P. Muller (1978: 23-25) this point was first argued by Richard Simon in 1678, later followed by Wellhausen. A detailed discussion is offered by Duhm (1897: viii). In his opinion, the frame-story was written during a quiet period in Israel, when 'folk' sacrifices were still customary, prior to the centralization of the cult and the priestly doctrine of sacrifices, and when the Chaldeans were still a small nomadic tribe. His hero believed in God and accepted his sufferings with love, whereas the poetic dialogues reflect a later period of misfortune, whose hero is an Edomite who rebels against God. Fohrer (1963: 29) opens his discussion of the frame-story with the unequivocal statement that it was not written by the author of the book, but stands in its own right. According to his approach, the original frame-story is from the period that preceded the Exile, and its background is the folk sources of the Pentateuch, from the ninth and eighth centuries BCE. Against this theory see Hurvitz (1974) who, on the basis of linguistic analysis, fixes the date of the story as the post-exilic period. Von Rad (1972: 209) states that the dialogues were introduced into the story hundreds of years after its composition.

7.   See Hoffman 1981. The essential points are the following: the presentation of Job as a perfect saint, the promise of Satan that 'he will curse thee to thy face', and Job's fear that 'It may be that my sons have sinned, and cursed God in their hearts' are inconsistent with the tendency of the prologue as such, but are necessary for the general purpose of the book, and particularly for the needs of the dialogue. The representation of Job as absolutely righteous creates a kind of laboratory situation in which to examine the subject of recompense by eliminating the simplistic solution—i.e., that he suffers because he sinned. The sins of the sons are alluded to for the opposite

should only be noted that, in the wake of the story of 'The Eloquent Peasant', which we discussed above, the combination of a prose plot with poetic sections concerning the injustice and justice perpetrated by a ruler is not foreign to the culture of the ancient Near East. From this viewpoint too there is no justification for separating the frame-story of the book of Job and the poem. The frame-story also fits well into the aesthetic norm of the book as a whole—it, too, reflects a tendency towards symmetry and clear structural lines. I will therefore focus only upon the question as to whether the entire story is authentic, or whether one may discern therein secondary layers. In the light of the hypothesis formulated above, this examination will be conducted from the point of view of the tension between mimesis and anti-mimesis.

In the wake of Duhm, who denied the original connection between the poetic chapters and the frame-story, many scholars have also cast doubt upon the unity of the story itself, and have identified at least two distinct stages in its development. Alt distinguished two distinct passages concerning the restoration of Job—42.7-10 and 12-17—concluding that it is impossible that both of them came from the hands of the same author. He likewise noted certain contradictions between them—the concluding section, 42.12-17, knows neither of the three friends or of Job's illness, its author being aware only of the story of the loss of property—1.13-19. Alt concluded from this that there had been an independent story—1; 42.12-17—to which was added a fragment of another independent story—2; 42.7-9. In the second story the friends, like Job's wife, tried to persuade him to curse his creator, and it was for

reason: to leave an apparent opening also for the other solution, so as to preserve tension during the course of the dialogues. The promise of Satan, 'surely he will bless [i.e., curse] you to your face' allows for the test of righteousness to be removed to the literary realm and allows for Job to say whatever critical words may occur to him— provided he does not 'bless' God. Against that, there is no substance to the claim of certain scholars that there are contradictions between the details of the frame-story and the dialogues. My assumption that the frame-story and the dialogues were written by the same author is shared by many other scholars, including Driver and Gray 1921: xxxv-xxxvii; Dhorm 1926: lxxv-lxxxv; Segal 1942; Rowley 1970: 8-12; Weiser 1959: 7-11; 1961: 289. Weiss refrains from contending directly with other views, but it follows from the general tone of his words that he holds the frame-story to be an inseparable part of the book as a whole. See, for example 1959: 88-92. Y. Kaufmann (1960: II, 608) seems to hedge his bets; in any event, he states that the author of the dialogues knew how to weave an 'organic connection' between the story and the poems.

this reason that God directed against them the words: 'for you have not spoken of me what is right, as my servant Job has' (42.8). The present reworking has altered this important detail and turned it around (Alt 1937). Following Alt, further conjectures have been proposed, distinguishing two or more levels within the frame-story. Additional contradictions which he noted are that Satan is 'forgotten' in the conclusion, and there is a stratum in which there is no mention of Job's wife.[8]

In fact these contradictions are only apparent, resulting from the arbitrary division of the story in two. As it stands, the story is free of contradictions. The principal difficulty—the absence of Satan in the epilogue—remains even when it is divided into two or more layers. One can see that the scholars attempted to apply here the same method as is used by the documentary hypothesis regarding the composition of the Torah, despite a fundamental difference in the data: here there are no real contradictions, nor is there any linguistic basis for drawing a distinction between independent sources. The linguistic unity of the story is absolute, and any attempt to search among the verses in order to find 'foreign' linguistic influences (such as that of Fohrer) is forced and unconvincing. Under such circumstances, one may only speak of minor inconsistencies, for which one also needs to find a suitable explanation. In my opinion, such an explanation may be found in the contrapuntal aspect of the book.

---

8.   According to Snaith (1968: 4-7), the original story consisted of 1–2.10; 42.10-17. Similarly Gordis 1965: 73-74. Maag (1982: 19-20, 92-94) likewise thinks that the original story consisted of 1–2.10 and 42.11-17. The rest was added later, in his opinion, by the author of the dialogues. Weiser (1959: 266-70; 1961: 290) believes that the differences between 42.7-10 and 11-16 may betray traces of two stages of editing. Brandwein (1966) stated that the initial formulation is as follows: 1.1-5, 13, 21; 42.11-17; at a second stage there were added the passages concerning Satan—1.6-12, 22 (a transitional verse); 2.1-13; 42.7-9. According to Horst (1969: ix, and in his commentary to chs. 1–2) the original core consisted of 1 and 42.11-17; while at a second stage were added 2 and 42.7-10. According to Pfeiffer (1941: 667-70) one may distinguish three editings of the story, the first version of which was Edomite: (i) 1.1-5, 13-19; 2.7b-10; 42.10-17; (ii) 1.6-12, 20-22; 2.1-7a; (iii) 1.22; 2.10-13; 42.7-10. Fohrer (1963: 29-32) argues that one can identify four strata: to the first stratum there were added, following the Exile, the heavenly scenes, as well as a wisdom reworking (1.1, 21; 2.3, 10); at this stage, one may detect the influence of the priestly style (1.8; 2.10; 42.16-17). Thereafter, the author of the poetic sections made use of the story and added the friends (2.11-13; 42.7-9). A similar view was expressed by Williams 1971. For a summary of the different opinions, as well as a defence of his own view, see Fohrer 1983: 19-36.

In terms of mimesis, one may divide the frame-story of Job in two. The major part, 1–2.7, 42.12-17, is anti-mimetic, while the other verses contain definite mimetic elements; it is these which arouse the sense of inconsistency. In defining the former as 'anti-mimetic', I mean to say that the author deliberately wrote a story that seemingly declares of itself 'I am not true', 'I am not an imitation of any reality'.

This anti-mimetic mood is created primarily by the numerous schematic and symmetrical elements which we noted earlier, which I shall reiterate here in brief: (i) typological numbers; (ii) repetitions of the number seven; (iii) linguistic formulae repeated in explicitly anti-mimetic circumstances (1.15, 16, 19, as well as 1.7-11; 2.2-6);[9] (iv) the chiastic relationship between the portrayals of happiness and the portrayals of disaster; (v) the equal result of all the disasters (only one remains to tell the tale); (vi) the exact doubling of Job's wealth (42.12); (vii) the number of years he lived after the disaster—one hundred and forty years.

To these one should add other elements that lend the opening story an anti-mimetic character. These include its location in the land of Uz (1.1), to which the exegetes present two basic approaches. There are some who venture an exact identification of the land of Job, suggesting such locations as northern Edom,[10] the environs of the city of Nahor in the area of the middle Euphrates,[11] or Aram.[12] Alongside geographical interpretations, Weiss has noted the linguistic relation between the word עוץ and the 'wisdom concept...of עצה ("counsel" or "advice"), in order

9. Regarding the verbatim repetitions, Driver and Gray argued that, 'The writer relies on repetition rather than variation for emphasis and effect' (1921: 1). The data are correct, but their explanation is in my opinion inadequate. The repetitions are not only for emphasis, but also for the deliberate creation of anti-mimesis.

10. Such as R. Abraham ibn Ezra, particularly according to Lam. 4.21. This exegetical tradition is also given in an addition to the book in the version of the LXX, according to which Job lived in the land of Uz on the border of Edom (ἐν μὲν γῇ κατοικῶν τῇ Αὐσίτιδι ἐπὶ τοῖς ὁρίοις τῆς Ιδουμαιας και Ἀραβίας...) while further on there appear the names of the kings of Edom according to Gen. 36.31-35. Kahana holds likewise in his commentary on Job 1.1 (1924); Driver and Gray (1921: 2) point toward eastern Palestine, in Edom or Haran.

11. According to Gen. 22.21, which mentions Uz son of Nahor, brother of Abraham. See R. Saadya Gaon's commentary on this verse (Qafah 1973), as well as Mazar (1946). On the location of Nahor, see Melamet, 'Nahor', *EncBib*, V, 1968, pp. 807-808.

12. Thus Rashi; Tur-Sinai, Job, *EncBib*, I, 1955, p. 242; see also Josephus, *Ant.* 1.6.4. For more on the identification of Uz, see Zafrir, 'Uz', *EncBib*, VI, 1971, pp. 106-107.

to express that Job is the archetype of God-fearingness and fear of sin within the world of "wisdom"' (Weiss 1959: 2). I tend to believe that he is correct. There is no necessary contradiction between the geographical and symbolic interpretations: the author chose Uz both because he knew it as the name of a real place and because of the associations which it elicits. This choice reflects the problematic nature of the prologue narrative: as the background to a book in which mimesis fulfils an important role, the plot needed to be rooted in actual reality; but, for reasons which I shall clarify below, it was likewise important that the author emphasize anti-mimetic elements in the opening story. He thus made use of a known name, but one that was not widespread. There are some who have raised doubts as to whether he himself knew the exact location of the land of Uz (e.g. Driver and Gray 1921: 2), suggesting that he deliberately chose a name that strengthened the anti-mimetic tendency. Maimonides seems to have had this in mind when he said:

> ...in which figures the equivocal word *Uz*. It is the name of an individual: 'Uz his first-born' [Gen. 22.21]; and also the imperative of a verb meaning to reflect and meditate: עוצו עצה [take counsel together; Isa. 8.10]. It is as if Scripture said to you: Meditate and reflect on this parable...
> *(Guide for the Perplexed*, 3.22; Pines 1963: 486-87)

The addition to the Septuagint (above, n. 11) manifests a tendency to strengthen the mimesis, to anchor the story in a known and actual reality. That is, the Greek translator was also aware of the legendary quality of the story as it appears in the traditional text. The presentation of Job's righteousness in hyperbolic language, not used regarding any other personality in the Bible—'blameless and upright, one who feared God, and turned away from evil'—also gives the opening the colours of a legendary tale.[13]

The absence of any mention of Satan in the concluding section is surprising, if one thinks in mimetic terms; this fact is not even adequately explained by the conjecture that his is a secondary figure in the story. However, it seems to me that this too involves an anti-mimetic tendency, which comes to suggest that in the prologue too one ought not to see either Satan or anything associated with him as reflecting a real event. Indeed, the tableau of the sons of God with Satan among them is unique

13. The Sages took note of this: 'He [the Satan] said to Him, "Master of the Universe, I have travelled over the whole earth and have found none so faithful as your servant Abraham"'. And further, 'Said R. Yohanan, 'Greater is that which is said about Job than that said about Abraham...' (*b. B. Bat.* 15b).

in the Bible, albeit its general lines are reminiscent of some other scenes. The closest of these is 1 Kgs 22.19-22:

> I saw the Lord sitting on his throne, and all the host of heaven standing beside him on his right hand and on his left; and the Lord said, 'Who will entice Ahab'…Then a spirit came forward and stood before the Lord, saying, 'I will entice him…I will be a lying spirit in the mouth of all his prophets'. And he said, 'You are to entice him, and you shall succeed; go forth and do so'.

Likewise in Zech. 3.1-2:

> Then he showed me Joshua the high priest standing before the angel of the Lord, and Satan standing at his right hand to accuse him. And the Lord said to Satan, 'The Lord rebuke you, O Satan!…Is this not a brand plucked from the fire?'

But in both these passages, unlike the case in Job, it is God who dictates Satan's moves or rebukes him. In Job, God himself is seduced by Satan—something so sharply contradictory to the conventions of the Bible that it is impossible to interpret it, except as a way of saying that such a thing never happened.[14]

All these features create a distinctly anti-mimetic story. Indeed, from the exegetical aspect we find that the Rabbis properly understood the author's intentions when they stated that 'Job never was and was never created, but was a parable' (*b. B. Bat.* 15a). Moreover, it would seem that the circumstances which led the Sages to deny the actual existence of Job (or at least of his sufferings, as in *j. Sot.* ch. 5) are similar to those which led the author to fashion the story of Job in an anti-mimetic fashion. That is to say, he was thereby allowed maximum freedom to shape the data of the story into an experimental-theoretic system for the examination of various doctrines of recompense: when the righteous man, his happiness and his suffering are 'absolute', one may examine the subject in a 'purer' way, as we have already noted. The anti-mimetic fashioning of the frame-story, as opposed to the mimesis of the debates, also supports the author's ironic stance vis-à-vis the solution to the problem of theodicy *per se*. Like irony, anti-mimesis also makes it easier for the author to express himself freely, as it is anyway only a legend.

---

14. See R. Johanan's words of astonishment: 'Were it not written, it would be impossible to say it: Like a man who is tempted and is tested' (*b. B. Bat.* 16a). Compare Weiss's discussion (1959: 33-48), which sees Satan as an expression of the thoughts of God.

This likewise suggests the irrelevancy of the account of Job's restoration to the issue of principle discussed in the debates, which was in truth never properly resolved.

On the face of it, one might argue that a story which seems in our eyes to be anti-mimetic was not necessarily understood as such by the author and his readers, whose alleged 'innocence' did not allow them to draw a sharp distinction between 'reality' and 'legend'. However, this argument is inappropriate in the light of the extensive tradition of biblical narrative, which knows very well how to shape a mimesis of everyday life without any legendary embellishment, and in which the miraculous is presented as exceptional and not as a routine event. An explicit example of the ability of the later biblical narrator to depict an archaic social setting, analogous to that of the book of Job, in strictly realistic lines, free of anti-mimetic elements, is the book of Ruth—but this is not the place to elaborate upon this point.[15]

From an overview of the frame-story as a whole, one also learns of the author's ability to distinguish between two types of stories. The frame-story is not all of a piece. The anti-mimetic details we have noted are concentrated in certain specific passages: 1.1–2.7, and 42.12-17. That is to say, towards its end—from 2.8 on—the prologue begins to assume mimetic coloration; the schematic elements disappear, being replaced by descriptions of realia and of expected psychological reactions: sitting in mourning in the ashes; scratching with potsherds; Job's angry response to his wife, attesting to his fear that, if she continues to goad him, he may end up saying things that verge on cursing of God; the arrival of the friends, who come to comfort him and sit with him in silence, 'for they saw that his suffering was very great'. The same holds true for the beginning of the epilogue—42.7-10—which is also mimetic in character. On the face of it, these data seem to confirm the speculations regarding two different strata, according to which the mimetic story of the friends was added to an alleged older anti-mimetic stratum—but things are not so. First of all, this is not an adequate explanation for all of the problematic data, such as the absence from the epilogue of Satan and of

---

15. See recently Zakovitch 1982: 3-14, on the nature of the narrative; on pp. 30-31 there is a brief comparison between the book of Ruth and the frame-story of Job. On the late date of Ruth (ca. fifth century BCE), see pp. 33-35; and see also Brenner 1988: 85-118 (on its literary nature) and pp. 119-63 (on its late date). The literary nature of the book of Ruth also confutes the argument of Duhm (above, n. 6), that a peaceful and pastoral story could not have been written at such a late period in Jewish history.

Job's wife. Second, the story of the friends (2.11-13; 42.7-9) and the mimetic sections of the frame-story (2.8-13; 42.7-10) do not completely overlap. Third, the frame-story is free of contradictions and makes use of uniform language; hence, there is no ground for dividing it into strata. There is an alternative explanation for the literary differences which we have noted, which fits one of the outstanding characteristics of the book—namely, the tension between the mimetic and anti-mimetic tendencies.[16]

As against the advantage to be gained from fashioning the story of Job as an unrealistic legend, there is also a need to lend mimetic character to the debates, as only thus can the reader identify with Job (or with his friends)—this being the advantage of a dramatic work over an anthology. Therefore, one needs to move from a situation 'which never was and was not created' to the mimetic situation of the cycle of debates. So as to make this transition as smooth as possible, it already occurs within the frame-story, rather than in the 'seam' between it and the debates. And indeed, the mimetic sections of the frame-story create a mimetic framework for the debates, while the book as a whole is placed within an anti-mimetic framework:

Frame-Story		*Debate Cycle*	*Frame-Story*	
Anti-Mimetic	Mimetic	Mimetic	Mimetic	Anti-Mimetic
1.1-2.7	2.8-13	3–42.6	42.7-10	42.11-17.

The counterpoint within the story itself thus bridges between the mimetic and anti-mimetic dimensions of the book. The introductory story contains within itself the code to the constant tension that charac-

---

16. Fullerton (1924: 117) sees the relation between the legendary nature ('Volksbuch', 'a Sunday School story') of part of the frame-story and the sophisticated nature of the book as disharmonious. According to him, 42.10-17 spoils the book as a whole from the religious viewpoint, because it is beyond any possible 'spiritual harmony' with the dialogues: they reflect the view of the friends that suffering is no more than temporary, an approach that was rejected by the author. Fullerton concludes from this that it is a late addition. But on second thought, he says, 42.10-17 may nevertheless be original, being offered by the author in order to satisfy the orthodox view (1924: 135). A similar distinction is drawn by Gordis (1965: 8) regarding the book as a whole: the prose was composed for the simple believer, while the poetry was for the philosopher. A study of the frame-story according to the criteria set forth for the examination of folk-tales by Vladimir Propp appears in an article by Fontaine (1987). Even though it is not the purpose of this article to prove the integrity of the story, it too supports this conclusion.

terizes the book as a whole: between the most strident anti-mimetic manifestation, its rigid structure, and its mimesis.

We therefore find that, in accordance with the hypothesis set forth at the beginning of this chapter, the frame-story in its entirety is authentic, and one cannot distinguish any later additions therein.

2. *The Third Cycle of Debates*

A decisive majority of scholars of the book of Job share the view that the third cycle of the debates, as it has come down to us, is corrupted or incomplete.[17] This view is based first and foremost upon structural considerations: there is no speech by Zophar; the speech by Bildad is extremely short, only six verses long (ch. 25); on the other hand, the final speech by Job extends over six chapters (chs. 26–31), and is far longer than any of his speeches in the previous cycles. Moreover, certain chapters within this speech seem to deviate from the character of the book as a whole (ch. 28), while others (chs. 26, 27) are inconsistent with Job's statements elsewhere. Segal is perhaps the only scholar who accepts the texts as they are, explaining that the brevity of Bildad's speech and the absence of Zophar's third speech derive from the author's wish to suggest that the friends had run out of arguments. The length of Job's remarks, as a substitute for the answers of the friends, likewise follows from this.[18]

Examination of the third cycle in the light of the hypothesis formulated at the beginning of this chapter leads to the conclusion that the author did not intend to shape it in this manner, since breaking the anticipated structure does not advance any mimetic function. The mimesis during the course of the debates revolves around four axes, which we have designated 'unifying elements': the tendency towards exacerbation, the binding features within the debate, the moulding of the characters, and the trial motif. These were examined in the fifth chapter of the present study, in which we observed that several chapters—namely, chs. 18,

17. Thus Duhm 1897: xiv; Gordis 1965: 98-99; Maag 1982: 154; Y. Kaufmann 1960: II, 604-605; Fohrer 1963: 35-36; Dhorm 1926: xliv-liii; Driver and Gray 1921: xxxviii-xl; Kahana 1924: 13; Horst 1969: xi, who designates chs. 24–27 as a 'konglomerat', following Fohrer 1963: 35; Weiser 1961: 20-21.

18. Segal 1942. Weiser (1959: 20-21) is prepared to accept a harmonistic explanation for the brevity of the third speech of Bildad, ch. 25, and the absence of the third speech of Zophar, but not for the other questions raised by the third cycle.

20, 24, 25, 26, and 28—do not manifest the mimetic tendency regarding even one of these axes. However, chs. 18 and 20 fit well into the structure of the second cycle; hence, we attributed the absence of mimesis therein to the lack of a tradition of shaping secondary characters and to the difficulty encountered in making maximum use of the possibilities offered by the complex structure of the book. Taking into consideration the 'circle of historical exigencies' of the author, there is hence no basis for the claim that they are corrupted or mislocated. Chapter 24 also fits into the anticipated structure of the third cycle, as part of Job's answer to Eliphaz's words in ch. 22; according to our hypothesis, there is no justification for claiming that it is in the wrong place, despite its exegetical difficulties.[19] True, it does not relate to the suffering of Job nor to Eliphaz's indictment in ch. 22, but this may be attributed to the gradual loosening that takes place in the connections among the speeches, as we noted above; or, to put it differently, on the strengthening of the catalogic-anthological element in the book.

The same is not true of the block of chs. 25–28. It does not meet the strict demands of structure and, as we have already noted, there is no basis for the theory that a tactic of structural deviation was used there as a deliberate means of expression. Hence, one must reject the possibility that the brevity of the speech of Bildad and the absence of Zophar's speech reflect a mimetic fashioning of a dying debate, in which the arguments of the friends ultimately peter out. Moreover, we have already observed that, although the mimetic fashioning of the characters weakens in the second cycle of debates, the formal framework is by contrast stubbornly preserved. In the third cycle, in which the unifying mimetic elements become even weaker, it would be reasonable to expect that every effort would be made to preserve the fastness of the connective framework even more strictly, yet it becomes clear that even this disintegrates. Nor does the block of chs. 25–28 as extant contribute to the creation of tension between mimesis and structure, a factor con-

19. The subject seems to be the description of the wicked who exploit and steal (vv. 1-16) and their cursing by Job (vv. 17-25—according to the division of Gordis 1965: 271-72). Fohrer (1963: 370-74) divides the chapter into four independent poems—(i)1-4, 10-12, 22-23; (ii) 5-8; (iii) 13-17; (iv) 18-21. Dhorm, in his commentary on the chapter (1926), states that only vv. 1-17 (in a different order) and 26 belong to the speech of Job, while the rest are part of the reconstructed speech of Zophar. I accept the view of Gordis that, precisely because of the difficult language of the chapter, which allows us to place it within almost any context, one must exercise restraint in proposing alterations.

tributing to the doubts concerning its place within the book. This doubt is strengthened in the light of the contents of 27.8-23, which attribute to Job an outlook inconsistent with his words thus far—namely, that God repays the wicked according to their just deserts.[20]

It follows from all these considerations that the block of chs. 25–28 as it presently stands is blemished: Bildad's speech is not merely brief, but truncated; the absence of Zophar's speech is a shortcoming, and not the result of planning; the same holds true for the unusual length of Job's final speech. In order to explain this situation properly, we shall need to examine closely the chapters which constitute this block. But first of all, we need to distinguish between chs. 25–27 and ch. 28.

The relationship of ch. 28 to the book as a whole is problematic: it is a closed intellectual and literary unit, as shall be clarified below. We have already noted that this is the only chapter that does not at all touch upon subjects related to recompense or theodicy—the righteous, the wicked, prosperity, catastrophe, causality, the doctrine of recompense; unlike the rest of the book, this chapter does not contain any emotional element, nor any expression of mutual tension between Job and his friends, nor rebellion against the conduct of the creator, nor even lamentation over bitter fate; there is no direct speech of God, nor any direct appeal by him to Job, as in chs. 39–41 (such as: 'Gird up your loins like a man...'—38.3-6; 'Have you commanded the morning since your days began, and caused the dawn to know its place'—v. 12; etc.). It is therefore difficult to imagine that the chapter was originally composed either as a speech of Job,[21] or of one of the friends,[22] or of God.[23] Rather, it stands entirely by itself. However, this evaluation does not yet imply any particular conclusion concerning the identity of its author.

From the linguistic viewpoint, ch. 28 is not markedly different from the other poetic chapters, and the same holds true with regard to its other aesthetic qualities. True, the lexicon of words used therein is unusual, and its style and structure are clearer than is characteristic of

20. According to Gordis (1965: 98), in 27.7-13 Job recounts what his faith was before the disaster; however, this answer is unacceptable to me. In any event, he also admits that vv. 13-23 are not in their right place and are part of a mislocated speech of Zophar. For more on this chapter, see below.

21. As in the present version, which according to Segal (1942: 84) is the original.

22. According to Graetz, Hoffmann and Stuhlmann (as cited in Driver and Gray 1921: 233). See Pfeiffer 1941: 672. Kaufmann (1960: II, 605) thinks that ch. 28 was the end of the speech of Elihu, that is, an integral part of the original book.

23. Thus, for example, Kahana 1924: 15; Tur-Sinai 1972: 238.

the debates generally (see below), but these data can be explained in terms of its distinctive subject.

It is thus understandable why scholars were divided regarding its authorship. There are some who think that it was written by the author of the book, while others hold that it was not by the author of the book,[24] and yet others hedge, saying that the entire book has one author, but that ch. 28 was written at a later stage, perhaps long after the rest of the book had already taken shape.[25] Before taking a stand on this question, a few words are in order concerning the chapter itself and its place in the book.

The key word of this chapter is 'wisdom' (חוכמה). It is repeated three times, always in a prominent place: twice in the repeated refrain, 'But where shall wisdom be found (come)? And where is the place of understanding?' (vv. 12, 20), and the third time in the final verse. One may therefore state that wisdom is the subject of the poem, albeit not one that is stated at the outset.[26] The opening stanza, vv. 1-11, is concerned with the ability to find the most hidden treasures—gold, iron, precious stones—by overcoming obstacles and dangers. The passage does not specify of whom it is speaking, using neutral language: יזקו ('which they refine', v. 1); יקח ('is taken', v. 2); הוא...שם ('put...he', v. 3); שלח ידו...הפך ('puts his hand...overturns', v. 9); בקע...ראתה עינו ('cuts out...his eye sees', v. 10); חבש...יצא אור ('binds up...brings forth to light', v. 11). The identification of the subject of these verbs thus becomes a kind of riddle,[27] whose solution one needs to search out. The reader becomes a participant in the experience of searching, which is the main theme of the second stanza. Who then is the subject of the first stanza? Taking the literal meaning of the phrases 'refine...is taken...put... overturns...his eye sees', etc., at face value, it is clearly speaking of humankind. The great accomplishments portrayed are not so remarkable that they cannot be ascribed to mortal human beings. Nevertheless,

---

24. Such as Duhm 1897: xiv; Driver and Gray 1921: xxxviii; Fohrer 1963: 392; Maag 1982: 195; Westermann 1956: 104-107; Weiser 1959: 198-99.

25. Thus Snaith 1968: 69-71; Dhorm 1926: xcvii; Rowley 1970: 13-14; Gordis 1965: 278; and others.

26. Thus Fohrer (1963: 390) thinks that the original poem opened with the repeated chorus 'and where shall wisdom be found.

27. Thus Westermann 1956: 104-105. I do not share his view that the chapter is a secondary expansion of a brief riddle (vv. 12, 20) and its double solution: positive (23) and negative (13, 21).

some scholars and exegetes have stated that it speaks of God,[28] and in this it seems that they have fallen into the trap which the author has set for them in the riddle, by hinting that humans are unable to resolve every mysterious thing with certainty. In any event, for those who understand the subject to be humankind, the question in v. 12 comes as a complete surprise: 'But where shall wisdom be found?' Has not human wisdom just now been portrayed? The answer given in the second stanza is negative. Not only has humankind not found wisdom, but it is so much beyond their attainment that they are unable to even assess it properly (vv. 16-19). Thus, the question in v. 20 invites the opposite answer to that suggested by its identical number in v. 12. The tendency now is to answer, no one knows the place of wisdom. But this too is surprisingly rejected further on: 'God understands the way to it, and he knows its place' (v. 23). The chapter therefore uses a tactic which might be described as 'the unexpected turnabout': the reader is led to one conclusion, but then is suddenly shown an error, and is redirected to the opposite conclusion.[29] It becomes clear that humanity's ability, as great as it may be, is substantively different from that of God: the latter determines at will the laws governing the world, while the most humans can attain is the use of this lawfulness. But the tactic of the unexpected turnabout does not end with v. 23. The reader arrives at the end of the chapter with the feeling that he or she has understood it properly: wisdom is not the lot of humanity, but of God alone. Then suddenly there comes the final verse, and that conclusion too is turned on its head: humans do possess wisdom—'Behold, the fear of the Lord, that is wisdom; and to depart from evil is understanding' (v. 28). The tactic of composition of the chapter well fits its message: anyone who misunderstood the meaning

28. See R. Ibn Ezra, in his commentary on v. 4, 'they open shafts in a valley...', as well as to v. 9, 'Man puts his hand to the flinty rock, and overturns mountains by the roots'. Also Rashi to v. 3 '"put an end": the Omnipresent'; and to v. 11: '"He binds up the streams": in the creation of the world, when he subdued the lower waters'. Likewise also Kimhi, in *Mezudat David*. Dhorm (1926: 400), Weiser (1959: 196), Gordis (1965: 279), Fohrer (1963: 389), Driver and Gray (1921: 238), and others, following AV and Luther, expanded the translation to v. 3 ('put an end to darkness') by adding the word 'man', thereby detracting from the riddle-character of the first stanza.

29. For more on the literary use of this tactic, see Hoffman 1992. The Mesopotamian story of the servant and the master ('The Pessimistic Dialogue') is likewise built upon a similar literary approach.

of the verse three times in succession should not claim to be wise![30]

This reading turns ch. 28 into a theoretical work touching upon two subjects, which over the course of time became specific disciplines within philosophy: epistemology and semantics. Regarding the former, the lesson to be drawn is that the limited quality of knowledge is an immanent human quality, not subject to correction by means of learning. Concerning the latter area, the lesson is that errors and mistaken views not infrequently stem from inaccurate use of concepts—in this case, that of 'wisdom'. The term relates to a quality of God, so that anyone who considers it in relation to humankind in isolation from the fear of God will necessarily arrive at a mistaken understanding.[31] If this chapter is indeed intended to warn against inexact use of language, there may in fact be room for a distinction[32] between 'Wisdom' (החוכמה; i.e., with the definite article), mentioned in vv. 12, 20—which is the exclusive domain of God—and 'wisdom' (חוכמה)—that is, the fear of God, which is accessible to man.

The conclusions that follow from this brief analysis with regard to the authorship of ch. 28 and its place in the book are not unequivocal. The epistemological aspect *per se* is not alien to the book as a whole. Statements containing speculations on the nature of human wisdom are scattered throughout the speeches preceding ch. 28, from some of which there follows by implication a sceptical position regarding the nature of human 'wisdom'. For example: 'He takes the wise in their own craftiness' (5.13); 'But oh, that God would speak...and that he would tell you the secrets of wisdom' (11.5-6); 'Wisdom is with the aged, and understanding in length of days. With him are wisdom and might, he has counsel and understanding' (12.12-13); 'Hast you listened in the counsel of God? And do you limit wisdom to yourself?' (15.8); 'How you have counselled

---

30. It follows from this that the definition of v. 28 as a late addition contradicts both its literary nature and the ideational message of the chapter, as opposed to the view of Duhm 1897: 137 ('prosaische Zusats'); Fohrer 1963: 392; Driver and Gray 1921: 245; Dhorm 1926: 414; etc.

31. Hints of ideas belonging to the realm between philosophy and semantics may also be found in Psalm 1. Despite a certain similarity, the view presented here is different from that which claims that the chapter speaks of two kinds of wisdom, 'practical-human' as against 'theoretical-divine'. See Driver and Gray 1921: 244-45; Kahana 1924: 146; and others.

32. Thus Gordis 1965: 100. A distinction between two kinds of wisdom, 'regular' and 'deep', was already drawn by Samuel b. Meir in his harmonistic inter-pretation of the book of Ecclesiastes. See on this Japhet and Salters 1985: 52-53.

him who has no wisdom' (26.3). In the speech of God, too, even though
it does not refer explicitly to human wisdom, humankind's ability to
know is challenged. We find that ch. 28 is written on the same scale as
the book as a whole, and does not create disharmony. Nevertheless, as
has been noted above, it constitutes an independent unit.

In light of these considerations, I propose borrowing the term 'cadenza',
from the realm of music, to describe the position of this chapter in the
book. This term is used to refer to 'a virtuoso improvization without
orchestral accompaniment, brought immediately before the conclusion
of an aria...applied also to the concerto...Generally speaking the soloist
himself composes the cadenza, but with the decline of the art of
improvisation towards the end of the 18th century composers began to
compose the cadenzas to their own works.'[33] One can of course have a
concerto without a cadenza, the latter not being an integral part of it, but
it is richer with it; it is set off from the concerto by the interruption of
the playing by the orchestra as a whole in favour of one solo instrument.
This instrument is not brought in from the outside, but has already
played a central role in the work; it creates an interlude in the 'natural'
development of the work without disturbing it. In practice, the soloist
may choose the particular cadenza which he wishes to play, or even
compose his own. In any event, the issue of the authorship of the
cadenza is secondary to that of the interpretation of the work as a
whole. The representation of ch. 28 as a 'cadenza' is intended to present
it as a known and existing artistic phenomenon, and to define its position
in the book more exactly: is it an alien body from the structural viewpoint? Yes, in so far as the cadenza is a foreign presence in the work.
Should it be seen as part of one of the speeches of one of the speakers?
No, it stands by itself. Does it contribute to the literary continuity of the
book? No, but neither does it detract from it. Is it part of the overall
orchestration, of the problem of recompense in its various aspects? No,
but it does entail the development of one motif, which is not alien to the
weave of the book as a whole.

The question as to whether ch. 28 is a later addition also needs to be
examined from another point of view: namely, the catalogic-anthological
nature of the book of Job, which we discussed earlier *in extenso*.
The term 'later addition' is foreign to an anthology. Even were we to
know the history of the editing of the book of Psalms and to be able to

33. Y. Hirschberg, 'Cadenza', *EncHeb*, XXIX, 1977, p. 160. Gordis (1965: 278)
defines ch. 28 as a 'musical interlude'.

distinguish its different stages, we would be unable to describe any particular psalm as an 'addition' merely because it had been included within the collection at one of the later stages of editing. The term 'later addition' is only of exegetical benefit in one of two contexts. (a) When a work has a single, clear message, as opposed to the passage which is suspected of being an addition. In such a case, one needs to decide whether, in interpreting the work as a whole, one needs to take into consideration the message that follows from that passage, or whether it is preferable that it be seen as a foreign body, and not allow it to influence our understanding of the work as a whole. A striking example of such a case is the concluding verses of the book of Ecclesiastes: are they an addition, or ought one perhaps to interpret the entire book as leading in one fashion or another towards the conclusion: 'Fear God, and keep his commandments' (12.13)? (b) If one wishes to map certain ideas chronologically, or if one is attempting to sketch the development of one or another outlook. Examples of this may be brought primarily from the prophetic literature: for example, are the eschatological prophecies in Isaiah 2 and 11 later additions, or do they represent an idea which was already known during the eighth century BCE? Neither of these contexts is relevant to the question of the status of ch. 28: first, because the chapter does not contradict the book as a whole; secondly, because, as we have already stated, the author of the book explicitly refrains from taking an unequivocal stance regarding the problem of recompense—a tactic which is among the basic foundations of his poetics. Finally, there is in any event no way to determine whether there is a gap between the date of its composition and that of the other writings in the book.

It follows from this that the identity of the author of ch. 28 is of only marginal importance from every conceivable viewpoint, and in any case we do not have the tools to establish it. The same is not true regarding the question as to who chose to incorporate the wisdom poem within the book. If the author of the book was responsible for this decision (whether he himself wrote it, or whether he took it ready-made), we may credit him with another innovation in the development of biblical literature—namely, the breaking of the structural framework and the interruption of its mimetic continuity by the introduction of an independent element—the 'cadenza'. However, the examination we have conducted thus far forces us to reject this possibility. It is difficult to assume that someone who took the trouble to construct such an orderly and systematic structure, which as we have seen itself involves a literary innovation, would introduce another innovation whose main feature is the breaking of that self-same structure, and for other than mimetic reasons; particularly as this break confutes the solution found by the author to the artistic problem as we have defined it pertaining to his freeing himself from the catalogic model. In other words, on the basis of the hypothesis presented at the beginning of the chapter, it seems unreasonable that the author of the book should incorporate a chapter which breaks the structure without contributing to the mimesis, or even to the tension between the two.[34]

If so, may one attribute this compositional innovation to a redactor? My answer to this question is dialectical; *post factum*, yes—as we can see; *ab initio*—no, as he evidently did not intend to do so. Had the editor wished to give this chapter an unusual structural status, he certainly would have incorporated it within the organized cycle of debates, as thereby its difference would be explicit, rather than within a problematic block, in which the uniqueness of ch. 28 is also obscured. It is incorporated where it is precisely because the lack of a fixed pattern in the third cycle exposed the anthological aspect of the book, and thereby paved the ground for assimilating a chapter lacking in context. Under these circumstances, ch. 28 could equally well be part of the 'nachlass' of the author or the work of another author, or even of the editor himself. But perhaps, one may suggest, this wisdom poem was consciously incorporated with the status of a 'cadenza', at a stage when the structure of the third cycle was still intact and not yet corrupted. My negative answer to this possibility will be argued further on in the course of this discussion.

These conclusions clarify one of the features which led me to my choice of the phrase 'blemished perfection' to describe the book of Job. The definition of the wisdom poem as a 'cadenza' provides a kind of justification for its artistic place within the book, and even a recognition

---

34. This reason also applies to those who attempt to grasp the stick at both ends (see n. 26); to argue that the author of the book is responsible for the incorporation (and composition) of the chapter, while explaining its departure from the norms of the book on the grounds that it was written after the book had already been fully shaped. Since if its incorporation reveals a lack of sensitivity to the nature of the work in general, for which reason one cannot assume that the author was responsible for it, why should one assume that the sensitivity of the same author diminished over the course of time when he added the chapter?

of the breakthrough in the realm of composition, a breakthrough that contributes to the wholeness of the work. On the other hand, one cannot ignore the fact that ch. 28 is inconsistent with the immanent pattern of the book, and that in this respect it contains a blemish. The fact that an artistic norm of 'cadenza' was created over the course of generations contributes retrospectively to our perception of the 'wholeness' of the book. This situation is the opposite of that implied in our earlier statement, namely, that the author exploited only some of the possibilities which were created by the structure of the book. There, our retrospective judgment led scholars to define some of the data in the book as a 'blemish' (and to propose changes); it was precisely their evaluation thereof within the framework of 'the circle of historical exigencies' that made it clear that there was no reason why the author should behave otherwise.

Unlike ch. 28, chs. 25–27 bear a clear relationship to the primary theme of the book of Job—God's righteousness. Nor are they independent literary units; rather, they are filled with the same sort of emotional baggage as is characteristic of the other chapters of the debate, their style, too, being similar to that of the other chapters of the book. For this reason, unlike ch. 28, there is no reason to doubt the identity of their author, and we only need to ask: (a) How is one to understand their location and editing? (b) Is it possible to reconstruct the 'original third cycle'? There are only two possible answers to the first question: either the third cycle of debates has come down to us corrupted, or it was never properly shaped to begin with. Obviously, one can only speak of reconstruction if we adopt the first option.

There is a certain inner logic to the theory that the block of chs. 25–27 was fashioned and arranged in an orderly way, like its predecessors, but became corrupted during the course of the transmission of the book. The contents of this block are not unequivocal, a factor which could have led to the mixing of the order of its various passages and to errors regarding their attribution to one or another speaker. If this is so, then the scholarly attempts to reconstruct its original sequence on the model of the two previous cycles of debates are in order. The lack of agreement as to the correct reconstruction does not negate the methodological justification for attempting to create one.[35]

35. The following are several examples of proposed reconstructions of the original speeches in chs. 23–27. (a) Maag 1982: 154; (b) Gordis 1965: 98-99; (c) Y. Kaufmann 1960: II, 604-605; (d) Fohrer 1963: 34-36, 361-88; (e) Dhorm

However, the theory that it was corrupted is not necessarily correct, and it seems preferable to me to assume that this block was never properly fashioned or ordered. The theory that the original sequence was corrupted contradicts the rule of giving preference to the difficult reading (*praeferenda lectio difficilior*):[36] moreover, why should the order of chapters have become confused, when their schematic order is so definite and anticipated? And if this happened, why did not any of the redactors or early copyists of the book take the trouble to correct it, at least according to the formal arrangement of chapters within the strict pattern known from the previous cycles? It is true that this last puzzle may be resolved by the assumption that they refrained from correcting it out of respect for the (confused) written text. But if this is so, then the other theory is preferable: namely, that the author never properly completed his work, so that what we have is no more than an incomplete outline, raw material from which he intended to create the structure of the third cycle. An answer to the question as to why he did not succeed in completing his entire work will take us beyond the realm of scholarly speculation to that of historical romance, which we must forego. It is sufficient to assume that the redactors saw these outlines as materials intended by the author for his book, and therefore incorporated them within the incomplete cycle, without, however, attempting to do that which the author did not manage to do. This theory, rather than its alternative, explains the attitude of respect toward the extant text: the earliest copyists refrained from altering it because they had a tradition

1926: xlvii-lii (the details of their proposals are given below). For further suggestions, see Driver and Gray 1921: xl; Dhorm 1926: xlviii-liii. I have not given the proposal of Reddy, who recombines the speeches freely as he sees fit (see above).

Job	Bildad	Job	Zophar
(a) 23.1–24.12	25.1-6; 24.13-25	26.1-4, 27, 23-26	27.7-23
(b) 23–24	25.1-6; 26.5-14	26.1-4; 27.2-13	27.13-23.
(c) 23–24	25.1-6; 26.5-14	26.1-4; 27.2-6, 11-12	27.7-10, 13-23
(d) 23.1-17	25.1-6	26.1-4; 27.1-6, 11-12	–
(e) 23–24.17	25.1-6; 26.5-14	26.1-4; 24; 27.2-12	24.10-24; 27.13-23

36. On this principle, see Tov 1990: 229-31. However, it is somewhat qualified, like the other rules pertaining to matters of text, which one should see as at most guide-lines for methodological preferences. Thus, I accept Tov's remarks that 'this rule is correct in principle' but 'it is problematic'. However, at least one of the difficulties cited by Tov regarding the application of the rule does not exist in the present case: here, unlike many other examples, the sequence of passages and their arrangement may be defined as a 'solid version' in an objective way.

that the book had come down thus from its author. According to this hypothesis, he completed writing chs. 29–31 and 38–42 (on 32–37, see below) before fashioning the third cycle, because the end of the book was clearer to him, whereas the shaping of the middle of the third cycle in a form that would go beyond that of an anthology on the subject of recompense was put off, and was never completed.

This assumption seems consistent with the stance presented above, namely, that the confrontation with the catalogic and anthological model represented a significant aesthetic problem, whose solution is reflected in the book: the various literary units in chs. 25–27 are anthological materials which required reworking. This reworking was meant to have organized them around unifying mimetic elements, make the contents fit the respective speakers, and thereafter arrange them following the formula of the other cycles of debate. But it is clear that this labour was never completed: Bildad's speech remains brief and unrefined; in ch. 26 one finds (see Appendix VII) only one unifying mimetic element—the links to the debate in the opening verses; ch. 27 is the most refined of them all—we have found it to contain (see the above appendix) three unifying elements, but it is clearly not properly incorporated within the structural system, and part of it may have been intended as a framework for the third speech of Zophar. The conclusion is that there was no room for reconstruction of the block of chs. 25–27, because it never existed in any different form, and its re-editing would therefore have nothing to do with its original arrangement.[37] For this reason, it is clear why we earlier rejected the possibility that ch. 28 was incorporated in its place before the third cycle became corrupted: it was never 'uncorrupted'.

The headings of the speeches in the third cycle are difficult in their own right. (a) What need is there for a heading to ch. 27, which according to what is said there is a continuation of the speech of Job begun in the

---

37. Driver and Gray (1921: xl) likewise concluded that there is no justification for rearranging chs. 25–27, if only for a practical reason: while they contain a mixture of material from the speeches of Job, Bildad, and Zophar, part of these have been lost, and hence we do not have sufficient data at hand to reconstruct the original. Gordis (1965: 18) warns against excessive correction of the book, but cannot resist the temptation to rearrange the block of chs. 25–27. Fohrer (1963: 35) takes a path of his own: he uses part of the material to reconstruct the 'original' source (see above), while defining another part as four independent and later poems (24.1-15; 26.5-14; 27.7-10, 13-23; 27.7-10; 28.1-28) which are unconnected to the words of the friends. It seems to me that this approach suffers from the same faults as the two theoretical approaches which wrestle with the difficulties of this block of chapters.

previous chapter? (b) Why is there no heading to ch. 28? (c) Throughout
the book, the formula 'Then X answered and said' (צופר/בלדד ויאמר/
אליפז/איוב ויען; thus in chs. 4–23; 32.6–42.6) is used repeatedly; how
then are we to explain the formula 'And Job again took up his discourse,
and said', which appears in chs. 27 and 29 alone?

The absence of a heading in ch. 28 may indicate that the editor who
incorporated it felt that its contents did not suit any of the speakers and,
as the poem originally had no heading, he left it that way. I am unable to
propose a satisfactory solution to the other two problems. However, I
would like to mention several considerations which will explain the
difficulty involved in deciding about this matter. One might speculate
that the unusual formula for the headings of chs. 27 and 29 indicates a
different editor. But if so, why did this editor not choose the regular
formula used for headings in the book (as was indeed done by the
author of the speech of Elihu, as we shall see below)? If one argues that,
due to the unusual length of Job's speech in the present redaction, the
author chose a special formula to remind the reader who the speaker is,[38]
one needs to explain the fact that the speech in chs. 26–28 is nevertheless shorter than those of Job in chs. 6–7, 9–10, 12–14, and 23–24, in
each of which there is only one opening heading. Alternatively, one
might speculate that the later editor deliberately chose an unusual
heading for ch. 27 in order to indicate that he found it without any
heading, and that it was he who assigned it to Job. But if so, why does
the same heading appear in ch. 29 as well? To conclude from this, in the
name of consistency, that this heading is from the same editor, and that
here too he wished to note that he found the chapter unattached, is like
allowing the tail to wag the dog: we have found that ch. 29 seems to be
in its proper place, that the things said there suit Job, and there is no
doubt that its original heading attributed it to Job. Under such circumstances, one cannot allow a doubtful solution to a marginal problem to
force things in favour of a complicated theory. Therefore, one must
remain content with a general model for the solution of the problem of
the headings, and to conclude that the book underwent more than one
redaction, that various contradictory editorial tendencies left their mark
upon the final text, and that not every detail can be fully explained.

---

38. As in the speech of Elihu; albeit there, as mentioned, the formula used is the
standard one; see 32.6; 34.1. Only in 36.1 is there a change, 'And Elihu continued to
say' (ויסף אליהוא ויאמר).

3. *The Speech of Elihu, Chapters 32–37*

It is widely accepted by scholars that Elihu's speech was incorporated within the body of the book at a later stage. Some believe that it was written by the author of the book himself,[39] while others atribute it to another author.[40] Only a small number of scholars see it as an integral part of the original version of the book, as it came from the author's hand.[41]

The conclusions reached in the previous chapters concerning the authenticity of the speech of Elihu appear to be ambivalent. On the one hand, we have seen that it departs in a striking way from the symmetrical pattern of the book and from the model of the cycles of debates; that, unlike the speech by God, which is also structurally deviant, the deviation of the speech of Elihu cannot be explained in terms of the need to emphasize the extraordinary nature of the speaker. The failure to mention Elihu in the frame-story exacerbates even further the break between his speech and the book as a whole. All these strengthen the view that the speech is not authentic. On the other hand, other conclusions reached seem to point in the opposite direction, namely: that the speech as a whole deals with the subject of recompense; that there is the highest concentration therein of words from the area of law and justice (see below, Appendix VI and the attached graph), which is the most stable mimetic unifying element in the book; that there is a close and explicit connection, in terms of both content and vocabulary, between the words of Job and the friends and the speech of Elihu; that the figure of Elihu is more distinctly shaped than any other figure, excepting that of Job himself, and thus fits in well with the mimetic tendency of the book.

But the contradiction between these data is only apparent, and in fact all of them tend toward the same conclusion: that the speech was written at a later stage in order to be added to an earlier edition of the book.[42]

---

39. Thus Gordis 1965: 104-16; Snaith 1968: 8, 72-85.

40. Thus Duhm 1897: xiv (who for some reason also attributes to this author a number of additions to the body of the book, such as 4.8-11; 8.14-19; 11.6, 24-28; 20.21); Maag 1982: 19; Fohrer 1963: 40-41, 445-46; 1983: 94-114; Kahana 1924: 14, who sees in Elihu's speech the beginning of exegesis of the book of Job; Tur-Sinai 1972: 275; Kraeling 1938: 127; Weiser 1959: 217-18; Dhorm 1926: c-ciii; Horst 1969: xi; and others.

41. Thus Budde 1913: xxxv; Y. Kaufmann 1960: II, 609; Segal 1942.

42. Kraeling (1938: 127) notes the duplications between the speeches of Elihu

Study of the speech may perhaps lead us to a closer understanding of the motivations of the author of the addition. At first glance, these seem to stem from considerations of content, both ideational and literary.

One would have assumed that the author of the speech saw fit to exploit the anthological nature of the book in order to expand it by the addition of further positions concerning the matter of recompense, which he did not find in the version that he had at hand. However, examination of Elihu's speech indicates that this was not its main function. We have already seen that it does not contribute much new to the subject of recompense, the little there is being confined to a small number of verses.[43] Had the author wished to add a further anthological item of limited scope, he presumably could have incorporated it more effectively in one of the speeches of the friends .

Another possible conjecture is that the author introduced a new figure who delivered a long speech in order to express his own views more emphatically, so that they would not be lost in the speeches of one of the friends as an additional anthological detail. However, in the absence of any substantial differences between the views expressed in the speech of Elihu and those found in the rest of the book, this theory must also be rejected. Moreover, the shaping of the figure of Elihu as a quarrelsome person, as one who thinks that all wisdom is to be found with him, creates from the very outset a certain aversion to him, and contradicts this solution.[44]

and Eliphaz. He concludes from this that the author of the speech of Elihu was familiar with an edition of the book that did not include the words of Eliphaz. This is an extremely strange conclusion, which assumes that the duplications came about by chance. But there is in fact, as we have seen, a clear literal connection between the speech of Elihu and the other speeches. The extensive relation specifically to the words of Eliphaz is to be explained on the basis of the fact that both his words and his figure are the most well-formed in the book, as we have seen.

43. See Maimonides' view that the entire speech was only written in order to introduce the idea of the 'interceding angel' (33.23-30). Gordis (1965: 105, 114) believes that the innovation of the author of the speech lay in his emphasizing the educational element in the suffering brought upon humanity by God, and likewise points to 33.19-28 as the 'heart of Elihu's speech'. Similar to him is Fohrer 1983: 110.

44. Y. Kaufmann (1960: II, 606) sees in Elihu the image of the author himself; if so, his words represent the view of the book of Job itself. This view differs from my own view that in principle the author did not come to present any one specific, clear-cut solution to the problem of recompense. On the contrary, if he wished to say anything of his own, it was that the problem has no solution. Moreover, if the author of

One must therefore conclude that the purpose of adding the speech of Elihu was fundamentally literary. Its author evidently found in the book of Job a ready-made vehicle capable of absorbing more material than it already contained, and perhaps even inviting additions. The author of the speech of Elihu sought to exploit this vehicle in order to give vent to his own artistic-aesthetic drives (in the sense of: 'For I am full of words, the spirit within constrains me'—32.18), and not necessarily in order to innovate in the intellectual sense.[45] Sporadic additions to the words of the friends would have been inadequate to satisfy this impulse; hence, he chose a new figure for whose moulding he was responsible from beginning to end. In terms of the inner tension between the sporadic-catalogic elements and the unifying-mimetic elements in the book, the speech of Elihu strengthens the latter. This is accomplished by placing added emphasis upon certain unifying elements, particularly those of extensive quotation from the entire book, which tie it and bond it together into a single whole. These considerations lead me to the conclusion that the adding of the words of Elihu was prompted by the chaotic situation of the third cycle of speeches, particularly that of the truncated speech of Bildad and the absence of the speech of Zophar. Support for this theory is found in several of Elihu's remarks, in which he justifies his joining the debate by the silence of the other friends. Thus, in the heading to his speech, we read, 'And when Elihu saw that there was no answer in the mouth of these three men, he became angry' (32.54). Also: 'Behold, I waited for your words...behold, there is none that confuted Job, or that answered his words, among you' (vv. 11-12). This being the case, there was a need to work in a speech at the end of the third cycle in order to close the gap in the literary framework. *Ipso facto*, it needed to be shaped as a bridge between the debates and the answer by God, and

the book indeed wished to suggest a 'correct solution', it would be natural for him to attribute it to God. According to Kaufmann, both the speech of Elihu and that of God belong to the original body of the book. Gordis (1965: 112) likewise thinks that the author attributed great importance to the ideas of Elihu, which were directed against 'orthodoxy' (as opposed to Pfeiffer 1941: 673, who thinks that the speech was added specifically for orthodox reasons), and hence did not place in God's mouth (42.7-9) any condemnation of Elihu.

45. I agree with Greenberg (1987: 297) that Elihu's words, with their flowery rhetoric, add colour to the book, but their substantive contribution to the discussion is very slight. I do not share his opinion (as shall be explained below) that the author of the book may have himself composed the speech, creating an additional figure in order to further demonstrate his rhetorical talent.

indeed such is its structure. The first part of the speech touches upon the
words of the friends, while the second part anticipates the speech of
God. Alongside quotations from things that have been said thus far in
the course of the debate, the first part also relates to subjects which
arose previously, such as the appearance of God (33.14-16; compare
4.12-16) and specific sins of Job (34.6-10; compare 22.1-14). The second
part, 36.26–37.24, is no more than a summary (or, in terms of its position in the book, an anticipation) of the speech of God. Thus, 36.26: 'the
number of his years is unsearchable', alludes to the beginning of God's
speech: 'Where were you when I laid the foundation of the earth?'
(38.4), while the descriptions of celestial phenomena—rain, clouds, sea,
light, etc.—further on in ch. 36 parallel ch. 38. 37.8: 'Then the beasts go
into their lairs, and remain in their dens' (and 'Who teaches us more
than the beasts of the earth, and makes us wiser than the birds of the
air?'—35.11) parallels the description of the animals in chs. 39–41.[46]

However, there is a literary price that must be paid in order to attain
the greater coherence of the book and to express the artistic impulse of
the author of the speech of Elihu in this manner, which in quite a few
respects seems forced. We have seen that the relation of the speech to
the trial motif is purely external—primarily verbal—without contributing
at all to its development. We have suggested that the shaping of a new
figure in addition to those of Job and Eliphaz is opposed to what is
required by the very nature of the book; the demonstrative and exaggerated connection to the other speeches is in fact anomalous and disturbing, as if to cry out and say, 'the speech of Elihu is an inseparable
part of the book'. It is likewise inconsistent with the norms of subtle
allusive connection established within the work. The entrance of an
additional friend without any expectation of his sudden appearance or
disappearance runs contrary both to dramatic mimesis and to the
structure, a contradiction which does not contribute to the tension

---

46. There is a different explanation for the relation between the speech of Elihu
and 40.6-14; see below. Hence, Fohrer's opinion (1983: 102-103) that the block in
36.27–37.13 is not part of the original speech of Elihu is refuted by the parallel
structure of God's speech and that of Elihu. See further Kraeling (1938: 127), who
sees chs. 32 and 36–37 as an addition. Fohrer justifies this with the argument that,
according to Elihu's approach, the praises of God are to be derived only from human
life and not from nature. But in fact these views do not conflict, and in many passages,
both in the book of Job (as we have seen) and outside it (for example, in Psalms 8;
104) humanity and nature are together invoked as proofs of the greatness and mercies
of God.

between these two tendencies, but only disturbs it.

If the speech of Elihu was indeed added primarily to tighten the book in the light of the weakening of the third cycle of the debates, and if the means used by its author contradict several of the poetic characteristics of the book, then we may assume that the speech was not written by the author of the book as a whole. And if indeed this addition betrays inadequate sensitivity to the poetics of the book, then it may not be ascribed to its author at all, not even as a late stage of a 'second edition, expanded and reworked by the author'.[47] It is only natural that the innate sensitivity of a later author to the poetics of a work not his own would be less than that of the original author.

4. *The Speech of God, Chapters 38–41*

We have seen that, despite its departure from the dominant model in the book, God's speech out of the whirlwind does not break the anticipated symmetry, as its striking structural position is called for by the very nature of the speaker. In other respects as well, we have seen that the there is no good reason to doubt its authenticity: its unusual contents should be understood in the light of the need to place in the mouth of God a unique sort of speech, rather than to suffice with the reformulation of ideas which were already previously articulated by human beings, nor to describe him as apologizing or submitting to Job's demand to stand with him in judgment. We have also seen that God's appearance in the wake of Job's pleas fits what we know from ancient Near Eastern literature—it is so in 'I Will Praise the Lord of Wisdom', and in a different way also in 'The Eloquent Peasant'. This poetic convention is

---

47. As against Snaith 1968: 8, 72-85, and Gordis 1965: 104-16. According to Snaith, the author of the book added the speech of Elihu in the third edition, and out of a good feel for drama did not allude to the appearance of this new friend in the earlier chapters. But if what we have here is indeed a good feel for drama, why did the author not include him in the first edition? And why is Elihu not mentioned after his speeches, in ch. 42? Gordis has noted the connective function served by Elihu. He is the one who heralds the appearance of God, like Elijah the prophet in Mal. 3.23-24. Yet even if we accept this comparison, it does not strengthen Gordis's view that the speeches of Elihu 'were added years after the bulk of the book had been written. Having written the praise framework in an earlier period, when the dialogue was composed, the poet would feel no need in later years (at the time of his maturity or in old age) to recast the text by reference to Elihu' (1965: 112). For further comparisons between the words of Elihu and the book of Malachi, see Dhorm 1926: clxvii.

also well anchored in the petitional hymns, in which God is initially presented as remote from the worshipper and not listening to him (as in Ps. 13.2; 22.2-3; 28.1 and many others), while in the end he comes to his aid (e.g., in 6.10; 17.15; 22.25; etc.). The appearance of God also enhances the tension between structure and mimesis: within the framework of the strict pattern—three cycles of human debates—there is no room for the speech of God, while the mimetic development of the trial motif creates an anticipation of a reaction on the part of 'the other party'. It follows from this that examination of the book based upon the principles that we have established leads to the conclusion that God's answer is an inseparable part of the original version of the book.[48] For that reason, I will only briefly address the question of the unity of the speech at hand: can we distinguish between authentic material and additions within it? Any such distinction must be based upon literary and substantive arguments. On the basis of such arguments, many scholars arrived at the conclusion that only the first part of the speech, chs. 38–39, is authentic, while the second, chs. 40.15–41.26, is a late addition.[49]

Scholars have noted the different literary character of the two sections. There is no focused series of rhetorical questions in the second, as there is in the first, and it only elaborates upon the description of two beasts, the Behemoth and the Leviathan, as opposed to some forty natural and zoological phenomena mentioned in the first block. For this reason, the first block alone has a strongly polemical tone. They further note that the Behemoth and Leviathan are mythological animals, and in any event are not native to the land of Israel, unlike the animals in ch. 39. The main substantive argument is that Job expresses regret before God twice, in 40.3-5 and 42.2-6, and that this is an unnecessary and sur-

48. Against those who think that the speech as a whole is a late addition, such as Volz 1911: 2, 79-80; Kraeling 1938: 141-64, 205. Arguments against this theory may be found among other places in Driver and Gray 1921: lviii-lxiii; Dhorm 1926: lxxxv-xcviii; Gordis 1965: 117-23. For reasons explained above I find no foundation for the assumption (as does, for example, Dhorm 1926: xcvii) that the author himself added the speech of God, albeit at a later stage.

49. A detailed justification of this, as well as of the possibility that the descriptions of the animals and of the Leviathan alone are not original, may be found in Driver and Gray 1921: 351-52. See Duhm 1897: xiv; Budde 1913: xxiv, 254-56; Fohrer 1963: 486-87; Oorschot 1987: 214. Oorschot's study is devoted entirely to the speech of God, and one finds therein a detailed summary of the various views, which are classified into groups. Oorschot himself claims to have proven that, in addition to the original version, one may distinguish three separate levels of additions.

prising repetition: why did not God make peace with Job immediately after his first apology, since the second, so they argue, adds nothing to it.

I believe these claims to be disproven. We have already seen that God's words do not contain any direct or substantive answer to the problem of recompense, and that in this respect there is no difference between the two sections. I have also explained the literary logic in the rapid posing of rhetorical questions, meant to increase Job's feelings of helplessness and fear of his creator. By dividing God's speech in two, the author has created a convenient framework in which to give free vent to a different artistic direction than that to which he confined himself in the first part of the speech: namely, detailed and extensive portrayals, in which reality and imagination are intermingled with one another. We find that the nature of God's answer—and this comment applies to the answer as a whole—serves well not only the underlying idea, but also the aesthetic need of the author as an artist. The question as to which is cause and which is effect must of course remain unanswered. The division of the speech into two units also serves well the mimetic tendency of the book. Had Job reneged on his struggle too quickly, this would have contravened his rebellious, fighting character as it is shaped through the entire course of the book. On the other hand, had he been represented as entirely rejecting God's words, this would go against his image as a mortal being with human weaknesses, who is prepared to forego theoretical solutions to the dilemma he has presented, provided that he be relieved of his physical and social suffering. Such a reaction on Job's part would also block the way against the story of the restoration of his fortunes, which is extremely important to the author as an existentialist solution to the problem of Job. The division of the speech of God, including the growing, albeit non-explicit, threat in the second part of the speech (be careful about continuing to rebel against One who has suceeded in subduing monsters like the Behemoth and the Leviathan!) provided a suitable means for the author to present an appropriate reaction by Job. The argument that there is no real difference between Job's two apologies, from which it follows that one of them, together with the second half of God's speech, is not authentic, is based upon a mistaken interpretation of the passages. There is a clear difference between the words 'Behold, I am of small account; what shall I answer thee? I lay my hand on my mouth. I have spoken once, and I will not answer; twice, and I will proceed no further' (40.4-5), and the second admission. The first words contain no expression of regret. On

the contrary, there is still a note of protest therein: you have come to
frighten me—and I know that it is thus, and I cannot answer you anything ('For he is not a man, as I am, that I might answer him'—9.32); in
the end, there is no more than a promise to cease challenging God. Not
so in the case of the second apology, 42.1-6. One finds there an explicit
confession of at least one error—speaking through lack of understanding
('Therefore I have uttered what I did not understand'—v. 3), coupled
with pain over the very fact of wishing to enter into judgment with God
('"Hear, and I will speak; I will question you, and you declare to
me"'—v. 4). The decisive conclusion is 'Therefore I despise [myself
(?)], repent/regret of dust and ashes' (v. 6)—a sentence containing at
least one clear word of regret—וניחמתי—'and I repent/regret'. There is
thus a certain mimetic logic in the extension of Job's withdrawal over
two graduated answers, to show that he did not easily let go of his own
truth. The formulation of the answers is also mimetic. The first is
evasive,[50] as mentioned; the second is ambiguous: for what does Job
repent? What is 'I despise [myself (?)]'? What is 'I repent/regret for dust
and ashes'?[51] It makes no sense for someone to express full repentance

50. See R. Saadya Gaon's commentary on 40.3: 'These words from him [i.e.,
Job] are considered [mere] words, so that those hearing them will not apprehend what
his intention is in them, which is that the author, when he tells he who is opposite him
that I am unable to answer you, these words may take two interpretations...But since
the one hearing these words of Job does not understand from them what his intention
is in them, there was needed a third word from God, informing him that these balanced
things are not correct, and that so long as you insist upon this, you still attribute [to
him] injustice in judgment, in giving your hearers some doubt regarding this...'
51. Rashi found here an expression of broken-heartedness and deep regret: 'I am
disgusted with my life, and I would be comforted were I to dwell in the grave, to
return to the dust and ashes from which I was taken'. Ibn Ezra interpreted, 'I am disgusted with all my words, and I would be that I am dust and ashes, for I am contemptible, as in the reason, "I am dust and ashes..."' R. Levi Gersonides interprets
this as regret over the very mourning which Job had practised, 'For in my opinion,
because of me this trouble has come upon me, and when I attempt to attach myself to
God, may He be blessed, this evil will leave me'. Some contemporary exegetes have
also suggested similar directions. See, for example, Greenberg (1987: 299) who
writes of 42.2-6: 'Job now submits unequivocally'. But there are those who have
noted the ambiguous nature of these words, such as Driver and Gray 1921: 373. For
a detailed discussion of the possible meanings of this verse, see Morrow, who concludes that the various opposed interpretations reflect 'an ambiguity that has been
deliberately structured in 42:6 by the Joban author' (1986: 212). Muenchow discusses the verse from an anthropological viewpoint. According to him, the moment

in such evasive language. In formulating Job's answer in this manner, the author must have intended to leave open the question as to whether Job was really convinced by God's inconclusive speech, and throws the ball back to each one of us: if I was convinced—there is no reason to conjecture that Job was not convinced by it; but if I am unconvinced—I cannot assume any differently with regard to Job.

God's two speeches and Job's two responses are therefore required by considerations of mimesis and, based upon the hypothesis formulated at the beginning of this chapter, there is no reason to question their authenticity. I am nevertheless unable to free myself of doubt regarding the authenticity of the direct appeal of God to Job in 40.6-14. This section, unlike the other portions of the speech, deals directly with the problem of recompense. The harshness and directness of this appeal (e.g. 'Will you even put me in the wrong? Will you condemn me that you may be justified?', 40.8) strongly contrast, both on the literary and substantive level, with the ignoring of Job in the rest of God's speech. Moreover, how is one meant to interpret the 'suggestion' of God that Job himself run the world—'Have you an arm like God, and can you thunder with a voice like his?...Then will I also acknowledge to you...' (vv. 9-14)? There are only two possibilities: either the author intended to admit that God is not successful in entirely subduing the wicked, even though he attempts to the best of his ability, and there is no one who can do so better than him; or else it is an entirely cynical remark. Neither of these two interpretations are consistent with the nature of the book as a whole. The first is totally opposed to the basic understanding of God's omnipotence, and it is unreasonable to assume that either the author or any later writer would set out to deny it. Hence, we must see these words as a cynical provocation placed by the author in God's mouth, directed against Job. If this is so, this statement deviates from the rest of the book, as nowhere else does it cross the line from the realm of irony, sharp as it may be, to that of open cynicism. It is as if the author knew well the speech of God, but does not rely upon the reader's understanding, or refuses to allow him or her too much exegetical freedom. He therefore sees fit to interpret the speech in an unequivocal, almost vulgar manner. Thus, the irony which surrounds the speech of

Job says these things he 'sinks down to the ground' (1986: 609), and thereby humiliates himself and demonstrates profound shame of his deeds. But even someone who is prepared to accept this view need not interpret Job's act as an expression of the depth of his feelings of regret.

God—which, as we have seen, is characteristic of the author's stance throughout the book as a whole—is here exchanged for aggressive and unequivocal cynicism.[52] This is a clear departure from the mimesis of the speech of God based upon demonstrative ignoring of Job, in order not to create a situation of direct polemic between God and humanity.

This being so, in my view this passage is not part of the original version of the book. The relation between it and the rest of God's speech is like that between the words of Elihu and the rest of the book: the author of the speech of Elihu—knowing well the words of Job and the friends, understanding the key role of the trial motif in the book, and being aware of the irony that accompanies the debate—determines the nature of his speech accordingly, but exaggerates by over-emphasizing each of the characteristic traits of the book. In brief, Elihu's speech contains such a high concentration of 'characteristic features' that it itself becomes an exception. For this reason, I would propose attributing 41.6-14 to the author of the speeches of Elihu. Even the technique is similar: the quotation of earlier passages. It is in this light that one ought to explain the duplication between 40.6-7 and 38.1, 3. Compare also the words of Elihu, 'Of a truth, God will not do wickedly, and the Almighty will not pervert justice...Shall one who hates justice govern? Will you condemn who is righteous and mighty?' (34.12, 17) with those of God, 'Will you even put me in the wrong? Will you condemn me that you may be justified?' (40.8). And compare Elihu's 'After it his voice roars; he thunders with his majestic voice' (37.4) with God's 'and can you thunder with a voice like his? Deck yourself with majesty and dignity' (40.9-10).[53] This conclusion is consistent with that arrived at in our discussion of the trial motif in 41.6-14 (above, Chapter 5).

5. *Summary and Conclusions*

Our examination of the book of Job on the basis of the hypothesis formulated at the beginning of this chapter led us to the conclusion that

---

52. Gordis writes of 40.9-14: 'The climax of this divine irony, infinitely keen yet infinitely kind' (1965: 119).

53. I do not ignore the measure of circularity in the argument based upon these examples. As I explained above, the author of the speech of Elihu quotes abundantly from the passages which were before him, while here I wish to infer from the similarity of language that the speech of Elihu and the words of God in 40.6-14 are by the same author. But perhaps in truth it is not impossible that the author who quotes the words of others will also make use of his own words.

the following writings are late additions: chs. 28, 32–37, 40.6-14. We likewise concluded that the third cycle of debates was never completed, and that chs. 25–27 may be seen as a collection of fragments whose writing and editing were never completed. Hence, there is no basis for speaking of a 'reconstruction' or 're-editing' of the third cycle of debates. One must likewise reject any pretence of improving the redaction of the book as a whole based upon the assumption that its present arrangement has been corrupted. Any such alteration is entirely subjective, as is witnessed by the large number of suggested corrections. Attempts at reconstruction lead to a deconstructionist reading of the book; I have already expressed, in the introductory chapter of this study, my reservations in principle regarding this approach towards a literary work.

It seems to me that the conclusions we have reached regarding the question of what is authentic and what is additional to the book of Job, derived from the application of one general assumption based upon the poetic norms that the book established for itself, are significant. Nevertheless, I do not pretend that these conclusions are a necessary result of objective considerations. Our general axiom was formulated on the basis of one reading of the book, albeit not the only possible one. Our judgments as to what contributes to mimesis, to structure, or to the tension between the two, carefully reasoned as they may be, are not 'objective', and cannot be so. The hypothesis on whose basis we attempted to distinguish between original source and addition cannot be programmed for a computer, into which one feeds data and expects to arriveat irrefutable conclusions. We are not entirely free of the hermeneutic circle which forces us to interpret the entirety of the book on the basis of its details, and to understand the details in the light of the whole. But by its very contribution to the weighing of all the phenomena in the book on the basis of the same criteria, our method succeeds in placing a dam (or perhaps one should use the more modest metaphor of filter) against absolute subjectivity and arbitrariness.

The exegetical significance of these conclusions does not lie in the realm of ideas: the positions expressed in the appended chapters do not substantially differ from those in the original part of the book. Nor should one exaggerate the importance of the final lesson that the book of Job comes to teach us since, as we have already explained, its author shaped it as a kind of vessel which can carry a wide range of positions concerning the subject of recompense, the choice among which is of only secondary importance in his eyes. Consequently, from the intellectual viewpoint there is no great significance to the distinction between source and addition.

Nevertheless, the distinction among the different levels in the book of Job teaches us that it, like the other books of the Bible, absorbed further additions even after its main body had already been shaped. These additions, the earliest exegetical stratum of the book of Job, shed light upon the intra-biblical means of exegesis—and this is not the place to expand upon the subject, which is deserving of study in its own right.[54] Neither may we draw any conclusions from what we have found in the book of Job for other books in the Bible, but must simply integrate what follows from this with the results of other studies on the subject, as only thus can we arrive at a complete picture. Were we briefly to characterize this early exegesis of the book of Job, we might say the following: that it is an exegesis that does not engage in polemics with the text, even if it does not agree with it. It presents its own outlook within the ongoing flow of the text, particularly stressing those positions acceptable to it for which it found an echo within the scripture, most especially, the axiomatic status of God's justice. It does this through an intuitive grasp of the fundamental literary character of the work, and with the intention that the additions be incorporated as an integral part therein. Nonetheless, the exegete does not overly trouble himself to hide his involvement so that it is unrecognizable. In so doing, he seems to reflect a principled position which finds in the catalogic element of the book a kind of legitimation, if not invitation, to contribute to the anthology and to expand it.

---

54. Such as Fishbane's study. I agree with his statement (1985: 525) that the roots of the Jewish exegesis are to be found in the Bible itself.

Chapter 9

CONCLUSION

The book of Job is the largest and most 'artistic' dramatic work in the Bible. This is not intended as a value statement—that is, as implying that it is the best, greatest or most important work—but simply as a literary characterization. If we understand 'art' as implying that the artist places the emphasis upon the 'how', which to a significant degree determines the 'what', we are justified in saying that the author of the book of Job enjoyed far greater artistic freedom than other biblical authors. The shaping of the stories within the biblical historiography—concerning the patriarchs, the conquest of the land, the kings and the early prophets—was limited by standards of 'historical truth', as this was passed down in the tradition of the generations. That is, its authors were unable to name their heroes as they wished: they could not, for example, decide that David was the son of Solomon, even were it to serve some important artistic purpose, nor were they free to create a dramatic climax by inventing a story about the murder of Moses during the course of a rebellion against him. Their art, as has already been noted by many people, had to be expressed in the context of their confrontation with given literary material.[1] Not so the author of Job. He was able to choose his heroes, their names, the background to their activity, their style of speech, and their theological outlook. His relation to the ancient legend of Job, which he freely chose out of artistic considerations, was extremely

---

1.   See, for example, Licht 1978: 9-23; Sternberg 1985: 25-26, 30-41, 81-83. For an opposing post-modernist speculation on the relationship between the historical event and its means of conveyance in writing, see White, who defines himself as a 'genuine pluralist...radical relativist' (1986: 486). In the course of an engagement with other views, he suggests the possibility that generic models which are understood in the consciousness of the historiographer, according to which history is necessarily 'a given sequence of events' (p. 489), determine for him the very presentation of the events and the choice of historical 'truth' and 'falsehood'.

tenuous, and he was able to use its details as he wished. In other words, the fashioning of the 'how' was determined almost exclusively by the 'what' and *vice versa*, both determined by the author himself. My own approach in this work was determined by this understanding of the book of Job: notwithstanding the emphasis which I placed upon the research method required by involvement in an ancient book, an ancient biblical book, an ancient Near Eastern book, I chose many examples, phenomena and terms from a variety of fields of creative art—music, painting, sculpture—and not only specifically literature. At the beginning of the discussion I posed a question from the realm of art: what is the nature of the aesthetic problem which the book of Job set out to solve? In the light of the answer to this question which I suggested, the book of Job may be characterized as a collection of writings concerning the problem of theodicy. Its artistic fashioning is intended to provide the author with maximal freedom of expression, to articulate unconventional dialectical positions, to lend the work a special value beyond that of an anthology by forcing the reader to adopt an emotional and intellectual stance towards the problem of theodicy.

This description of the book was arrived at by comparison with both other biblical literature and with ancient Near Eastern literature. The comparisons contributed to our understanding of its literary characteristics, to an acquaintance with the circle of exigencies which determined its literary image and the nature of its theoretical innovations, and to the shaping of a method of relating to it, based upon the norms which it established for itself. The understanding of these norms helped us to clarify the problem of its difficult language and to formulate a stance concerning the relation between the extant text and the original version. This emphasis upon comparison was a consequence of the principled stance expressed in the theoretic framework which I set forth initially. Among other things, I argued that the book of Job—like every work of art—must be understood against the background of the time of its composition. There followed from this the need for comparisons with ancient literature, which was part of the cultural world of the author of the book.

Nevertheless, I did not formulate the subtitle of this study as 'The Book of Job against the Time of Composition'. It was not for purely stylistic reasons that I chose the formula, 'The Book of Job in its Context', but precisely because of its ambiguity. It is not only the time of composition of the first, original text that constitutes the background of the book of Job. The ancient exegete who added the speech of Elihu thereby extended the field of the background of the book; hence, I attempted to ascertain his motivations as well. The exegesis written thereafter also constitutes a part of the background of the book for later readers, as it is impossible entirely to separate the understanding of the book at the time of its composition from the manner in which it was understood over the course of generations. The same holds true with regard to contemporary scholars who interpret and criticize the book in the light of the aesthetic norms of Western culture, thereby bringing this as well within the realm of 'the background of the book of Job'. It follows from this that an understanding of the book against the background of its time of composition requires familiarity with its background in the broadest possible sense. I have therefore attempted to find a way of distinguishing between the general perception of the book by contemporary scholarship, and the cultural anachronism heaped upon it by generations of exegesis. For that reason, I have included within the term 'background' not only 'I Will Praise the God of Wisdom', but also the *Poetics* of Aristotle. Whereas the former may shed light upon the status of the author regarding his work, the latter may help us to clarify the approach of later researchers to him.

The Bible as a whole constitutes the background to the book of Job in a somewhat different sense. It follows from this also that the approach known as 'canonical interpretation', which seeks to view each book in the Bible in retrospect in terms of its context as part of the canon, is justified in principle. Nevertheless, I have not dealt with this approach, because it is inconsistent with the theoretical framework established for this work. However, within those limits I have seen fit to view the book of Job in terms of its relation to the biblical oeuvre which came in its wake. Beyond the interest entailed in examining its possible influence upon the development of the latter from the literary and intellectual viewpoint, it may also prove useful in examining retrospectively the validity of several exegetical statements concerning the book itself, particularly if we wish to avoid literary, intellectual and artistic anachronism. Thus, for example, I utterly rejected the suggestion that God's answer be read as a kind of aesthetic manifesto, especially as this idea has no continuity in biblical or early post-biblical literature.

And indeed, examination of the book of Job from this point of view indicates that, despite the fact that no similar work was ever written thereafter, neither in the Bible nor in Second Temple literature, in a certain sense there is a clear sequel. The book expresses a quest for a path that allows for the shaping of writings concerning a specific subject, while avoiding the simplification and nondescript nature of an anthology. And indeed, in at least two books composed after the book of Job, which are similarly of a personal rather than a national character—namely, the Song of Songs, and Ecclesiastes—one finds a similar tendency.

The anthological character of the Song of Songs is self-evident, and several of its manifestations have already been noted on the level of the small literary unit. In terms of the book as a whole, one may note the lack of any clear connection among the various poems, as well as the lack of any clear dramatic sequence—that is, one may read the poems in an arbitrary order, without in any way altering one's understanding of them. Nevertheless, these songs are united by two connecting threads giving it a coherency beyond that of a mere anthology on a given subject. One thread is that of the two primary characters—the lover and the beloved/sister—surrounded by the secondary figures—the daughters of Jerusalem, the guards, the keepers of the city, the brothers. Two of them—at times this seems to refer to the two primary figures, but this is not always clear—even have names: Solomon (1.11; 3.7, 11; 8.12), and the Shulammite (7.1). Thus, the book uses a known figure in order to spin the crimson thread upon which are woven the poems—hints of plot which yet do not combine into a clear story: a shepherdess with whom the king falls in love, suspicion of unfaithfulness, abandonment, etc. Nearly everything said about the Song of Songs applies in equal measure, as we have seen, to the book of Job. If we add to this the explicit relationship of each of these works to ancient Near Eastern literature, it becomes clear that we may reasonably state that the Song of Songs confronted literary problems similar to those found in the book of Job, and used similar means for their solution.[2]

The relationship of the book of Ecclesiastes to the book of Job is of a similar nature. It too is a collection—in this case, of wisdom sayings and thoughts. Here too, there is no flow of contents between the different units, and even the inner arrangement of most of them may be altered without harming their meaning or understanding. But neither is it a simple anthology like the book of Proverbs, because everything there is ascribed to one figure, who even shares with the reader part of his

---

2. Fox (1985) arrived at similar, albeit not identical, conclusions regarding the literary nature of the Song of Songs independent of any connection to the book of Job.

autobiography (1.12–2.10) and many of his spiritual experiences (2.11-26; 3.9–4.17; and other thoughts expressed in the first person). Thus, the author sketches the outlines of a figure who, like Job, invites the reader to take a personal stance towards him, rather than to rest content with an intellectual position towards the abstract ideas which he expresses.

Even if this tendency to go beyond the technical solution of an anthology in order to create a unified collection of writings is most characteristic of the period following the destruction of the First Temple, and with regard to works of a personal nature, such as as Job, Ecclesiastes and Song of Songs, it is not unique to them. Even prior to the period of the book of Job, it found expression in the fashioning of that literature which bore a national character. An explicit example of this may be found in the creation of the Pentateuch. In this book, an attempt was made to organize various literary elements—traditions concerning creation, stories of the patriarchs, poems, collections of laws, genealogical lists, and the like—around a central dramatic axis.[3] A similar picture emerges with regard to the Deuteronomistic historiographic literature, particularly the books of Kings, and thereafter, in a tighter way, in the chronistic historiography of the books of Chronicles. There too we find a variety of kinds of literary sources edited around a clear dramatic axis. It may be that the final stages in the editing of the prophetic books should also be perceived from this perspective. This is not the place to elaborate upon these comparisons; my sole purpose is to point out the manner in which the book of Job, as presented in this work, integrates within a general tendency in the development of biblical literature.

The book of Job is a trail-blazer in a number of respects, which we discussed in the course of our study. The principal innovations, which to a large extent determined the nature of the novelty of the book of Job in general, are as follows. (a) The 'anthological' materials crystallized in the book were the authentic work of the author and not ready-made proverbs or traditions. Thus, the initial data, which were imposed upon those who shaped the Torah and historiographic literature, were in his

---

3. This is not the place for an extensive discussion of the question as to the state in which the Torah literature existed at the time of the Babylonian exile and the early post-exilic period, prior to being fashioned into one book. In any event, even Kaufmann, who struggles to advance the date of the 'Torah literature', distinguishes between it and the 'book of the Torah', which he fixes at the period of 'the time of the Exile and the beginning of the Second Temple period' (Y. Kaufmann 1960: I, 212-20; the quotation is from p. 217).

case the result of choice, based upon the best means of achieving his artistic and intellectual goal. (b) These materials were woven around a non-historiographical dramatic axis, as was not the case in the Torah and historiographic literature; this was done in the course of a unique structural and generic fashioning of the book. (c) A retrospective intellectual examination of the book of Job also places it as a landmark within the development of biblical thought,[4] particularly as the harbinger of the book of Ecclesiastes.

I would almost be tempted to say that, without the book of Job, the book of Ecclesiastes could not have so crystallized its outlook concerning theodicy—except, of course, that it is impossible to predict the path of the spirit. It is sufficient to compare the cry of Job, 'he destroys both the blameless and the wicked' (9.22) with the sober observation of Qoheleth that 'in the place of justice, even there was wickedness, and in the place of righteousness, even there was wickedness. I said in my heart, God will judge the righteous and the wicked...' (3.16-17); or Job's 'The earth is given into the hand of the wicked; he covers the face of its judges—if it is not he, who then is it?' (9.24) with Qoheleth's 'If you see in a province the poor oppressed and justice and right violently taken away, do not be amazed at the matter; for the high official is watched by a higher, and there are yet higher ones over them' (5.7). Some of the things said in the book of Ecclesiastes sound as if they are a concealed dialogue with the book of Job, whose goal is to sharpen the protest concerning the issue of theodicy. Following a description of his great wealth (which, unlike that of Job, involves much pampering and great luxury), Qoheleth relates of himself: 'So I became great and surpassed all who were before me in Jerusalem' (2.9), similar to what is said of Job ('so that this man was the greatest of all the people of the east'—1.3). But unlike Job, who raised the issue of recompense through his own distress and disaster—a factor which weakens, if only apparently, the objective force of his arguments—the author of Ecclesiastes places his

---

4.　See on this the recent paper by Janzen (1987), who emphasizes the role of the book of Job in giving new directions ('transformations') to Israelite faith. Regarding this matter, it is also worth noting the words of von Rad (1972: 237-39), who casts doubt upon the influence of the book of Job (and Ecclesiastes) upon Israelite thinking. He even asks whether the learned Ben-Sira (notwithstanding his remarks concerning the righteous Job in his 'praise of the fathers of the world', 49.9) read the book. And if he read it, did he understand its depths? And if so, how is it that it did not shake the unproblematic piety expressed in the Proverbs of Ben-Sira?

words in the mouth of an omnipotent king, to teach us the essential character of the problem of theodicy. It thereby also suggests his ironic attitude to the 'solution' implied in the restoration of Job's fortunes. This stands out particularly in the light of Qoheleth's stance towards his offspring—'I hated all my toil in which I had toiled under the sun, seeing that I must leave it to the man who will come after me; and who knows whether he will be a wise man or a fool? Yet he will be master of all for which I toiled...' (2.16-17); and also: 'a man to whom God gives wealth, possessions and honour...If a man begets a hundred children, and lives many years, so that the days of his years are many...I say that a stillbirth is better off than he' (6.2-3). Are Qoheleth's words, 'for God is in heaven, and you upon earth; therefore let your words be few' (5.1), an echo of Job's pathetic desire to speak with God? And is his warning, 'Be not righteous over much' (7.16) an ironic allusion to the 'life experience' of Job, who was 'overly righteous', and was overtaken by disaster for precisely that reason? Similarly, the epistemological sayings of Qoheleth, whose sense is that we do not and cannot know the truly important things with certainty ('also he has put eternity into man's mind, yet of that he cannot find out what God has done from the beginning to the end', 3.11), are a direct sequel to the epistemology of the book of Job, particularly that of the response of God.

Qoheleth exacerbated the paradoxes presented by Job in the area of theodicy and carried them to absurdity. This intellectual development returns us to the question of the place of the book of Job in the sequence of literary development. The dramatic framework of the debates in the book of Job, which was suitable for the presentation of contradictory views concerning the question of divine justice without taking any one explicit position, does not suit the extreme and unequivocal outlooks which Ecclesiastes wished to present. He thus developed a path of his own: harsh statements, not in the framework of a debate between different speakers, but presented as unquestioned truths by a wise king. The speculative character required by the nature of the subject is itself preserved by sowing contradictory sayings here and there, as fruitful material for further thought.[5] By doing so, the author took a further step

---

5.   Many people have noted the internal contradictions within Ecclesiastes, and this is not the place to elaborate upon them. Against those who attribute this to the anthological nature of the book, its sayings having been gathered from different sources, there are others who explain that the author's method was to present a given view for discussion, so as to refute it thereafter. Others seek to resolve the difficulties

in the direction of discursive philosophical thought. One may assume that Qoheleth was influenced by Greek philosophy, but it seems doubtful whether, had it not been preceded by the book of Job, his thought would have taken root in Judaism to the extent of being canonized, albeit admittedly only after severe differences of opinion.[6]

In conclusion, allow me to add something concerning the title of this work—'A Blemished Perfection'. I noted in the preface that this title was chosen because it unites both an aesthetic-principled statement and a fitting description of the book of Job. In the course of the work I attempted to shed light upon several aspects of this claim.

We saw that the book of Job does not contain any orderly presentation of the problem of theodicy. There is no systematic discussion of its various aspects, nor a clear and unequivocal preference for one or another approach to it; it contains numerous repetitions of things which have already been said. Were one to judge the book as a philosophical tract, one might well describe these features as 'defects'. The same is true if the book is judged as a dramatic work, with regard to the structure, the means of development of the plot, the shaping of the characters, etc.—as we have noted during the course of the discussion. However, I would argue that not only do these 'faults' not detract from the wholeness of the book, but they even create it. Considered theoretically, this derives from the complete identity in an artistic work between form and content: is Job's faith whole or defective? The answer given to this question by the book of Job is ambiguous (or, if you prefer, it is itself blemished). Eliphaz, the dogmatic believer, together with his friends of the same ilk, are presented as those who do not speak 'what is right', unlike Job (42.7; see the discussion of the figure of Eliphaz above). True, Job is only forgiven after he has expressed regret (note that I do not say: 'regretted') for his harsh speech, which God nevertheless describes as

in a harmonistic way. See, for example: Gordis 1951: 95-109; Whybray 1980; Fox 1987.

6. An explicit expression of the need to give legitimation to the book of Ecclesiastes is its conclusion, 12.9-14. I agree with the view that this is an addition, and not part of the original work. As we have seen in the speech of Elihu, here too the book is interpreted by means of an addition. However, it seems that here the exegete used the method of twisting the original syntax (סרסהו ופרשהו) with regard to the author's intention. The discussion from the first or second century CE regarding the question as to whether or not Ecclesiastes renders the hands impure (*m. Yad.* 3.5; etc.) indicates that the debate concerning its canonic status had not been forgotten even hundreds of years after its composition, in the fourth–third centuries BCE.

'right'. Thus, doubts, struggles, and bold rebellion which do not lead to clear theological decisions—all these cannot remain in the realm of faith and beliefs alone without finding aesthetic expression. To paraphrase a well-known saying of R. Nahman of Braslav, one might say there is no greater artistic wholeness than a blemished form that expresses a broken heart.

Another view of the blemished perfection of the book of Job may be seen through a double viewpoint—that of the time of its composition, and that which it acquired over the course of generations. This double perspective involves more than a little dialectic. In at least one case, that of ch. 28, we have seen that, whereas if judged against the background of the time of its composition it would need to be counted among the 'blemishes' of the book, when viewed with a certain distance we are able to see it as representing a certain dimension of aesthetic innovation. On the other hand, we have noted other data which cannot be viewed as faulty against the background of the time of its composition, but may be seen as such in retrospect.

As being a 'blemished perfection' is a primary element in the book, the corruptions and additions therein also enjoy a special status. The very statement that a given datum is the result of textual corruption or is a later addition suggests that it is out of place, for only thus could one distinguish its secondary nature. But by this it shares an immanent characteristic of the book, and does not deviate from its coherency. For this reason, it seems doubtful to me whether the book of Job would be any more complete were it to be corrected with the intent of bringing it closer to its original version. Again, in a paradoxical sense this holds true even when applied systematically to the correction of everything that is understood by one or another scholar as an 'incorrect reading', of the type which certainly occurred in this book as in every other biblical text. We find that even linguistic obscurity is an immanent feature of the book, and the dispersing of this mist is more likely to harm than to help.

The matter of 'blemished perfection' may be summarized by means of two comparisons to a phenomenon in the realm of the plastic arts—the torso, the statue lacking in head or limbs. As a first example, we may consider what is possibly the best-known torso of all, 'Venus de Milo'. This statue was evidently created in the fourth century BCE and its later copy came down to us as a torso, without arms (the possibility that the complete statue included another figure, perhaps that of Cupid, does not concern us here). This being so, one cannot dispute the statement that

'Venus de Milo' is a defective work of art. Does this contradict the statement that it is a perfect work? In the eyes of students of art, the perfection of the statue is not affected by the state in which it has come down to us—and I refer here not to the original statue, but to that which is extant. Even were there agreement regarding the exact posture of the arms before they were cut off, no one would argue that they ought to be reconstructed because without them the statue is not whole. We may apply this by way of analogy to various suggestions for emendation of the book of Job: even were agreement to be reached among all of the scholars as to the location of one or another addition or corruption and the proper means of restoring the original, such a reconstruction would not contribute to the wholeness of the book. Yet in neither case does this conclusion detract from or diminish the value of searching out the difference between the original and what has come down to us, because the very fact of discussion of this question contributes to understanding of the work.

A second example is that of the sculptural motif which developed in the wake of Greek statues of the type of 'Venus de Milo'—namely, the fashioning *ab initio* of a headless/armless torso. Again, for illustrative purposes, I will mention the well-known sculpture of August Rodin, 'Torso of a Woman' (1910). This statue was originally designed without the woman's hands or, to formulate it differently, the 'blemishes' in the work are an immanent part of its perfection, exactly as in the book of Job. On the face of it, there is a decisive difference between the two examples: in the former, the blemish is quite definite, being the result of damage caused by time rather than the result of some premeditated planning, whereas in the second, the artist planned the defects in the woman's body from the outset. But in fact, there is not such a great difference here. Rodin created his torso as he did because he observed the aesthetic perfection of the Greek statues which had come down to us defective. By doing so, he reduced the gap between *ab initio* and *post factum*, between faults and 'faults' in a work of art: neither of them necessarily detracts from its perfection, but are an inseparable part of it. This does not, of course, negate the paradoxical nature of the combination 'blemished perfection', for which reason I find the image so suitable for the book of Job.

APPENDIXES

Appendix I: *Catalogic Classifications in the Book of Job*

Key:
A—Catalogue of the universe and its wonders
B—Catalogue of organs of the body
C—Catalogue of types of human beings
D—Catalogue of sins

Catalogue	Job	Eliphaz	Bildad	Zophar	Elihu	God
A	3.1-19	–	–	–	37*	38–41*
	9.5-10			28 (?)		
	24.14-17*					
	26*					
B	3.9-12**	–	–	20.9-16	33	40–41
	10.3-19**					
	16**					
	29**					
C	3; 12	–	–	–	–	–
	19.13-21					
	29–30					
D	24; 31	22	–	–	–	–

*   in a hymnal context
* * in a dirge context

Appendix II: *The Tendency towards Exacerbation in the Speeches of the Friends*

Key:

1. The numbers indicate the degree of severity with which the friends judged Job in their speeches. The point of departure is Eliphaz's speech in the first cycle, the numbers ascending in direct proportion to the subsequent degree of severity.
2. The sign + is intended to add to the degree of severity represented by that number, but as it stems primarily from slight variations of nuance there is no justification for making it a full number higher.
3. The numbers under the heading 'general impression' refer to the severity of the speech as a whole, whatever its components; i.e., a kind of average of the data in the previous columns.

Friend	Opening	Doctrine of Recompense	Conclusion	General Impression
1st Cycle				
Eliphaz	1	1	1	1
Bildad	2	2	2	2
Zophar	3	3	3	3
2nd Cycle				
Eliphaz	4	1+	4	3+
Bildad	(2?)	–	4	3
Zophar	–	–	4	3
3rd Cycle				
Eliphaz	5*	3	3	4+
Bildad	–	1	–	?

* The direct appeal to Job which is characteristic of the openings (of the speeches) here continues until v. 13 (and is renewed towards its conclusion, v. 21), and is therefore indicated here by the term 'opening'. This degree of severity in the third speech is explained above, p. 137 n. 22.

Appendix III: *The Connections between the Speeches*

Key: This table distinguishes between the purely technical connections (Column A) and the substantive connections between the speeches (Column B). The numbers indicate the number of verses in which such connections are found.

Speaker	Cycle I		Cycle II		Cycle III	
	A	B	A	B	A	B
Eliphaz	1	6	4	–	1	–
Job	9	6	–	–	–	
Bildad	1	–	1	–	–	–
Job	–	3	4	–	5	–
Zophar	2	–	–	–		
Job	3	3	8	–	–	–

Summary of Level of Connection:

	Group A	Group B	Total
Cycle I	7	21	28
Cycle II	23	0	23
Cycle III	6	0	6

Appendix IV: *Key Words from the Area of Justice*

שפט   8.3; 9.15, 19, 20, 24, 32; 12.17; 13.18; 14.3; 19.7; 21.22; 22.4; 23.4, 7; 27.2; 29.14; 31.13; 32.9; 34.3, 5, 6, 12, 17, 23; 35.2; 36.6, 17; 40.8.

עד   10.17; 16.8, 19.

ריב   9.3; 10.2; 13.6, 8; 23.6; 29.16; 31.35; 33.13; 40.2.

נקי   4.7; 9.23, 28; 17.8; 22.19, 30; 27.17.

צדק   4.17; 6.29; 8.3; 9.2, 15, 20; 10.15; 12.4; 13.18; 15.14; 17.9; 22.3; 32.1, 2; 33.12, 26, 32; 34.5, 17; 35.2, 7; 36.3, 7; 40.8.

חטא   5.24; 7.20; 8.4; 10.6, 14; 13.23; 14.16; 22.19; 25.4; 27.5, 6, 17; 29.14; 31.6; 33.27; 34.37; 35.3, 6.

פשע   7.21; 8.4; 13.23; 14.17; 31.33; 33.9; 34.6, 37; 35.6; 36.9.

עון   7.21; 10.6; 11.6; 13.23; 14.17; 15.5; 22.5, 13; 31.10, 28, 33; 33.9.

עות   8.3; 19.6; 34.12.

רשע   3.17; 8.22; 9.20, 22, 24, 29; 10.2, 3, 7, 15; 11.20; 15.6, 20; 16.11; 18.5; 20.5, 29; 21.7, 16, 17, 28; 22.18; 24.6; 27.6, 13; 32.3; 34.8, 10, 12, 17, 18, 26, 29; 35.8; 35.6, 17; 38.15; 40.8, 12.

Appendix V: *Occurrences of Words from the Realm of Justice in the Book*

Chapter	Speaker	Number of Occurrences	Chapter	Speaker	Number of Occurrences
1	Prologue		22	Eliphaz	8
2	Prologue		23	Job	3
3	Job	1	24	Job	1
4	Eliphaz	2	25	Bildad	1
5	Eliphaz	1	26	Job	–
6	Job	1	27	Job	7
7	Job	3	28	Job	–
8	Bildad	5	29	Job	3
9	Job	15	30	Job	–
10	Job	9	31	Job	7
11	Zophar	2	32	Elihu	4
12	Job	2	33	Elihu	6
13	Job	8	34	Elihu	19
14	Job	4	35	Elihu	7
15	Eliphaz	4	36	Elihu	5
16	Job	3	37	Elihu	–
17	Job	2	38	God	1
18	Bildad	1	39	God	–
19	Job	2	40	God	5
20	Zophar	2	41	God	–
21	Job	5	42	Epilogue	–

Appendix VI: *Summary of Appearance of Words of Justice by Distribution Among the Speakers*

Speaker	Number of Words	Average per Chapter
Job	76	3.8
Eliphaz	15	3.75
Bildad	7	2.33
Zophar	4	2
Elihu	41	6.83

Chart for Appendix VI: *Distribution of Key Words from the Realm of Justice*

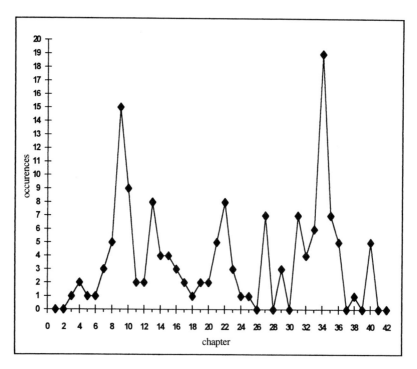

Key: The horizontal axis represents the number of the chapter. The vertical axis represents the number of key words found in the chapter.

Appendix VII: *Binding Elements in the Book of Job*

The symbols + and - indicate the presence or absence of a given element, as noted in the discussion. The lack of either symbol indicates that the element in question could not by its nature have been found in that particular chapter. Hence, for example, the item 'tendency to exacerbation' is not pertinent to the frame-story or the speeches of Job, for reasons noted in the course of our discussion. In the column, 'connections of debate', we have indicated by the sign + those chapters in which the number of verses connecting between the different speeches was not less than the average among all the chapters examined (4–31) This average was determined on the basis of Appendix III, and comes to slightly more than two verses per chapter (58 : 28). In the columns 'moulding of the figures' and 'trial motif', the signs indicate the conclusions reached in the course of our detailed discussion of the contribution of each chapter to the item in question.

Chapter and Speaker	Tendency to Exacerbation	Connections of Debate	Moulding of the Figures	Trial Motif
1–2			+	+
3 Job			+	-
4 Eliphaz	+	-	+	+
5 Eliphaz	+	-	+	+
6 Job		+	+	+
7 Job		-	+	+
8 Bildad	+	-	-	+
9 Job		+	+	+
10 Job		-	+	+
11 Zophar	+	+	-	+
[Summary:	4	3	8	9 = 24]
12 Job		+	+	+
13 Job		+	+	+
14 Job		-	+	+
15 Eliphaz	+	+	+	+
16 Job		+	+	-
17 Job		-	+	-
18 Bildad	-	-	-	-
19 Job		+	+	-
20 Zophar	-	-	-	-
21 Job		+	+	+
[Summary:	1	6	8	5 = 20]

Chapter and Speaker	Tendency to Exacerbation	Connections of Debate	Moulding of the Figures	Trial Motif
22 Eliphaz	+	-	+	+
23 Job	-	+	+	
24 Job		-	-	-
25 Bildad	-	-	-	-
26 Job		+	-	-
27 Job	+	+	+	-
28 Job		-	-	-
29 Job		-	+	+
30 Job		-	+	+
31 Job		-	+	+
[Summary:	2	2	6	5 = 15]
[3 Cycles:	7	11	22	19 = 59]
32 Elihu		+	+	+
33 Elihu		+	+	+
34 Elihu		+	+	+
35 Elihu		+	+	+
36 Elihu		+	+	-
37 Elihu		+	+	-
[Summary:		6	6	5 = 17]
Total:	7	17	28	24

Appendix VIII, A: *Comparison of Distribution of hapax legomena in the Books of the Bible*

Key: This table gives the distribution of words that have been classified as *hapax legomena* by the mediaeval exegetes (according to Cohen 1978: 101-105); by Cohen himself (1978: 108-43); and according to the double classification of Greenspahn (1977: 252) into absolute *hapax legomena* (a) and general *hapax legomena* (b). Since the number of *hapax legomena* must be examined relative to the size of the corpus as a whole, I have also cited the number of such words relative to the total number of words in the entire corpus (Column II). The calculation is given in percentages, with the result multiplied by one thousand, so that the expression reached is in whole numbers. The number of words is based upon Even Shoshan 1979: I, xxxviii. The number of words in each part of the book of Isaiah is based upon my own calculation. The division of Isaiah into two parts is based upon the general scholarly consensus regarding this matter, there being no argument with the fact that the latter half was written following the destruction of the First Temple. I saw no need to distinguish among the books given under the heading 'other books', because the results that would be received from such a division would not be significant to the subject at hand. The Song of Songs and Lamentations were separated from the corpus of 'other books', because the findings therein are significant, and it is worthwhile that they not be lost.

	I				*II*				
Book	*Number of hapax legomena*				*Average Relative to All Words*				*Total Number of Words*
	Mediaeval	*Cohen*	*Greenspahn*		*Mediaeval*	*Cohen*	*Greenspahn*		
			a	*b*			*a*	*b*	
Pent.	38	62	36	299	84	77	45	374	79,847
Form. Pro.	17	27	26	150	24	33	37	216	69,359
Isa. 1–39	10	22	29	–	99	219	289	–*	10,026
Isa. 40–66	8	17	14	–	116	246	203	–*	6,894
Jeremiah	7	11	43	83	32	50	198	382	21,673
Ezekiel	12	24	14	127	62	125	73	664	19,123
Minor Pro.	8	15	17	107	55	104	118	746	14,339
Psalms	12	20	33	159	61	102	169	816	19,479
Proverbs	7	11	10	70	101	159	144	1,012	6,912
Job	16	26	39	149	190	309	464	1,775	8,393
Song of Songs	6	15	14	36	479	1,199	1,119	2,877	1,251
Lamentations	1	2	6	21	67	134	402	1,408	1,491
Other Books	17	23	50	189	36	49	108	409	46,114

* Greenspahn does not distinguish between the two parts of the book of Isaiah in his classification of *hapax legomena* of type (b)

Appendix VIII, B: *Weighting of the Data according to an Average of All Methods of Classification*

The weighting given here is that of the data given in the second half of the previous table, and pertains to the seven corpuses which contain the greatest number of *hapax legomena*.

Song of Songs	1,418
Job	684
Lamentations	502
Proverbs	354
Ezekiel	231
Isaiah 1–39	202
Isaiah 40–66	188

Appendix IX: *Deviation of Distribution of hapax legomena from Statistical Prediction*

Key:

1. The table is based upon the data given by Greenspahn 1977: 253.
2. I have only offered data pertaining to those books whose deviation is high, that is, in which the number of *hapax legomena* is greater than that average statistical prediction for the Bible as a whole.
3. In columns [a] are given the data pertaining to absolute *hapax legomena* and in columns [b] that pertaining to the overall number of *hapax legomena*.
4. The listing is in descending order of deviation for absolute *hapax legomena*.

Book	*Predicted Number of hapax legomena*		*Actual Number*		*Statistical Deviation*	
	a	*b*	*a*	*b*	*a*	*b*
Job	7.60	39.55	39	149	130.73	302.89
Cant.	1.25	6.52	14	36	130.05	46.46
Isa. 1–39	9.24	–	29	–	40.70	–
Lam.	1.42	7.39	6	29	14.77	63.19
Proverbs	6.53	33.95	10	70	1.84	38.28
Ezekiel	17.98	93.46	21	127	0.51	12.04

Appendix X: *Distribution of Foreign Words in the Bible according to Barr*

Key:

1. The table is based upon Barr 1968: 320-37.
2. The table indicates the number of words in each book that are explained on the basis of their meaning in Semitic languages other than Hebrew.
3. I have not taken into account words from Semitic languages on whose basis only a very small number of words have been explained, such as Ethiopic, as in any event their number is too small to alter the overall relative picture.
4. The numerical expression in the right-hand column is based upon Appendix VIII A (see above).

Corpus	*Total Number of Foreign Words*	*Relative to Total Number of Words*
Pentateuch	25	31.3
Former Prophets	31	44.7
Isaiah 1–39	27	269.3
Isaiah 40–66	19	275.6
Jeremiah	17	78.4
Ezekiel	16	83.6
Minor Prophets	38	265.0
Psalms	41	210.4
Proverbs	25	361.6
Job	55	655.3
Other Books	19	38.9

Appendix XI: *Distribution of Metaphors in the Book of Job, Chapters 3–14*

ch. 3:	3, 4-5, 6, 7, 8, 9, 10, 16, 21, 23, 24	= 12
ch. 4:	3, 4, 8-9, 10-11, 12, 14, 19-21	= 11
ch. 5:	3, 4, 5, 6, 7, 11, 12, 13, 14, 16, 18, 19, 21, 23, 24-27	= 18
ch. 6:	2-3, 4, 7, 9, 12, 14-20, 22, 23, 26, 27, 30	= 18
ch. 7:	1, 2, 5, 6, 7, 12, 13, 19	= 8
ch. 8:	2, 4, 6, 9, 13, 14-18, 20, 22	= 12
ch. 9:	6, 7, 8, 18, 20, 23, 24, 25, 26, 30-31, 34	= 12
ch. 10:	3, 8-11, 15, 16, 17, 22	= 9
ch. 11:	2, 4, 6, 10, 12, 13, 14, 15, 16, 17, 20	= 11
ch. 12:	2, 5, 18, 20, 21, 24, 25	= 7
ch. 13:	4, 10, 12, 14, 21, 24, 25, 26, 27, 28	= 10
ch. 14:	2, 6, 9, 12, 14, 16, 17, 18-19, 20, 21	= 11
	Total Number of Verses:	299
	Total Number of Metaphors:	139
	Average Metaphors per Verse:	0.46

Appendix XII: *Distribution of Metaphors in Psalms 1–22*

ch. 1:	1, 3-4	= 2
ch. 2:	3, 9	= 2
ch. 3:	4, 8	= 2
ch. 4:	3	= 1
ch. 5:	5, 9, 10, 11, 12, 13	= 6
ch. 6:	5, 7, 8, 11	= 4
ch. 7:	2, 3, 4, 7, 13-14, 15, 16, 17	= 8
ch. 8:	7	= 1
ch. 9:	4, 5, 6, 8, 14, 15, 16, 17	= 8
ch. 10:	1, 2, 3, 4, 5, 8, 9, 15, 18	= 9
ch. 11:	1, 2, 3, 6, 7	= 5
ch. 12:	3, 4, 5, 7	= 4
ch. 13:	2, 3, 4	= 3
ch. 14:	3, 4, 6	= 3
ch. 15:	1	= 1
ch. 16:	1, 4, 5, 6, 8, 11	= 6
ch. 17:	1, 2, 5, 6, 8, 9, 11, 12, 14, 15	= 10
ch. 18:	5, 6, 15, 17, 20, 28, 29, 30, 33, 34, 37, 40, 41, 43, 46, 49	= 17
ch. 19:	3, 5, 6, 8, 9, 11	= 6
ch. 20:	2, 3, 9	= 3
ch. 21:	3, 7, 9, 10, 11, 13	= 6
ch. 22:	5, 7, 9, 10, 13-17, 21, 22, 30	= 8

Total Number of Verses in these Chapters:	309
Total Number of Metaphors:	119
Average Metaphors per Verse:	0.38

Appendix XIII: *The Spelling of the Verb* יסף *in the* Hif'il *Form*
(Freedman 1969: 35-44)

Corpus	Number of Occurrences	Plene	Defective
Pentateuch	38	6	32
Former Prophets	48	23	25
Later Prophets	27	24	3
Writings (excluding Job)	37	26	11
Total	150	79	71
Job	11	3	8

Appendix XIV: *Distribution of Foreign Semitic Words in the Books of the Bible*
(based on Barr 1968)

Corpus	*Ugaritic*	*Akkadian*	*Aramaic*	*Arabic*	*Total*
Pentateuch	3	3	1	18	25
Former Prophets	7	6	4	14	31
Isa. 1–39	3	4	2	18	27
Isa. 40–66	–	3	4	12	19
Jeremiah	2	5	1	9	17
Ezekiel	1	5	3	7	16
Minor Prophets	3	3	6	26	38
Psalms	10	6	6	19	41
Proverbs	7	4	1	13	25
Job	9	2	8	36	55
Other Books	6	5	–	8	19
Total:	51	46	36	180	313
Percentage:	16.3	14.7	11.5	57.5	100

Appendix XV: *Distribution of Word-Pairs Defined as 'Ugaritic' in the Books of the Bible (based upon Fisher 1972)*

Key: The data are in descending order of distribution of word-pairs. The numerical expression in the right-hand column is based upon the method used in Appendix VIII. The numbers given at the side are the total number of words in those books not noted in the previous tables.

Book	*Number of Word-Pairs*	*Distribution Relative to Number of Words*	
Joel	30	3,100	[total words: 697]
Psalms	588	3,018	
Job	250	2,970	
Proverbs	165	7,832	
Micah	32	2,290	[total words: 1,395]
Amos	40	1,940	[total words: 2,053]
Hosea	44	1,849	[total words: 2,379]
Isaiah	306	1,808	
Jeremiah	168	775	
Ezekiel	126	659	
Pentateuch	448	615	

Appendix XVI: *Distribution of hapax legomena in the Book of Job*

Key:
1. The table is based upon Greenspahn 1977: 253 (see Appendix VIII)
2. The table refers to absolute *hapax legomena*, and is arranged by descending order of distribution.

Literary Block	Predicted Number of hapax legomena	Actual Number	Deviation
God	0.83	13	178.44
Job	3.49	15	61.50
Eliphaz	0.75	5	24.08
Elihu	1.16	5	12.71
Bildad	0.32	2	8.82
Prose	0.69	1	0.14
Zophar	0.33	0	0

Appendix XVII: *Distribution of Motifs of Recompense in the Book of Job*

Key:

1. In the column 'causality' I have cited those cases in which causality touches only tangentially upon the subject of recompense. Passages that touched upon this subject directly are noted in the right-hand column, under the heading 'recompense'. I have also included under the heading 'causality' those statements regarding the arbitrary behaviour of God in the world, because they are a kind of polemic against the conventional understanding of causality in general, and of moral recompense in particular.
2. The definitions of the units are not to be seen as being of significance, beyond setting very weak boundaries within the flow of verses relating to a central subject. So as to avoid unnecessary confusion, several motifs are cited in one unit, rather than dividing them into small sections.
3. It is self-evident that a passage speaking of recompense generally mentions the righteous or the wicked, or both. So as to avoid duplication, I have only cited such cases in the column of recompense, while the columns 'righteous' and 'wicked' only pertain to the description of the way of life of the righteous or the wicked.

Unit	Righteous	Wicked	Suffering	Happiness	Causality	Recompense
1–2	+		+	+	+	+
3	+	+				
4–5	+	+	+	+	+	
6	+	+	+			
7	+	+				
8	+	+	+	+		
9	+	+	+	+	+	
10	+	+				
11	+	+				
12	+					
13	+					
14	+					
15	+	+				
16–17	+					
18	+	+				
19	+	+				
20	+	+				
21	+	+				
22	+	+	+			

A Blemished Perfection

Unit	Righteous	Wicked	Suffering	Happiness	Causality	Recompense
23	+					
24	+					
25	+					
26	+					
27	+	+	+			
28						
29	+	+				
30	+					
31	+					
32						
33	+					
34	+					
35	+					
36	+					
37						
38–39						
40.1-14	+					
40.15–41.26						
42.1-6	+					
42.7-17	+	+				

Appendix XVIII: *Distribution of the Word* צדיק *('Righteous') and its Parallels*
in Psalms, Proverbs and Job

Word	Job	Distribution in Psalms	Proverbs
צדיק	7	50	65
תם	7	2	1
ישר	7	17*	16
זך	2	–	2
ירא אלהים	3	3	1
סר (מרע)	3	1	1
נדיב	3	6	5
נקי	5	2	1

*   Includes ישרי לב (upright of heart)—7 times in Psalms

Appendix XIX: *Distribution of the Word* רשע *('wicked') and its Parallels*
in Psalms, Proverbs and Job

Word	Job	Distribution in Psalms	Proverbs
רשע	25	81	78
אנשי רשע	1	–	–
עריץ	1	3	1
עול	4	–	–
פעל/חרש און	4	15	2
אנשי און	1	1	–
זורע עמל	1	–	–
אויל	2	1	17
שכח אל	1	1	–
חנף	6	1	1
מרעים	1	9	1
פתה	1	–	1

BIBLIOGRAPHY

Allen, T.W.
1910   'The Homeric Catalogue', *JHS* 30, pp. 292-322.
Alt, A.
1937   'Zur Vorgeschichte des Buches Hiob', *ZAW* 55, pp. 265-68.
Alter, R.
1981   *The Art of Biblical Narrative* (New York: Basic Books).
1985   *The Art of Biblical Poetry* (New York: Basic Books).
Andersen, F.I., and A.D. Forbes
1986   *Spelling in the Hebrew Bible* (Rome: Pontifical Biblical Institute).
Andersen, F.I.
1976   *Job* (TOTC; Downers Grove, IL: Inter-Varsity Press).
1991   Review of J. Barr, *The Variable Spelling of the Hebrew Bible*, in E.J.
            Epp (ed.), *Critical Review of Books in Religion* (Atlanta: Scholars
            Press).
Arend, M. (ed.)
1989   *R. Kera's Perush le-Sefer Iyov* (*Commentary on the Book of Job*)
            (Jerusalem: Mossad Harav Kook).
Arpali, B.
1977   'Mivneh u-Mashma'ut be-Shirat Yehudah Amihai' ('Structure and
            Significance in Yehuda Amihi's Poetry') (Doctoral dissertation, Tel-
            Aviv, Tel-Aviv University).
Aufrecht, W.E. (ed.)
1985   *Studies in the Book of Job* (Waterloo, Ontario: The Canadian
            Corporation for Studies in Religion).
Bar-Efrat, S.
1979   *ha-'Izuv ha-Omanuti shel ha-Sippur ba-Miqra* (*Narrative Art in the
            Bible*) (Tel-Aviv: Sifriat Hapoalim [English Edition: JSOTSup, 70;
            Sheffield: Almond Press, 1989]).
Barr, J.
1968   *Comparative Philology* (Oxford: Oxford University Press).
1974   'Philology and Exegesis', in C. Brekelmans (ed.), *Questions disputées
            d'Ancien Testament* (Leuven: Leuven University Press), pp. 39-61.
1985   'Hebrew Orthography and the Book of Job', *JSS* 30, pp. 1-33.
1986   *The Variable Spelling of the Hebrew Bible* (Oxford: Oxford University
            Press).
Battersby J.L., and J. Phelan
1986   'Meaning as Concept and Extension: Some Problems', *Critical
            Response* 12, pp. 605-15.

Baumgärtel, D.F.
1971   *Der Hiobdialog* (BWANT, 61; Stuttgart: W. Kohlhammer Verlag).
Baumgartner, W.
1971   *Die Klagegedichte Jeremia* (BZAW, 32; Berlin: Töpelmann).
Beardsley, M.C.
1958   *Aesthetics* (New York: Harcourt, Brace & World).
Ben-Amos, D.
1980   'The Concept of Motif in Folklore', in V.J. Newall (ed.), *Folklore Studies in the Twentieth Century* (Woodbridge: Brewer).
Bentzen, A.
1959   *Introduction to the Old Testament*, I (2 vols.; Copenhagen: G.E.C. Gad, 5th edn).
Bergstrasser, G.
1929 [1918]   *Hebräische Grammatik* (2 vols.; Leipzig: J.C. Hinrichs).
Berlin, A.
1983   *Poetics and Interpretation of Biblical Narrative* (Sheffield: Almond Press).
Bezek, Y.
1984   *Ẓurot u-tekhanim be-Mizmorei Tehillim* (*Structures and Contents in the Psalms*) (Jerusalem: Devir).
Bialik, H.N.
1966   'Revealment and Concealment in Language', trans. J. Sloan, in *An Anthology of Hebrew Essays*, selected by I. Cohen and B.Y. Michali, I (Tel-Aviv: Massada), pp. 127-35.
Black, M.
1962   *Models and Metaphors* (Ithaca, NY: Cornell University Press).
Blanchot, M.
1959   *Le Livre à venir* (Paris: Gallimard).
Blummerde, C.M.
1969   *Northwest Semitic Grammar and Job* (Rome: Pontifical Biblical Institute).
Bonnet, H.
1978   'Dichotomy of Artistic Genres', in Strelka (ed.) 1978, pp. 3-16.
Booth, W.C.
1974   *A Rhetoric of Irony* (Chicago: Chicago University Press).
Bowra, C.M.
1930   *Tradition and Design in the Iliad* (Oxford: Clarendon Press).
Boyd, J.D.
1968   *The Function of Mimesis and its Decline* (Cambridge, MA: Harvard University Press).
Bradi, H., and M. Wiener
1946   *Mivḥar ha-Shirah ha-ʿIvrit* (*Selection of Hebrew Poetry, a Short Edition*) (ed. H.M. Habermann; Jerusalem: Rubin Mass).
Brand, G.
1979   *The Central Texts of L. Wittgenstein* (Oxford: Blackwell).
Brandwein, H.
1966   'The First Stages of the Legend of Job' (Heb.), *Tarbiz* 35, pp. 1-8.

Brenner, A.
1988   *Ahavat Ruth (Ruth and Naomi)* (Tel-Aviv: Sifriat Poalim; Hakibbutz
            Hameuchad).
Briggs, E.G.
1907   *The Book of Psalms* (3 vols.; ICC; Edinburgh: T. & T. Clark).
Brin, G.
1975   *'Iyunim be-Sefer Yehezqel (Studies in the Book of Ezekiel)* (Tel-Aviv:
            Hakibbutz Haeuhad).
Buber, M.
1960   *The Prophetic Faith* (New York: Harper & Row).
Budde, K.
1913   *Das Buch Hiob* (HKAT; Göttingen: Vandenhoeck & Ruprecht).
Carroll, R.P.
1986   *Jeremiah* (OTL; London: SCM Press).
Cassuto, M.D.
1959   *Perush 'al Sefer Shemot (A Commentary on the Book of Exodus)*
            (Jerusalem: Magnes Press).
1971   *The Goddess Anat* (Jerusalem: Magnes Press).
Catford, J.C
1965   *A Linguistic Theory of Translation* (London: Oxford University Press).
Ceresko, A.R.
1980   *Job 29–31 in the Light of Northwest Semitic* (Rome: Pontifical Biblical
            Institute).
Chadwick, H.M.
1960   *The Growth of Literature* (Cambridge: Cambridge University Press).
Cohen, H.R.
1978   *Biblical Hapaxlegomena* (Missoula, MT: Scholars Press).
Cooper, L.
1962   *Aristotle, On the Art of Poetry* (Ithaca, NY: Great Seal Books).
Cox, D.
1978   *The Triumph of Impotence* (Rome: Pontifical Biblical Institute).
Craigie, P.C.
1979   'Parallel Word Pairs in Ugaritic Poetry', *UF* 11, pp. 135-40.
Crenshaw, J.L.
1970   'Popular Questioning of the Justice of God in Ancient Israel', *ZAW*
            82, pp. 380-95.
Croce, B.
1922   *Aesthetic as Science of Expression and General Linguistics* (London:
            P. Owen-Vision Press).
1965   *Guide to Aesthetics* (trans. with an Introduction, P. Romanell;
            Indianapolis: Bobbs–Merrill).
Cross, F.M.
1973   *Canaanite Myth and Hebrew Epic* (Cambridge, MA: Harvard
            University Press).
Dahood, M.
1957   'Some Northwest-Semitic Words in Job', *Biblica* 38, pp. 306-20.

1973	'Ugaritic and Phoenician or Qumran and the Versions', in H.A. Hoffner (ed.), *Orient and Occident* (Neukirchen–Vluyn: Neukirchener Verlag), pp. 53-58.

Daily, T.
1993	' "And yet he Repent"—Job 42.6', *ZAW* 105, pp. 174-204.

De Man, P.
1982	'Sign and Symbol in Hegel's Aesthetics', *Critical Inquiry* 8, pp. 761-75.

Deissler, A.
1955	*Psalm 119 (118) und seine Theologie* (Munich: K. Zink).

Derrida, J.
1979	'Living On: Border Lines', in H. Bloom (ed.), *Deconstruction and Criticism* (New York: Continuum), pp. 75-176.

Dhorm, E.
1926	*A Commentary on the Book of Job* (London: Nelson).

Dick, M.B.
1979	'The Legal Metaphor in Job 31', *CBQ* 41, pp. 37-50.
1983	'Job 31: The Oath of Innocence and the Sage', *ZAW* 95, pp. 31-53.

Donner, H., and W. Röllig
1964	*Kanaanäische und Aramäische Inschriften* (3 vols.; Wiesbaden: Otto Harrassowitz).

Driver, G.R.
1953	'Hebrew Poetic Diction', in G.W. Anderson (ed.), *Congress Volume* (VTSup, 1; Leiden: Brill), pp. 26-39.
1956	*Canaanite Myths and Legends* (Edinburgh: T. & T. Clark).
1960	'Problems in the Hebrew Text of Job', in N. North and D.W. Thomas (eds.), *Wisdom in Israel and in the Ancient Near East* (VTSup, 3; Leiden: Brill), pp. 72-93.

Driver, S.R., and G.B. Gray
1921	*The Book of Job* (ICC; Edinburgh: T. & T. Clark).

Duhm, B.
1897	*Das Buch Hiob* (HKAT, 16; Tübingen: Mohr).

Eichrodt, W.
1964	*Theology of the Old Testament* (London: SCM Press).

Eissfeldt, O.
1964	*Einleitung in das Alte Testament* (Tübingen: Mohr, 3rd edn).

Ellenbogen, M.
1962	*Foreign Words in the Old Testament* (London: Luzac).

Else, G.F. (ed.)
1957	*Aristotle's Poetics: The Argument* (trans. G.F. Else; Cambridge, MA: Harvard University Press).

Even, Y.
1980	*Ha-Demut ba-Sipporet* (*Characters and Characteristics in Literature*) (Tel-Aviv: Sifriyat Poalim).

Even Shoshan, A.
1979	*New Biblical Concordance* (Heb.) (Jerusalem: Kiryat Sefer).

Ewald, H.
1854	*Das Buch Ijob* (Göttingen: Vandenhoeck & Ruprecht, 2nd edn).

Fairclough, H.R. (ed.)
1929 *Horace Satires, Epistles and Ars Poetica* (Cambridge, MA: Harvard University Press).

Fisch, H.
1990 *Poetry with a Purpose: Biblical Poetics and Interpretation* (Bloomington, IN: Indiana University Press).

Fish, S.
1980 *Is there a Text in this Class?* (Cambridge, MA: Harvard University Press).

Fishbane, M.
1971 'Jeremiah IV 23-26 and Job III 3-13: A Recovered Use of the Creation Pattern', *VT* 21, pp. 151-167.
1985 *Biblical Interpretation in Ancient Israel* (Oxford: Clarendon Press).

Fisher, L.R. (ed.)
1972 *Ras Shamra Parallels*, I (Rome: Pontifical Biblical Institute).

Fohrer, G.
1963 *Das Buch Hiob* (KAT, 16; Gütersloh: Gütersloher Verlaghaus).
1983 *Studien zum Buche Hiob* (BZAW, 159; Berlin: de Gruyter)

Fokkelman, J.P.
1975 *Narrative Art in Genesis* (Assen: Van Gorcum).
1986 *Narrative Art and Poetry in the Books of Samuel* (Assen: Van Gorcum).

Fontaine, C.
1987 'Folktale Structure in the Book of Job: A Formalist Reading', in E.R. Follis (ed.), *Directions in Biblical Hebrew Poetry* (JSOTSup, 40; Sheffield: JSOT Press), pp. 205-232.

Forster, E.M.
1927 *Aspects of the Novel* (London: Edward Arnold).

Fosster, F.H.
1932 'Is The Book of Job a Translation from an Arabic Original?', *AJSL* 49, pp. 21-45.

Fox, M.V.
1977 'Frame-Narrative and Composition in the Book of Qohelet', *HUCA* 48, pp. 83-106.
1981 'Job 38 and God's Rhetoric', *Semeia* 19, pp. 53-61.
1985 *The Song of Songs and the Ancient Egyptian Love Songs* (Madison, WI: University of Wisconsin Press).
1986 'Egyptian Onomastica and Biblical Wisdom', *VT* 36, pp. 302-10.
1987 *Megillot Shir ha-Shirim Ruth ve-Eikhah* (*The Song of Songs, Ruth and Lamentations*) (Olam Ha-Tanakh, 16; Ramat-Gan: Revivim).
1989 *Qohelet and his Contradictions* (JSOTSup, 71; Sheffield: JSOT Press).

Fox, M.V. and J. Klein
1987 *Shir Hoshirim* (*The Song of Songs*) (Olam Hatanach 16; Jerusalem: Revivim).

Freedman, D.N.
1969 'Orthographic Peculiarities in the Book of Job', *Eretz-Israel* 9, pp. 35-44.
1972 'Acrostics and Metrics in Hebrew Poetry', *HTR* 65, pp. 367-92.

| 1987 | 'Acrostic Poems in the Hebrew Bible, Alphabetic and Otherwise', *CBQ* 48, pp. 408-31. |

Fullerton, K.
| 1924 | 'The Original Conclusion of the Book of Job', *ZAW* 42, pp. 116-36. |
| 1930 | 'Double Entendre in the First Speech of Eliphaz', *JBL* 49, pp. 320-74. |

Gardiner, A.H.
| 1947 | *Ancient Egyptian Onomastica* (2 vols.; Oxford: Oxford University Press). |

Gemser, B.
| 1960 | 'The Rib or Controversy Pattern in Hebrew Mentality', in N. North and D.W. Thomas (eds.), *Wisdom in Israel and in the Ancient Near East* (VTSup, 3; Leiden: Brill). pp. 120-37. |

Gerhart, M.
| 1988 | 'Generic Competence in Biblical Hermeneutics', *Semeia* 49, pp. 29-44. |

Gese, H.
| 1958 | *Lehre und Wirklichkeit in der alten Weisheit; Studien zu de Spruchen Salomos und zu den Buche Hiob* (Tübingen: Mohr). |

Gombrich, E.H.
| 1960 | *Art and Illusion* (New York: Phaidon Press). |

Good, E.M.
| 1965 | *Irony in the Old Testament* (Philadelphia: SPCK). |

Goodwin, D.W.
| 1969 | *Text and Restoration Methods in Contemporary USA Biblical Scholarship* (Naples: Istituto orientale di Napoli). |

Gordis, R.
1951	*Kohelet: The Man and his World* (New York: Schocken Books)
1965	*The Book of God and Man* (Chicago: Chicago University Press).
1978	*The Book of Job: A Commentary* (New York: Jewish Theological Seminary).

Grabbe, L.
| 1977 | *Comparative Philology and the Text of Job* (Missoula, MT: Scholars Press). |

Gray, J.
| 1970 | 'The Book of Job in Context of N.E. Literature', *ZAW* 82, pp. 251-69. |

Greenberg, M.
1969	*Understanding Exodus* (New York: Behrman House).
1972	'Narrative and Redactional Art in the Plague Pericope' (Heb.), in B. Uffenheimer (ed.), *The Bible and Jewish History* (Tel-Aviv: Tel-Aviv University), pp. 65-75.
1981	'Reflections on the Theology of Job' (Heb.), *Petahim* 55/56, pp. 52-57.
1987	'Job', in R. Alter and F. Kermode (eds.), *The Literary Guide to the Bible* (Cambridge, MA: Belknap), pp. 283-303.

Greenspahn, F.E.
| 1977 | 'Hapax Legomena in Biblical Hebrew' (Doctoral dissertation, Waltham, MA, Brandeis University). |

Greenstein, E.L.
| 1989 | 'Deconstruction and Biblical Narrative', *Prooftexts* 9, pp. 43-71. |

Guillaume, A.
1964   'The Unity of the Book of Job', *ALUOS* 4, pp. 32-52.
1968   *Studies in the Book of Job* (ed. J. Macdonald; Leiden: Brill).
Haezrachi, P.
1954   *The Contemplating Activity* (London: George Allen & Unwin).
Halperin, S.
1978   *'Al ha-Poetiqa le-Aristo (On Aristotle's 'Poetics')* (Tel-Aviv:
            Hakibbutz Hameuchad).
Hillers, D.R.
1964   *Treaty Curses and the Old Testament Prophets* (Rome: Pontifical
            Biblical Institute).
Hirsch, E.D., Jr
1967   *Validity in Interpretation* (New Haven, CT: Yale University Press).
1986   'Coming with Terms to Meaning', *Critical Inquiry* 12, pp. 627-30.
Hoffman, Y.
1977   *ha-Nevuot 'al ha-Goyim ba-Miqra (The Prophecies against Foreign
            Nations in the Bible)* (Tel-Aviv: Hakibbutz Hameuchad).
1979a   'Between Convention and Strategy' (Heb.), *Hasifrut* 29, pp. 89-99.
1979b   'The Believer in the Book of Job' (Heb.), in E. Ha-Menachem (ed.),
            Hagut Bamiqra 3 (Tel-Aviv: Don), pp. 84-94.
1980   'The Use of Equivocal Words in the First Speech of Eliphaz', *VT* 30,
            pp. 114-19.
1981   'The Relation between the Prologue and the Speech-Cycles in Job',
            VT 31, pp. 160-70.
1983a   'Irony in the Book of Job', *Immanuel* 17, pp. 7-21.
1983b   *Yeẓi'at Miẓrayim be-Emunat ha-Miqra (The Doctrine of the Exodus in
            the Bible)* (Tel-Aviv: Tel-Aviv University, University Publishing
            Projects).
1986   'The Transition from Despair to Hope in the Laments of the
            Individual' (Heb.), *Tarbiz* 55, pp. 161-72.
1992   'Psalm 104' (Heb.), in M. Fishbane and E. Tov (eds.), *Shaarei
            Talmon* (Winona Lake, IN: Eisenbrauns), pp. 13-24.
Holbert, J.C.
1983   'The Rehabilitation of the Sinner; The Function of Job 29–31', *ZAW*
            95, pp. 229-237.
Holladay, W.
1986   *Jeremiah*, I (Philadelphia: Fortress Press).
Hölscher, G.
1952   *Das Buch Hiob* (HAT, 12; Tübingen: Mohr).
Hornby, R.H.
1965   'Catalog Verse', in *Encyclopaedia of Poetry and Poetics* (Princeton:
            Princeton University Press), p. 106.
Horst, F.
1969   *Hiob 1–19* (BKAT, 16; Neukirchen–Vluyn: Neukirchener Verlag).
Huberman-Scholnick, S.
1982   'The Meaning of משפט in the Book of Job', *JBL* 101, pp. 521-29.

1987   'Poetry in the Courtroom: Job 38–41', in E.R. Follis (ed.), *Directions in Biblical Hebrew Poetry* (JSOTSup, 40; Sheffield: JSOT Press), pp. 185-204.

Hurvitz, A.
1974   'The Date of the Prose-Tale of Job Linguistically Reconsidered', *HTR* 67, pp. 17-34.
1991   *Sheqe'ei Hokhmah be-Sefer Tehilim* (*Wisdom Language in Biblical Psalmody*) (Jerusalem: Magnes Press).

Irwin, W.A.
1933   'The First Speech of Bildad', *ZAW* 51, pp. 205-16.

Jacobsen, T.
1939   *The Sumerian King List* (Chicago: University of Chicago Press).
1976   *The Treasures of Darkness: A History of Mesopotamian Religion* (New Haven, CT: Yale University Press).

Janzen, G.J.
1987   'The Place of the Book of Job in the History of Israel's Religion', in P.D. Miller, Jr (ed.), *Ancient Israelite Religion: Essays in Honor of Frank Moore Cross* (Philadelphia: Fortress Press), pp. 523-38.

Japhet, S., and R. Salters
1985   *Perush R. Shmuel ben Meir (Rashbam) la-Qoheleth* (*The Commentary of R. Samuel Ben Meir [Rashbam] to Qoheleth*) (Jerusalem: Magnes Press).

Jellicoe, S.
1968   *The Septuagint and Modern Study* (Oxford: Clarendon Press).

Jongeling, B.
1974   'L'Expression *my ytn* dans l'Ancien Testament', *VT* 24, pp. 32-40.

Kahana, A.
1924   *Sefer Iyov* (*Commentary on the Book of Job*) (Tel-Aviv: Meqorot).
1960   *Ha-Sefarim ha-Ḥizoni'im* (*The Pseudoepigrapha*) (Tel-Aviv: Devir).

Kallen, H.M.
1918   *The Book of Job as a Greek Tragedy Restored* (New York).

Kant, E.
1987 [1790]   *Critique of Judgment* (trans. W.S. Pluhar; Indianapolis: Hackett).

Kaufman, S.A.
1988   'The Classification of the North West Semitic Dialects of the Biblical Period and Some Implications Thereof', in *Proceedings of the Ninth World Congress of Jewish Studies: Panel Sessions, Hebrew and Aramaic Language* (Jerusalem: World Union of Jewish Studies), pp. 41-57.

Kaufmann, Y.
1960   *Toldot ha-Emunah ha-Yisra'elit* (*The History of the Israelite Faith*) (4 vols.; Jerusalem and Tel-Aviv: Bialik Institute and Devir).

Kautzsch, E.
1902   *Die Aramäismen im Alten Testament* (Halle).

Kierkegaard, S.A.
1989 [1841]   *The Concept of Irony* (ed. and trans. with Introduction and Notes, H.V. Hong and E.H. Hong; Princeton: Princeton University Press).

Klein, J.
1982   ' "Personal God" and Individual Prayer in Sumerian Religion',
            Archiv fur Orientforschung Beiheft 19, pp. 295-306.

Knapp, S., and W.B. Michael
1982   'Against Theory', *Critical Inquiry* 8, pp. 723-42.

Koch, K.
1953   'SDK im Alten Testament' (Doctoral dissertation, Heidelberg,
            Theologische Fakultie).
1969   *The Growth of the Biblical Tradition* (London: A. & C. Black).
1983   'Is There a Doctrine of Retribution in the Old Testament', in
            J. Crenshaw (ed.), *Theodicy in the Old Testament* (Philadelphia:
            Fortress Press), pp. 57-87.

Kraeling, E.G.H.
1938   *The Book of the Ways of God* (London: SPCK).

Kramer, S.N.
1960   ' "Man and his God"; A Sumerian Variation on the "Job" Motif', in
            N. North and D.W. Thomas (eds.), *Wisdom in Israel and in the Ancient
            Near East* (VTSup, 3; Leiden: Brill), pp. 170-82.

Kraus, H.J.
1961   *Psalmen* (2 vols.; BKAT; Neukirchen–Vluyn: Neukirchener Verlag,
            1961).

Kugel, J.
1981   *The Idea of Biblical Poetry* (New Haven, CT: Yale University Press).

Kuhl, C.
1953   'Neuere Literarkritik des Buches Hiob', *TRev* 21, pp. 163-205.

Lambert, W.G.
1960   *Babylonian Wisdom Literature* (Oxford: Oxford University Press).

Leddy, M.
1986   'Validity and Reinterpretation', *Critical Inquiry* 12, pp. 616-26.

Lefevere, A.
1975   *Translating Poetry* (Assen: Van Gorcum).

Lessing, G.E.
1962 [1766] *Laocoon: An Essay on the Limits of Painting and Poetry*
            (Indianapolis: Bobbs–Merrill).

Levi, W.A.
1978   'Literature and the Imagination: A Theory of Genres', in Strelka (ed.)
            1978, pp. 17-40.

Licht, J.
1976   'Mimesis as a Literary Feature in Biblical Narrative' (Heb.), in J. Licht
            and G. Brin (eds.), *Ha-Ûevi Yisrael* (Tel-Aviv: Tel-Aviv University),
            pp. 133-42.
1978   *Storytelling in the Bible* (Jerusalem: Magnes Press).

Lichtheim, M.
1973   *Ancient Egyptian Literature* (3 vols.; Berkeley: University of
            California Press).

Loewenstamm, S.E.
1965   *Masoret Yeẓiat Miẓraim be-Hishtalshelutah* (*The Tradition of the
            Exodus in its Development*) (Jerusalem: Magnes Press).

Lowth, R.
1787   *Lectures on the Sacred Poetry of the Hebrews* (Hildesheim: G. Olms).
Luzzatto, S.D.
1969 [1876]   *Perush Shada'l 'al Yirmiyah Yeḥezqel Mishlei ve-Iyov* (*Luzzatto's Commentaries on Jeremiah, Ezekiel, Proverbs and Job*) (Jerusalem: Maqor).
Maag, V.
1982   *Hiob* (Göttingen: Vandenhoeck & Ruprecht).
MacKenzie, R.A.F.
1959   'The Purpose of the Yahweh Speeches', *Biblica* 40, pp. 435-45.
Margalit, B.
1989   *The Ugaritic Poem of AQHAT* (Berlin: de Gruyter).
Marino, A.
1978   'A Definition of Literary Genre', in Strelka (ed.) 1978, pp. 41-55.
Mays, J.L.
1987   'The Place of the Torah-Psalms in the Psalter', *JBL* 106, pp. 3-12.
Mazar, B.
1946   'The Origin of the Sons of Nahor', *Zion* 11, pp. 3-16.
McFall, L.
1989   *The Enigma of the Hebrew Verbal System* (Sheffield: Almond Press).
McKane, W.
1970   *Proverbs* (OTL; London: SCM Press).
1986   *Jeremiah*, I (ICC; Edinburgh: T. & T. Clark).
Michel, W.L.
1987   *Job in the Light of Northwest Semitic*, I (Rome: Pontifical Biblical Institute).
Morrison, J.C.
1968   *Meaning and Truth in Wittgenstein's Tractatus* (The Hague: Mouton).
Morrow, W.
1986   'Consolation, Rejection, and Repentance in Job 42.6', *JBL* 105, pp. 211-25.
Mowinckel, S.
1962   *The Psalms in Israel's Worship* (Oxford: Blackwell).
Muenchow, C.
1986   'Dust and Dirt in Job 42.6', *JBL* 108, pp. 597-611.
Muller, C.
1969   'Lexical Distribution Reconsidered', in L. Dolezel and R.W. Bailey (eds.), *Statistics and Style* (New York: American Elsevier Publications), pp. 42-55.
Müller, H.P.
1978   *Das Hiobproblem* (Darmstadt: Wissenschaftliche Buchgesellschaft).
O'Connor, K.M.
1988   *The Confessions of Jeremiah* (Atlanta: Scholars Press).
Oorschot, J. van
1987   *Gott als Grenze* (BZAW, 170; Berlin: de Gruyter).
Orlinsky, H.M.
1957   'Studies in the Septuagint of the Book of Job, I', *HUCA* 28, pp. 53-74

1958   'Studies in the Septuagint in the Book of Job, II', *HUCA* 29, pp. 229-
                271.

Patte, D.
1990   *The Religious Dimensions of Biblical Texts* (Atlanta: Fortress Press).

Perdue, L.G.
1991   *Wisdom in Revolt: Metaphorical Theology in the Book of Job*
                (JSOTSup, 112; Sheffield: JSOT Press).

Perry, M.
1979   'Literary Dynamics: How the Order of a Text Creates its Meaning',
                Poetics Today 1, pp. 35-64.

Pfeiffer, R.
1926   'Edomite Wisdom', *ZAW* 44, pp. 13-25.
1941   *Introduction to the Old Testament* (New York: Harper & Brothers).

Pines, S. (ed.)
1963   *Maimonides' Guide for the Perplexed* (trans. S. Pines; Chicago:
                University of Chicago Press).

Pope, M.
1973   *Job* (AB; Garden City, NY: Doubleday, 3rd edn).

Porter, J.R.
1965   'The Legal Aspects of the Concept of "Corporate Personality" in the
                Old Testament', *VT* 15, pp. 361-80.

Qafah, J.D. (ed.)
1973   *Perush Rav Saadiah Gaon la-Sefer Iyov* (*R. Saadia Gaon's
                Commentary on the Book of Job*) (Jerusalem: Mosad Harav Kook).

Rabbe, P.R.
1991   'Deliberate Ambiguity in the Psalter', *JBL* 110, pp. 213-27.

Reddy, M.P.
1978   'The Book of Job: A Reconstruction', *ZAW* 90, pp. 59-94.

Reichert, J.
1978   'More Than Kin and Less Than Kind: The Limits of Genre Theory',
                in Strelka (ed.) 1978, pp. 57-79.

Rendsburg, G.A.
1982   'Evidence for a Spoken Hebrew in Biblical Times' (Doctoral
                dissertation, Ann Arbor, University Microfilms).
1990   *Linguistic Evidence for the Northern Origin of Selected Psalms*
                (Atlanta: Scholars Press).

Reventlow, H.G. von
1969   'Gattung und Überlieferung in der "tempelrede Jeremias": Jer. 7 und
                26', *ZAW* 81, pp. 315-52.

Richards, I.A.
1936   *The Philosophy of Rhetoric* (New York: Oxford University Press).

Robinson, H.W.
1936   'Corporate Personality in Ancient Israel', in *Werden und Wessen des
                Alten Testaments* (BZAW, 66; Berlin: de Gruyter), pp. 49-62.

Rogerson, J.W.
1985   'The Hebrew Conception of Corporate Personality: A Re-
                Examination', in B. Lang (ed.), *Anthropological Approaches to the
                Old Testament* (Philadelphia: Fortress Press), pp. 43-59.

Römer, W.H.P., and W. von Soden
1990   *Weisheitstexte, Mythen und Epen: Texte aus der Umwelt des Alten Testament*, III (Gütersloh: G. Mohn).

Rosmarin, A.
1985   *The Power of Genre* (Minneapolis: University of Minnesota Press).

Rowley, H.H.
1970   *Job* (London: Nelson).

Sacks, S.
1964   *Fiction and the Shop of Belief* (Berkeley: University of California Press).

Sapan, R.
1981   *Ha-Yiḥud ha-Taḥbiri shel Lashon ha-Shirah ha-Miqrait (The Syntactic Uniqueness of the Language of Biblical Poetry)* (Jerusalem: Kiryat Sefer).

Schwartz, Y. (ed.)
1969   *Perushei Rishonim 'al Sefer Iyov (Ancient Commentaries on The Book of Job)* (Jerusalem: Maqor).

Segal, Z.M.
1942   'The Book of Job' (Heb.), *Tarbiz* 13, pp. 73-91.
1949   'The Parallels in the Book of Job' (Heb.), *Tarbiz* 20, pp. 35-48.

Shirley, S. (trans.)
1989   *Spinoza, Tractatus Theologico-Politicus* (Leiden: Brill).

Simon, U.
1969   'The Secondary Characters in Biblical Narrative' (Heb.), in *Proceedings of the Fifth World Congress of Jewish Studies*, I (ed. P. Peli; Jerusalem: World Union of Jewish Studies), pp. 31-36.

Simpson, R.H., and J.F. Lazenby
1970   *The Catalogue of the Ships in Homeric Iliad* (Oxford: Clarendon Press).

Smith, G.V.
1990   'Job 4.12-21: Is it Eliphaz's Vision?', *VT* 40, pp. 543-63.

Snaith, N.
1968   *The Book of Job* (London: SCM Press).

Soll, W.M.
1989   'Babylonian and Biblical Acrostics', *Biblica* 69, pp. 305-23.

Sternberg, M.
1985   *The Poetics of Biblical Literature* (Bloomington, IN: Indiana University Press).

Strelka, J.P. (ed.)
1978   *Theories of Literary Genre* (Yearbook of Comparative Criticism, 8; University Park, PA: Pennsylvania State University Press).

Talmon, S.
1988   'Literary Motifs and Speculative Thought in the Hebrew Bible', *Hebrew University Studies in Literature and the Arts* 16, pp. 150-68.

Thompson, K. Jr
1960   'Out of the Whirlwind', *Interpretation* 14, pp. 51-63.

Todorov, Z.
1976   'The Origin of Genres', *New Literary History* 8, pp. 159-70.

Toury, G.
1979   'Translated Literature: System, Norm, Performance' (Heb.), *Hasifrut* 28, pp. 58-69.

Tov, E.
1990   *Biqoret Nusaḥ ha-Miqra (The Textual Criticism of the Bible)* (Jerusalem: Bialik Institute).

Tur-Sinai, N.H.
1941   *Sefer Iyov (Commentary on the Book of Job)* (Jerusalem: Hebrew University Press).
1972   *Perush le-Sefer Iyov (Commentary on the Book of Job*, rev. edn) (Jerusalem: Rubin Mass).

Tzevat, M.
1966   'The Meaning of the Book of Job', *HUCA* 37, pp. 73-106.

Van Den Broeck, R.
1978   'How Can Metaphor Be Translated?' (Heb.), *Hasifrut* 27, pp. 44-53.

Volz, P.
1911   *Weisheit (Das Buch Hiob, Spruche und Jesus Sirach, Predig)* (Gottingen: Vandenhoeck & Ruprecht).

Von Rad, G.
1960   'Hiob xxxviii und die altägyptische Weisheit', in N. North and D.W. Thomas (eds.), *Wisdom in Israel and in the Ancient Near East* (VTSup, 3; Leiden: Brill), pp. 293-301.
1972   *Wisdom in Israel* (London: SCM Press).

Weimer, J.
1974   'Job's Complaints: A Study of its Limits and Form, Content and Significance' (Doctoral dissertation, New York, Union Theological Seminary).

Weiser, A.
1959   *Das Buch Hiob* (ATD; Göttingen: Vandenhoeck & Ruprecht).
1961   *Introduction to the Old Testament* (London: Darton, Longman & Todd).

Weiss, M.
1959   *Ha-Sippur 'al Reshito shel Iyov (The Story of Job)* (Jerusalem: Iyyunim, The Jewish Agency).
1967   *Ha-Miqra ki-demuto (The Bible and Modern Literature)* (Jerusalem: Mosad Bialik).
1984   *The Bible from Within: The Method of Total Interpretation* (Jerusalem: Magnes Press).

Westermann, C.
1956   *Der Aufbau des Buches Hiob* (Tubingen: Mohr).

White, H.
1986   'Historical Pluralism', *Critical Inquiry* 12, pp. 480-93.

Whybray, R.N.
1980   'The Identification of and the Use of Quotations in Ecclesiastes', in J.A. Emerton (ed.), *Congress Volume* (VTSup, 32; Leiden: Brill), pp. 435-51.

Williams, J.G.
1971   'You Have Not Spoken Truth of Me', *ZAW* 83, pp. 231-55.

Wiseman, D.J.
   1980   'A New Text of the Babylonian Poem of The Righteous Sufferer',
            Anatolian Studies 30, pp. 101-107.
Wolfers, D.
   1990   'The Lord's Second Speech in the Book of Job', *VT* 40, pp. 474-99.
Yule, G.U.
   1944   *The Statistical Study of Literary Vocabulary* (Cambridge: Cambridge
            University Press).
Zakovitch, Y.
   1979   *'Al Sheloshah ve-'al Arba'ah': Ha-Degem ha-Sifruti Sheloshah ve-*
            Arba'ah ba-Miqra (*The Pattern 'For Three...and For Four' in the*
            Bible) (Jerusalem: Makor).
   1982   *Ḥayyei Shimshon* (*The Life of Samson*) (Jerusalem: Magnes Press).
   1990   *Ruth* (Heb.) (Mikra Le-Yisrael; Tel-Aviv: Am Oved and Jerusalem:
            Magnes Press).
Zemach, E.
   1970   *Astetiqah Analitit* (*Analytical Aesthetics*) (Tel-Aviv: Daga).
   1988   'What did the Lord Answer to Job?' (Heb.), *Moznaim* 61, pp. 14-17.

INDEXES

INDEX OF REFERENCES

OLD TESTAMENT

A Blemished Perfection

Eichrodt, W. 217
Eissfeldt, O. 19
Ellenbogen, M. 185
Else, G.F. 40
Even Shoshan, A. 319
Even, Y. 133
Ewald, H. 148

Fisch, H. 56
Fish, S. 14
Fishbane, M. 106, 300
Fisher, L.R. 199, 327
Fohrer, G. 36, 104, 149, 156, 164, 268,
  270, 276, 277, 279-81, 285, 287,
  289, 290, 292, 294
Fokkelman, J.P. 16
Fontaine, C. 275
Forbes, A.D. 193
Forster, E.M. 133
Fosster, F.H. 190, 198, 199
Fox, M.V. 27, 64, 77, 84, 87, 103, 112,
  182, 249, 304, 308
Freedman, D.N. 32, 49, 188, 189, 191-
  93, 325
Fullerton, K. 117, 220, 225, 227, 275

Gaon, R.S. 202, 271, 296
Gardiner, A.H. 86
Gemser, B. 144, 146
Gerhart, M. 24
Gersonides, R.L. 118, 296
Gese, H. 37, 268
Goethe, J.W. 18
Gombrich, E.H. 24
Good, E.M. 212, 219
Goodwin, D.W. 32
Gordis, R. 19, 35, 145, 148, 156, 159,
  162, 164, 218, 268, 270, 275-82,
  285, 287, 289-91, 293, 294, 298,
  308
Grabbe, L. 149, 183, 199
Gray, G.B. 19, 35, 56, 118, 119, 122,
  126, 133, 141, 145, 148, 149,
  154-56, 164, 165, 180, 187, 217,
  269, 271, 272, 276, 278-81, 286,
  287, 294, 296
Gray, J. 37, 84, 160
Greenberg, M. 70, 249, 291, 296

Greenspahn, F.E. 179, 181, 182, 206,
  319, 321, 328
Greenstein, E.L. 14
Guillaume, A. 189, 190, 194-99, 202
Gunkel, H. 18, 19, 22

Haezrachi, P. 26, 29, 30, 45, 113
Halperin, S. 40, 41
Hillers, D.R. 107
Hirsch, E.D. Jr 23, 27
Hirschberg, Y. 282
Hoffman, Y. 24, 64, 78, 94-96, 117,
  122, 134, 143, 192, 212, 248,
  268, 280
Holbert, J.C. 157
Holladay, W. 235
Holscher, G. 149
Homer 90, 91
Horace 23
Hornby, R.H. 85
Horst, F. 270, 276, 289
Huberman-Scholnick, S. 144, 167
Hurvitz, A. 49, 268

Irwin, W.A. 123

Jacobsen, T. 219, 262
Janzen, G.J. 212, 306
Japhet, S. 281
Jellicoe, S. 180
Jongeling, B. 155
Joyce, J. 200

Kahana, A. 56, 119, 122, 126, 133,
  141, 148, 154, 158, 162, 189,
  194, 202, 218, 244, 271, 276,
  278, 281, 289
Kallen, H.M. 39, 45
Kant, I. 24
Kara, R.J. 119, 133
Kaufmann, Y. 19, 35, 55, 56, 189, 217,
  269, 276, 278, 285, 289-91, 305
Kautzsch, E. 195
Kierkegaard, S. 212, 213, 220
Klein, J. 77, 247, 261
Knapp, S. 28
Koch, K. 169, 225, 251
Koenig 19